Navigating Failure

THE
LUTHER
HARTWELL
HODGES
SERIES

ON
BUSINESS,
SOCIETY,
AND THE
STATE

WILLIAM H. BECKER, EDITOR

Navigating Failure

BANKRUPTCY AND

COMMERCIAL SOCIETY IN

ANTEBELLUM AMERICA

Edward J. Balleisen

THE UNIVERSITY OF NORTH CAROLINA PRESS

CHAPEL HILL AND LONDON

The paper in this book meets the guidelines for
permanence and durability of the Committee on
Production Guidelines for Book Longevity of the
Council on Library Resources.

Library of Congress Cataloging-in-Publication Data

Balleisen, Edward J. Navigating failure : bankruptcy
and commercial society in Antebellum America /
Edward J. Balleisen.

p. cm. — (The Luther Hartwell Hodges series on
business, society, and the state)

Includes bibliographical references and index.

ISBN 0-8078-2600-6 (cloth: alk. paper)

ISBN 0-8078-4916-2 (pbk.: alk. paper)

1. Bankruptcy—United States—History—19th
century. 2. United States—Economic conditions—
To 1865. 3. Social mobility—United States—
History—19th century. I. Title. II. Series.

HG3766B22 2001   332.7'5'097309033—dc21

00-061537

05 04 03 02 01   5 4 3 2 1

For Karin

Contents

Illustrations

Table, Maps, Figure

Table

Maps

Figure

Acknowledgments

Writing this book has left me decidedly among the ranks of debtors. Indispensable financial support has come from the Andrew W. Mellon Foundation, Yale University, the University of the Witwatersrand, Johannesburg, and the Duke University Arts and Sciences Research Council. Archivists and librarians at Yale's Sterling, Mudd, and Law School Libraries, Columbia University's Division of Rare Books and Manuscripts, the New-York Historical Society, the New York Public Library, and the Baker Library at Harvard Business School greatly contributed to my work, guiding me through the intricacies of their respective collections. The assistance of Robert Morris, John Celardo, and the rest of the staff at the Northeast branch of the National Archives was particularly important. Their efforts, both in Bayonne, New Jersey, before the archive's move, and then in Manhattan, greatly expedited my examination of the voluminous federal bankruptcy records that serve as the book's evidentiary touchstone. Florence Thomas taught me how to use a database program that proved extremely useful, and Deborah Breen, Noeleen McIlvenna, and Gwenn Miller ably helped with the final production of the manuscript.

My fascination with nineteenth-century business failure dates back almost a decade, when I began this book as a dissertation under the supervision of an extraordinarily supportive faculty committee. Nancy Cott encouraged me to think about the social implications of bankruptcy and to explore the nineteenth-century economy from the perspective of the people who experienced its opportunities and dangers. Bill Cronon provided crucial assistance in formulating a methodological approach to antebellum bankruptcy records and in developing a narrative framework. My dissertation director, David Brion Davis, had a tremendous impact on my development as a scholar, continually offering perceptive criticism and trenchant suggestions about how I might link my findings with broader developments in American culture. His remarkable knowledge of nineteenth-century American society has enriched this book immeasurably.

In Johannesburg, where I wrote my dissertation and began the process of turning it into a book, Bruce Murray, Charles van Onselen, Phil Bonner, Peter Delius, Paul Le Hausse, and the other historians at Wits helped to orient the foreigner in their midst. Their companionship eased the task of writing so far away from home. More recently, my colleagues at Duke both greatly facilitated my adjustment to the life of an assistant professor and offered unstinting encouragement as I completed the manuscript.

Making sense of antebellum bankruptcy has drawn me into several historiographies, including American business, legal, social, and cultural history. In seeking to bridge subdisciplinary divides, I have greatly benefited from intellectual exchanges with historians in all of these fields. Discussions with Trudi Abel, Sven Beckert, Edward Countryman, John Demos, Richard Ellis, Margot Finn, Eric Foner, Emily Greenwald, Nancy Hewitt, David Montgomery, Scott Sandage, David Waldstreicher, David Weiman, Elizabeth White, and Jim Wooten enriched my analytical approaches to antebellum economy, society, and culture. The final manuscript also bears the marks of helpful critiques that I have received from legal history workshops at Yale and the University of Chicago, as well as conference sessions at the annual meetings of the American Historical Association and the American Society of Legal History.

In addition to my dissertation advisers, numerous people have commented on various incarnations of the manuscript, including Jim Campbell, Ann Fabian, Leif Haase, David Moss, Richard Ross, and Rachel Seidman. Since my first years at college, Stan Katz has served as a mentor to me. Throughout this study, he has furnished invaluable guidance to the historical study of legal institutions. Carol Sheriff tenaciously worked her way through complete drafts of both the dissertation and the revised manuscript; the finished product owes much to her understanding of the nineteenth-century commercial classes and her high standards for historical rhetoric. Peter Coleman brought his erudition in debtor-creditor law to early versions of Parts I and II, and Tony Freyer and Bruce Mann similarly engaged with later drafts of particular chapters, each magnanimously sharing his insights about the intersections between America's economic culture and its law. My colleagues Jack Cell, Peter English, Larry Goodwyn, Cynthia Herrup, Alex Keyssar, Syd Nathans, Kristen Neuschel, and Peter Wood have all commented on the revised manuscript, collectively challenging me to refine the scope of my arguments about commercial society and to place my findings within a broader international context.

The assessments of three anonymous reviewers for the *Business History Review* sharpened my discussion of "vulture capitalism" in Chapter 5; I am grateful for the *Review*'s permission to reprint the article that first appeared in that journal. The initial outside reader for UNC Press, now known to me as Christopher Clark, provided a model evaluation of my dissertation, offering exceedingly helpful suggestions for remolding it into a book. Lewis Bateman expressed faith in my research from the moment I first discussed it with him, providing all the assistance for which a first-time author could hope from an acquisitions editor. Mary Caviness did a superb job of preparing the manuscript for production.

Over the past decade family and friends have contributed to my work in ways large and small. An avid reader of nonfiction and especially history, my father, Donald Balleisen, eagerly read the chapters I completed before his death, dishing out criticisms with characteristic bluntness. My mother, Carolyn Balleisen, has offered both the perspective of a lawyer with experience in contemporary bankruptcy law and thoughts about the interests and concerns of a general audience. My sisters, Ellen Balleisen and Wendy Finger, my brother-in-law, Michael Finger, and my in-laws, Joy and Lionel Shapiro, have offered constant and much appreciated encouragement. A number of friends and relatives graciously gave me a place to stay during research trips, including my sister Ellen, David Moss and Abby Rischin, Geoff and Dale Norman, Arthur Kimmelfield and Marilyn Braverman, and Andrew Clarkson. Ellen deserves a special mention, given the number of times I imposed on her while doing research in Bayonne and New York City. In the last few years, my sons Zachary and Aaron have never hesitated to lure me away from writing for much-needed breaks.

Karin Shapiro has shaped this book in more ways than I can count. She has shared insights about American history and the craft of writing about the past. She has listened to one damn story about bankruptcy after another, always challenging me to relate individual experience to patterns of behavior and a larger social context. Many of my arguments took shape during our walks around New Haven, Johannesburg, and Durham. Every draft of every chapter was subjected to her considerable acumen as an editor. Perhaps most important, her enthusiasm and companionship have helped to make the creation of this book a pleasure.

Navigating Failure

Risk and Wreckage in
Antebellum America

In the city of New York there are probably about two thousand applicants for the benefit of the bankrupt law. The schedules, containing the necessary description of the affairs of these individuals, are about ten thousand in number, and form a library of the most remarkable and instructive character. . . . In these documents we are presented with a perfect picture—drawn with all of the stern fidelity of legal accuracy and precision—of the actual condition of society, the errors, follies, vices, and indiscretions of men—the course and progress of finance, morals, and religion.

It is indeed difficult to describe the full interest and importance of these most curious of all auto-biographies. What a world of sagacious speculation, and sober reasoning, and painful moralizing, and philosophical reflection, is opened up to the thoughtful reader of one of these magic volumes. The whole history of a man's career, with all its bounding hopes, its disappointments, its hypocrisies, its shiftings, its doublings to escape the dreaded exposure, its positive frauds—all this condensed into the formal record of a legal document.

—*New York Herald*, December 14, 1842

On the morning of February 2, 1842, William W. Campbell opened an office at No. 12 John Street, in the middle of New York City's bustling mercantile quarter. Campbell did a thriving business that day and continued to do so for the next thirteen months. Week after week, grocers, jobbers, brokers, and dealers of every description paraded into his office. Joining them were agents, clerks, and self-proclaimed gentlemen, stagecoach drivers and cartmen, manufacturers of everything from iron rails to carpets, customhouse officers and tavern keepers, doctors and druggists, carpenters, shoemakers and tailors, butchers and bakers, the occasional boardinghouse keeper or milliner, and particularly lawyers.

These representatives of nearly every walk of New York City life came to William Campbell or sent their attorneys to him because he held out the prospect of absolution and redemption. Campbell, though, was no man of God. He emulated neither antebellum revivalists like Charles Finney nor self-proclaimed prophets like William Miller, each of whom heralded the upcoming millennium. Instead of attracting people on the basis of spiritual reputation, Campbell owed his authority and popularity to the appointive powers of Samuel Rossiter Betts, judge of the United States Court for the Southern District of New York, who had made him a commissioner under the 1841 United States Bankruptcy Act. The salvation that so many New Yorkers hoped to find on John Street was economic and legal release—the ability to cleanse themselves of their debts, to wipe away the stain of misfortune, and to begin life anew, freed from the crippling claims that financial misfortune had created.[1]

The scenes in Campbell's office had their counterparts throughout New York's southern federal district, and throughout the rest of the nation as well. As long as the bankruptcy system created by the 1841 act endured, most Americans could find a federal bankruptcy official within a day's ride. From the second day of February in 1842 until the repeal of the Bankruptcy Act on March 3, 1843, more than 41,000 people made the trip to one of these officials.[2] Although some petitioners were creditors who sought to force a debtor into involuntary bankruptcy, the overwhelming majority were bankrupts who promised to give up all but a small portion of their worldly goods in the attempt to procure economic rebirth.

Applicants for relief under this legislation had come to realize, much to their chagrin, that participation within a market economy brought financial dangers as well as opportunities. Entrepreneurship frequently entailed great risks in the rapidly commercializing world of nineteenth-century America. Without sufficient capital resources and business savvy, antebellum proprietors could be cruelly exposed by competition, accident, or the pressures of a financial crisis.

Petitioners under the 1841 Bankruptcy Act were by no means the only Americans to discover this economic reality in the decades before the Civil War. Business failure permeated the nineteenth-century United States. Amid a chaotic economy in which almost all business owners found themselves entangled in complex webs of credit, at once debtors to suppliers and creditors to customers, insolvency constituted an omnipresent counterpart to the narratives of economic achievement so often lauded by the era's pundits and politicians. No sector of the antebellum economy was immune from bankruptcy. Throughout the era, farmers from every part of the country lost their land because they could not make mortgage payments, while large numbers of artisans and manufacturers found themselves unable to meet their obligations. In the biggest cities and the smallest hamlets, a host of mercantile firms experienced bankruptcy. Corporations proved no more immune to the vicissitudes of trade than partnerships and individual proprietors, as banks, transportation companies, and chartered manufacturing firms failed with great regularity. Alongside all of these economic wrecks stood myriad broken land speculators. In the thousands, Americans bet heavily on the future of city lots and rural tracts, usually with borrowed money. When the bubbles of real estate booms invariably burst, droves of speculators went to the wall.[3]

By the 1840s and 1850s, the notion that there was a high rate of bankruptcy in the United States had become part of the received wisdom about America's tumultuous economy. A contributor to *Hunt's Merchants' Magazine* offered a typical appraisal in 1860, remarking that in America, "most men sooner or later [go] bankrupt and fail in their business undertakings; not merely merchants and tradesmen, but even farmers, and those of all occupations." Although antebellum commentators noted the dangers posed by every kind of market-based activity, they emphasized the risks faced by merchants. According to almost every person who publicly discussed bankruptcy in the middle decades of the century, the overwhelming majority of mercantile businesses failed. The most common estimate, repeatedly asserted both before and long after the Civil War, was that over ninety-five of every one hundred such ventures ended in bankruptcy.[4]

This statistic overstated the frequency of antebellum insolvency, though not by so much as to vitiate the basic claim that failure was endemic. Historians who have surveyed credit reports on businesses during the 1840s and 1850s have invariably found ample evidence of widespread bankruptcy, whether in Boston, New York, Baltimore, western Massachusetts, rural Pennsylvania, central New Jersey, or San Francisco. When considered in the aggregate, the work of these scholars suggests that among antebellum proprietors directly involved in market exchange, at least one in three and perhaps as many as one in two eventually succumbed to an insupportable load of debt.[5] A lithograph of New York City's Liberty Street from 1836 or 1837 testifies to the reasonableness of such approximations. Of nine firms depicted in the lithograph, four endured bankruptcy within the next five years. As one American writer observed in an 1834 novel, the antebellum "wheel of fortune" was "constantly moving; some are making, and some are braking."[6]

All of these encounters with business failure cumulatively left far-reaching marks on the nineteenth-century United States, simultaneously helping to consolidate a brand of capitalism that encouraged risk taking and innovation, and leading large numbers of Americans to seek havens from the dangers associated with independent proprietorship. *Navigating Failure* explores several dimensions of these opposing processes, reconstructing the antebellum experience of bankruptcy by commercially inclined Americans—people who placed themselves foursquare within the world of the marketplace and who framed their ambitions according to the terms of a market society. My goals in this study are several: to recapture the

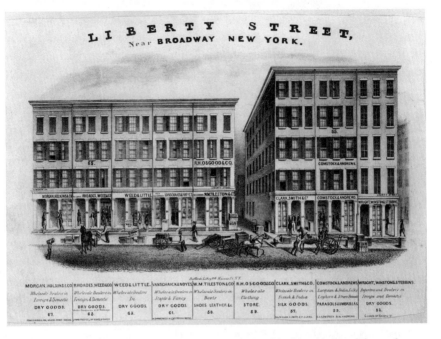

FAILURES IN LIBERTY STREET. Four of the nine firms depicted in this mid-1830s lithograph—Rhoades, Weed & Co., Weed & Little, Van Schaik & Noyes, and Comstock & Andrews—had gone bankrupt by 1842, suggesting the pervasiveness of business failure in antebellum America (The Metropolitan Museum of Art, Bequest of Edward W. C. Arnold, 1954, The Edward W. C. Arnold Collection of New York Prints, Maps and Pictures).

economic roots and social experience of individual bankruptcy; to assess the consequences of widespread insolvency for business and legal culture; and to trace the impact of business failure on the evolution of America's urban middle class.

There are many historical narratives to be told about economic failure in nineteenth-century America. This one revolves around a single episode in the history of American bankruptcy—the operation of the 1841 Bankruptcy Act that attracted so many insolvent Americans into the offices of federal court officials like William W. Campbell. Within that episode, this book turns especially on the bankruptcy proceedings that occurred in New York's southern federal district, which encompassed New York City, Long Island, and the lower Hudson Valley.

I focus on the 1841 Bankruptcy Law partly because it coincided with and emanated from powerful transformations in the scope and character of American capitalism. Widespread business failure, of course, presented challenges to Americans long before and long after the early 1840s. In late colonial Philadelphia, at least a third and most likely a higher proportion of merchants failed at some point in their lives. Since the Civil War, the American economy has continued to generate a high incidence of commercial insolvency, especially for unincorporated small-scale concerns and new business ventures, regardless of their form of organization.[7] But the antebellum decades witnessed an acceleration in the growth of market relations that made bankruptcy a social, cultural, and political problem of particularly great intensity. During these years, American entrepreneurs forged an increasingly national "credit system" and ever more integrated and competitive markets for goods and services, all of which helped to usher in the modern business cycle. Together, these processes democratized the specter of insolvency, bringing its anxieties and perplexities to a greatly expanded population of market-oriented proprietors.

For many historians, these developments constitute a "market revolution," in which capitalist institutions and associated habits of mind overturned previously dominant precapitalist social structures and mind-sets in a compressed period of intense historical change. This perspective has sustained compelling critiques from numerous scholars, summarized effectively in two recent essays by Richard Bushman and Naomi Lamoreaux. As Bushman stresses, proponents of the "market revolution" thesis excessively underplay the breadth of engagement with networks of long-distance trade in the eighteenth and early nineteenth centuries; and as Lamoreaux shows, those proponents often mischaracterize the values and practices of eighteenth- and early-nineteenth-century proprietors who vigorously directed their economic activities toward markets, thereby exaggerating the cultural divide between them and ostensibly precapitalist participants in locally based household economies. Yet even in the absence of a model postulating economic "revolution," it is clear that during the first several decades of the nineteenth century, the United States underwent a dramatic expansion in market-based production, distribution, and consumption.[8]

As more and more Americans either embraced or found themselves enmeshed in commercial networks, larger numbers of individuals confronted the dilemmas posed by bankruptcy. What happened to contractual and moral obligations when firms could not pay their debts? How did one determine whether bankrupts were culpable for their financial reverses, and how should the business community and the legal system punish insolvent proprietors, if at all? Should legal institutions seek to restrain entrepreneurial impulses that increased the likelihood of financial ruin, or rather accommodate them as, on the whole, facilitating economic growth? Nothing in antebellum America fixed attention on such questions as much as great financial panics, like the ones in 1837 and 1839 that precipitated tens of thousands of commercial insolvencies and unleashed an upsurge of political support for a comprehensive federal bankruptcy system, eventually resulting in the passage of the 1841 Federal Bankruptcy Act. More than any other legislation during the era, this statute reflected a nationwide conversation about how the law should treat insolvencies and insolvents. As a result, the politics surrounding this act, its judicial implementation, and its impact on debtor-creditor relations nicely illustrate enduring conflicts about how to handle business failure.

I additionally concentrate on the 1841 act, and particularly its workings in southern New York, because of the phenomenal court records that it generated there. These documents have enabled me to piece together hundreds of personal histories about nineteenth-century Americans who sustained financial ruin, including the careers of numerous individuals whose business dealings extended far beyond southern New York, and scores of others whose failures occurred in other parts of the nation. This collection of biographies offers such enlightening vistas on the attempts of the commercial classes to make their way through the shifting landscape of American capitalism that it both serves as the book's evidentiary compass and primarily guides its narrative framework.

As the *New York Herald* proclaimed, the southern New York bankruptcy records are extraordinarily rich. These "most curious of all auto-biographies" provide a wealth of evidence about the causes of financial ruin from the 1820s through the early 1840s; they reveal the responses of bankrupts and their creditors to insolvency in that period, both informally and through legal institutions; and they document the substantial economic opportunities that antebellum business failures created, both for the people directly involved in bankruptcy administration and for individuals who speculated in the sale of assets from insolvent estates. All of these topics receive close treatment in Part I and Part II. Part III tracks the postfailure lives of southern New York bankrupts, in some cases following their economic careers into the 1870s and 1880s. This investigation, based primarily on credit reports and local histories, tests the ability of antebellum bankrupts to dust themselves off and rejoin the scramble for riches and social status.

A methodological approach largely dependent on collective biography calls for some discussion of dramatis personae. The 503 bankrupts whose commercial careers constitute the heart of this study encompass a broad cross section of antebellum entrepreneurs, reflecting considerable diversity in demographic profile, cultural background, occupation, extent of business, and geographic location at the time of failure.[9] All but nine of these insolvents were men, reflecting male domination of most segments of the era's commercial economy, and a large majority were native-born Americans. Although some had barely reached adulthood when they suspended payments to their creditors or had already attained an age well beyond the era's normal life expectancy, most were in the prime of their lives, possessing both meaningful business experience and a likely work future of at least a decade.

Roughly three-quarters were married, of whom a sizable majority had at least one dependent child.

This group adhered to a variety of faiths and political opinions. Religious inclination, as suggested by book inventories and descriptions of rights to church pews, was overwhelmingly Protestant, with Episcopalian, New Light Presbyterian, Dutch Reformed, Methodist, Baptist, and Quaker congregants particularly in evidence. Several bankrupts manifested deep-seated commitments to the reform causes of revivalist antebellum Christianity, including Sabbatarianism, temperance, and missionary work in the western states. Despite the preponderance of Protestants in the sample, a few bankrupts counted Hebrew prayer books among their possessions and others probably owed their allegiances to the Catholic Church. Political affiliation, where indicated by newspaper subscriptions, possession of portraits of political leaders, or the attainment of public office, was split fairly evenly between Whigs and Democrats.

The commercial endeavors that brought these individuals to bankruptcy court spanned nearly the full gamut of the antebellum economy, embracing almost every sort of mercantile venture imaginable, an array of manufacturing concerns and crafts, the various professions, and the art of tilling the soil. Almost half of the sample went bankrupt as merchants and just under a third as manufacturers, subcontractors, or artisans. Far smaller proportions failed as professionals, brokers, service providers, farmers, and speculators. The scale of their enterprises ranged from private banking that transacted business worth millions of dollars, to peddling and shoe repair, which at the best of times barely kept their practitioners in the ranks of independent proprietors. Some bankrupts' commercial dealings linked them to suppliers and customers throughout the United States and the Atlantic world. Others confined their economic relationships to the immediate neighborhood of an urban ward or a rural village. About one in seven pursued extensive businesses or grand speculative schemes that eventually created debts in excess of $100,000, while one in six reported pecuniary obligations totaling less than $3,000. Most of the bankrupts fell in between these two groups, running country stores, wholesale establishments, small manufactories, modest to substantial workshops, or middling professional practices. Single proprietorships or partnerships were by far the most common form of business organization, though a few bankrupts had engaged in corporate ventures of one sort or another.

A substantial majority of the failures endured by these individuals were of relatively recent vintage. Half occurred between 1840 and 1842, and over 40 percent between 1837 and 1839 (the years of financial panic). Still, almost 10 percent took place earlier, between 1823 and 1836, allowing comparison of insolvencies that transpired during prosperous periods with those precipitated by hard times. When

TABLE 1. Amount of Debt Owed by Southern New York Bankrupts, 1842–1843

Debt ($)	($N = 503$) Number	Percentage
0–500	2	0.4
501–1,000	11	2.2
1,001–1,500	13	2.6
1,501–3,000	46	9.1
3,001–5,000	71	14.1
5,001–10,000	55	10.9
10,001–25,000	98	19.5
25,001–50,000	59	11.7
50,001–100,000	53	10.5
100,001–250,000	33	6.6
250,001–500,000	23	4.6
500,001–1,000,000	3	0.6
1,000,001–2,500,000	2	0.4
more than 2,500,000	1	0.1
debt amount unclear[a]	33	6.6

[a]Includes thirty involuntary bankrupts whose case-files do not provide evidence of debts, and three voluntary bankrupts whose list of debts are dominated by uncertain amounts.

court clerks inscribed their names onto bankruptcy dockets, two-thirds resided in the great cities of New York or Brooklyn, one-sixth lived in Ulster or Dutchess County, particularly in the river towns of Kingston and Poughkeepsie, and the rest were scattered throughout the lower Hudson Valley and Long Island. Slightly more than one-fifth of the sample, however, failed *outside* Judge Betts's jurisdiction, usually beyond New York's borders. Among these migratory bankrupts were individuals who had failed in every region of the country and in nearly every state, almost always in mercantile hubs on or close to the nation's rapidly expanding transportation network.[10]

The commercial quests of these business owners before, during, and after insolvency bring the antebellum economy to life, suggesting the often wrenching manner in which the era's proprietors fathomed such abstract processes as market integration and the business cycle. Through their economic odysseys, one gains a sense of how commercially minded Americans tried to tack between the shoals of an expanding market society, sometimes with continual futility, sometimes with mixed fortunes, and sometimes with eventually remarkable success. These individual journeys further provide a means of exploring the interconnections among several instructive stories about the development of nineteenth-century American capitalism—tales of commercial law that proved friendly to insolvent business owners,

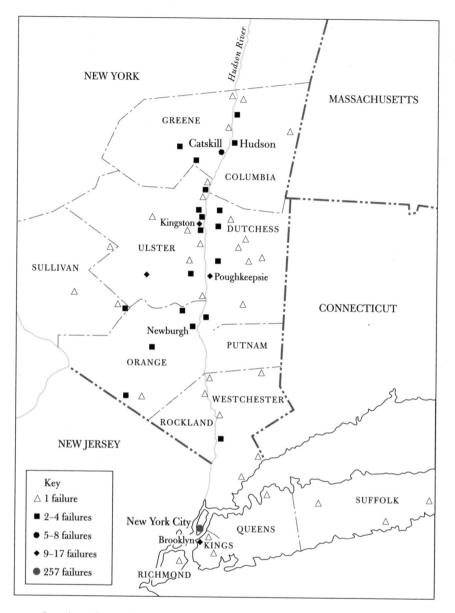

MAP 1. Locations of 399 Failures by Members of the Sample within Southern New York, 1823–1843

and of powerful stigmas that still bedeviled them; of cultural collisions between nationalist legal reformers committed to a smoothly functioning capitalist order and socially rooted proprietors who cared particularly about their own local networks; and of social responses to the omnipresent flux within the era's marketplaces and commercial classes. Ultimately, I will suggest, these intersecting tales help to

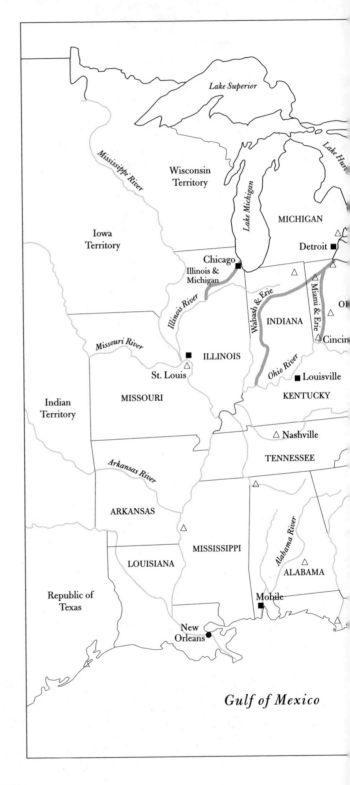

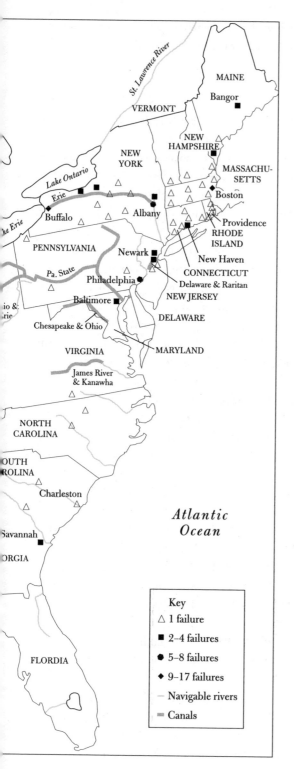

MAP 2. Locations of 129 Failures by Members of the Sample outside of Southern New York, 1828–1842

explain how a society that defined citizenship largely in terms of proprietorship came, in fairly quick order, to accommodate the rise of corporate enterprise.

Petitioners under the 1841 Federal Bankruptcy Act could consider themselves lucky not to be facing the European legal requirements then in force. In addition to permitting voluntary applications and allowing anyone to receive a discharge, regardless of occupation, the 1841 statute gave creditors no means to block the granting of a bankruptcy certificate unless the petitioner had committed an act of fraud specified in the law. Reckless financial management or wholesale incompetence did not constitute a bar to a full release from the obligation of past debts.[11] Across the Atlantic, where small-scale property owners and aspirant entrepreneurs possessed less political influence, bankruptcy laws were not so generous. Throughout Europe, imprisonment for debt was common and formal bankruptcy discharges were only available to merchants, who could not initiate legal proceedings themselves. Those proceedings usually subjected failed entrepreneurs to a searching examination of their commercial affairs, in which a judicial finding of excessively speculative behavior usually led to stiff penalties. Even in the absence of such a ruling, European bankruptcy laws made the granting of a discharge dependent on the explicit consent of a large proportion of creditors. In several countries, released bankrupts also continued to incur civil disabilities until they paid their old debts in full.[12]

Lenience toward antebellum American bankrupts extended well beyond the terms of the 1841 Bankruptcy Law. In the wake of financial crises, especially after the panics of 1819, 1837 and 1839, and 1857, many state governments enacted stay and appraisal laws to provide relief for struggling debtors. The former slowed down legal mechanisms of debt collection by requiring lengthy delays between the granting of debt judgments and the auction of debtors' assets; the latter prohibited court-mandated sales of real estate unless they brought in a significant percentage of what local assessors adjudged to be the true value of the land. From the 1820s onward, a growing number of states dramatically curtailed the use of imprisonment for debt, essentially restricting the institution to instances in which a debtor was guilty of gross fraud. During the same period, most state legislatures expanded the range of property that was exempt from execution for debt. By the 1850s, exemptions increasingly included not only basic clothing, furniture, and household goods, but also the tools of a debtor's trade, some livestock, the debtor's dwelling house, and forty or fifty acres of surrounding land.[13]

Comparatively easy handling of debtors also characterized state insolvency processes and the antebellum law of assignments, despite several rulings by the U.S. Supreme Court early in the century that limited the power of state governments to extend relief to debtors. As a result of those rulings, state legislatures lacked the constitutional authority to pass insolvency laws that operated retrospectively or restricted the claims of out-of-state creditors. But states could establish insolvency courts with the power to free applicants from the legal obligation to pay creditors who resided in-state. Although the states that did enact insolvency statutes often required that creditors consent to discharges, they placed few other barriers in the way of applicants. American approaches to assignments for the benefit of creditors similarly placed debtors in a relatively privileged position. These legal instruments transferred a person's assets to a trustee or trustees, who then liquidated the property and distributed the proceeds to creditors. Except in a few states, failed debtors could make a creditor's access to dividends from such trusts dependent on a legal release from any obligation to pay the outstanding part of the claim. In a number of jurisdictions, makers of assignments could even designate different classes of creditors, specifying that members of a preferred class would receive full payment before other creditors received a cent.[14]

The legal treatment of bankruptcy in the United States astonished European visitors such as Alexis de Tocqueville. Tocqueville toured America several years before the Bankruptcy Act of 1841 smoothed failed proprietors' paths to new economic starts. He nonetheless was forcibly impressed by the "strange indulgence that is shown to bankrupts" throughout the American union. "In this respect," the French visitor maintained, "the Americans differ, not only from the nations of Europe, but from all the commercial nations of our time."[15]

Even if nineteenth-century American law accorded insolvents "strange indulgence" when juxtaposed to the harsher demands of European jurisprudence, the personal consequences of antebellum business failure remained considerable. The crucial psychological reference point for the period's bankrupts was the premium that their own society placed on economic independence, not the status of their counterparts in Paris, Hamburg, or St. Petersburg. For white adults in the land of democratic government and "self-made men," economic self-direction constituted a crucial badge of honor. Farmers who cultivated their lands; artisans who produced goods in their own workshops; manufacturers who superintended their own factories; merchants who oversaw commercial operations in their own counting-houses—these were the prototypical citizens of the American republic. Furthermore, many antebellum Americans desired far more than simple proprietorship, harboring ambitions for affluence and the lofty social position that accompanied success in business.

Bankruptcy, at least for a time, transformed assertions of independence into pretense and aspirations of wealth into delusion. Financially troubled antebellum debtors discovered how vulnerable they were to pecuniary reverses, how dependent they were on commercial reputation and indulgence from creditors, and how anxious they could become as they tried to fend off looming insolvency. Once outright failure actually took place, liquidation of assets generally followed. Whether such liquidation occurred through sheriff's sales, under the auspices of private assignees, or according to the terms of the 1841 Federal Bankruptcy Act, the result was the same—loss of legal title to property and the concomitant requirement of moving down in the world. In addition, legal releases from debts, however valuable, did not instantaneously bring forth new entrepreneurial openings. On the contrary, personal histories of failure usually tarnished public standing and restricted access to capital and credit, greatly complicating the efforts of former bankrupts to return to the business world.

Comparative generosity in the antebellum law of debtor and creditor did not transform insolvency into a trivial event, with limited implications for individuals who became swamped by unpayable obligations. For tens of thousands of nineteenth-century Americans, bankruptcy represented dashed hopes and circumscribed prospects. Indeed, in a society that endlessly celebrated entrepreneurial success, business failure could exact a substantial psychological toll, not infrequently leading those who endured it to the whiskey bottle or the insane asylum.

For a great many nineteenth-century Americans, insolvency also imparted compelling instruction about the nature of risk in a market society, which often profoundly shaped postfailure careers. Bankrupts did not necessarily encounter a single financial curriculum, as there were many paths to insolvency in the turbulent nineteenth-century economy. Nor did they draw the same conclusions from pecuniary embarrassment or adopt a uniform strategy in the effort to overcome legacies of failure. Nonetheless, I have identified telling patterns in the multifarious experience of antebellum bankruptcy and the variegated responses to it—patterns that reveal much about the attempts of commercially oriented Americans to navigate a world increasingly driven by market exchange. Three interrelated themes stand out in this regard: 1) the variable and shifting meanings of "economic independence" in capitalist culture; 2) the importance of familial and social networks to business success, and the resulting clash between two competing versions of commercial morality— one premised on special financial obligations to one's closest business associates, and another, formulated by apostles of an integrated, national economy, that mandated equal treatment to everyone in the marketplace; and 3) the manifold interconnections between widespread financial calamity on the one hand, and capitalist dynamism and innovation on the other.

The cultural implications of personal independence have attracted considerable attention from scholars of the nineteenth-century United States. Over the past several decades, historians have explored myriad contexts in which strong commitments to economic autonomy served as a counterpoint to the onward march of

American capitalism. The emphasis has been on relatively self-sufficient farmers, who took great pride in their status as self-employed producers and whose keenest desire was to ensure that their children would be able to enjoy a similar way of life; or on skilled urban artisans and journeymen, who bemoaned the bastardization of their crafts resulting from production for mass markets and who struggled to avoid the demeaning life of permanent, alienating wage labor.[16] For all of the insights that this varied scholarship has furnished, it largely skirts consideration of economic independence as an ideal *within* antebellum commercial society.

In a host of ways, the biographies of antebellum bankrupts that I present here underscore the strength of personal autonomy as a social and cultural value before the Civil War. Ironically, the drive for self-employment itself constituted a major cause of failure. A determination to commence business, despite inexperience and limited capital resources, rendered countless young proprietors vulnerable to financial reverses. As insolvency loomed on the horizon, emotional attachment to the status associated with self-employment also kept numerous business owners from capitulating in the face of daunting financial difficulties. Rather than restricting damage to creditors by formally suspending business, many failing business owners plunged into risky schemes, hoping against hope to recoup their losses. Such attempts usually only delayed the moment of financial reckoning and resulted in even greater loads of debt.

A rhetoric of autonomy further played a central role in increasingly successful efforts to improve the legal position of insolvent debtors. Supporters of state insolvency laws, national bankruptcy reform, and abolition of imprisonment for debt all stressed the oppressive and dependent conditions faced by individuals who had failed. Thousands of these Americans, according to antebellum champions of debt relief, were harassed at every turn by grasping creditors. Unable to transact business and vulnerable to endless legal suits, bankrupts faced the equivalent of perpetual bondage. If, however, American legislators fashioned statutory mechanisms that gave failed debtors the ability to gain discharges from their obligations, the "enslaved" would receive emancipation. Legal obliteration of past debts would create new economic persons, once again able to go into business.

When antebellum Americans did receive a discharge from their debts, either through private releases from creditors or public mechanisms like the national bankruptcy system created by the 1841 act, they often demonstrated aspirations consistent with this vision of financial resurrection. The impulse to return to the marketplace as an independent proprietor was commonplace among nineteenth-century bankrupts. Failed businessmen routinely found a way to reenter the world of commerce on their own responsibility, in many cases because they possessed skills that attracted credit, or because they chose an enterprise that did not require much capital.[17] Thus this history of antebellum bankruptcy highlights the enduring allure of economic self-direction in nineteenth-century America, even in those parts of society and culture most affected by the growth of a market economy.

Yet my research also reveals striking transformations in the way that some commercially minded Americans, and especially a number of onetime bankrupts, thought about personal independence. Business failure often prompted reconsideration of the best means to achieve and maintain the status associated with proprietorship, leading many of those who endured it to reorient their business and investment strategies, with priority placed on the limitation of risk. The most common tactics were to eschew speculative ventures, to refuse to expand without a sufficient capital base, and to try wherever possible to curtail reliance on credit. Former bankrupts who adopted these principles accepted constraints on their potential profits in order to improve the odds that they would be able to sustain their status as solvent proprietors. In these instances, bankruptcy led individuals to adopt financial prudence as a watchword, but not to forsake the conceptual link between economic autonomy and business ownership.

For other Americans, the common occurrence of insolvency encouraged a more radical rethinking of what economic independence signified in a society so dominated by market exchange. Throughout the nineteenth century, America's commercially inclined writers and orators glorified the values of Emersonian self-reliance and the rugged individualist who embodied those values, risking all and gaining a commercial or manufacturing empire. By the 1840s, though, the nation's magazines and journals included dire warnings about the dangers of autonomous economic activity alongside their tributes to the wildly successful self-made man. In the aftermath of the financial crises that rocked America during the late 1830s, a number of social commentators began to compare proprietorship unfavorably with salaried employment, extolling the latter as a means of attaining personal independence. These writers essentially redefined autonomy in terms of security and freedom from the anxieties that so often beset the owners of business ventures. Significant numbers of bankrupts may have internalized this message or adopted similar views on their own. After failing, they carved out careers as white-collar employees, finding niches within America's commercial society, but avoiding the worries and dependencies that often accompanied business ownership. Both of these consequences of antebellum economic failure—the embrace of prudential business philosophies and the turn to salaried work—profoundly influenced the development of America's urban middle class.

Although market-oriented residents of the antebellum United States generally esteemed economic independence, and although nineteenth-century American capitalism increasingly emphasized detached interactions between self-interested, autonomous agents, most of the era's businesses, including most of those that failed, were embedded in dense social networks. A communal web surrounded enterprise throughout the country, in eastern seaports and inland villages, among economic elites and middling proprietors. Even as impersonal market exchange was fostered by heightened application of the division of labor, development of a sophisticated banking system, growth of large, anonymous cities tied to ever-expanding hinterlands, and transformations in the law of negotiable instruments, intensely personal relationships continued to mediate entrepreneurial schemes and strategies.[18]

As several historians have shown, the formation of antebellum business partnerships in commerce and manufacturing usually reflected kinship links or the ties forged in fraternal orders, religious congregations, and circles of informal business association. Relatives, patrons, and mercantile friends also furnished entrepreneurs with other forms of aid. Loans and business introductions from these sources often eased the opening of an enterprise, while endorsements smoothed access to working capital, either from banks or note brokers. My evidence about postfailure careers amplifies evaluation of the significance of such assistance. Helping hands from family and friends often proved indispensable to bankrupts, enabling fresh starts, warding off additional descents into insolvency, and even laying the groundwork for postfailure prosperity. I demonstrate that failed entrepreneurs regained lost economic ground with sufficient frequency to buttress contemporaneous perceptions of the United States as a land of fluctuating fortunes. But full-fledged pecuniary redemption came most readily to insolvents who enjoyed well-placed social and familial connections, a finding that offers a new measure of the salience of class position in structuring nineteenth-century business opportunities.[19]

Bonds of family and friendship, like the magnetic pull of self-employment, guided antebellum entrepreneurs as they contemplated failure. Bankruptcy exposed crucial tensions between the moral obligations that Americans owed to kith and kin and the duties owed to impersonal creditors. Throughout the antebellum decades, these tensions shaped the advice that commercial commentators meted out to bankrupts and their creditors, the choices made by legislators and judges in tinkering with the law relating to insolvency, and the actions of bankrupts. Although the growing importance of impersonal economic exchange greatly influenced informal codes of commercial honor and legal standards of financial rectitude, the demands of relatives and friends frequently governed the behavior of failing debtors. In the face of impending bankruptcy, antebellum Americans habitually tried to protect the interests of those close to them, occasionally by fraudulently conveying or concealing assets, more commonly by making preferential payments to favored creditors. Yet many bankrupts simultaneously took pains to portray their conduct as equally concerned with the claims of all their creditors, mindful that a reputation for financial shenanigans could limit postfailure business opportunities, especially outside the circles of family and business cronies.

In addition to forcing thousands of individuals to confront the ethical conundrums of participation in a complex modern economy, antebellum bankruptcies and the degree of tolerance exhibited toward many former bankrupts markedly contributed to the dynamic character of nineteenth-century American capitalism. This argument might seem odd, since in the short term, business failures stopped economic activity in its tracks. Failed mercantile or manufacturing concerns suspended their operations—they entered into no contracts, shipped no goods, and made no payments. Business suspensions, in turn, meant unemployment for firms' employees and often financial difficulties for their creditors, especially if they were depending on payments to meet their own obligations. During financial panics and commercial depressions, these ramifications made bankruptcies a primary means by which slowdowns percolated through the economy. Yet over the longer term, I suggest that endemic insolvency and the ability of bankrupts to gain legal absolution from old debts unleashed a range of economic energies.[20]

One link between antebellum bankruptcy and capitalist innovation lay with financial opportunities created by the process of insolvency itself. In any economy, a business failure almost always creates a financial and legal mess. When circumstances multiplied that mess several thousandfold, as was the case in the nineteenth-century United States, new avenues of profit making presented themselves. Someone in antebellum America had to sort out the wreckage left by bankruptcies, selling assets and distributing dividends to creditors. Individuals who took on such chores expected to receive compensation for their troubles. So too did the lawyers or court officials who worked to hash out the legal implications of any given failure. By the early 1840s, a number of persons, including several former bankrupts, found it worth their while to specialize in bankruptcy law or administration. Other entrepreneurs capitalized on surging demand for information about the financial standing of the nation's businesses or about the legal procedures and doctrines relating to insolvency. In addition, the avalanche of antebellum failures engendered a whole new kind of speculation—in the assets of bankruptcy estates. This undertaking required careful sifting among the remains of an insolvent business owner. Among the rubble of a bankrupt's holdings, among all the book account debts marked "doubtful" and all the seemingly worthless land claims in Illinois or Mississippi, which ones might turn out to be valuable? A new class of bargain-hunting scavengers made it their business to seek out the answers to such queries and to profit from their investigations. The emergence of these vulture capitalists and their eventual acceptance in antebellum commercial culture stand as instructive measures of evolving self-consciousness about the mechanisms of a capitalist economic order.

The give and take that occurred between antebellum debtors and creditors in the context of bankruptcy, moreover, honed rhetorical skills that proved essential in a volatile economy. Court processes pertaining to insolvency regularly served less as a formal means of dispute resolution and more as the platform for multifaceted negotiations between failing Americans and the holders of claims against them. Typically parties to such negotiations used the likelihood of eventual legal outcomes or the prospect of mounting legal costs as levers to arrange private settlements. In the unstable economy of nineteenth-century America, an ability to cajole payments out of debtors, to wheedle easier terms out of creditors, and to wield lawyers and legal proceedings effectively toward both of these ends was as important to pecuniary success as salesmanship or technical know-how. Individuals who cultivated aptitude in these matters greatly improved their chances of prospering in the antebellum marketplace.

Perhaps the most important connections between antebellum bankruptcy and the release of capitalist energy manifested themselves in postfailure career strategies. Not every former bankrupt sought a haven from risk after insolvency. Discharge from past obligations encouraged a number of highfliers to redouble their entrepreneurial efforts. These bankrupts typically sought to breech prevailing commercial boundaries, either by expanding the domain of market transactions, developing new products, or devising new methods of distribution. On occasion such efforts produced spectacular postfailure success; more commonly they led only to new accumulations of unpayable obligations. Collectively, the ventures of risk-taking former bankrupts helped to consolidate a business culture predicated on "creative destruction," in which a multitude of entrepreneurs mounted ongoing assaults on prevailing forms of economic activity, at once seeking profits and envisioning, if not always realizing, a continuous process of social "improvement."[21]

Navigating Failure, then, explores the culture of American capitalism through the prism of one of its most enduring features—the widespread inability of individuals and firms to pay their debts. Such a perspective enriches our understanding of how Americans adjusted economically, socially, and culturally to the advent of a thoroughly integrated market society. It further suggests why so many Americans who were touched by business failure directed their energies toward making the capitalist system work for them and their families, rather than challenging that system outright.

Placing the biographies of market-oriented bankrupts at center stage inevitably obscures some aspects of America's nineteenth-century experience with insolvency.

The pages that follow offer scant discussion of failures by corporations and still less analysis of debt repudiations by municipalities and state governments. I concentrate neither on imprisonment for debt, nor on the defaults of purchasers of public lands, nor on the significance of stay laws, homestead exemptions, and mechanics' lien laws, all issues of central importance within the period's state and national politics. By the same token, this book does not delve into the bitter meanings of insolvency for antebellum slaves, who frequently endured family separations as a result of their owners' inability to make good on financial obligations.

I have additionally chosen not to focus on two crucially important responses to bankruptcy in nineteenth-century America—attempts to escape the reach of a growing market society, and efforts to oppose market expansion through politics. The standard method of escape involved physical flight, particularly in rural America, where foreclosure sometimes led insolvent farmers to migrate westward in the hopes of starting again on land isolated from transportation routes and networks of long-distance trade. Less commonly, sustained financial difficulties helped to inspire socialist experimentation, as with the transcendentalist writer Bronson Alcott, or spiritual odysseys with anticapitalist overtones, as with the founder of Mormonism, Joseph Smith. For Alcott, incessant battles with personal indebtedness greatly contributed to a long-standing search for economic alternatives to capitalism, most clearly exhibited in his commitment to the short-lived Massachusetts utopian community, Fruitlands. In Smith's case, a familial history of financial struggle and outright commercial failure almost certainly influenced his patriarchal and communitarian religious philosophy, which repudiated the individualism and materialism so fundamental to the workings of the antebellum marketplace.[22]

Insolvency, moreover, often sparked anger and resentment about the injustices spawned by an integrated market economy, emotions that powerfully shaped the rhetoric and agenda of the antebellum Democratic Party. Some of the most vehement and influential critics of the antebellum financial system, including Andrew Jackson and Thomas Hart "Old Bullion" Benton, the long-serving senator from Missouri, owed their economic views at least partly to early commercial trials. Jackson and Benton both almost experienced bankruptcy as young adults, the former because a partner in a real estate deal defaulted on his obligations, the latter because of financial entanglements with a bank that failed during the panic of 1819. These incidents left the two men with deep suspicions about the credit arrangements that fueled America's explosive commercial growth, which undergirded their later political opposition to concentrated economic power.[23]

Fears of bankruptcy similarly shaped the political impulses of a portion of the antebellum electorate, especially among farmers and urban artisans who prized economic self-direction above the pursuit of riches or the consumption of luxuries. Harboring great apprehension of crippling indebtedness, significant numbers of small-scale producers witnessed the swift pace of antebellum commercial development with alarm. In their minds, the ever-encroaching credit system simultaneously encouraged corrupting speculation, placed excessive power in the hands of individuals who controlled the flow of credit, and exposed petty proprietors to unnecessary financial risks. These citizens warmed to Jacksonian attacks on economic aristocracy and the "Monster" Bank of the United States, emerging as one of the major constituencies of the Democratic Party.[24]

Insolvency, then, emboldened some residents of the nineteenth-century United States to resist the incursions of a thoroughly commercial world. But this particular dimension of America's past encounters with economic failure has drawn considerable scholarly investigation. If we are to understand the complex processes by which ordinary people created a market society in the United States, despite ever-increasing harvests of ruined business owners, we need as well to fathom the ways in which bankruptcy encouraged many individuals to rethink their place within a capitalist economy. To that end, the motif of capitalist adaptation features particularly prominently in this book.

The nineteenth-century marketplace was filled with smothered dreams and re-kindled aspirations. It offered persistently cruel judgment for some American entrepreneurs, presented others with only temporary obstacles to later prosperity, and gave still others a grand opportunity to scavenge off the economic carcasses around them. The brutal fact of ever-present business failure demanded the creation of institutions to cope with it, whether embodied in private arrangements or legislatively mandated judicial processes. High rates of bankruptcy further ensured much soul-searching about the moral dimensions of capitalist enterprise and the risks that such enterprise entailed. To see what antebellum failure wrought, one must begin where failure did—in the misfortunes and mistakes that at least momentarily overwhelmed the era's bankrupts.

Part 1

The Roots of Misfortune

"Now, Uncle, do not commit the common fault of judging the community by a few.
There are hundreds of worthy honest men, who have accumulated a competency
by years of toil and honest industry, and who see themselves now suddenly reduced
to ruin without any error of their's—all that fail are not ambitious speculators."

"Pretty near all. No man can *fail* who is prudent, and cautious."

—E. R. S., "The Pressure of the Times: A Commercial Story,"

Ladies' Companion (1837)

Chapter 1

Perils of the Credit System

Bankruptcy . . . is like death, and almost as certain.
—"The Chances of Success in Mercantile Life,"
Hunt's Merchants' Magazine (1846)

Antebellum social commentators carried on a running quarrel about the culpability of all the bankrupts in their midst. Did individuals who found themselves overwhelmed by debts bring about their own failures, or was financial disaster the result of circumstances beyond any reasonable foresight? Contemporary observers came to greatly different conclusions on the matter. A November 1841 sermon by the Reverend John T. Brooke, rector of Cincinnati's Christ Church, typified charitable interpretations of the nation's many bankruptcies. Addressing his congregation on the "morality of the credit system," Brooke conjured up a world filled with bankrupts struck down by misfortune. The reverend's sermon observed that "there are many honest failures in business, which ordinary prudence cannot prevent." Denying that bankrupts were necessarily to blame for their predicaments, Brooke preached that "the very elements or other causes alike uncontrollable, may war against a man's interest and success." While cautioning against excessive reliance on credit relationships, the Cincinnati rector intimated that the very structure of American trade and commerce made at least some bankruptcies inevitable.[1]

Many antebellum writers, however, took the opposite view, echoing Puritan and republican suspicions that individuals who violated the sanctity of contracts almost invariably possessed some telling personal defect. Thomas Greaves Cary, an influential member of the Boston business community, exemplified those who located the causes of insolvency in the breasts of those who failed. Three years after Brooke preached his sermon on debt and the credit system, Cary gave a widely circulated address to the Boston Mercantile Library Association. His major goal was to explain "the causes of frequent failure among men of business." Brushing off the common presumption that bankruptcies primarily resulted from an unavoidable run of bad luck, Cary argued that "the failures that arise from inevitable misfortune alone are not so numerous as they are generally supposed to be." Instead, he maintained that "in most cases insolvency is caused by mistakes that originate in personal character." According to this Boston industrialist, bankruptcy usually turned out to be the child of fraud or mismanagement.[2]

People like Cary did not deny that bankrupts suffered unexpected reverses; they simply rejected arguments that the most important determinants of those reverses lay outside of individuals' control. Commentators such as Brooke, by contrast, suggested that the source of a bankrupt's losses often resided in forces, whether social, economic, or providential, against which he had little if any ability to protect himself. Both of these views offer insights into the causes of antebellum failure, and hence the experiences that shaped the responses of Americans to insolvency.

As this chapter demonstrates, the basic workings of antebellum capitalism ensured that hundreds of thousands of Americans would carry heavy loads of debt; the fundamental character of the economy further guaranteed that crippling losses would visit a large proportion of those Americans. The failures of most individuals who appeared on the southern New York bankruptcy dockets in 1842 and 1843 stemmed from structural economic faults that were frequently difficult to foresee. The suddenly tight credit markets of 1837 and 1839, the great panics that conditions of tight money created, and the "dull times" that followed the second of these revulsions all took their toll on the era's businesses, as did the pressures of capitalist competition and the inscrutable fluctuations of demand within particular markets.

But as Chapter 2 will make clear, independent proprietors in antebellum America did not share the same likelihood of suffering financial ruin. Some individuals were particularly vulnerable to bankruptcy, both in times of depression and prosperity. Any business owner who practiced poor methods of accounting, who lacked experience with the complexities of buying and selling on credit, or who transacted a relatively large amount of business on a relatively small capital base stood an especially good chance of failing. So too did consumers who consistently lived beyond their means. Antebellum bankruptcies resulted as much from inexperience, greed, and an initial shortage of capital as they did from the structural imperatives of a capitalist economy.[3]

Awash in an Ocean of Credit

As the Revolution of 1776 receded into memory, Americans increasingly organized their work and consumption according to the incentives of market capitalism. More farm families grew crops or raised livestock with an eye toward sale. A greater proportion of artisans abandoned production based on custom orders, seeking instead to turn out more standardized goods for a larger market. Simultaneously, Americans in both town and countryside experienced growing material wants, which soon became growing material needs. Eager to match the productive capacities of the nation's farms, workshops, and manufactories with the wants and needs of the nation's consumers, thousands of Americans entered into business as merchants of one sort or another.[4]

Together, burgeoning market-oriented production and surging demand for foodstuffs and consumer goods eventually fostered dramatic economic growth. In the decades after the War of 1812, Americans produced more cotton, more grain, more livestock, more textile goods, more coal, more lumber, more machinery, more of just about everything. As the century progressed, most free Americans had greater and greater amounts of income to spend, and they spent it on more and better housewares, nicer homes, fancier furnishings and clothing, or the clearing of unimproved land for themselves or their children.[5]

The expansion of America's market economy depended crucially on what contemporaries such as Reverend Brooke referred to as "the credit system"—an intricate tangle of obligations that extended throughout the country, financing production, distribution, and consumption of the nation's goods and services. Credit had such allure prior the Civil War for several reasons, the most important of which concerned a dearth of specie and capital. The new republic was, in the terminology of modern economic theory, a developing economy, richer in potential than actual stores of wealth. American monetary reserves, especially before the discovery of gold in California, were not sufficient to meet the demand for funds by the nation's producers, entrepreneurs, and consumers. In both town and countryside, circulating coin fell well short of commercial requirements. Credit arrangements filled the gap, with promissory notes, bills of exchange, and banknotes furnishing the bulk of the money supply. The vastness of the United States and long cycles of agricultural and manufacturing production further contributed to the dominance of credit in the antebellum economy. Since goods often had to travel long distances to reach their ultimate markets, direct transfers of specie were both inconvenient and expensive, even when coin was abundant. Credit instruments greatly eased the transit of crops and processed articles. Farmers, artisans, and factory operators also incurred substantial expenses before they were able to vend their output. Loans from suppliers, banks, or marketing merchants tided over countless proprietors during the interval between production and sale.[6]

Thus the antebellum economy was structured as much around borrowed money and promises of payment as it was around the routes of rivers, roads, canals, and, by the 1840s, railroads. The extensive reach of credit, in turn, constituted a crucial precondition for the failure of so many businesses. Any attempt to appreciate the viewpoint expressed by the Reverend Brooke requires close attention to the manner in which antebellum enterprise was yoked to the credit system.

For many commercially oriented Americans, simply embarking on a course of independent enterprise required access to credit. Lacking the resources to finance their dreams, individuals like Alfred Carpenter, Andrew Merwin, and Daniel Greene had to raise funds in order to set their ambitions in motion. In the case of Carpenter and Merwin, the latter's father served as creditor, lending over $2,600 to enable the pair to open a New York City dry goods firm in 1837. Daniel Greene's venture assumed grander proportions. Based in East Greenwich, Rhode Island, during the early and mid-1830s, Greene and several partners gained legislative incorporation for manufacturing ventures ranging from the production of cotton broadcloth to the bleaching and laundering of clothes. The Rhode Island manufacturers then borrowed money from local banks and New York City merchants as a means of getting their operations up and running. Throughout the antebellum decades, thousands of schemes gained a listing in a city directory only because of the infusion of someone else's capital.[7]

Whether or not proprietors borrowed money to enter the antebellum economy on their own account, they almost universally relied on credit in the course of daily business operations. Entrepreneurs generally did not pay rent, wages, or transportation charges in advance, nor did they immediately settle accounts for professional services.[8] Even more important, most business owners did not supply cash when they bought stock or supplies, nor demand cash when they sold merchandise, agricultural produce, or finished articles. Instead, they took on debt as purchasers and extended credit as sellers. At the forefront of these transactions were individuals who made their living through mercantile exchange.

Although business dealings drew just about every American merchant into the nation's web of credit, the complexity of financial entanglement varied significantly. Specialization over the first decades of the nineteenth century created a bewildering array of commercial niches, differentiated by size and function. A person who thought of himself as a merchant in 1835 might have been a traveling peddler, the keeper of a country store, a small-scale city grocer or dry-goods retailer, a wholesale jobber devoted to one particular line of goods, such as textiles or hardware, a large-scale importer of European manufactured goods, or an equally large exporter of American agricultural products.[9] These enterprises required greatly differing engagement with mercantile credit.

The business of Aaron Abrahams, an immigrant vendor of jewelry and hardware, typified the credit relationships of small dealers in the world of antebellum commerce. Originally from Poland, Abrahams first emigrated to England, leaving there for New York City around 1834. For a time he ran a store in New York but eventually opted for peddling as a livelihood. In November 1841, he bought almost $3,000 worth of jewelry and cutlery from five New York City dealers. Promising payment for the goods in the spring, the peddler traveled to Charleston, South Carolina, and then across the South to St. Louis, selling his wares for cash as he went.[10] The arrangement between Abrahams and his suppliers reflected an unusually straightforward mercantile relationship. He bought goods on credit, which he hoped to sell for cash at enough of a mark-up to justify the investment.

More complicated networks of credit permeated the commercial life of most antebellum merchants. The failed partnership of David Boyd and Martin Pond demonstrates a characteristic pattern of debts for a rural outpost of the nation's burgeoning system of trade. In the mid-1830s, Boyd & Pond operated a country store in Jamestown, Alabama. The pair confronted over $13,000 in debts by the time they closed down in 1838—considerably more than Abrahams owed and typical for bankrupt storekeepers, but a modest amount in comparison to the business handled by large merchants in the nation's biggest cities. A clear majority of the $13,000 was due on credit purchases from New York City dry goods merchants, crockery dealers, and purveyors of hardware. Unlike Aaron Abrahams, who demanded cash for his trinkets and knives, Boyd & Pond sold much of their wares "on time"—that is, they allowed their customers to buy goods with a promise to pay in the future.[11] The Jamestown firm extended the chain of credit one step further than Abrahams, and so had to worry about collecting debts owed to them as well as paying obligations that they incurred.

Still more complex credit arrangements characterized the mercantile affairs of eastern wholesalers or importers, such as the New York City partnership between Edward and Henry Heyer. A major distributor of hardware before its failure in August 1842, Heyer & Heyer kept a wide range of goods—everything from nails, screws, and locks to guns, anvils, mousetraps, and cutlery. They bought these goods from merchants and manufacturers in New York City, throughout New England, and from Sheffield and Birmingham in Great Britain. After assembling stock, the firm attracted credit-based business from New York City retailers and storekeepers in nearly every part of the country. Whereas Boyd & Pond bought almost exclusively from merchants in one city and sold to a local population, Heyer & Heyer had to keep track of credit relationships with suppliers throughout the North Atlantic trade basin and customers in almost every state of the American union. In addition, the hardware dealers' obligations to English suppliers often had to be settled in pounds, necessitating the drafting or purchase of international bills of exchange.[12]

The commercial activities of Aaron Abrahams, Martin Pond, and the Heyer brothers suggest the basic outlines of the credit system as it pertained to merchants. The businesses of other antebellum proprietors usually took on a similar character. Boardinghouse keepers such as Angeline Brown, who failed in New York City during 1842, bought provisions on time and extended credit to tenants. Artisans like the bankrupt Brooklyn shoemaker William Watson procured raw materials with promissory notes or on account. The great majority of antebellum manufacturers also relied heavily on credit. As the Englishman Francis Grund noted in an 1837 travel account, America's "system of credit, established in manufactures and commerce, extends also to the business of the mechanic, and in some instances even to the workman."[13]

The intricacies of that system frequently stretched beyond the interconnected threads of debt created by the purchase or sale of goods and services on time. Matters could become more intertwined as the result of two common business practices—discounting and endorsing. The business of Frederick J. Conant illustrates how discounting worked. A dry goods jobber based in New York City during the mid-1830s, Conant marketed his goods throughout the country, particularly to storekeepers in the Old Northwest and the South. He sold a substantial proportion of his stock on credit, asking for payment in four to six months, like most antebellum wholesalers. In 1836, however, the jobber wanted hard cash from his credit sales before the promissory notes from his customers would mature. His solution was to get the notes discounted. Lacking the connections or credit to persuade bank officers to provide this service for him, Conant went to New York City note brokers, who charged between two and five times the 6 percent annual interest levied by banks. (The higher rates reflected the greater risk presented by borrowers who had been shunned by the discount committees of banks.) These financiers "shaved" the country notes for Conant, giving the jobber a percentage of their face value in cash or their own promissory notes, and gaining ownership of the commercial paper in return. By discounting the notes of his customers, Conant, along with thousands of other antebellum entrepreneurs, hoped to expand his business without raising additional capital. Of course, taking advantage of discounting facilities meant that the dry goods wholesaler ceded some of his profit to note brokers, assuming that his customers made good on their obligations. If they did not, he incurred a range of new debts, since he would be liable to the brokers, or to a subsequent holder, for any unpaid note.[14]

While discounting allowed a creditor to transform accounts receivable into cash, endorsements enabled a prospective debtor more readily to gain access to credit. For all the borrowing and lending of money and goods in the antebellum economy, those in a position to lend did not grant advances to any would-be borrower. Nor did they proffer loans without thought as to the terms of arrangement. Creditors, whether individuals, partnerships, or corporations, generally lent money with the intent of making a profit.[15] When a supplicant enjoyed excellent credit, lenders might very well furnish money on the basis of a simple promise to pay. If the person requesting a loan did not boast such high financial standing, or if the lender wished special protection against nonpayment, the latter often demanded security. Creditors frequently demanded a mortgage on property owned by a would-be borrower, such as real estate, stock, or furniture. Alternatively, lenders might ask for actual possession of collateral—usually intangible property like stock certificates or promissory notes.[16] Another way to increase the security of an obligation was to get the debtor to borrow someone else's credit, chiefly by persuading a third party to co-sign, or endorse, the loan.

Requirement of an endorsement could occur in just about every kind of ante-bellum financial transaction but was especially common in the discounting of commercial paper, the granting of accommodation loans (straightforward loans of cash that were unrelated to the regular course of trade), and the purchase of real estate on credit. Close business associates provided one crucial source of financial guarantees, as commercial confidants regularly furnished one another with a signa-ture on a note, secure in the knowledge that they would be able to ask for a similar favor in turn. Some proprietors could rely on the aid of partners or the backing of patrons, such as former employers. Otherwise, debtors in need of bolstered credit had little choice but to seek out the assistance of relatives, playing on their sense of familial duty.[17] Endorsements, like discounts, multiplied the interlinked strands within the credit system.

The pervasiveness of commercial indebtedness meant that the economic for-tunes of antebellum proprietors were inextricably bound up with one another. Manufacturers and urban importers depended on the remittances of wholesalers; wholesalers on timely collections from retailers and artisans; retailers and artisans on eventual payment from consumers; discounting banks and note brokers on disbursements by drawers of promissory notes and acceptors of bills of exchange; and endorsers on the pecuniary fidelity of friends or relatives. In time, this interde-pendence spread over the full length of the United States. Throughout the ante-bellum decades, a large cast of boosters, politicians, and entrepreneurs worked feverishly to refashion the connections between points on the American map. Their efforts produced a fleet of steamboats on the nation's rivers and coastlines, a vastly improved road network, hundreds of miles of canals, and thousands of miles of railroads. Collectively, these internal improvements laid the foundation for far-reaching economic integration, extending the chains of credit over a wider and wider area, and linking the fates of New York City hardware dealers and Jamestown, Alabama, storekeepers.[18]

In embracing commercial credit, market-oriented participants in the antebellum economy evinced considerable optimism about the future—their own, that of the individuals with whom they did business, and that of American commerce as a whole. Antebellum entrepreneurs had no doubt that their efforts would create profits, enabling them safely to anchor their businesses in a sea of credit trans-actions. So long as British and American banks, European suppliers, and domestic mercantile houses gladly extended loans and discounted commercial paper, this optimism looked to be more than warranted. When times were flush, prosperity traveled with the nation's transportation routes, as merchants diffused easier credit terms and registered strong demand for the products of field, manufactory, and workshop.

During good economic times, Americans tended to view the credit system as an unmixed blessing. The magic lubricant of credit quickened the pace of the antebellum economy, reducing the capital resources necessary to start enterprises, lowering requirements of working capital, and expanding potential markets. In its absence, far fewer individuals would have been able to enter the business world, existing enterprises would have encountered barriers to growth, and the creation of a consumer society would have slowed, since Americans would have had a more difficult time purchasing the burgeoning products of domestic and European manufacturers. The "credit system," as the Albany Republican Committee noted in 1837, "has extended our commerce over the whole world—peopled our wilderness—built our cities and villages—founded our colleges and established our schools. It has given us national wealth and individual prosperity."[19]

But universal dependence on credit also made Americans more susceptible to the shifting currents of the overall economy or the misfortunes of the firms with whom they transacted business, and thus more likely to undergo financial shipwreck. If, for example, enough customers neglected, refused, or lacked the ability to pay the bills owed to a rural storekeeper, that proprietor could not so easily make good on his debts to eastern wholesalers. If sufficient numbers of a jobber's customers encountered analogous difficulties, the wholesaler was going to have problems in satisfying the claims of his own suppliers. The same exertion of economic "pressure" could work in the opposite direction. Should a seaport jobber find himself in economic difficulties, he would almost certainly dash off imploring letters to the retailers he supplied, alternately requesting and demanding remittances on their accounts. Economic hardships anywhere along the chain of credit could quickly migrate up and down the chain, tracing the very same paths that in other times spread economic growth. The nation's rapidly growing postal system could bring news of bank and mercantile failures as easily as requests for new orders of calico or crockery. Credit fueled the antebellum economy; it further ensured that Americans throughout the land would stand exposed if their confidence in the profitability of enterprise proved even momentarily misplaced.

Panic, Deflation, and Hard Times

No events produced more antebellum bankruptcies than the periodic financial crises that buffeted the American economy, ushering in periods of sustained commercial depression. The remarkable economic growth between 1815 and 1860 occurred not as the result of gradual, steady expansion of production and consumption, but through the far more wrenching oscillations of boom and bust.

During the prosperous part of the business cycle, sanguine expectations, usually related to the emergence of new economic vistas, such as the reopening of trans-atlantic trade after the War of 1812, the settlement of the trans-Appalachian frontier, and the construction of grand transportation projects in the 1830s and 1850s, stimulated a free flow of credit from both European and domestic sources. Sooner or later, though, the short-term views of leading commercial figures dimmed, either because they confronted pressure from their own creditors or because of worries about accumulating excesses in American consumption and investment. Prominent investors, bankers, and merchants then looked only to curtail their own potential losses. The resulting squeeze could ripple across the Atlantic and into the American hinterland within weeks.[20]

Contemporaries referred to the most severe revulsions of credit as "panics." As a panic took hold, fear of impending ruin generated desperate attempts to collect debts, runs on banks, and the collapse of both land values and stock prices. Antebellum America experienced four great panics—in 1819, 1837, 1839, and 1857—as well as a series of less severe monetary contractions.[21] In the case of bankrupts who appeared on federal court dockets under the 1841 Bankruptcy Act, the financial crises of the late 1830s and the ensuing deflation were the most important proximate causes of failure.

The prelude to the panics of 1837 and 1839 was overbrimming confidence in American development, which manifested itself in several quarters. During the 1830s, some of America's most steadfast commercial champions resided within the borders of its former colonial ruler. Excellent harvests spurred British economic growth in the period, buttressing both the income of consumers and their demand for cotton textile goods. This heightened demand for textiles led to increased orders by British manufacturers for American cotton, an increased price for the staple, and liberal extension of credit to merchants and farmers engaged in the business of growing and distributing the South's main crop. As long as the trans-atlantic cotton market boomed, British investors and exporters also turned to American securities and American markets with relish. The former gobbled up state bond issues, while the latter flooded eastern seaports with manufactures, invariably sold on generous terms.[22]

British exuberance over American prospects was more than matched in the United States. State governments borrowed millions in the 1830s to fund canal and railroad construction. By the thousands, speculators and settlers bought land at government auctions or through private sales, usually relying on debt-based financing. American merchants at every link in the country's distribution system emulated the credit policy of British exporters, stimulating domestic consumption and helping to produce a massive merchandise trade deficit. All of these activities gained support from an inflow of specie into the American economy, which largely resulted from a favorable dollar-pound exchange rate and the willingness of British mercantile houses to carry over accounts with their American buyers. Specie reserves in the United States nearly tripled between 1832 and 1836, underpinning a remarkable expansion of bank credit and circulating banknotes.[23]

The combination of robust British growth, monetary inflow, and confidence in the American economy proved to be a potent mixture. Together they produced an economic boom, with increased output and rapid rises in commodity prices and the market values of stocks and land. Neither British growth, currency expansion, nor faith in America's economic performance lasted forever, though. Britain endured average to poor wheat harvests in 1835 and 1836, which cut into incomes and textile demand. By the winter of 1836, dimming economic conditions and a rapid depletion in the Bank of England's specie reserves persuaded leading British bankers and merchants to rethink their generous stance toward American debtors. The Bank of England's governors led a reversal of mercantile policy, raising the institution's discount rate from 3 to 5 percent and sharply curtailing loans to British merchants engaged in the American trade. Credit quickly became both expensive and elusive for these firms.[24]

Tight credit hit American markets with the speed of the first packets to reach the United States with news of the change in British financial markets. Instead of rolling over old loans or generously granting credit, as they had done for several years, British firms now pressed their American correspondents for payment. Many importers lacked the funds to meet these demands and had to scurry about American money markets in search of loans to satisfy their creditors across the Atlantic. With this increased demand for money in the fall and winter of 1836, short-term interest rates offered by banks and brokers shot up. Seekers of discounts in New York City had to pay at least 2 percent a month for accommodation by October 1836.[25]

Alongside these ruinous rates of interest, American merchants confronted plummeting cotton prices as the winter of 1836 stretched into the new year. A drop in the British demand for textiles coincided with the Bank of England's new loan policy to stifle British orders for American cotton. By April, cotton fetched only 70 percent of its average 1836 price. Faced with a rapidly declining return on their cotton holdings, extremely high interest rates, and insistent British creditors, a number of American cotton merchants succumbed to the strain. Unable to pay their debts, they become insolvent. The earliest failures occurred in New Orleans during March 1837; others soon rocked the whole of the Old Southwest.[26]

Since the initial firms that failed had credit relationships with a multitude of commercial houses in eastern cities, the impact of their failures soon spread to the eastern seaboard. Hundreds of eastern merchants had conducted their businesses on the assumption that their southwestern debtors would make good on their obligations. When those debtors failed, the eastern firms found themselves facing similar pressures—a loss of expected income, an inability to borrow additional funds at less than exorbitant rates, and demands from their creditors for payment of maturing debts.

J. & L. Joseph & Co. was one of the first eastern houses to feel the brunt of southwestern failures. Comprised of Joseph Joseph, Solomon Joseph, and Moses Henriques, all of whom would apply for bankruptcy in 1842, Joseph & Co. operated one of the largest exchange brokerages in the nation. The firm cast a wide commercial net, contracting debts well into the millions of dollars. Among the brokerage house's many activities were the discounting and collection of country debts for New York City merchants, the marketing of domestic stock and bonds to Americans and Europeans, and the buying and selling of both foreign exchange and commercial paper relating to transatlantic trade. Pressed by its many American and European creditors from early in 1837, Joseph & Co. did not have the resources to withstand the March failure of a chief New Orleans debtor, the cotton brokerage firm of Herman, Briggs & Co. The latter firm owed the New York City brokers well over $1 million. When prospects for prompt and full remittance of this sum disappeared, Joseph & Co. lost all hope of avoiding bankruptcy. On March 17, the firm officially stopped payment to its far-flung creditors.[27]

Once a firm as influential as Joseph & Co. succumbed to the financial pressure instigated by the Bank of England, already shaken commercial confidence quickly degenerated into full-scale panic. As the onetime New York City mayor and diarist Philip Hone noted, the failure of this brokerage house "occasioned great consternation in Wall Street." The Josephs had conducted an "enormous" business, maintaining business relationships with a great many "merchants, jobbers, grocers, and other regular dealers." All of these mercantile firms now faced the likelihood of substantial losses.[28]

Faith in American commerce and industry evaporated as banks and other creditors began to fear widespread insolvency. Samuel Swartwout, then the customs collector of New York Port, captured prevailing sentiment in an April 8 letter to a close business associate in Texas. Marveling at the stupendous crash of the Josephs, Swartwout described a commercial scene in which "[e]verybody will fail—all H——l will fail."[29] In such a fearful environment, the holders of debt almost universally sought to squeeze payment out of the individuals and firms who owed them money. As more and more firms felt this pressure, and as additional credit became next to impossible to obtain, debtors sought to sell assets in order to pay the claims against them.

These attempts at liquidation only intensified the crisis. Willing sellers of real estate, stocks, and furniture suddenly found a dearth of would-be buyers. Throughout the 1830s Americans had been all too happy to accept commercial paper and banknotes as payment for goods and debts. By March 1837, bits of paper did not

CREDIT CONTRACTION AMID FINANCIAL CRISIS. This cartoon illustrates the drying up of credit in the wake of a commercial panic (*Harper's Weekly*, Oct. 24, 1857, Rare Book, Manuscript, and Special Collections Library, Duke University).

BANK DIRECTOR TO MERCHANT.—"Do as we do; take care of yourself."

look nearly as inviting as hard pieces of silver and gold. Individuals who had reserves of hard currency or other unimpeachable assets would no longer part with them easily. Moreover, the future prospects for continued rises in the value of land, stock, and goods ceased to look so good. The combination of a greatly increased supply of assets for sale and a greatly diminished demand for them produced a predictable result—precipitous declines in market value. As early as April 21, Philip Hone reported that almost all bank stocks had fallen well below par and that most canal and railway stocks fetched around one-half of their price a year previously. Real estate was in even worse straits. Upper Manhattan lots that had sold for $480 in September 1836 went for only $50 a scant seven months later. The diarist and mainstay of New York's high society could only marvel at the blasted fortunes in his midst, which "have melted away like the snows before an April sun."[30] Such momentous declines greatly complicated the problems faced by debtors struggling to stave off impending failure; they also weakened the financial position of other owners of land and stocks. Throughout March and into April, every day brought at least a handful of New York City firms to their knees. As each firm stopped payment, its creditors had to reckon with lost income and the increased pressure they would now face in taking care of their own obligations.

A general loss of confidence in banking institutions exacerbated the parlous financial situation. At the same time that New York City banks curtailed credit and sought repayment on outstanding loans, their own creditors became uneasy about the ability of the institutions to maintain payment in specie. Banking practice presupposed that all the holders of banknotes would not come calling for specie payment at once. With the commercial world suddenly lurching from the announcement of one mercantile failure to another, New Yorkers entertained serious doubts about the continued solvency of the city's banks. Toward the end of April, bank cashiers had to work feverishly and after regular business hours to meet the demand of patrons who wished to exchange banknotes for gold or silver. Early in May, the demands became too great for the banks to handle and bank directors agreed among themselves to stop payment in specie. A similar sequence of tight credit, mercantile failure, intensifying commercial pessimism, and bank suspension played itself out in cities and towns across the nation. By the end of May, banks throughout the United States had stopped paying out specie.[31]

The commercial panic of 1837 took its toll on thousands of American businesses. Many individuals and firms did not survive the most pressure-filled months of April and May. On April 8, the New York *Journal of Commerce* cataloged ninety-eight of the biggest local firms brought down by the crisis to that date. The list included five foreign and domestic exchange brokers, such as Joseph & Co., thirty dry goods jobbers, sixteen commission merchants dealing in shoes or clothing, twenty-eight real estate speculators, and eight stock brokers. The combined amount of debts owed by these firms exceeded $60 million. A host of medium-sized firms and small traders similarly fell victim to the pressure of the times.[32]

Despite the financial devastation wrought by this crisis, it did not send American commerce immediately into depression. Ironically, the general bank suspension that began in May initially worked to ease the enormous pressure confronted by so many of the nation's debtors. Freed from the obligation to redeem any banknote in specie, banks could now extend a more liberal policy toward individuals and firms who already owed them money or toward applicants for new loans.[33] English creditors similarly exercised renewed leniency, as the Bank of England steadily improved its position over 1837 and dropped its discount rate accordingly. After credit eased in London, British traders willingly provided new commercial credits to American merchants. British investors, moreover, followed the lead of the country's merchants and continued to plough their resources into American securities, especially those financing internal improvements. Able to rely on these investments to fund bond issues, state governments dramatically increased their expenditures on transportation projects, injecting cash into the American economy. Renewed

British credit and vigorous spending on public works spurred demand for American goods and raised prices for commodities, stocks, and land. As a result, American debtors found themselves far more able to make their payments. By the spring of 1838, the American financial system had recovered sufficiently that most banks returned to a standard of specie payment on demand.[34]

Recovery, however, did not last long. By the fall of 1839, commercial crisis had once again gripped the North Atlantic. The roots of the crisis mirrored those that precipitated the panic a few years previously. Hit by another poor wheat harvest in 1838, the British economy began to bleed specie when the country had to import grain to feed its growing population. As in 1836, the Bank of England responded to the depletion in its reserves by increasing interest rates. In the summer of 1839, the bank's discount rate topped 6 percent. The combination of falling British incomes and tight British credit soon rocked American markets. With diminished incomes, the British demanded less cotton. With restricted credit at home, British merchants tightened the credit they offered abroad. At the same time that these fluctuations beset the British economy, American cotton growers brought in a bumper crop. Weak British demand and strong American supply worked to drive down the price of cotton. American merchants now found themselves caught in an all-too-familiar bind, facing plummeting prices and extraordinarily tight money markets. Enough firms cracked under the pressure to recreate the drama of widespread commercial failures, shattered business confidence, and bank suspensions.[35]

Unlike in the months following the earlier panic, though, quick relief was not forthcoming from British creditors. Ongoing difficulties in the British economy encouraged banks and merchants to shy away from American business. Equally important, British investors soured on American prospects, drastically cutting off the flow of capital to the transportation schemes of the states. Deprived of the ability to borrow from abroad, state governments could no longer afford to continue dozens of construction projects. By early 1840, work on most internal improvements had ground to a halt and many states had great difficulties making the payments on outstanding bonds. Nine states eventually defaulted on bond issues from the 1830s; Arkansas, Michigan, Mississippi, and the territory of Florida all repudiated at least part of their debts. The defaults and repudiations only served to worsen already damaged American prospects for European credit.[36]

Without significant aid from across the Atlantic, American markets entered the new decade beset by deflation. Debtors looked to sell whatever they owned in order to make payments to their creditors. Real estate, stocks, slaves, commercial paper, and furniture all poured onto the nation's markets, as hundreds of thousands of Americans struggled to avoid a liquidity crisis. Buyers were even less easy to find now than they had been in 1837. The "visions of [a] glorious future" no longer "filled the imaginations of the multitude" as they had only a few short years previously.[37] With supply stretching far beyond demand, the market values of all these assets moved steadily downward. Chicago properties brought only one-sixth of their 1836 prices in 1842. Real estate in New York City also experienced sharp, if not nearly as precipitous, declines in value. In the seven years after the height of the mid-1830s boom, city tax assessments of all privately owned New York properties fell more than 30 percent. Stocks plunged as well; railroad shares in 1843 were worth only around one-half of their pre-1839 crash level.[38] Throughout the country, propertied Americans watched the nominal value of their assets eaten away by the inexorable workings of a deflationary economic environment.

The prices of commodities tumbled alongside the values of town lots, farms, and stock, largely as the result of monetary contraction. In the mid-1830s, the stock of specie in domestic circulation had almost tripled; now, with Americans greatly distrustful of banks, the proportion of specie held by the public increased. With far fewer gold and silver coins in their vaults, banks had to limit both their loans and their issuance of banknotes. This diminished monetary supply, along with tight British mercantile policy, worked to slash the credit available to Americans throughout the country. As each link in the transatlantic mercantile chain confronted tougher conditions of payment, and as so many antebellum proprietors and consumers struggled to cope with what they already owed, demand for all kinds of goods fell away. From the height of the pressure in October 1839 through much of 1843, businessmen throughout the nation complained of "dull times" and poor business prospects. Prices during that four-year stretch plummeted by approximately 40 percent, one of the sharpest deflations in American history.[39]

Thousands of Americans who survived the most difficult days of general commercial crisis still confronted serious threats to their solvency during the years of deflation. Lightening one's debts was a difficult proposition when the nominal value of assets and commodities evaporated and the pace of trade slowed considerably. Even if merchants, artisans, or manufacturers were able to maintain a decent level of business, they received less for their exertions than they did during the heady days of the mid-1830s. Debts from those years were contracted during times of high prices; after the fall of 1839, debtors would have to pay those obligations with far more expensive dollars. Deflation was not an unmixed financial curse for antebellum proprietors; wages and rents fell at more or less the same rate as land values and wholesale prices, and the prices that merchants or manufacturers had to pay for goods declined alongside the payments that they received from customers. Declines in cost for labor, supplies, and overhead, however, often failed to compensate for the other financial worries that a slack economy presented antebellum businesses.

Chief among those worries was the weak demand that permeated American markets throughout the early 1840s. Firms with a substantial investment in goods that no one wanted to buy faced particular difficulties in meeting their obligations. The travails of Reuben Tower's Sons indicate the perils of soft markets to firms struggling under a heavy load of debt. Located in Waterville, a small town in Oneida County, New York, Reuben Tower's Sons consisted of Charlemagne and Julius Tower, the two eldest sons of the firm's deceased namesake. Charlemagne and Julius oversaw the manufacture and distribution of whiskey and brandy. The firm made its liquor at a Waterville distillery; they also fattened cattle off of the distillery's waste products and maintained a New York City store, where an agent supervised the distribution of liquor throughout the country. Reuben Tower's Sons managed to satisfy its creditors during the panics of the late 1830s and through the first two years of the next decade; the firm's distillery continued to fill barrels with spirits, and its New York City store found buyers willing to pay enough to keep the concern afloat. As late as June 1841, Charlemagne expressed confidence that although "the markets are dull and prices very low," the business would "find the year 1841 a year of profit."[40]

A scant nine months later, the markets had become considerably more dull, and the partnership confronted a bevy of creditors demanding payment. On April 1, 1842, the firm faced debts of around $60,000, half of which comprised unsecured bank discounts. The Waterville distillers did not lack assets, possessing around $15,000 in liquor ready for market, $2,000 in raw materials, over $9,000 in claims against customers, and several shipments of liquor consigned to dealers in cities around the country. But demand for alcohol had slackened to such an extent that the Towers could not raise the funds to continue their business. In mid-March, the firm's Cincinnati correspondent informed them that liquor was no longer sellable there, in Indianapolis, or in St. Louis for cash—only for barter and at very low prices. Cash sales were possible in New York, but only at the extraordinarily low price of 16 1/2 cents per whiskey barrel, more than a third less than the prices that had prevailed only a few years earlier. With such depressed markets, the Towers lacked the resources to pay their maturing liabilities. On April 10, they stopped making payments to their creditors and began notifying them of their failure. Myriad Americans saw their businesses collapse as a result of a similar set of circumstances.[41]

In addition to weak markets, American proprietors in the early 1840s had to contend with depreciating currencies and an avalanche of bad debts. With so many banking institutions tottering on the edge of solvency, a significant proportion of the nation's money supply traded at substantial discount, especially when notes had traveled great distances. Throughout the period of deflation, many business owners were able to collect payments only in devalued currency that was unwanted by their own creditors.[42]

All too often, moreover, individuals and firms struggled to pay their debts in any form of money. As the bankruptcy of R. Hoe & Co. makes clear, even firms that produced goods in high demand could become insolvent if sufficient numbers of customers did not remit the sums they had contracted to pay. Led by brothers Robert and Richard, R. Hoe & Co. manufactured some of the most sought after printing presses and circular saws in antebellum America. Throughout the worst economic times of the 1830s and early 1840s, the Hoes received orders from every section of the country and from as far away as Havana, Cuba. Collecting from their hundreds of customers, however, proved to be a vexing proposition. From the spring of 1837 until their failure in late 1842, the Hoes constantly faced "*confounded protests*" that "upset all our calculations." Some customers could not pay immediately or in cash; others failed after the Hoes had discounted their notes, placing "the whole burden and loss" upon the New York City machinists. Since the business relied on extensive credit when ordering its supplies, and since the firm continually discounted the notes of its debtors, shortfalls in collections seriously threatened its ability to meet its engagements. Eventually, "repeated disappointments in . . . receipts" left Richard and Robert Hoe owing their creditors over $250,000 and forced them into bankruptcy court. The machinists shared their place in the bankruptcy docket with numerous other individuals who owed their financial ruin to the surfeit of bad debts in a deflationary economy.[43]

Bankruptcies such as those endured by the Tower brothers and the Hoes are inexplicable without reference to the jarring dislocations of the early-nineteenth-century transatlantic business cycle. Absent financial panic, the process of general liquidation, and sharp deflation, neither concern would have confronted serious threats to solvency. Had liquor markets remained firm, Reuben Tower's Sons would have received a great deal more cash income; had so many of the Hoes' customers not been stymied by weak demand or their own bad debts, the machinists would have experienced no problems in cash flow. As the New York City newspaperman William Leggett observed in May 1837, complete "prostration of commercial confidence" felled "many a sound and solvent" proprietor, each of whom found himself "arrested by inevitable necessity, in the midst of a prosperous career."[44]

A Multitude of Commercial Hazards

The risks of independent economic activity in pre–Civil War America did not begin and end with commercial panics or dull times. Many antebellum bankrupts suffered financial losses that were either unrelated to the strains of a fluctuating national and global economy or only partly attributable to cyclical downturns. Proprietors who participated in the credit system confronted a slew of financial snares and pitfalls.

The pressures of competition created some of the most widespread obstacles to

SCHEDULE B, REFERRED TO IN THE ANNEXED PETITION.

The Property of the Petitioner consists of the following particulars:

	Dollars.	Cents.
A promissory note of William Riddle dated July 10th 1839 for $343.30 for goods sold to him on which note $100 was paid on 1st January 1842	243	30
An account against J. S. Phillips for merchandize consigned to him and by him sold amounting to about	250	00
An acceptance of Judge Guyon of Vicksburg Mississippi received from Harvey Mitchell for goods sold to him — now in the hands of J. S. Yerger of Vicksburg for collection	100	00
One due bill of Thomas B. Hooper formerly of Louisville dated March 19th 1839 for money loaned to him by me	44	00
An acceptance dated April 18th 1840 of the firm of Thompson and Griffith formerly of Louisville in the State of Kentucky for goods sold to Jeremiah Edrington of Louisville	10	00
A promissory note of Richard Hall dated March 6th 1840 for goods sold to him — balance due thereon	93	44
A promissory note of William J. Hamlet and Co (dated October 18th 1836) formerly of Memphis in the State of Tennessee for goods sold to them	71	37
A due Bill of R. J. Gardner formerly of Louisville dated 1st May 1839 for money loaned to him	12	63
A promissory note of John Farrow of Louisville in the State of Kentucky dated November 25th 1841 for goods sold to him	57	00
A promissory note of Bradford P. Hall formerly of Louisville in the State of Kentucky dated March 28th 1842 for goods sold to him	12	00
Together with sundry small amounts due on the Book accounts of the Petitioner, which he cannot state from recollection, and cannot ascertain with certainty as his books are in the State of Ohio.		
The following household furniture, remaining at Wheelersburgh in the State of Ohio,		
Bedding worth about	20	00
One Work table	10	00
One Guitar	16	00

A CATALOG OF BAD DEBTS. The asset schedule of George Gunn, a failed Louisville, Kentucky, lumber dealer, furnishes a typical list of worthless claims against customers. Gunn notes that as a result of the "[b]ankruptcy of the several individuals therein mentioned, it will be impossible to collect" any of these debts (C-F 918, National Archives and Record Administration, Northeast Region, New York City).

solvency, posing an ever-present financial threat to a wide range of antebellum businesses. Relative ease of entry into many fields of endeavor meant that entrepreneurs generally did not have a market to themselves. When antebellum Americans found a profitable economic niche, other individuals wasted little time in attempting to share the business. Manufacturers and artisans strove to copy successful production techniques; merchants looked to extend their trade into proven markets. Over time, a mushrooming population, growing incomes, and expanding consumption meant that the American economy could absorb additional output, and in many sectors additional businessmen. But in the short term, proprietors who made similar goods, sold similar products, or provided similar services vied with one another for a relatively fixed amount of business.

The regional and national economic integration spurred on by transportation improvements created one particularly powerful source of competition. Wider markets intensified economic rivalries at the same time that they broadened opportunities, for much the same reasons. As artisans and manufacturers in northeastern cities and towns began to expand their operations, producers located elsewhere felt their presence in ways previously unimaginable. Danbury, Connecticut, hatters, Lynn, Massachusetts, shoemakers, and New York City tailors all found ways to make their products more cheaply, mostly by subdividing work tasks and harnessing cheap wage labor. They and the makers of many other consumer goods then marketed the fruits of their workers' labor as far and wide as the nation's new means of transport would profitably take them. Local artisans often could not match the prices of these "imports" and suffered financially as a result. Eastern farmers encountered analogous pressures from the tillers of land in the newer areas of western New York and the Old Northwest. As trans-Appalachian farmers gained the ability to ship their produce over canals and rails, richer western soils soon gave them clear advantages over their eastern agriculture brethren. Northeastern farmers, in particular, experienced a declining ability to meet the low prices of western grain.[45]

Competitors most directly threatened the solvency of businesses when other concerns lured away customers or forced ruinous reductions in the price of goods for sale, as in the case of two New York City merchant tailors, George Andrews and Jeremiah Lamphier. Through 1841 and early 1842, Andrews and Lamphier did their best to stay afloat in the notoriously cutthroat world of the Manhattan ready-made men's clothing trade. The pair purchased buttons and bolts of material from city dry goods dealers, relying on the willingness of the merchants to extend credit. They then paid a chief cutter, four male cutters, and around a dozen female seamstresses to turn the yards of material into caps, vests, pants, and coats, most likely in a garret workshop. Finally, they ran a city store where they tried to vend the finished goods, offering credit as an inducement to individual customers.

With hundreds of similar establishments in New York City, and with dozens of larger manufacturers and distributors also in Manhattan, Andrews and Lamphier faced a terrific battle for the business of local shoppers. Their willingness to extend book credit to customers reflected a concession to the realities of the New York City marketplace—antebellum New Yorkers had so many clothiers from which to choose that marginal clothing proprietors had to offer generous terms of payment in order to secure trade. These two merchant tailors also enjoyed little or no flexibility in pricing their goods. If the quotations for their vests and pantaloons went above the prices in the many clothing stores down the block or across town, few customers would have had qualms about walking out of Andrews & Lamphier's shop empty-handed. But charging market rates and allowing shoppers to buy goods on credit did not provide the income needed to maintain a viable business. By the time of their failure in the spring of 1842, Andrews & Lamphier owed over $7,000 to New York City dry goods merchants for raw materials and borrowed money, as well as almost $500 to their employees. Counterbalancing the debts were $942 in claims against customers and $1,500 worth of dry goods and finished articles of clothing. Liquidation of these assets barely provided enough money to pay the firm's back wages.[46]

Andrews and Lamphier were by no means the only southern New York bankrupts who failed while running a business in a particularly competitive part of the antebellum economy. Dozens of furniture makers, carpenters, masons, stonecutters, and shoemakers found their way into Judge Betts's court; so too did scores of dry goods jobbers and grocers. In each of these trades, proprietors confronted a profusion of competitors; as a result, those proprietors generally had to hustle for customers, extend generous credit, and seek to cut expenses wherever possible. Inevitably, many of these businessmen were unable to drum up enough business or trim their costs sufficiently to meet all of their pecuniary obligations.[47]

In addition to competition, thousands of antebellum businesses faced seemingly never-ending liquidity problems. Such continual shortfalls in cash flow often stemmed from the structure of the credit system that enabled many individuals and firms to enter business in the first place. Suppliers tended to provide businesses with relatively short-term credit, often only three to six months. Customers, by contrast, generally asked for much longer terms of payment. Rural consumers particularly demanded credit of up to a year, as their incomes were tied to the rhythms of agricultural production. This difference placed many firms in an almost perpetual financial bind, since their debts came due before their assets matured. Many antebellum businesses never found a satisfactory solution to this problem in finance.[48]

The plight of John Dayton, a New York City dry goods jobber, illustrates the way in which conditions of credit could turn into a financial vise. Dayton and his partner, Thomas Schuyler, began their enterprise in the spring of 1841, having persuaded a larger New York City firm to sell them $500 worth of goods. The pair negotiated a host of other credit purchases soon thereafter and began to seek out customers. These newcomers to the nation's busy dry goods market had little difficulty in finding buyers, selling freely to New York City tailors and to merchants and tailors in upstate New York and across the Old Northwest. In order to attract customers, though, Dayton & Schuyler extended generous credit, more generous than the three months offered by their own creditors. After only six months had passed, they had no way to meet their maturing debts, which totaled over $6,000. Although their customers had provided them with notes, the firm's creditors had demanded most of these assets as collateral. Unable to buy further goods on credit and without the means of borrowing additional funds, Dayton & Schuyler stopped payment in September 1841.[49] The credit system permitted people like John Dayton to become proprietors in their own right; but that same network of credit could quickly transform those new proprietors into bankrupts.

The most common strategy to bridge the financing gap between the maturation of debts and assets was the one adopted by Frederick Conant—to get the notes of customers discounted. Discounting, however, could prove expensive, especially at the interest rates charged by note brokers. And as Conant and countless other antebellum entrepreneurs discovered, this expedient furnished no assistance whatsoever if enough customers defaulted on their obligations. Several of the rural storekeepers who bought dry goods from Conant neglected to pay their accounts in 1836, leaving the wholesaler with over $20,000 in debts to discounters, and eventually no option but to suspend his business. In this instance and numerous others, crippling liquidity problems occurred during a period of general prosperity. Bad debts could sink an enterprise in good times as well as during panic or deflation.[50]

If competition or cash flow problems did not ensnare an antebellum proprietor, reverses might come from other sources. In his sermon on the morality of the credit system, the Cincinnati rector John T. Brooke listed "the very elements" as one contributor to the nation's bankruptcies. He spoke with good reason. Among the applicants for bankruptcy in New York's southern federal district were victims of fire, shipwreck, and flood.[51]

Of all such "acts of God," none created more bankrupts than the New York City fire of December 16, 1835. Breaking out in the heart of Manhattan's commercial district on a bitterly cold night, the blaze destroyed "seventeen of the most valuable blocks" in the city. Contemporary estimates of damage ranged between fifteen and twenty million dollars. Few businesses failed directly after the conflagration, as New York City's banks offered credit to firms whose stores or warehouses had been reduced to rubble. For many mercantile firms, though, the extension of funds only "postponed the payday to a more convenient season." The financial panics at the end of the decade brought death blows to several firms that had been weakened by "the great conflagration."[52]

Yet another danger to antebellum balance sheets came from the individuals with whom proprietors worked. Some entrepreneurs suffered grievous losses as the result of frauds committed by partners or employees. Business in pre–Civil War America depended extensively on personal trust. Lenders trusted the individuals and firms to whom they granted credit, particularly when borrowers offered no collateral. Endorsers trusted the individuals who asked them to cosign loans. Perhaps the greatest degree of trust was required of partners and of confidential employees like clerks and collecting agents. These individuals had intimate knowledge of a business's operation and easy access to its cash, goods, and other assets. Antebellum businessmen generally went into partnership with people and employed confidential clerks whom they felt would look out for the interests of the firm. They did not always choose advantageously.

William Hillyer's two failures demonstrates the ease with which the fraudulent actions of a partner or an employee could lead to financial ruin. A merchant, Hillyer had the misfortune to experience embezzlement twice, once by a partner and once by his confidential clerk. In March 1837, Hillyer commenced a New York City partnership in dry goods jobbing with Alexander P. Lane. A short four months later, Hillyer and Lane parted company, each wishing to pursue other enterprises. The pair agreed to dispose of the firm's assets, pay off their creditors, and then go their separate ways. Lane, however, did not abide by the agreement. In November 1837, he absconded from Manhattan with over $4,000 in merchandise and about the same amount in promissory notes from New York City merchants and store-keepers in upstate New York. Hillyer's business position in New York City became severely compromised by Lane's disappearance. Seeking to escape angry creditors, he left the city himself in December and set up shop in Louisville, Kentucky, again as a dry goods dealer. This time an employee took the opportunity to separate Hillyer from his assets. In the summer of 1838, the unfortunate dry goods merchant traveled from Louisville to Philadelphia in order to place orders with that city's jobbers. He left his chief clerk, Jervis Hubbell, in charge of the Louisville store. When Hillyer returned in September, he discovered to his great consternation that Hubbell had followed in the footsteps of Alexander Lane, quietly departing the Ohio River city with all of Hillyer's stock in tow. The combination of these two thefts left the merchant hopelessly insolvent. Although Hillyer's encounters with embezzlement were particularly punishing, other bankrupts sustained similar losses.[53]

Finally, American entrepreneurs before the Civil War constantly had to adjust their readings of market signals under conditions of great uncertainty. Attempts to gauge the potential demand for a new product or the future price of a standard commodity were inherently risky enterprises, whether general commercial activity was booming or depressed. The financial predicament of Lewis Feuchtwanger points to the perplexities surrounding the marketing of novel goods. A German immigrant and a chemist of considerable talent, Feuchtwanger moved around New York State in the 1830s, hawking drugs and chemicals. By the early 1840s, he had settled in Manhattan, where he tried to convince Americans to buy his "celebrated Poisons for the total extermination of bedbugs, moths, cockroaches, rats, and mice." Despite vigorous advertising in New York and the free distribution of samples to drug merchants in several other cities, demand for the chemist's wares remained limited. He failed in the spring of 1842. An analogous fate befell several early northeastern manufacturers of railroad equipment, whose estimations of the likely market for rolling stock proved to be excessively sanguine.[54]

Indeterminate market conditions also bedeviled Americans who produced or traded goods that tended to fluctuate markedly in value. Information about ante-bellum commercial developments was often sketchy at best, especially in the years before the widespread introduction of the railroad and the telegraph. Wrong guesses about the direction of the cotton market ruined large numbers of southern planters and cotton factors throughout the antebellum period; misjudged estimations of price movements and overall demand similarly created grave financial problems for market-oriented northern farmers and crop wholesalers.[55]

Antebellum proprietors faced a daunting array of financial hazards. Competitors posed an ever-present threat to business, while debtors had a disturbing habit of delaying payment or defaulting altogether. The forces of nature periodically endangered the sturdiest of human contrivances. Close associates and trusted agents sporadically bilked their partners or principals out of hard-earned income. And a fickle marketplace neither embraced every new product nor maintained predictable prices for basic commodities. The turbulent course of the American and transatlantic business cycle compounded all of these threats, subjecting antebellum firms to dramatic shifts in the supply of credit and the overall demand for goods and services. Given the range of impediments to economic success, the interdependence created by the credit system, and the frequency of insolvency, it is hardly surprising that some antebellum commentators, like the Reverend Brooke, sought to exonerate bankrupts from the charge that they were inexorably culpable for their failures.

Chapter 2

Guises of Financial Vulnerability

> In a country, where capital is difficult to be obtained, and among a people enterpris-
> ing to an extraordinary degree, it is probable that the business transactions bear a
> larger proportion in amount to the capital of merchants, than would be deemed
> prudent in most parts of Europe. . . . The speculations of individuals more fre-
> quently terminate in bankruptcy among us than in places where there is more capi-
> tal and less enterprise.
> —*American Quarterly Review* (1834)

For all the evidence lending itself to structural explanations of antebellum bankruptcy, Thomas Cary's emphasis on the personal responsibility of bankrupts also
merits a hearing. Although the scope and frequency of antebellum failure would not
have been possible without an economy based so profoundly on intricate networks
of credit and the rhythms of the capitalist business cycle, a significant proportion of
bankruptcies depended crucially on the inexperience, avarice, and outright folly of
the individuals who failed. Many more failures would not have happened if proprietors had been able to draw on more substantial resources when they began ventures or ran into difficulties. Even if the architecture of antebellum capitalism
guaranteed a conspicuous place for bankruptcy in the American marketplace, it did
not determine which businesses and individuals would collapse under intolerable
loads of debt. When the analytical focus shifts to the vulnerability of particular
individuals and firms, the arguments of people such as Thomas Cary offer a host
of insights.

Commercial Neophytes

Antebellum society greatly esteemed the independent proprietor. In a nation so
dominated by the realities of slavery and the ideals of republican liberty, white men
generally manifested a proud determination to avoid wage labor except as a temporary expedient. For some Americans, the value of economic autonomy encouraged
suspicion of capitalism—what one Philadelphia labor leader referred to as "this

system of self-interest and competition." Within isolated agricultural regions ill served by transportation routes, apprehensions about the growth of a market society encouraged farming strategies geared to neighborhood self-sufficiency; among the urban population of wage-earning artisans and journeymen, similar fears animated early union activity and the radical politics of Workingmen's Parties.[1]

For other residents of antebellum America, the ideal of self-direction gave rise to very different ambitions, essentially inviting an embrace of capitalist competition. To numerous farmboys, clerks, and young mechanics, the aspiration of economic independence encouraged an early leap into the commercial fray on their own financial responsibility. These individuals chafed at their status and often dreamed not only of self-employment but also of comfort and even wealth. In many instances, such restlessness was at least temporarily assuaged by a loan of capital from family members or business associates, or through the commencement of an enterprise in a field that had few barriers to entry. As a result, the ranks of American business owners before the Civil War were by no means limited to seasoned, well-entrenched proprietors.

Instead, the business community constantly had its complement enlarged by the entrepreneurial endeavors of relative novices, such as the young Horace Greeley. Greeley's career as an influential newspaper editor and national political operator began at the age of twenty-one, when he went into business as an independent printer. At the time, he could count on "a decent knowledge of so much of the art of printing as a boy will usually learn in the office of a country newspaper," roughly a year's additional experience as a journeyman in New York City, and no capital whatsoever. But he did have a sense that "the world was all before me" as well as a partner of similar age, who, while also without capital, possessed both "enthusiastic confidence" and some connections in New York City's world of print. These assets, along with the willingness of several suppliers to sell paper, type, and ink on time, launched Greeley as a businessman.[2]

When Americans like Horace Greeley embarked on commercial ventures, they frequently lacked the business acumen or financial resources to sidestep the pitfalls that threatened any antebellum enterprise. Freeman Hunt, editor and publisher of the influential mercantile periodical *Hunt's Merchants' Magazine*, offered a trenchant criticism of such premature entry into business in an 1856 collection of "maxims, morals, and miscellanies for merchants and men of business." Hunt concentrated his ire on youths who chomped at the bit to become full-fledged merchants. All too often, he complained, young clerks began to "conduct business on their own account" before completing a sufficient course of mercantile apprenticeship. Lacking a "perfect knowledge of business," the "cautious discrimination" that came with years of entrepreneurial training, and "the confidence of those around them," tenderfoot merchants overwhelmingly "waste[d] their capital." So long as an enterprise was governed by "practical ignorance and the want of proper business habits," "embarrassments" and outright failure loomed as near-certainties. Bankruptcy was especially likely when newcomers brought meager financial assets into their enterprises. As Hunt pointed out, would-be proprietors all too frequently began on their own before possessing "a sufficient capital or credit to compete successfully." Without an adequate stake of capital, businesses were extremely vulnerable both to unexpected losses and to liquidity problems.[3]

Viewed from this perspective, the short-lived business of John Dayton assumes a different significance. Dayton had begun his New York City dry goods jobbing venture with minimal business experience and virtually no capital. He simply bought materials on short-term credit and sold them on longer-term credit. Thus he possessed no reserves either to cushion the blow of bad debts or to pay his own obligations while he waited to collect from his customers. Dayton's business was all but doomed from the start. Horace Greeley's initial enterprise, which involved the printing of a new newspaper aimed at New York's working class, had a similar likelihood of success. With no seed capital to advertise or sustain short-term losses, the paper folded within a month, leaving its printers sorely tested to meet their obligations. To Americans who held uncharitable views of bankrupts, the willingness of individuals such as Dayton and Greeley to plunge ahead despite the odds against them merited harsh censure.[4]

Even considerable experience within a given trade did not mean that an individual had obtained the commercial skills requisite for success in business. Several years as a journeyman or a mercantile clerk might still not have provided an aspiring proprietor with crucial elements of a business education, such as a thorough grounding in accounting. The complexities of commercial transactions in an economy dominated by credit made good bookkeeping essential. Without a knowledge of accounting principles and a fixed habit of applying them, business owners could easily find themselves lost in a sea of credits and debits, unaware of impending financial weakness. Only by constantly referring to a set of up-to-date ledgers could businessmen gain an accurate reading as to the position of their enterprises. So long as they took such readings, proprietors usually had the time to head off potential trouble, either by limiting the extent of business, pressing debtors for payment, or cutting personal expenditure. When individuals neglected their ledgers, the ineluctable result was a "want of correct information of their own standing, and consequently of the qualifications necessary to direct business operations." According to the *Philadelphia Merchant*, such negligence explained "the failure of nine-tenths of the Insolvents in every Commercial City in the world."[5]

While the *Merchant*'s statistics seem far-fetched, there is no question that an absence of good accounting practices contributed to numerous antebellum bankruptcies. A dearth of bookkeeping acumen was particularly apparent in the insolvency of James Alden, a New York City dry goods merchant. Alden was twenty-eight years old when he failed toward the end of 1842. Although he possessed promissory notes and accounts receivable seemingly worth more than his debts, most of his assets turned out to be worthless. Alden explained that his financial difficulties resulted partly from ignorance about accounting. "I understand dry goods business," he maintained during a court deposition, but "am not a very good accountant, was not educated to accounts, and have no knowledge of accounts but what I have acquired myself." Without such knowledge, Alden was unable to calculate whether his business was profitable at any stage of its existence. He bought goods on credit as long as he could find willing sellers and struggled to find the money to pay his various obligations as they came due. Through September 1842, he managed to satisfy his creditors; shortly thereafter, the toll of unanticipated losses became too great and he stopped making payments.[6]

This approach to bookkeeping practices was far from unusual in the antebellum United States, especially before the 1840s and 1850s, when accounting primers became more widely distributed and commercial schools more common.[7] Confessions of lackluster methods of maintaining accounts were regular features of antebellum bankruptcy applications. In one especially revealing apology, a Kingston, New York, bankrupt who had been unsuccessful as a storekeeper, canal boatman, blacksmith, and baker claimed to have "conducted his affairs as most mechanics did—he did not pretend to keep a list of his debts before him nor did he know the amount of his indebtedness; his credit enabled him to borrow whatever he required when other resources failed." The Kingston man did not do a much better job of keeping track of his assets, as the bankruptcy assignee for Ulster County reported that the "derangement of the Bankrupt's Books and papers" made an accurate statement of his property impossible. Such carelessness diminished a proprietor's control over finances, just as the *Philadelphia Merchant* had suggested. Unaware of their financial position, business owners like James Alden and the Kingston baker missed crucial warnings about looming difficulties and were particularly susceptible to eventual embarrassment.[8]

"The Ambition to Be Rich"

The itchiness of many inexperienced Americans to run their own economic affairs had its counterpart in the alacrity with which less callow proprietors chased after the grail of speedily obtained wealth. "It is so hard for any man, be he merchant, or be he drayman, to be content with his earnings," complained the Jacksonian political economist William Gouge in 1833. "We are all so anxious to become rich in a hurry." In striving to amass a fortune quickly, a legion of antebellum Americans pursued schemes that promised enormous returns, regardless of risk. As Thomas

Cary observed, these individuals did not trust to a "cautious integrity" that "gets on slowly," nor limit their indebtedness in light of their "ability to pay." Instead they desired all the credit that "the world are willing to give," because those facilities seemed to be a surefire means to affluence. Sadly for all the would-be magnates, "unforeseen changes" in the commercial world usually plunged them, "with all that [they] have, into a sea of troubles where [they] must eventually sink."[9]

Cary and other antebellum critics of bankrupts made an instructive distinction between two kinds of "great undertakings" that made Americans particularly likely candidates for insolvency—speculation and overtrading. The first of these follies reflected "visions of great and sudden changes in the value of property." The speculator borrowed money to buy a given asset, betting that strong demand would bring about swift appreciation.[10]

Outlets for speculative impulses beckoned throughout the antebellum landscape, as people in every part of the country plotted out the likely direction of future growth. Land, whether in the form of city lots, town lots, settled farms, or unimproved pieces of wilderness, especially attracted the attentions of American speculators. They also gave considerable attention to commodities like cotton or coffee, ventures in manufacturing, transport, or mining, banking or insurance stock, and state bonds. Although trading in these assets remained a constant feature of the era's economy, it peaked during periods of inflation and easy access to credit, like the early to mid-1830s.[11]

Antebellum commentators portrayed that interval as a time when free Americans were besotted with speculation. "All classes," maintained a short-story writer for a high-toned New York magazine, "became smitten with a sudden criminal passion of being rich. . . . They thought no more of the gradual accumulation of wealth by labor, but would escape the curse imposed on Adam. A fortune must now be made in a day."[12] True to this characterization, scores of southern New York bankrupts joined in the speculative frenzy that overwhelmed the country prior to the panics of 1837 and 1839. The background of these bankrupts, though, does not wholly support contemporary perceptions that the "flush times" enticed Americans of "all classes" to gamble on rising values of land, stock, and commodities.

The bankrupts who most vigorously pursued investments outside of their regular field of business tended to be merchants, brokers, lawyers, and builders— people at the forefront of capitalist enterprise, with access to credit and knowledge about the world of finance. Among these big-time operators, debts for land and stock purchases frequently totaled over $50,000, an enormous sum at a time when long-serving urban clerks or skilled artisans might earn only $300 to $400 in an entire year.[13] George Denison Strong, a New York City gentleman, held typical debts for a large-scale speculator. Strong owed more than $400,000 when he petitioned for bankruptcy in June 1842. Well over one-fourth of that sum represented purchases of several hundred city lots in Brooklyn and New York City, and stock in New York City banks, upstate New York railroads, and a Brooklyn ferry company. Other bankrupts cast their speculative gaze further afield. Brooklyn lawyer Peter Clark compiled land-related debts in excess of $300,000 during 1835 and 1836, complementing his purchases of lots in Buffalo with parcels in upstate New York, northeastern Pennsylvania, and Virginia. Bankrupts like Strong and Clark dreamed of mammoth fortunes founded on boldness and decision; instead of comfort and ease, their speculative operations only netted them a fortune's worth of debt.[14]

These would-be empire builders were by no means representative of all speculators among southern New York bankrupts. Petitioners with less access to credit, or perhaps more temerity, joined the quest for speculative riches in a more moderate fashion. But bankrupts who pursued less grandiose schemes came overwhelmingly from the same occupational groups as the most active speculators. Even apparent exceptions frequently turn out to fit within the generalization. Edward Kellogg, for example, filed for his discharge as a farmer from New Canaan in Columbia County. A little over half of his $25,000 in debts resulted from the purchase of Binghamton, New York, land in 1832 and 1836. During those years, however, Kellogg was a dry goods merchant in Binghamton. Few of the speculators who applied for bankruptcy in southern New York came off the farm or out of the workshop.[15]

At least a handful of artisans among New York City bankrupts did succumb to speculative temptations. Land purchases in upstate New York lay at the heart of the butcher Andrew Wheeler's financial troubles. Joseph and Lemuel Brewster, brothers and copartners in a hatting firm, also found their way to embarrassment via real estate investments, particularly for lands in Illinois. For the bookbinder Charles Starr, a harebrained manufacturing scheme in Poughkeepsie served as the main cause of insolvency. Each of these failures, however, reinforces the claim that bankrupt speculators had intimate links to the dynamic world of antebellum business enterprise. Wheeler, Starr, and the Brewsters had attained the status of master artisans years before they embarked on the ventures that ruined them. Each had become comparatively wealthy, and each became active in community business organizations.[16]

The failures of these four men does point to one sense in which destructive speculation swept across American society during the 1830s. The mania that prevailed in those years took in pillars of the community, men who deeply engaged in philanthropic activities and were profoundly committed to a benevolent, Christian capitalism, alongside individuals who made no pretense of caring for much of anything but their own wealth. Wheeler, Starr, and the Brewsters all took an active role in the "benevolent empire," the collection of antebellum evangelical organizations that sought to reshape social institutions and individual hearts according to

Schedule A referred to in the preceding Petition

The debts and liabilities of the petitioner are as follows viz:

To Athearn Cyrus Tobacconist. Buffalo New York and James Provost residence unknown. on a joint and several bond with James A Salisbury deceased given to secure the payment of the purchase money of a lot on 6th Street Buffalo 100 feet front dated Jan'y 1. 1836 payable in 5 annual instalments with interest accompanied with my mortgage on same Lot for **$2080.00**

To Avery Ebenezer R. farmer, Erie Co. N.Y. On a decree in the Eighth Chancery Circuit for balance due on a joint and several bond, with Phineas B. Sherwin Benjamin Clark. Hanchurst Addington & George W. Baker. accompanied with my mortgage on about 5 acres of land in Buffalo, at the corner of Main and North Streets. Said Decree was docketed against me and others April 10th 1838. E. Ford Solicitor for Complt. for **$5804.56**

To Ainsworth Stephen H. farmer Avon. Genesee Co. N.Y. or Bloomfield in said Co. on a Bond & Mortgage for purchase money on a lot corner of Allen & Franklin Streets Buffalo. 100 feet front for the sum of $1090. payable $390 in 6 months, from date April 10. 1836. & $800 in 12 mo' from date **$1090.00**

" Same. Bond & Mortgage for purchase money of lot on Delaware Street for $2107.30 payable $1000 in 18 mo' from date April 12th. 1836. $700. in 30 mo' from date and $407.30 in 6 mo' from date with interest **$2107.30**

" Same. On my Note dated April 30. 1836 in part payment of 69 feet front on Hudson Street Buffalo at 3 mo' payable at Commercial

REMNANTS OF LAND SPECULATION. Peter Clark's debt schedule tells a characteristic tale of debt-financed real estate purchases gone sour (C-F 462, National Archives and Record Administration, Northeast Region, New York City).

Christian principles. All four men were on the board of the New York City Temperance Society as early as 1829, while Joseph Brewster and Charles Starr busied themselves for years in the distribution of religious tracts. (Starr, in his bankruptcy filing, proudly noted the ownership of both a family Bible given by the American Bible Society "for long continued and faithful service" and a complete set of American Tract Society tracts, a "complimentary present" from the organization.) These reformers celebrated capitalist enterprise, so long as it toed the line of Christian precept and embodied hard work, craftsmanship, and the sober accumulation of wealth.[17]

Had these four artisans resolutely followed their own script for economic success, they most likely would never have found themselves in the lists of bankrupts published by the New York City newspapers. The ways in which Andrew Wheeler and Charles Starr departed from that script suggest just how strong the pull of speculation could be in the 1830s. At some time in either 1835 or 1836, Wheeler agreed to join a group of New Yorkers who believed that an upstate New York village was on the verge of a boom in land prices. The group purchased $35,000 worth of Cattarangus County land and $7,000 worth of Randolph Village Company stock, offering almost nothing in the way of down payments. The details surrounding these deals are murky in Wheeler's bankruptcy petition, because, as the butcher lamented in a preface to his list of assets, he had never been aware of their particulars. If one can take the statement at face value, Wheeler risked his once comfortable economic position on land deals about which he knew next to nothing.[18]

Charles Starr's indiscretions even exceeded those of Wheeler's. Like the butcher, Starr entered into a speculation with other New Yorkers, though in a manufacturing company rather than in land. (He also invested in ten Harlem lots on his own). In August 1836, the bookbinder united with two New York City merchants to buy a one-half interest in the partnership of Frederick Goodell and Thomas Harvey, mechanics who owned and ran the aptly named Poughkeepsie Screw Company. As a part of the deal, Starr and his partners agreed to assume the debts of the firm, represented by the mechanics to be around $50,000, and to support the pair's living requirements. In return, Harvey promised to "devote his time and skill to the perfecting of certain inventions or useful machines, which were thought to be of great utility." By early January of the next year, Starr and his compatriots had discovered to their horror that the Poughkeepsie inventors actually owed debts in excess of $120,000; even worse, the mechanics had disappeared, leaving the New Yorkers without any prospect of realizing the valuable patent rights they had so readily believed would come their way.[19]

These artisans were not the only New York reformers to have their economic wings clipped by speculative ventures. Two New York City merchants who were among the most active leaders of metropolitan benevolent organizations also landed in bankruptcy court because of investments that went awry. The philanthropic career of one of these merchants, Marcus Wilbur, stretched back into the 1810s and included work in the Sabbatarian movement, the Young Men's Missionary Society, tract societies, and especially in the Society for the Promotion of Collegiate and Theological Education at the West. These activities did not stop Wilbur from land speculation, particularly in rural Illinois parcels. Loans associated with those investments represented a majority of his $20,000 in obligations. The other bankrupt reform leader, Arthur Tappan, was both more influential than Wilbur and considerably more well known. Tappan, along with his brother Lewis, could lay claim to the highest rank in the "benevolent empire's" Christian army. From missionary societies to Bible and tract organizations, from educational philanthropy to the antislavery movement, the Tappans contributed time, leadership, and money. But all of this effort on behalf of the impending Christian millennium did not save brother Arthur's finances from the baneful impact of ill-judged speculation. In 1838, Tappan allowed himself to get roped into a land scheme by Daniel Pomeroy Jr., a friend and fellow New York merchant. Tappan received title to 270 parcels of land in Brooklyn for his participation but also accumulated around $100,000 in unpayable debts.[20]

For all their commitment to evangelical capitalism and a Christian commonwealth, men like Wheeler, Starr, Wilbur, and Tappan proved far from immune to the seductive charms of seemingly easy money. Their confidence in the schemes of the era, as with so many of their contemporaries, proved disastrous. The shards of that trust, left in the petitions of southern New York bankrupts, corroborate the contemporaneous descriptions of speculative mania. After a long visit to the United States in the mid-1830s, the British social commentator Harriet Martineau wrote of Chicagoans buying land rights to a piece of wilderness in the morning, only to sell them in the afternoon for a cool profit. "The rage for speculation" seemed everywhere to Martineau, "infect[ing] the whole people."[21] Even if that infection did not manage to pass through the portal of every free residence in the American union, it reached far and wide and, once the bubble of inflation had burst, created thousands of bankrupts.

Unlike speculation, overtrading occurred within the scope of a proprietor's regular operations. The overtrader relied on credit to extend a business's normal operations beyond the prudent limits of its capital. So long as firms were able to convince suppliers to sell on credit, they might enlarge the range of their business accordingly, regardless of the capital that undergirded their transactions. An 1850 letter to *Hunt's Merchants' Magazine* laid bare the dangers of pursuing such a course. The correspondent conjured up a representative overtrader, a merchant who managed to turn $25,000 in capital into annual transactions of over $400,000, "spread broad cast over the nation." The keys to this feat of mercantile multiplication were "buy[ing] and sell[ing] on long credits, [and] depending on discounts to keep the links of his operations entire." So long as "all is fair weather, his affairs proceed smoothly." But this hypothetical merchant made his solvency dependent on continued clear commercial skies; any "sudden revulsion" in commerce would almost certainly lead to protested discounts, insistent creditors, and unending embarrassments. Like the newcomer to business who hoped to make profits despite his lack of capital, the overtrader set himself up for a liquidity crisis.[22]

Despite the dangers, a profusion of antebellum businessmen did not hesitate to expand their businesses as quickly and fully as possible, squeezing every last dollar of available credit from lenders and suppliers. For individuals like Jonathon Amory and Henry Leeds, "overtrading" was a basic premise of their commercial operations. The business practices of these two partners indicate how close an actual bankruptcy could come to mirroring the descriptions of the contributor to Freeman Hunt's journal.

Amory and Leeds began a partnership as New York City commission merchants in 1837 with $25,000 given to Amory by his father-in-law, a Boston physician who had made his fortune as a planter in British Guiana. Leeds and another partner promised to put in an additional $35,000 but neglected to add more than $4,000. Nonetheless, the threesome soon built up a massive business. They accepted textile shipments from European textile manufacturers and New York City dry goods jobbers on consignment, arranging sales to merchants throughout the United States. By 1838, the firm disposed of over $1,800,000 a year in merchandise. Even though the partnership never took title to the goods they marketed and served only as a middleman between manufacturers and storekeepers, they operated on a tiny capital base relative to the amount of business they transacted. With comparatively few reserves to fall back on, Amory & Leeds had next to no hope of enduring a spate of reverses; and such reverses were not long in coming. Bad debts piled up during the difficult economic climate of late 1839; equally important, Leeds withdrew thousands of dollars in partnership funds to sustain a wide array of faltering real estate speculations. The combination of worthless debts and plunging land values left the firm strapped to pay their creditors. By June 1840, the firm had to cease operations. Shortly after they suspended, a committee of creditors estimated that the pair's financial obligations exceeded their assets by around $350,000.[23] Amory & Leeds fell victim to a commercial crisis and a deflationary economy; but like other overtraders and speculators, their risky strategies of wealth-getting made them particularly exposed to derangements in American markets.

Merchants proved to be the most egregious antebellum overtraders. But artisans, manufacturers, and agriculturalists also fell victim to a version of overtrading,

though one better described as undercapitalization. Even if artisanal and manufacturing firms could pay for tools and machinery with their own resources, they often
had to meet daunting expenses for labor and raw materials. Since most artisans and
manufacturers bought supplies and sold finished products on credit, they faced
potential liquidity problems. Possession of sufficient working capital warded off
such difficulties, enabling firms to meet obligations while waiting for collections.
Unfortunately for the owners of many workshops and manufactories, they could not
call upon such reserves. The result was vulnerability to economic downturns.
Similar financial weaknesses beset numerous farmers and southern planters who
expanded productive capacity to the utmost reach of their credit, only to find
themselves swamped by an accumulation of debts before their investments had paid
sufficient returns.[24]

In the case of both speculation and overtrading, the degree of financial reckless-
ness depended crucially on the ratio between an investor's or business's capital and
overall indebtedness. Antebellum speculators who did not risk more than they
owned might incur worrying losses, but they were not likely to face insolvency. The
New York City lawyer and real estate developer Samuel B. Ruggles typified speculators who avoided bankruptcy in the wake of panic and dull times. Ruggles had
invested heavily in New York City building projects since the mid-1820s. The sharp
decline in the real estate markets in the late 1830s and early 1840s left him pressed to
satisfy his creditors; but he owned enough properties that he was able to meet his
obligations by liquidating a portion of his assets.[25]

Ruinous extension of business similarly required a relatively slender capital base
for the amount of trade a firm undertook. One antebellum commercial observer
enjoined proprietors never to let their financial obligations exceed one-half of their
capital. Pursuing such a course would keep business from turning into a "game at
hazard" in which players "risk[ed] what is in reality not [their] own." Another
onlooker, paying closer attention to the different kinds of enterprises in the American economy, suggested that a skillful urban wholesaler might safely conduct business worth "three or four or even five times the amount of his capital."[26]

Given the turbulence of the antebellum economy, many bankrupts would have
done well to consider something like these principles as a guide to business practice. Had John Dayton waited to begin his jobbing venture with one-tenth the sum
that Amory & Leeds brought to their commission business, he would have avoided
the liquidity problems that strangled his fledgling partnership. Had the latter firm
kept its commercial pretensions more in line with its resources, it would have been
far better placed to survive the trials of panic and deflation.

As with the era's many broken-down speculators, an "anxious spirit of gain" was
often as responsible for the bankruptcies of overtraders as commercial crisis or dull

markets. The "ambition to be rich," Thomas Cary pointed out in his 1845 address, "often defeats itself."[27] Impatience to achieve that ambition, more than any other individual trait, heightened an antebellum proprietor's chances of failure.

Consumption Run Rampant

The growth in market production after the War of 1812 had its counterpart in expanding market consumption. Throughout the decades that followed renewed peace with Great Britain, a torrent of European and American manufactures cascaded into the premises of urban retailers and country storekeepers, and then into American homes. Prompted partly by rising incomes and dramatic declines in transportation costs, partly by urbanization and the desire of myriad farm women to escape the drudgery of domestic manufacturing, and partly by the ceaseless marketing activities of American merchants, this upsurge depended on strong currents of credit extension.[28] The emergence of a debt-propelled consumer society presented market-oriented families with a challenging task—to balance purchases of calico, cast-iron kitchenware, and parlor furniture against household financial resources.

Through both works of fiction and the commercial press, a number of antebellum writers exhorted their audience to cultivate restraint in this exercise, while lamenting the inability or refusal of many Americans to do so. Blending pragmatic evaluation of the marketplace's seductions with republican concerns about luxury as a progenitor of dissipation, these commercial commentators urged Americans to adopt rigorous limitations on expenditures.[29] "Is She Rich?," an 1842 short story by T. S. Arthur that appeared in *Godey's Lady's Book*, exemplifies fictional cautions against extravagance, which generally sought to influence the attitudes of women within the commercial classes.

The tale begins with two young clerks, each with ambition but little in the way of means, discussing the merits of potential brides. Henry Richmond restricts his interest to women from wealthy families, since he desires both the capital to begin his own business and an immediate high style of living. Henry's friend, Charles Hammond, responds with the argument that he would prefer a wife who would be able to withstand poverty, since America was a country where "wealth is held by a very uncertain tenure." In accordance with their respective principles, Henry marries a woman who owns a great deal of property, while Charles weds a woman who possesses excellent character. Henry and his wife, Eveline, then "commenced the world with quite a dash," moving into an expensive house, keeping several servants, and entertaining lavishly. Before two years had passed, a combination of business reversals and household expenses leaves young Henry ruined. Charles, by contrast, married to the "modest, intelligent" Caroline Wentworth, continues on a steady climb to respectability and independence. The couple live in "a quiet, economical, but very comfortable and genteel way," waiting for Charles's new venture into business to pay its slow but sure dividends.[30]

This story's basic message was repeated over and over again in advice manuals and mercantile periodicals, where authors sought to reach a mostly male readership. A widely reprinted article from the *Providence Journal* offered typical commentary. After presenting statistics to demonstrate the remarkable impact of compound interest on even the most modest savings, the author identified "long and rigid economy" as a critical element in the accumulation of wealth. By the same token, a lack of thrift made "the opposite result of bankruptcy . . . frightfully certain." The article concluded with a rueful declaration that "the general prevalence of an unrestricted indulgence in showy habits of dress and of living . . . cause[d] the failure of nine-tenths of the men who embark in business."[31]

Despite the emphasis that antebellum commentators placed on excessive consumption as a well-trod path to insolvency, failures resulting primarily from reckless personal expenditure were less common than those brought about chiefly by inexperience, speculation, or undercapitalization.[32] Nonetheless, consumption-related obligations did contribute something to the overwhelming majority of antebellum bankruptcies. Like most antebellum Americans, bankrupts consistently took advantage of the ability to buy on credit. Almost every bankrupt in southern New York owed debts that arose through the purchase of goods and services. And in at least some instances, the taste for high living that so worried writers such as T. S. Arthur constituted a major cause of financial crisis.

The career of Frederick E. Westbrook, a New Yorker who only narrowly avoided bankruptcy, serves as a case in point. Westbrook kept an extraordinary diary between 1840 and 1843, meticulously chronicling a slide into almost irretrievable debt. He began his journal with a long disquisition on his prior career, recalling that he spent the late 1820s and early 1830s in Fishkill, a town in Dutchess County and most likely the place where he grew up. Throughout those years Westbrook tried his luck as a merchant in partnership with a cousin. The endeavor did not go too well, and in 1832 he left the concern so as to avoid getting too "deeply involve[d]." He had stayed long enough, though, to incur a debt of $2,000 to his cousin as his share of the firm's debts. Westbrook then moved to New York City, where he was able to secure a position as a clerk to Samuel Betts, the federal judge who would later preside over bankruptcies in southern New York. The diarist stayed in that post through the end of 1839, using part of his salary to pay off his obligations in Fishkill. Although the clerkship provided reasonable compensation, he eventually chose to resign because its great demands were impairing his health. Westbrook next turned his attentions to the law and to real estate investments, studying for the bar and renting out two city properties that his wife, Catherine, brought with her when the two married in 1838. By November 1840, he had passed his bar examination and opened a city law office.[33]

Unfortunately for the new attorney, both his law business and his rental properties proved less remunerative than he had hoped. From quarter to quarter, Westbrook kept a watchful eye on expenditures, obsessively calculating his expenses for garments, board, furniture, rent, and travel, both from the time he had moved to Manhattan in 1833 and from the date of his marriage. He compared these sums to his income over the same period, always finding his financial situation growing worse. In spite of continual protestations that he economized wherever possible and only bought goods at discounts, the amount that Westbrook owed to various creditors grew every year. At the end of 1840, he owed $1,777; a year later, the total had reached $3,600; by New Year's Day, 1843, Westbrook owed just over $8,700 and worried greatly about insolvency.[34]

Family expenditures accounted for almost all of these debts. Frederick and Catherine Westbrook traveled regularly, down the coast to Washington, D.C., immediately after their marriage and up the Hudson River valley in the summers that followed. Catherine had access to most of the money that came in from her properties and used it to buy what she wanted. For his part, Frederick spent considerable time buying furniture for the couple's home. The most expensive expenditures of all, however, resulted from Westbrook's determination in early 1841 to build a home in which to place all the furnishings. Enticed by the seemingly rock-bottom prices of the New York housing market, he bought a plot on 21st Street and contracted with a builder to begin work. Westbrook spent most of the next eight months supervising construction. He received a superb dwelling for his efforts, one with an especially deep foundation and with walls made from the very best Cocksackie and Philadelphia bricks. But the lawyer also chalked up another $6,000 in expenses.[35]

This enterprise took its toll on Westbrook's finances. As early as the summer of 1842, mounting debts and insistent creditors had led him to ruminate about impending bankruptcy. On July 2, he penned a confession of economic sins. Finding himself "alone in this large House," he bemoaned ever thinking of building his grand home. His "expectations blasted," Westbrook set down a narrative of his "pecuniary troubles." He first discussed "the prostration of business" afflicting the United States during the past handful of years and the impact of national depression on his insubstantial legal business, as well as on the returns to his investments in property. But he did not stop there. "My Embarrassments," Westbrook continued, "have been caused . . . as well [by] my living in a style conformadable [*sic*] to the manner in which my wife was brought up—which was unfortunately beyond my means." He could only conclude this explanation for the "misfortunes that I now so deeply deplore" by reflecting on his relationship with "the Ruler of the Universe." Interpreting his afflictions as just retribution for "past omissions and transgressions," the attorney judged that "man in his best estate is born for trouble."[36]

Westbrook's recognition of moral failure becomes all the more poignant when juxtaposed next to his extended discussion of New York City's social scene in the winter of 1840. On January 29, the diarist contrasted the dearth of parties given by New Yorkers that season with "more prosperous times," when "extravagance in dissipation and gaiety of all kinds prevailed." He heaped scorn upon the improvident entertainments put on by "the class whose imaginary fortunes enabled them to spend money upon the ruins of others," men whom Westbrook labeled "Broken-down Speculators and Stock Gamblers." Not content to restrict his criticisms to these scenes of "inordinate vanity," the attorney chided those "intoxicated in their imaginary Wealth" for "adopting that style of living . . . which is known in our Republican land as being the First in point of extravagance." He ended this pronouncement by commenting that "no truly sensible man would make such a fool of himself." Two and a half years later, possessed of a large dwelling built on "imaginary Wealth," Westbrook had good reason not to think himself particularly sensible.[37]

There were antebellum bankrupts who qualified for Westbrook's definition of a fool, having failed in large measure because their habits of consumption consistently outpaced their income. In the case of John Adams, a New York City painter and glazier, insolvency probably resulted from a fondness for alcohol. When Adams petitioned for bankruptcy in 1842, half of his $1,608 in debts were owed to grocers, neighborhood traders who often specialized in the sale of ardent spirits.[38]

Other southern New York bankrupts owed their pecuniary downfalls to more expensive tastes. As the bankruptcy of James Watson Webb demonstrates, spendthrift ways could contribute to economic failure despite the enjoyment of a considerable income. An influential member of the Whig Party and editor of the *Morning Courier and New York Enquirer*, Webb possessed a comfortable salary. He nonetheless struggled to satisfy his many creditors for years. Webb owed much of his pecuniary difficulties to land speculation during the frenzy of the mid-1830s. Participation in a number of real estate schemes saddled the newspaperman with tens of thousands of dollars in debts. But throughout the 1830s and into the early 1840s, Webb continued to pursue, in the words of his biographer, "the conscious display of the good life." In 1838, after his investments had begun to sour, he moved his family to a large country estate in Westchester County. Ignoring his financial position, the Whig editor always traveled in style, regularly dined at New York's finest establishments, and wore only the best clothes. Had Webb responded to the defla-

tion of the late 1830s with a policy of personal austerity, he still would have battled to pay his creditors. By eschewing any attempt at economy, he made bankruptcy inevitable.[39]

In his *Practical Treatise on Business*, Edwin Freedley recounted a story that compressed most of the financial dangers to antebellum proprietors into a single parable. Originally told by a Newburyport minister, the tale concerned the prospects of a New England farm lad who wished to go into business for himself. The boy bought three calves, each for six dollars and on three months credit, with the intention of selling them for a profit in a distant market. In reflecting on the young drover's "chances of success," the clergyman first observed that failure could result from "accident," such as "his calves dying, or escaping, or being stolen." Absent such misfortunes, the venture might miscarry from "a want of judgment as to the value of calves[,] so that he finds the butchers will not give cost"; or because he places his four-legged merchandise in the hands of agents or a partner "who prove dishonest"; or as a result of an unexpected surge in the supply of cattle, which precipitates "a great depression in . . . market price at a time when he must sell."

Should the lad agree "to sell to a butcher on credit," the undertaking's financial vulnerabilities multiplied. Any general market dislocation, such as a sudden "contraction of the currency," could ripple throughout the economy, threatening the butcher's solvency, and hence the boy's. If instead he took paper money in payment for his livestock, he ran the risk that "the banks explode," leaving him essentially penniless. Alternatively, excessive confidence in the outcome of his investment might lead him to embrace "extravagance in living," which "will certainly ruin him," or to speculate through "the purchase of a lot" on credit, which, in the event of "falling property," would "compel him to make an assignment."

After cataloging such an extensive list of perils to his farm lad's undertaking, the New England minister concluded his discussion with a consideration of his likely gains should the boy manage somehow to avoid the pitfalls placed in his path. "Suppose, finally," the divine suggested, that "he sells his calves at a profit of two dollars each, over and above all expenses—gets safely home without being robbed, or losing his money—and pays his debt promptly." What is the result? "Why he has made six dollars, and is a successful merchant."[40]

This parable lays bare the complex relationships between structural economic hazards and threats to antebellum solvency that emanated from individual agency. All kinds of events may turn this lad's venture into an early failure—accident or lack of judgment, financial crisis or personal extravagance, sudden deflation or unwise speculation. The boy is particularly at risk, however, because he lacks experience and the capital resources to deal with reverses. Everything must go perfectly for his scheme to succeed. Few individuals who ended up on the southern New York bankruptcy lists were as exposed to financial trouble as the preacher's would-be cattle drover. But numerous petitioners faced long odds in their quests to achieve competency or wealth, and for many of the same reasons as did the hypothetical farm boy.

In some respects, the Newburyport minister's cautionary narrative offered maxims that would be recognizable to any generation of seasoned business owners in any capitalist society. Structural perils to solvency inhere in all capitalist economies, while managerial inexperience and undercapitalization render any venture a likely candidate for failure.[41] Despite the tale's universal qualities, it also unmistakably reflects the ambivalences of an agrarian society undergoing a rapid process of market expansion, in which small-scale proprietorship remained the norm.

One of the remarkable characteristics of the antebellum United States was the ability of so many people to emulate the lad of the parable and enter the marketplace as independent economic actors. Their entry into business would have been far more difficult without the "credit system." Extensive reliance on credit funded the internal improvements that linked the country's people and markets; credit additionally underwrote the exchange of goods across long distances, limited the need for transfer of specie, and enabled firms to increase their business beyond the confines of their capital resources. The fruits of the credit system, of course, did not unequivocally encourage individual proprietorship. By increasing the size of the market for American manufactured goods, the widespread use of credit aided a process of bastard industrialization that greatly increased the number of workers who toiled for wages.[42] Nonetheless, economic growth fueled by antebellum credit created business opportunities for hundreds of thousands of Americans. Equally significant, access to credit enabled many would-be farmers, artisans, and merchants to strike out on their own when their own resources would not have sustained such ventures.

At the same time that antebellum credit fostered untold business opportunities and unprecedented abundance, its weblike networks enmeshed American proprietors within an often unforgiving world of economic interdependence, competition, and financial obligation. The promise of the credit system went hand in hand with vulnerability and risk—with periodic market collapses, regular defaults by customers, and frequent business failures. As nineteenth-century Americans struggled to come to terms with the benefits and costs of capitalism, they increasingly found themselves grappling with the meaning and consequences of bankruptcy.

The resulting debates and controversies about insolvency took place on two distinct though interconnected levels. In instances of particular failures, bankrupts and their creditors faced a complicated process of sorting out financial wreckage. More generally, business owners, social commentators, politicians, and jurists wrestled with the task of setting cultural and legal ground rules for such events. In both contexts, commercially oriented Americans found themselves weighing the competing requirements of self-interest and moral obligation in a society that was at once capitalist and democratic. As they did so, the clashing discourses about the roots of failure—appeal to structural hazards and insistence on individual culpability—gave ample room for rhetorical maneuver, since each of these analyses drew on persisting features of America's economic order.

Part 2

The Institutional World of Bankruptcy

If no debtors were dishonest, and no creditors cruel, there would be no necessity for bankrupt laws. Such laws are designed to protect the creditor from fraud, and the debtor from oppression. From the dishonest debtor they wrest the property which he misapplies or craftily conceals from his creditors; and from the unfeeling and oppressive creditor they snatch the iron rod with which he smites his honest but unfortunate debtor. They give to the creditor a satisfaction of his demands to the extent of the debtor's property; and they give to the debtor a release of his person and future acquisitions from the burden of his past obligations.

—Joshua Van Cott, "A General Bankrupt Law," *Hunt's Merchants' Magazine* (1841)

Chapter 3

Dilemmas of Failure

> [W]ith every precaution reverses may come. Every man should admit the possibility of them, and should endeavour to prepare his mind for encountering them with fortitude, and resisting their undue action on the spirits.
>
> —John Frost, *The Young Merchant* (1839)

For sixty-seven of the seventy-two years between the ratification of the Constitution and the outbreak of civil war, American debtors and their creditors received neither guidance nor aid from a national bankruptcy system. Instead they confronted a bewildering array of state laws for the collection of debts, the protection of creditors' rights, and the relief of insolvent debtors. Confusing matters further, the law of creditor and debtor in any given state changed constantly. State legislatures regularly adopted or repealed statutes that affected debtor-creditor relations, while state courts periodically altered their interpretations of both statutory and common law. For the most part, bankruptcy law reflected the profound decentralization of political authority in the antebellum United States.[1]

Despite the varied and mutable legal terrain, a group of commercial moralists offered a clear set of instructions to their countrymen who had to deal with potential bankruptcies, either as hopelessly entangled debtors or anxious creditors. From the 1830s onward, this assortment of businessmen, ministers, writers of fiction, and representatives of the bar laid out consistent guides for appropriate responses to insolvency. Primarily New Light Calvinists who lived in northern cities and harbored Whig political sympathies, the champions of commercial rectitude included leading members of the nation's business community, such as Thomas Cary and Freeman Hunt, influential religious spokesmen, like Henry Ward Beecher, prominent members of the legal fraternity, such as Joseph Hopkinson, and widely read authors, such as T. S. Arthur and Sarah Hale. These individuals accepted the basic contours of America's entrepreneurial economy, generally viewing commerce as a vital agent of human progress and an indispensable testing ground for the development of individual character. They nonetheless fretted ceaselessly about the excesses of an expansive, fortune-hungry marketplace and wished to imbue antebellum commercial practice with the principles of mercantile honor and Christian benevolence. Their concern about business ethics represented just one dimension of a broader cultural evangelism, which sought to establish informal authority over social manners, aesthetic taste, and the tenor of public life.[2]

According to the self-appointed keepers of antebellum commercial morality, credit relationships created profound ethical obligations, and so imposed tough requirements on a person who encountered financial difficulties. Individuals who incurred liabilities had a duty, first of all, to keep a close eye on their pecuniary position, so that they could quickly spot potential problems. Whenever serious questions of solvency emerged, proprietors should immediately convene a meeting of their creditors, provide them with a full accounting of impending financial calamity, and place their economic fates in the hands of the people to whom they were indebted. If creditors did not offer extra time to make payments, debtors should no longer think of themselves as independent business owners; instead they should act as trustees for those creditors. Without delay, failing entrepreneurs should cease business operations and give up all of their property in order that their creditors might receive payments in proportion to the amount of their respective claims. The Philadelphia merchant John Sargeant reduced these stern recommendations to ten words in an influential 1839 address to the Mercantile Library Association of his city. In Sargeant's formulation, the guiding lights for a failing American were "a fair disclosure, a full surrender, and an equal distribution." By following these beacons, bankrupts could demonstrate the depth of their commitment to candor and fairmindedness in matters of finance, refuting any possible charges of manipulative scheming or out-and-out fraud.[3]

Moralists disseminated guideposts for the behavior of creditors as well. Just as debtors should strive to treat all of their creditors equally, the holders of claims against insolvents ought to respect the rightful interests of other parties. Rather than seek "an advantage over his neighbor," the creditor of a bankrupt should deem "his honor of more value than even the preference of a large percentage of pecuniary gain." Other prescriptions emphasized the duty of charity toward those who had suffered misfortune. If a supplicating debtor was likely to make good on his obligations given a reasonable extension of time, he deserved the deferment. Finally, when no extension would enable an honest individual to avoid bankruptcy, his creditors should handle the situation with humaneness. After ensuring that a bankrupt has surrendered all of his assets, creditors should willingly discharge him from his debts, allowing him the opportunity to begin life anew.[4]

In almost every particular, the commercial moralists' rules for bankrupts and their creditors mirrored long-standing injunctions in British commercial thought. Daniel Defoe laid the intellectual foundations of this approach to insolvency in his 1726 work, *The Complete English Tradesman*, drawing on his own experiences as a

FACES OF COMMERCIAL MORALISM: (clockwise from top left) Joseph Hopkinson (*National Cyclopedia of American Biography*, Lilly Library, Duke University), T. S. Arthur (frontispiece of T. S. Arthur's *Lights and Shadows of Real Life* [1853], Sterling Library, Yale University), Henry Ward Beecher (*National Cyclopedia of American Biography*, Lilly Library, Duke University), and Freeman Hunt (*Frank Leslie's Illustrated Newspaper*, Mar. 20, 1858, General Research Division, New York Public Library, Astor, Lenox and Tilden Foundations)

failed merchant. Over the subsequent century, Defoe's plea for honesty from bankrupts and beneficence from their creditors greatly influenced both British mercantile custom and English bankruptcy law.[5]

Although America's antebellum moralists occasionally made reference to British commentary on the rights and wrongs of reacting to a business failure, they rarely highlighted the lineage of their ideas, perhaps because of their pride in an autonomous American culture. Instead, they preferred to portray their counsel as flowing from the dictates of Protestant Christianity. As the Reverend J. N. Bellows proclaimed, the best way to locate "the maxims of trade" was a conscientious reading of "the Bible," for the good book stood as *the statute book of a republic.*" Henry Ward Beecher similarly implored creditors to act "with the lenity of christian men," and debtors to demonstrate a "manly honesty" that will work a "sustenance of religion."[6]

In addition to depicting the candid bankrupt and the humane creditor as exemplars of Protestant manliness, the oracles of proper commercial conduct appealed to enlightened self-interest—a move very much in keeping with their embrace of the entrepreneurial ethos. To debtors, they argued that obeying the demands of a Christian capitalism would make their lives after failure more hopeful, as creditors were likely to reward their integrity. To creditors, they pointed out that misfortune or mismanagement might one day place them in a position of insolvency, where they too would appreciate acts of kindness and liberality.[7]

At least some Americans took the moralists' advice to heart. When the combination of disastrous fire and commercial panic left Arthur Tappan's silk firm unable to meet its obligations in April 1837, the Christian philanthropist and his partners immediately gave public notice of the partnership's suspension and called a meeting of its creditors. Tappan and his fellow silk merchants laid out a detailed accounting of their finances and placed the business's fate in the hands of the individuals who possessed claims against them. The firm's creditors judged that with time Arthur Tappan & Co. would probably be able to meet its $1,100,000 in liabilities; as a result most of them agreed to renew their notes over an eighteen-month period.[8]

However admirable, the conduct of Arthur Tappan and the majority of his creditors was not typical, especially during periods of widespread economic pressure. Failing antebellum debtors frequently did not suspend their businesses at the first intimation of possible failure; they tended not to place themselves at the mercy of their creditors; and rather than fully surrendering their assets or striving to ensure an equal distribution among their creditors, they often sought to cushion the pain of their bankruptcy both for themselves and for those close to them. Creditors similarly strayed from the creed of the antebellum commercial moralists. Instead of looking out for other creditors, they displayed a penchant for trying to secure their own interests ahead of those of their fellow claimants.

Several aspects of antebellum commercial life militated against the urgings of the moralists. Amid a society that exalted the independent proprietor, many troubled debtors had great difficulty accepting that their business ventures were headed for outright failure. In addition, antebellum business culture, which made substantial accommodations to the great dependence of most proprietors on personal networks of credit, legitimated the impulse on the part of bankrupts to prefer the demands of favored creditors. The interconnected nature of the American economy further meant that most creditors periodically confronted daunting financial pressures of their own, which they ignored at their peril. Finally, state laws regarding the collection of debts encouraged creditors not to tarry in turning to the legal system to compel payment on overdue obligations.

Although commercial moralists proved unable wholly to reconstruct channels of decision making in the antebellum marketplace, they nonetheless succeeded in shaping the ethical norms professed by numerous proprietors who embraced the growth of a market society. Even when conduct under reverses followed other impulses altogether, these norms could guide failing debtors as they represented their financial predicaments to creditors and the public at large. And as we shall see over the next three chapters, the moralists' precepts increasingly influenced the development of numerous institutions, both formal and informal, that helped to structure the complex world of credit.

Obstacles to an Early Stop

When financial troubles beset antebellum businesses, their owners rarely thought first and foremost of an immediate suspension. Instead, most proprietors attempted to scrape together resources to pay debts as they came due, usually discounting commercial paper or seeking out straightforward advances of money. Banks provided one source of such loans, particularly to individuals who owned stock in them or who presented promissory notes that had been endorsed by someone of unimpeachable credit. Private brokers also stood ready to extend financial advances, though generally at high interest rates.[9] In many instances, though, strapped debtors looked for help from individuals who were close to them, such as business associates or relatives. Debtors particularly sought out friends and family members when they lacked the credit or the collateral to obtain assistance from other quarters. The practice of seeking such short-term loans was known as "shin-plastering" or "shinning"—so called because in the rush to obtain cash to meet a maturing obligation, a pressed debtor was likely not to notice "wheelbarrows, boxes, barrels, piles of brick, and other obstacles" in his way, and thus was "very apt to run furiously against them with his *shins*."[10]

In the early stages of a financial collapse, shinning might not prove especially difficult. Within a given circle of businessmen, informal loans of short duration were commonplace. The lag between the maturation of debts owed to creditors and those owed by customers encouraged a willingness among entrepreneurs to give advances to individuals whom they knew socially or through business dealings, often without interest. If the hardware dealer down the block asked for a week's loan of $500, a dry goods jobber might very well accede to the request, so long as the latter merchant was well acquainted with the hardware dealer and had $500 in cash that he could spare; the jobber knew that he would then be able to demand a similar favor. As Horace Greeley recalled of his early years as a debt-ridden New York City printer, "[Y]ou cannot ask favors, and then churlishly refuse to grant any,—borrow, and then frown upon whoever asks you to lend,—seek indorsements, but decline to give [them]." Antebellum entrepreneurs thus created myriad local credit circles founded on the principles of mutualism and flexibility.[11]

Charles Starr's response to pecuniary difficulties illustrates this feature of nineteenth-century business culture. After being lured into the disastrous manufacturing scheme in Poughkeepsie, the bookbinder and reformer struggled throughout late 1836 and most of 1837 to meet his obligations. Unable to come up with sufficient resources on his own, Starr looked to friends who might aid him. He turned most frequently to a former partner, Francis Shoals. Over the course of 1837, Shoals provided his onetime partner in bookbinding with "sundry sums" totaling more than $8,000. Starr also managed to extract $1,200 from fellow New York City reformer Marcus Wilbur and an additional $6,000 from a host of New York City merchants and artisans.[12]

Borrowing from business associates and friends, however, had its limits. As the financial position of a proprietor worsened, the need to borrow money increased while the number of friends willing to provide loans diminished. Similarly, whenever the money market tightened and the number of firms in search of accommodation mushroomed, individuals faced a more arduous task when they attempted to extract aid from their fellow artisans or merchants. In these circumstances, failing debtors tended to fall back on the resources of relatives.

The financial difficulties of George C. Thomas, a New York City dry goods jobber and real estate developer, demonstrate the role of family members as lenders of last resort. Along with a partner, Thomas had participated eagerly in the speculative mania of the mid-1830s, buying large tracts of real estate in several northern states. Overextension put the dry goods jobber under significant pressure in 1838, when he maintained his solvency by mortgaging his many properties with New York City banks and insurance companies. A year later, he complemented extensive bank discounts with over $40,000 in loans from fellow merchants. By 1840, Thomas found credit from financial institutions or business associates unavailable. His brother-in-law stepped into the financial breach, lending $20,000 to the dry goods firm and an additional $10,000 to Thomas individually. These loans only postponed insolvency. By August 1841, his business had stopped payment. Between individual and partnership debts, Thomas owed over $450,000. Businessmen who lacked the initial resources and connections of this dry goods jobber had even greater reason to rely on the financial support of relatives. Without significant

FRIGHTFUL WANT OF CONFIDENCE
BETWEEN FRIENDS.

"Ah! Jones, my dear fellow, how ——"
"No you don't! Nary red to lend!"

EXHAUSTING THE AVENUES
FOR SHINNING. Eventually,
as this cartoon suggests,
financially troubled debtors
received excuses, not loans,
from even their closest business associates and family
members (*Harper's Weekly*,
Nov. 21, 1857, Rare Book,
Manuscript, and Special
Collections Library, Duke
University).

property to mortgage or the ability to take advantage of cozy relationships with bank
directors, financially troubled proprietors had limited options. They might be able
to get a few notes discounted at a bank or with note brokers, and they probably
could shin for a while within their own business circles; but once serious financial
difficulties emerged, loans from family members typically constituted the only way
to avoid a suspension of payments.[13]

In addition to putting off the day of bankruptcy through shinning, failing proprietors sometimes hatched schemes to recoup the losses that had created their
financial problems. A common strategy was to extend business beyond previous
bounds, as the shoe manufacturer George Ferguson did during the early 1840s, in
the hope that new profits would make up for past miscalculation. From 1839
through 1842, Ferguson maintained a manufactory in the Westchester County
village of Tarrytown and a retail store in New York City. By the spring of 1841, he

was encountering difficulties in meeting his obligations, partly because of unwise loans made to business associates and partly because of the debts that he still owed as the result of an 1836 business failure in Buffalo. Ferguson's response was twofold. He regularly "borrowed money" in order to make his "payments punctually"; and he increased the output of his manufactory, hoping to improve his net income. Neither tactic proved sufficient to fend off insolvency. Shoe prices plummeted along with most other commodities in the winter of 1841–42, leaving the manufacturer in an even worse position. He suspended payments to creditors in April 1842. Numerous failing merchants and artisans similarly strove to beat back financial ruin through extension of business, usually without success.[14]

Entrepreneurs on the brink of insolvency additionally sought to extract whatever payments were possible from the individuals and firms that owed them and, at the same time, to plead for extensions from their creditors. The correspondence of Carlos P. Houghton, a New York City merchant during the late 1830s, offers particularly instructive testimony about the tense relations between a failing proprietor and his customers. Houghton and his partner, Daniel Day, began business in the spring of 1839 on the basis of Day's $3,000 stake. They aggressively bought manufactured goods on credit from local jobbers and manufacturers and sold the same products to merchants throughout western New York and the Old Northwest. Within six months, the pair of newcomers had contracted over $60,000 in obligations, which they found themselves pressed to pay.[15]

Houghton & Day soon transmitted that pressure to their own debtors. From June 1839 through April 1840, Houghton ceaselessly tried to coax or force payments out of the firms that had bought goods from him and his partner. The New York City merchant asked some debtors for early payment as a "favour," as Houghton & Day were laboring under "difficulties." To others he sent reminders of debts that were about to mature, requesting a prompt remittance since "the times are very hard . . . and it is nessecary [sic] for us to collect as fast as we can." From still others he demanded payments that were already past due, informing his debtors that "we are much in want of funds and depend upon our collections to meet our own obligations." If such language did not have the desired effect, Houghton adopted a more menacing tone. Amos Cornwall received a typical missive, in which Houghton proclaimed that "[w]e have borne so long that Forebearance [sic] is no longer a virtue"; unless immediate payment was forthcoming, A. Cornwall & Co. could expect a lawsuit. While all this energy undoubtedly paid dividends, the results were not enough to save Houghton & Day from its financial bind. By May 1840, the deluge of dunning letters had ceased and the firm had stopped its own payments.[16]

Many hard-pressed antebellum businesses combined insistent demands of customers with deferential supplications to creditors. Continually troubled by cash flow shortfalls throughout the late 1830s and early 1840s, for example, the New York machinists Richard and Robert Hoe did not take too kindly to excuses about "hard times" or requests for extensions of time from their debtors. During the same period, they regularly entreated their creditors to show them leniency about their own payments. On numerous occasions R. Hoe & Co. was forced to request extensions on obligations that were about to come due. Each time they did so, they carefully couched the appeal in terms of poor business conditions—"the embarrassing state of the times" made immediate payment difficult; "[e]verything continues so very dull here that it is impossible to make collections," and so impossible to send money at the moment; in light of "the present state of the money market," the firm needed a renewal on its paper; an extension was reasonable because "we cannot do more than we can do." A September 22 letter to Bostonian Samuel Ackerson summed up the firm's approach to creditors. Asking for additional time to pay a $500 note coming due in October, the machinists detailed their difficulties in collections and assured Ackerson of eventual payment. "All we wish," they beseeched, "is a little indulgence."[17]

Struggling antebellum entrepreneurs engaged in shinning, or gambled on expansion, or requested "a little indulgence" from creditors because they hoped that somehow, with a little more time, they would be able to dance out of failure's way. Occasionally these tactics proved successful; but all too often, they led to a "procrastination of the most expensive kind," simply delaying bankruptcy, increasing the amount that bankrupts owed, and shifting the composition of their obligations.[18] Why, then, were failing Americans so determined to turn their economic fortunes around and so disposed to reject the commercial moralists' pleas to concede financial defeat "manfully?"

The answer lies primarily with the culture of economic independence that dominated antebellum America and the mental strain caused by financial distress. Individuals did not become merchants or masters of workshops with the expectation that they would experience financial ruin; they embarked on ventures with the fervent intention of securing a decent income and an honorable social position. The acceptance of failure meant, at least temporarily, an end to self-directed work and the status that came with it, as well as a public declaration of one's inability to make good on contractual promises. Permanent suspension of business necessitated a search for employment or some other means of supporting dependents, such as taking in boarders. In most cases, it further compelled wide-ranging retrenchment—a move to less expensive accommodations, withdrawal of children from schooling—and a concomitant fall in social standing.[19]

All of these consequences rendered failed businessmen open to the charge of having lost their manhood, despite the fervent efforts of moralists to invest their prescriptions with the luster of courage, resolution, and honor. The figure of the "unmanned" bankrupt had loomed large in American business culture since the eighteenth century. During the colonial and revolutionary eras, merchants and social commentators often equated insolvency with weakness, vulnerability, and lost social identity. Such connotations continued to resonate in nineteenth-century discourse, as indicated by a satiric cartoon in *Harper's Weekly* published soon after the panic of 1857. This caricature depicts a Wall Street broker the day after his failure. Fearful of confrontations with angry creditors, he ventures out for his daily carriage ride only because he is obscured from onlookers by his wife's enormous skirts. The prospect of becoming the target of such lampooning did not encourage male proprietors to suspend business at the first signs of pecuniary difficulties.[20]

Disinclination to accept looming bankruptcy was often reinforced by fears of disappointing family members or bringing dishonor on one's religious group. In a culture predicated on material advancement, parents and wives frequently harbored deeply felt aspirations for sons and husbands. Acquiescence to insolvency risked chilling the confidence of a father in his child's "ultimate Success," shaking a spouse's faith in her mate's capacities as an economic provider, or confirming the suspicions of in-laws about the shortcomings of their daughter's husband. Antebellum bankruptcies could and did lead to family estrangements—especially the return of wives to their parents' homes, which occasionally precipitated custody disputes over children. For at least some devout proprietors, moreover, the prospect of failure elicited apprehension about its impact on their denomination's reputation. As one Methodist Episcopal merchant in Selma, Alabama, faced an avalanche of bad debts in mid-1839, he worried that his financial plight might wreak "serious injury to the cause of religion." Whatever his personal merits or intentions, this merchant fretted that "the church will suffer on my account." In light of all these considerations, many Americans found it easier to "struggle on" rather than confront the consequences of bankruptcy for themselves, their families, and their communities of fellowship.[21]

Benjamin F. Butler, the nation's attorney general from 1833 to 1837 and a prominent New York City attorney, summed up this psychology of denial during an 1840 meeting of merchants that considered a proposed national bankruptcy law. "[T]housands of upright men," Butler maintained, continued their labors in a "losing business" because they would not abandon "hope of a favorable turn in their affairs." These men could not make a "proper consideration" of their desperate situation; they were blinded by "pride" and "idle hopes of the future." Unable to come to terms with their misfortune or lack of judgment, they would not stop until "ruin the most overwhelming at last comes upon them."[22]

Butler's analysis mirrors portrayals of bankruptcy in contemporaneous fiction. Failing debtors in antebellum novels and short stories have little inclination to think through the relative merits of suspending their business or continuing it. Instead,

WHAT A BLESSING THESE LARGE SKIRTS ARE!

Mr. Coupon, of Wall Street, who had the misfortune to fail the other day, ruining his Creditors, might find it inconvenient to take the exercise his Constitution requires, but for the kindly shelter of his wife's skirts.

THE UNMANNING OF A BANKRUPT. This cartoon drew the common association between failure and loss of independent manhood (*Harper's Weekly*, Dec. 5, 1857, Rare Book, Manuscript, and Special Collections Library, Duke University).

they are wracked by fears—of an uncertain future, of social ostracism, of losses to trusting friends and relatives, and of painful consequences for wives and children. As a result, fictional proprietors on the road to failure generally embrace schemes to save their precarious financial position or at least put off the final day of reckoning. The prevailing image of the sinking businessman is that of a person who "walks to and fro in his office, with his head down and his hands in his pockets"; who "reads the newspaper paragraph but half through, and heaves a sigh when he sits down to pore over his cash-book or his bill-book"; whose "form shrinks," until his "coat hangs loose upon him."[23] These characters are prone more to nervous depression than to the dispassionate calculation of the best course of action for their creditors.

Commentary by antebellum specialists in "mental hygiene" complements fictional depictions. Superintendents of American insane asylums uniformly identified pecuniary reverses as a leading cause of insanity, usually ranked just below religious excitement and poor physical health. In elucidating the relationship between financial difficulties and psychological disturbance, physicians such as Edward Jarvis, Isaac Ray, and Samuel Woodward paid close attention to the unprecedented ambitions unleashed by America's democratic revolution. With so many ordinary people pursuing dreams of wealth and social distinction, these students of the human mind argued, restlessness and trepidation about economic status pervaded society. The urge to get ahead inevitably bred stress, especially among those who were most "exposed to . . . misfortunes connected with business, speculation, and money." In the event of "overtrading, debt, bankruptcy, sudden reverses, [and] disappointed hopes," the strain often became acute, sometimes developing into insanity.[24]

Newspaper accounts of suicides further suggest the emotional toll exacted by antebellum failures. Throughout the antebellum decades, papers in big cities and small towns regularly provided reports of individuals who responded to insolvency by taking their own lives. An early 1842 story about the self-destruction of Zephaniah Pells, a Dutchess County town collector, offers especially poignant testimony. As Pells explained in a "paper" that he left for those who would find him, he owed "two hundred and fifty dollars—gone I can't tell where—and I must take my life. . . . I am gone and forgotten—numbered with the dead, where creditors call upon me no more."[25] Suicide, of course, was far from the most common way of handling a growing stack of unpayable obligations; but its periodic occurrence underscores the psychological dimensions of pecuniary embarrassment. In the hindsight offered by commercial moralists, an early bankruptcy was the rational response to misfortune. The pressures bearing down on a failing proprietor, though, were not always conducive to cool and calm calculation.

Creditors in a World of Commercial Pressure

While troubled antebellum proprietors cast about for a means of avoiding failure, their creditors betrayed a predisposition for securing their own claims, regardless of the consequences for debtors or other claimants. Creditors who learned of a firm's financial difficulties and who wished to look out for their own interests had several options open to them. They could exert pressure, hoping that verbal or written requests would bring about payment. If this most basic tactic proved unavailing, they could ask for some means of legally securing their claim—either a pledge of collateral or a mortgage on real property or chattels.[26]

Alternatively, creditors could threaten or actually bring a lawsuit. In the most common action, a creditor would file papers with a local court alleging that the obligation of a debtor was both past due and unpaid. If the creditor proved the existence and legality of the debt, he received a judgment indicating as much. After judgment, he had the common-law right to an "execution" on the debtor's property. This process called for a sheriff to take possession of as much of a debtor's goods and real estate as necessary in order to satisfy the creditor's claim, to sell that property, and to transfer the resulting proceeds to the creditor, up to the amount owed plus court costs. In many states, the holder of an obligation that was past due could also ask a court to attach the property of a debtor in anticipation of a future legal judgment; usually such attachments required an affidavit that the debtor was either concealing himself to avoid the normal process of law or about to leave the state.

In the event that a debtor did not have easily discoverable real estate or chattels, creditors in a number of states, including New York, had the option of filing an action called a "creditor's bill." This suit would be brought in a chancery court after an unsuccessful attempt by a sheriff to levy on the property of a debtor. The bill would allege the inability of the sheriff to locate property under the normal judicial process and request the chancery judge to appoint a receiver over the debtor's estate. Assuming the bill was successful, the receiver would take legal title to all of the debtor's goods, including intangible property such as book accounts and commercial paper; he would then have power to reduce those assets to money, whether through collection or sale, and then pay the creditor. Finally, in several jurisdictions, antebellum debtors continued to be subject to imprisonment for debt unless they could post bail equal to the amount of the claim alleged against them.[27]

As antebellum creditors sought to collect on the obligations of financially strapped debtors, they relied heavily on all of these tactics. The records of southern New York bankruptcies are littered with descriptions of pledged assets, foreclosed parcels of real estate, attached household furnishings, debt judgments, judicially mandated sheriff's sales, and assets surrendered to court-appointed receivers. Few petitioners arrived in bankruptcy court without having endured substantial pressure from the people to whom they were indebted.[28]

The experience of Houghton & Day, the New York City dry goods firm that spent 1839 and the first few months of 1840 trying to squeeze payments out of customers, suggests the most compelling reason for antebellum Americans to hound debtors. Lenience or indulgence was an almost impossible stance for many firms to take, especially during a general financial crisis. Reliance on credit so pervaded the antebellum economy that almost every creditor was also a substantial debtor. Businesses that allowed their debtors a great deal of leeway might find themselves hardpressed to make their own payments. Even relative ineffectiveness in compelling the satisfaction of one's claims could prove disastrous to a firm's solvency. Firms such as Houghton & Day had little choice in the way they approached defaulting debtors. Either they pressed their customers as hard as they knew how or they gave up all hopes of continuing their own businesses.

Antebellum law reinforced the imperatives created by an interdependent, credit-based economy. Although varying in detail from state to state and over time within a given state, legal mechanisms for the collection of debts universally favored creditors who made early legal assaults on their debtors. A bona fide mortgage on real estate or chattels created a legal claim known as a lien. In case of nonpayment, mortgagors had the right to appropriate the property in order to satisfy their debts, no matter how many other creditors debtors might have or how much they might owe them. Holders of collateral had an analogous right to dispose of it for their own benefit, irrespective of other claimants. Similar principles regulated the legal implications of debt judgments. The first creditor to receive judgment and to levy execution on a debtor's property had a lien on that property—only after the first claim was satisfied would other judgment creditors have the opportunity to attack the remainder of the debtor's possessions.[29]

Antebellum jurists characterized the legal jockeying that resulted from debtor-creditor law as "a race of diligence."[30] Creditors who moved early received legal priority for their efforts; those who held back from stern measures could look forward to a growing list of uncollectible debts in their ledgers and account books. Even if individuals, firms, or corporations were not themselves in desperate financial straits, lenience to debtors could quickly lead to substantial losses. The judicial label was apt; creditors frequently competed to gain legal priority over one another.

On occasion, the scramble among creditors extended beyond a rush to the lawyer's office and the courthouse steps. In the case of one failing New York City dry goods dealer, Cassander Frisbee, creditors literally raced to pillage the bankrupt's store goods. Frisbee encountered difficulty in meeting his payments by October 1841. Shortly thereafter he became ill. A creditor took advantage of the merchant's subsequent absence from his store to apply pressure on his clerk, threatening him with legal action against the business if he did not relinquish stock equal to the value of their debt. The clerk acquiesced, standing by as the creditor's agent "repossessed himself of certain goods and carried them off." Word soon reached Frisbee's other creditors of this successful bullying. With the rumor "spreading rapidly" that all of Frisbee's assets were about to disappear, creditors flocked to the store, demanding a similar payment in kind. According to Frisbee's clerk, "the panic . . . was so great" that creditors managed to carry away the business's assets despite his attempts to stop them. A few days after the first repossession, "the store was stripped almost entirely of its assets." Similar fears animated the actions of creditors throughout the antebellum economy.[31]

In light of the weighty reasons for antebellum creditors to take a hard line with failing debtors, the extent of credit given those debtors seems puzzling. How could so many individuals provide financially distressed firms with credit? One explanation turns on the quality of information that undergirded antebellum commercial transactions. Many failing businesses maintained access to credit because their suppliers or endorsers did not know the true state of their affairs. The tactics of

Cassander Frisbee before his creditors descended on his store suggest the ways in which individuals in precarious straits could persuade firms to give them credit.

Frisbee's response to financial difficulties was a plan to extend his business in an attempt to reverse his misfortune. But to increase the volume of his business, Frisbee needed new and even greater amounts of credit, a difficult prospect given the troubles he had already encountered. He skirted this problem by having a business associate misrepresent his assets and financial position. In November, the dry goods dealer sought to negotiate a series of sales with the New York City agent of a German mercantile house. Since the agent wanted evidence of Frisbee's standing, the dry goods dealer referred him to a friendly creditor. That creditor vouched for Frisbee's resources, leading the agent to make the sale on credit terms. A scant month later, Frisbee had fallen victim to the demands of other creditors. Numerous antebellum proprietors adopted similar strategies to gain new sources of credit shortly before suspending business.[32]

The willingness of third parties to disseminate misleading information about failing debtors, and thus to shore up their credit, often reflected mutual advantage. Business associates who gave good references to potential creditors often held their own claims against troubled firms. By propping up their credit, such associates hoped to postpone insolvency long enough to collect their own debts. Houghton & Day fell victim to such a ploy. In early 1839, they were persuaded by several fellow New York City merchants that a Boston dealer named Stearns was a good risk. Stearns soon failed, leaving Houghton & Day with another bad debt. The Bostonian's other New York City creditors, by contrast, made sure that their interests were well secured.[33]

Credit given to many new, capital-poor proprietors reflected analogous considerations. The first suppliers to offer such businessmen credit sales could expect to receive payment, so long as other merchants could be persuaded to sell on similar terms. Even though would-be merchants like John Dayton and Thomas Schuyler began their enterprise with little chance of avoiding bankruptcy, their principal backers faced slight risk of loss. W. & J. Benjamin, Dayton & Schuyler's chief creditor, did not suffer at all from the latter partnership's failure, since they had received early payments for some claims and collateral for the rest. Only firms that followed the lead of W. & J. Benjamin found themselves stuck with uncollectible debts.[34]

In other instances, credit was forthcoming to failing debtors because lenders also faced a precarious financial position and needed credit in turn. Troubled businessmen could, on occasion, bolster each other's credit through the mutual endorsement of accommodation notes. By endorsing each other's notes, a pair of such business owners could conceal the desperate nature of their finances, at least for a time. So long as banks or brokers would discount the promissory notes, each debtor could obtain funds to make his other payments, and thus appear to be perfectly solvent. As long as each of the pair was able to meet his obligations without apparent difficulty, banks tended to discount their paper. Contemporaries referred to this practice as "flying the kite"—so called because the fictitious paper exchanged enabled each party to "raise" funds.[35]

When strategies of misinformation or obfuscation do not account for the provision of credit in the face of financial difficulties, the terms of the loan or sale sometimes provide an explanation. Note brokers who discounted commercial paper or otherwise lent funds exacted steep interest charges from customers known to be of questionable standing. Brokers attempted to balance the likelihood that risky borrowers would default with these high interest rates. Amory & Leeds, the New York City commission merchants who failed because of overtrading and speculation, faced typically rigorous terms from brokers. Their business lingered on through 1839 and into the middle part of 1840 in part because they borrowed money at rates between 1.5 and 3 percent a month—rates many times above New York State's legal limit of 6 percent annually.[36]

As an alternative to demanding high rates of interest, potential creditors of failing debtors often asked for legal security to back up proposed loans or sales. Once fortified by an offered mortgage on real estate or the pledge of commercial paper, store goods, or corporate stock, creditors were far more willing to extend credit to individuals who were struggling to side-step bankruptcy. A number of southern New York bankrupts managed to put off their suspensions by granting creditors this kind of security.[37]

In most instances, then, the assistance that individuals and firms on the verge of failure received did not conflict with the inclination of creditors to place their own interests ahead of their debtors' or fellow creditors'. Many providers of such assistance did not know they were giving it; others took measures to protect themselves against their debtors' likely failure. When Americans knowingly extended credit to distressed individuals or businesses without taking such precautions, the reason usually lay with the close relationship between lender and borrower. In such instances, the provider of loans or endorsements invariably was a relative or a business friend who responded to the bonds of mutual affection.[38]

Negotiation in the Midst of Failure

To a great extent the relationship between failing antebellum proprietors and their creditors resembled a game of cat and mouse. Debtors sought to hide their true circumstances from the holders of claims against them, especially outside the closest circles of family and friends; creditors, once apprised of those circumstances, did their best to pounce on whatever assets the debtors possessed. But debtor-creditor relations frequently assumed a more complicated character. The legal tools available to antebellum creditors, though extensive, had limitations. Debtors frequently proved adroit at exploiting those limitations, as well as the financial pressures bearing down on their creditors. As a result, debtors and creditors often found themselves tussling for advantage, relying on offers of settlement and compromise as well as threats and legal maneuvers. The most important drawbacks to legal recourse against a defaulting debtor were the monetary costs and delays inherent in the legal process. Turning to the law meant having to pay lawyers to prepare a case and appear in court; lawsuits also required the payment of court costs. In the event that creditors successfully attained both judgment and a sufficient execution to satisfy their claims, they would usually be able to recoup some of these expenses. But creditors could not always be sure that their legal efforts would pay dividends.

Several circumstances could transform reliance on the law into an exercise of throwing good money after bad. Competing creditors might beat a litigant to the courthouse, leaving little for other claimants.[39] Even if the holder of an obligation gained an early judgment and execution, a debtor's property might be already encumbered by mortgages, or already dissipated by the attempt to meet maturing debts.[40] Moreover, in those states where creditors retained the ability to subject a debtor to imprisonment, the petitioning creditor usually was responsible for paying the costs of feeding the prisoner.[41] To get a sense of how costly debt actions could be, one need only look at antebellum bankruptcy petitions. Efforts to enforce payment through the legal system frequently led to new debts, this time to lawyers.[42]

In addition to the costs and risks associated with legal action, creditors who relied on the courts had to wait for the wheels of justice to grind. Judicial process took time. Cases had to conform to the schedule of the court; defendants usually had to receive notice of motions so that they might prepare a defense; debtors who lost at the trial court had the option of appealing the decision; and most states required a waiting period between the moment at which creditors gained debt judgments and the time when they might levy on debtors' property. Some actions could take place only after a creditor had exhausted other legal options open to him. Thus in New York a litigant could not file a creditor's bill in chancery court unless he could prove that he had already received a judgment in the common-law courts and that the execution resulting from that judgment had not extinguished the debt. Even after the holder of an obligation received a warrant for a sheriff to take possession of a debtor's property, he was dependent upon the actions of that officer. Antebellum sheriffs did not always move quickly to sell out the worldly goods of their neighbors; nor did they always transfer the proceeds of a sale with dispatch.[43]

Postponements in the legal process of debt collection tended to multiply during periods of severe deflation. Democratically elected state governments had a penchant for passing debtor relief legislation when widespread economic distress followed events like the panic of 1819 or the commercial revulsions of the late 1830s. These enactments included stay laws, appraisal laws, and homestead exemptions. The first group of these measures increased the time that it took to move from a judgment to a judicially mandated sale; the second required that before such a sale, members of the community had to appraise the value of the goods to be sold, which set a floor under which the purchase price could not go; the third exempted some property from execution altogether. Some of these measures had short life spans, because of either legislative repeal or judicial rulings of unconstitutionality; others were more enduring. But as long as they remained on the books, they complicated the position of creditors.[44]

On the whole, the mechanisms of antebellum law did not give creditors immediate access to their debtors' property. Delays were particularly likely when a creditor did not already hold security or when a debtor actively opposed the legal maneuvers against him. As a result, reaching the property of a debtor through the courts often required substantial patience. Time, however, was a commodity that some antebellum creditors could ill afford.

In some contexts, two other constraints diminished the utility of enforcing a debt through the antebellum courts. First, many debts were small enough that legal moves did not seem to justify the expenditure of time and money to bring a suit. Second, a substantial amount of property owned by antebellum debtors was of limited use to their creditors. In particular, promissory notes and account book debts could be extremely difficult to reduce to cash, especially for someone who was not familiar with the business's customers and the circumstances surrounding each debt. Even when creditors could reach these kind of assets through legal process, they might not realize much from them.

Despite the willingness of creditors to use the courts to secure the payments due them, they were not unaware of the difficulties and expenses that came with lawsuits; those same problems did not escape the notice of debtors, who were themselves overwhelmingly creditors. As a result, many financially troubled businesses and individuals attempted to negotiate their way of out difficulty, most frequently by requesting extensions for their payments. Creditors were by no means always amenable to such entreaties. But under the right conditions, debtors received a hearing.

Renewals were most likely to be forthcoming if a firm seemed to have a strong likelihood of eventually making its payments and if creditors could afford the delay. During periods of general prosperity, both of these conditions often obtained, encouraging creditors as diverse as southern cotton factors, investors in western lands, and rural eastern storekeepers freely to extend their debtors' terms of payment.[45] Relatively solid businesses could arrange deferments even in the midst of economic slowdowns and widespread liquidation. For four years after the panic of 1837, R. Hoe & Co. successfully renegotiated a host of loans. Its creditors knew that the firm made the best printing presses and circular saws in the country; they accepted the firm's laments about problems in collections and manifested the faith that the machinists would overcome the drag of bad debts. The patience of creditors, of course, had limits. Eventually even a business with as strong a base as R. Hoe & Co. had to mortgage its property in order to keep the loans coming.[46]

Ironically, as soon as a failing business conceded financial defeat, its negotiating leverage increased significantly. If the firm's assets were not likely to cover all of its obligations, either some creditors would receive nothing, or many creditors would have to settle for less than the full value of their claims. Failed proprietors made use of this arithmetic in an attempt to pry concessions from the firms and individuals who held claims against them. Most commonly, business owners who had suspended payments offered to pay creditors some fraction of what they were owed, so long as those creditors signed a release for the remaining amount of their claims. Creditors who received such proposals had no obligation to accept; and if they refused, they maintained all of their legal rights. But the holders of obligations against a bankrupt debtor could not be sure how other creditors would respond. If enough creditors accepted terms, the debtor's entire estate might go to other parties before hold-outs moved their cases through the courts. As a result, settlement offers frequently received careful attention, especially from creditors whose claims were not yet due. Holders of promissory notes, bills of exchange, or mortgages that had not yet matured stood in a poor legal position relative to other creditors. These claimants had no legal standing to sue until their debtors were actually in default, and thus they stood little chance of winning a legal race of diligence. Compromise might furnish the only means of securing even a partial payment.[47]

Severe commercial pressure also made creditors amenable to settlement offers, another pattern illustrated by the actions of Houghton & Day. When Carlos Houghton sent off letter after letter to far-flung customers and agents, he showed little reluctance to threaten lawsuits or instigate them. But Houghton could not afford to reject proposed compromises out of hand. In desperate need of cash, the dry goods dealer was willing to consider such deals if he believed that holding out would yield no greater return.[48]

Creditors similarly tended to look kindly on compromise proposals if they did not see much chance of extracting full payment. Many holders of notes given by Dayton & Schuyler adopted such a position. Neither partner seemed to have property outside of the business, and the partnership had failed badly. As a result, the compromise offered by partner Thomas Schuyler a week or so after the firm suspended operations received serious consideration. Schuyler held out the

To all to whom these Presents shall come, or may concern, Greeting:

Know Ye, That I, Richard Mitchell, —
of Leicester in England —

for and in consideration of the sum of One hundred dollars (Ninety four 20/100 dollars in note and balance in Cash) — lawful money of the United States of America, to me — in hand paid by Jonathan Amory and Henry H Leeds of the city of New York Merchants — have remised, released, and for ever discharged, and by these Presents do, for myself my heirs, executors, and administrators, remise, release, and for ever discharge, the said Jonathan Amory and Henry H Leeds their heirs, executors, and administrators, of and from all, and all manner of action and actions, cause and causes of action, suits, debts, dues, sums of money, accounts, reckonings, bonds, bills, specialties, covenants, contracts, controversies, agreements, promises, variances, trespasses, damages, judgments, extents, executions, claims, and demands, whatsoever, in law or in equity, which against them or either of them I ever had, now have or which I, or my heirs, executors, or administrators, hereafter can, shall, or may have, for, upon, or by reason of any matter, cause, or thing whatsoever, from the beginning of the world to the day of the date of these Presents. — Saving however and without prejudice to my claim and demand against William Watson one of the members of the late firm of Amory Leeds and Company

In Witness whereof, I have hereunto set my hand and seal the Eighteenth — day of January, in the year of our Lord one thousand eight hundred and forty two —

Sealed and delivered in the presence of

M. Isaacs

Richd. Mitchell by
B Warburton Atty.

LEGAL RELEASE MANDATED BY DEBT COMPROMISE. One of dozens of releases negotiated by the New York City mercantile firm of Amory & Leeds, this document shows the standard form for privately arranged settlements between antebellum creditors and insolvent debtors (C-F 30, National Archives and Record Administration, Northeast Region, New York City).

prospect of a 50 percent payment, partly in cash and partly in goods; several creditors accepted the proposal.[49]

As adept as many failed Americans were at convincing their creditors to compromise claims, those debtors would have confronted a much more difficult task if antebellum law had not sanctioned a legal instrument known as a voluntary assignment for the benefit of creditors. Through such an assignment, a debtor transferred all or part of his assets to a third party, known as the "assignee"; this person agreed to act as a trustee over the debtor's estate, converting it to money and then distributing the proceeds to creditors.[50]

Voluntary assignments had a long lineage in the English common law and almost all of the American states recognized the ability to execute these instruments as an intrinsic aspect of property rights. There were legal constraints on assignments. Among other requirements, they had to involve a bona fide transfer of a debtor's property, the transfer had to be consummated by a written document, and the assignee or assignees had to be solvent and had to make a good faith effort to administer the trust. But so long as failing individuals and their assignees met these prescriptions, they could insulate all unencumbered property from the legal attacks of creditors.[51]

This protection further enhanced the negotiating position of debtors. Assignments commonly stipulated that any creditor who wished to receive a payment under it had to release the assigning debtor from all legal liability. Creditors who did not wish to meet this demand and who did not already hold security, such as a mortgage, had few options open to them. They could either attempt to attack the legality of the assignment or they could wait for the debtor to obtain new property, which they might then attack through the courts. Both approaches ran the risk of leaving a creditor with no payment whatsoever; the first additionally required investment in legal counsel and court costs.

Reliance on voluntary assignments to extract settlements from creditors drew heavy fire throughout the antebellum decades. Commercial moralists reviled the custom, arguing that it gave far too much power to individuals who had driven themselves and their creditors into a financial morass. Philadelphian Joseph Hopkinson offered a representative assault in his 1832 oration on commercial integrity. Hopkinson lamented the "almost universal" disregard of the principles that should regulate the actions of bankrupts. Rather than placing all property in the hands of creditors, the typical insolvent had a disturbing habit of becoming "the sole judge between himself and his creditors." He called his creditors only after making out an assignment that "dictates the terms" on which they may receive payment; and when he summoned them to a meeting, it was "not to consult them, not to learn their wishes and opinions about their own rights and interests, not to ask them what he shall do, but to inform them what he has done."[52]

Despite such criticism, the absence of national bankruptcy legislation throughout most of the antebellum period led thousands of failing Americans to "make a bankrupt law for [themselves]." Merchants in the largest cities relied most heavily on assignments, but the practice was common throughout the country. Insolvent debtors in town and countryside used this legal device to choose the person or persons who would superintend the liquidation of their assets, as well as to structure the terms for receiving any benefit from that liquidation.[53] As significant as these powers were, the utility of assignments did not end there; failing individuals and firms also used the instrument as one of many tools to favor their relatives and closest business associates over other creditors.

A Culture of Preference

Perhaps no admonitions of the commercial moralists received such short shrift as the calls for insolvents and their creditors to work out a pro rata distribution of debtors' assets to each and every person or concern holding claims against them. Failing debtors exhibited remarkable ingenuity in finding ways to prefer some creditors over others. The least complicated methods of preference involved payments of cash or goods immediately before announcing a suspension of business. But on the eve of failure, antebellum debtors also surrendered collateral, executed mortgages on real estate, machinery, and furniture, and transferred such assets outright.[54] Each of these actions gave particular creditors access to a given debtor's estate, enabling them to satisfy their claims while others would have to rely on either the remnants of property or the future earnings of the debtor.

An additional method of favoring a creditor relied on the legal mechanisms of debt collection. Delays and costs associated with those mechanisms hinged on active opposition by debtors, who could either ask for continuances, directly contest suits, or attempt to obstruct the work of sheriffs and court-appointed receivers. Whenever debtors did not fight debt actions or actually cooperated with them, legal costs and postponements fell away. Individuals and firms on the brink of failure routinely arranged preferences through such cooperation. These soon-to-be bankrupts confessed judgments to selected creditors, giving those claimants liens on their assets.[55]

In conjunction with these expedients, failing proprietors habitually drafted voluntary assignments that benefited some creditors far more than others. The maker of an assignment could achieve this end by setting up different classes of beneficiaries. After the assignee or assignees had converted enough property to declare a dividend, a preferential assignment instructed them to pay certain creditors in full before other claimants received a penny. In many instances, assignments included several classes of creditors, each class having to wait for payment until the more favored group had garnered a full share. Failing debtors also frequently appointed one or more of the favored creditors as assignee, ensuring that their interests would be well taken care of in the administration of the trust. The consequence of these arrangements was that preferred creditors often received full payment, while other creditors were lucky to garner a pittance.[56]

Antebellum courts generally upheld the legality of these provisions in the absence of statutory regulation, which was largely absent before the 1840s. As with the judicial sanction of both assignments in general and the ability of a debtor who had not suspended business to make payments to creditors in the order that he saw fit, the right of making a preferential assignment fell within the legal ambit of common-law property rights.[57] Legal doctrine concerning preferences, of course, does not by itself account for the widespread nature of the practice. For explanations of why antebellum debtors so often preferred some creditors shortly before or after their suspension of business, one must consider the pressure that creditors brought to bear on the people who owed them money, the customs and culture of the antebellum business community, and the bonds of affection and obligation that tied failing Americans to their families and business "friends."

Debtors were by no means wholly insulated from the legal and psychological assaults of creditors. The shrewdness that many troubled proprietors demonstrated as they fended off their creditors or delayed attempts at legal action did not mean that harried debtors were invulnerable to anxiety or stress. Debtors most easily circumvented the insistent demands of creditors when the latter resided at a comfortable distance. As both Houghton & Day and R. Hoe & Co. found to their intense annoyance, far-flung customers had a disturbing habit of responding to dunning letters with silence.[58] When a creditor or his agent was close at hand, though, debtors had to withstand threats delivered at close range. They occasionally gave way to the resulting strain.

The actions of Amory & Leeds, the New York City commission house that failed largely as a result of overtrading, demonstrate the ways in which a persistent creditor could elicit preferences. As the commission merchants struggled to keep their business afloat, they persuaded a prominent New York auction house, John Haggerty & Sons, to give them advances in the form of promissory notes. Amory & Leeds then sold the notes at a "ruinous" discount in order to raise funds to pay other creditors. By December 1839, the commission merchants owed John Haggerty & Sons over $124,000. Throughout the following months, the auctioneers hectored the recipients of their notes for payment, threatening dire consequences and lawsuits. At one point, the mercantile firm transferred a parcel of real estate as partial satisfaction of the debt; but as the property's estimated value was only $27,000, the transaction did not placate the auctioneers. By June 15, 1840, Amory & Leeds had little choice but to suspend operations, causing John Haggerty to press his claim all the more doggedly. The commission merchants soon rewarded his tenacity.

Among the firm's possessions at the time of its suspension were over $50,000 in linens and other textile goods that a British manufacturer had placed on consignment. These goods continued to belong to the British manufacturer, Thomas Taylor & Son; Amory & Leeds had authority to sell them only for the benefit of the consignors. But Thomas Taylor and his son lived in Barnsley, England, thousands of miles away. John Haggerty and his sons, by contrast, lived and worked within a short horse ride. A few days after their suspension, Amory & Leeds gave the New York City auctioneers the Taylors' lots of linen and sheetings.[59]

Other creditors persevered not so much as a result of wearing debtors down, but rather because the debtor did not see much point in trying to forestall the inevitable. Debtors frequently confessed judgment or made preferential payments when they had no reasonable defense against a threatened suit. Instead of attempting to drag out legal proceedings, thereby incurring their own legal costs, they cooperated with a diligent litigant.[60] The result was a priority of claim, usually to the detriment of other creditors.

If the badgering of creditors provides one explanation for the frequency with which failing Americans favored certain holders of claims against them, ingrained customs about the sanctity of "confidential debts" offers another. As American business culture developed in the decades that followed independence, numerous participants in the credit system came to accept the proposition that all debts were not equal. Two kinds of debts stood apart as imposing special obligations— money that was borrowed without interest and debts that arose as the result of endorsements.

Defenders of special treatment for these classes of creditors made two arguments on their behalf. The first, which appeared in Anglo-American commercial thought at least as far back as the 1770s, was that such benefactors extended the assistance of their bank accounts or their commercial reputations on the basis of "motives entirely disinterested." Individuals who lent a proprietor money without interest or endorsed his paper without exacting payment for the privilege did so in order to "promote his prosperity" without "any consideration moving toward themselves." When an American received benefits from such unselfish aid, he took on obligations of gratitude that far outweighed his duty to pay debts that emanated from normal business transactions. To forsake this duty of gratitude, according to one Alabama commentator, would be "the blackest of crimes."[61]

The second justification for favored treatment of no-interest lenders and sureties turned on the settled character of the practice. Since these preferences were of such long standing, creditors had to be presumed to know that if a customer failed, he would prefer such lenders and endorsers. Furthermore, the custom of preferring confidential debts gave rise to settled expectations on the part of individuals who loaned money or their name without charge. They acted in "the confidence, predicated upon almost invariable usage, that the party obtaining assistance in that manner, when overtaken by pecuniary distresses, will not permit [them] to suffer." In short, the demands of gratitude and the "tacit understandings" created by commercial usage legitimated special handling of confidential debts.[62]

Failing antebellum debtors frequently acted in accordance with the precepts that flowed from these justifications. A significant proportion of identifiable preferences given by southern New York bankrupts went to endorsers or suppliers of non-interest loans. Charles Starr's handling of financial woes was typical. When the time came to draft an assignment in November 1837, the New York bookbinder and advocate of reform took care of the friends who had helped him try to stave off financial ruin. Only after these associates received full payment would other creditors gain a nickel. Confidential creditors by no means always averted losses as the result of their financial aid; many southern New York bankrupts owed their own failures to the insolvency of individuals to whom they had lent money or given endorsements.[63] Nonetheless, the claims of confidential lenders and sureties generally received special attention when antebellum debtors gave up hope of avoiding insolvency.

The solicitous stances that insolvents typically adopted toward their confidential creditors makes the extensive assistance received by many distressed debtors even more comprehensible. Lenders or endorsers to a troubled proprietor often provided financial assistance in part because of the "tacit understandings" that surrounded confidential credit. Even without a specific agreement that confidential creditors would receive security, as through a mortgage, many providers of endorsements or interest-free loans discounted the desperate state of their debtors' predicament. If insolvency came, they believed, often rightly so, that they would receive special treatment.

Critics of preferences charged that the practice was largely responsible for the risky and mostly unsuccessful schemes undertaken by failing debtors. Without the props of endorsements, these critics argued, individuals on the verge of bankruptcy would have no further "chance in the lottery of speculation." Deprived of "delusive credit," the failing debtor would be more likely to suspend his business at an early season. These attacks, primarily made by large urban wholesalers who chafed at the ease with which bankrupt customers evaded payments to their faraway suppliers, had only limited impact in the 1820s and 1830s. In every region of the nation, extension of confidential credit and protection of confidential creditors flourished, largely as a result of widespread political support for "local control" over the disposition of a bankrupt's assets.[64]

The third primary spur to preferences reflected the intimate relationships between debtors and some of their creditors. Just as many antebellum Americans did not see all debts as being equal, most participants in the credit system viewed some creditors as being more important than others. Financial obligations to relatives or close business associates generally carried more weight than debts that resulted from more impersonal commercial transactions. Antebellum debtors cared more about the fortunes of people close to them; when presented with an opportunity to protect the finances of a father-in-law, a brother, or a close business associate, few hesitated to do so. Again and again the preferences granted by antebellum bankrupts went to family members or business friends.[65]

These three impulses for insolvent debtors to favor particular creditors often overlapped. Pressure from creditors was much harder to ignore when it came from a person who had extended credit-preserving endorsements, or from someone whom one could expect to see at family gatherings for years to come. In addition, the providers of endorsements or interest-free loans came overwhelmingly from the ranks of family and close business associates. In such instances, bankrupts confronted twin impulses—one created by the obligation of gratitude to confidential creditors, the other by bonds of fidelity to kith and kin.[66]

In the absence of strong laws against the favored treatment of individual creditors by Americans on the verge of failure, the pleas of the commercial moralists made remarkably little headway. As most failing debtors contemplated insolvency, they shakily stood their ground between the push of diligent creditors and the pull of personal obligations. The latter were particularly hard to brush off or ignore, since, as we will see, the future prospects of a bankrupt often depended crucially on the support he received from family and friends. In an economy where some creditors possessed considerable geographical advantage over others and in which many commercial transactions took place within families and close-knit business circles, preferential bankruptcies were the order of the day.

Skirting a Full Surrender

Many failing debtors went further than trying to protect the interests of favored creditors. These bankrupts chafed at the legal and moral obligations to yield absolutely all of their property in order to satisfy the debts that had overwhelmed them. Most states exempted at least some property from the legal reach of debtors, no matter how badly an individual had plunged into debt. Antebellum legal exemptions in New York State were like those of many states. When the sheriff came to levy on a debt judgment, a defaulting New York debtor was entitled to keep spinning wheels, weaving looms, and stoves in use; schoolbooks, family Bibles, and family portraits not to exceed fifty dollars in value; a church pew; a cow, two pigs, and up to ten sheep, including their fleeces; up to sixty days worth of stores and food; a limited amount of clothing, bedding, furniture, and cooking utensils; and tools necessary to the carrying on of a trade, not to exceed a worth of twenty-five dollars.[67] Throughout the country, individuals on the verge of bankruptcy sought to salvage more than what legal provisions like these granted them.

One particularly common way to protect assets from creditors was to conceal them. Tilly Allen successfully engineered such a feat after his failure in 1840. Allen failed as the operator of a canal line in Rochester; he executed an assignment there and then moved to New York City. While out of business in New York and before he petitioned for bankruptcy, the former canal freighter bought sixty-eight shares in a Maryland coal company. Allen did not list the stock on his bankruptcy petition, and neither his creditors nor the bankruptcy assignee ever discovered the omission.[68]

Other strategies of protecting property relied on technical features of antebellum property law. In order for a creditor to reach his defaulting debtor's assets, he had to show a court or a levying sheriff that the assets actually belonged to the debtor. Myriad failing debtors sought to frustrate their creditors by conveying property to someone else, almost always a relative. One southern New York bankrupt conveyed store stock to his father, who was about to head off to Texas; another arranged the sale of a house to her mother; a third assigned store goods to a clerk but kept possession of them, continuing to sell the stock as the clerk's "agent."[69]

Of all the strategies of concealment adopted by southern New York bankrupts, the most comprehensive were pursued by Henry Leeds. His machinations indicate the extent to which American debtors could use their understanding of antebellum law to protect their assets from creditors. When Leeds entered the partnership with Jonathon Amory in 1837, he did so with the explicit understanding that he might use the firm's resources and credit in his real estate ventures. Those speculations went back to at least 1833 and involved dozens of properties in New York City, Brooklyn, and New Brunswick, New Jersey, as well as several parcels on Long Island. Despite continual reliance on firm funds and firm notes, Leeds's financial position grew precarious as the real estate market dipped first in 1837 and then again two years later. By the early months of 1840, Leeds's operations had cost the firm over $66,000, greatly contributing to the business's insolvency.[70]

Several months before the partnership informed its creditors of its financial difficulties and began to negotiate settlements, Leeds sought to protect his real estate interests. Between December 1839 and March 1841, he conveyed the bulk of his properties to his widowed sister, Frances Keown, whom Leeds had supported since her husband's death in 1835. His brother Amos, a New York City coal dealer, also received a few New York City stores. The commission merchant then opened two bank accounts in his sister's name and had her sign a power of attorney, which enabled him to manage all the assets as her agent. For the next two years Leeds continued to squeeze income from his real estate empire, even though he owed hundreds of thousands of dollars to the creditors of Amory & Leeds. Acting behind the legal shield of his sister's ownership, he collected rents from tenants, deposited and withdrew monies from the bank accounts, and made mortgage payments.[71]

A final strategy for safeguarding property from creditors took advantage of the rights held by the wives of insolvent debtors. The common law as received by the American states provided married women with limited property rights. Under the doctrine of coverture, women lost all title to their property when they married. All real estate and chattels became vested in their husbands, who could use and dispose of those assets as they saw fit. Equally important, property that a wife brought into the marriage was legally available to a husband's creditors if that spouse defaulted on his obligations. There were, however, means of getting around these common-law strictures, means that some failing husbands exploited.[72]

After marriage, husbands could reserve property for a wife through the use of a trust. The husband would convey assets to a third party or third parties for the benefit of his wife and children. The trustee or trustees had legal control over the property, as well as the legal obligation to manage it in the interests of the bene-ficiary. If the creation of the trust was legal—if, for example, it did not represent a fraudulent conveyance motivated by a desire to hinder creditors—then the holders of claims against an insolvent husband had no way to reach the property contained therein.

Failing debtors made at least occasional use of trusts as a means of sheltering family assets from the impact of bankruptcy. The actions of New York dry goods and carpet dealer James H. Sackett nicely illustrate this gambit. In 1837, Sackett placed his wife's inherited Westchester County farm in a trust for her benefit. This transaction likely raised few eyebrows, as it came at a time when his firm had no difficulty making its payments. Three years later, though, the merchant added to the trust on the eve of a business suspension. Almost certainly impelled by impend-ing debt judgments, Sackett placed all his household furniture and all of the tools and implements on the Westchester farm in the hands of his wife's trustees. While of questionable legality, these later transfers worked as well as the first, ensuring that the Sackett family retained a sizable core of assets. Thus the granting of a separate estate for a wife served as an insurance policy against business reverses, a means of limiting the damage that economic failure would bring to one's family.[73]

Antebellum commercial moralists offered such consistent advice about the appro-priate responses to bankruptcy in part because they recognized the extent to which Americans flouted their principles. Henry Ward Beecher, like most of the moralists, had few illusions about either debtors or creditors. All too often, the antebellum debtor practiced "cunning tricks, delays, concealments, and frauds"; all too often, his creditors, fearful "that one should feast upon the victim more than his share, . . . rush upon him like wolves upon a wounded deer, dragging him down, ripping him open, breast and flank, plunging deep their bloody muzzles to reach the heart and taste blood at the very fountain." To Beecher and his fellows, sin pervaded the houses of American commerce.[74]

Through all of the preaching to errant entrepreneurs, America's spokesmen for commercial rectitude hoped to infuse the American economy with principles that would moderate its furious pace. The moralists coupled their exhortations to the failing debtor and his creditors with pleas for prudent business practices. Most importantly, they counseled proprietors to extend and ask for credit with great caution. Limiting the use of credit would slow down one's business but also make it safer, less prone to commercial pressure, and less susceptible to commercial temptation.[75] Some of the moralists also advocated the abolition of all legal machinery for the collection of debts. In their eyes, that machinery fostered an often delusive faith on the part of creditors, who placed excessive reliance on their ability to recover a debt through the law when weighing the advisability of granting credit. The repeal of debt-collection laws would make American commerce rest more solidly on trust between men; it would lead businessmen to conduct their affairs prudently, and thus promote "honor, integrity, and upright mercantile character."[76]

This appeal for a more restrained and considered business culture shared a good deal with the ethic of local exchange that pervaded segments of rural America in the early nineteenth century. As the historian Christopher Clark has demonstrated for the Massachusetts portion of the Connecticut River valley, the economic life of rural areas was often predicated on flexible principles for the settlement of debts. Local creditors generally refrained from forcing the issue of payment, and especially from turning to legal means of collection. When settlement of claims occurred, the means of payment would have to be agreed to by both parties, each taking due measure of the economic constraints faced by the other. This attitude toward credit was well suited for relatively self-sufficient communities that were dominated by interdependent families, each motivated primarily by the desire to provide offspring with sufficient land to reproduce a household economy. The ethic of local exchange lingered on in western Massachusetts at least into the 1830s; in parts of the country further removed from the urban engines of economic growth, it lasted well into the 1850s.[77]

Neither the older ethic of rural exchange nor the creed of the commercial moralists grafted easily onto the dynamic economy of antebellum America.[78] Each of these codes presupposed a relatively leisurely economy—the first structured around agricultural production, neighborhood trade, and the provision of homesteads to children; the second around a Christianized brand of measured capitalist exchange. As America's republican experiment stretched further into the nineteenth century, more and more of its citizens found neither pace to their liking. By the 1830s, the rhythms of the American economy increasingly militated against any notions of an unhurried commerce, in both urban and rural settings.

America's revolution in transport brought its residents closer together, collapsing both distance and time. Goods and information moved more quickly along the nation's new canals and railways, and commerce speeded up in turn. As complex networks of credit grew around the busy routes of domestic trade, leisurely approaches to financial settlements became impossible for a greater number of Americans—indulgence to debtors could easily lead to creditors' own financial crises.

At the same time that transportation projects reordered economic opportunities and constraints, thousands of Americans embraced ambitions in direct conflict with the precepts of local exchange or those advocated by the commercial sermonizers. As those spokesmen were well aware, proprietors in every part of the nation extended their operations in the pursuit of riches. Many of these businessmen granted credit to people they did not know well, since refusals would simply send business to competitors. The dangers associated with such commercial practices were often considerable, but in the eyes of countless merchants, manufacturers, and investors, the potential payoff justified the risks.

All the exhortation of the commercial moralists, then, did not lead to a thoroughgoing reformation of American business. And yet the significance of the moralists' vision extends beyond its service as a counterpoint to the behavior of Americans caught up in the tumultuous antebellum economy. Despite the frequent breach of the moralists' principles, contemporaries were aware of them and, to a point, accepted them as ethical standards.

Henry Leeds's behavior is once again illustrative. When he and his partner, Jonathon Amory, sat down to write a circular letter to their creditors on February 1, 1841, their language recalled the moralists' commandments throughout. They spoke of their honesty and forthrightness in calling a meeting of their creditors several months previously. No bankrupt mercantile business, they maintained, "could produce a more honest or candid statement" of its affairs. The pair further pledged that they were willing to "surrender all we possess," having no more than they had already offered. And they criticized the actions of some creditors who wished to hold out for an advantage, vowing that "we are in honor and justice bound to protect *equally*" each and every holder of a claim against them.[79]

Amory and Leeds made these declarations because they expected that their audience would respond favorably to them. Even though their actions belied their words in almost every particular, the commission merchants assumed that the precepts of the moralists had some currency. If they could convince creditors that their actions met those standards—if, in other words, they presented a skeptical mercantile audience with a sufficiently persuasive tale of evenhanded conduct amidst entrepreneurial struggle—the pair believed they stood an improved chance of arranging a compromise.[80] At one level, this episode underscores the extent to which theatricality and storytelling suffused nineteenth-century American capitalism. Just as antebellum commercial exchange depended partly on salesmanship— entertaining display, calculating manipulation of desire, and subtle adaptation to the personalities of potential customers—so the era's credit system rested partly on emotion-laden narratives conveyed between individuals at different points within a given network of obligations. Successful negotiation of individual or economywide financial crises often required skill in crafting the dunning letter, the plea for debt extension, or the bankrupt's explanatory circular to creditors, as well as deftness in evaluating or responding to such missives. To be effective, though, these forms of narrative communication usually had to fit a firm's conduct within the confines of conventional mercantile plots; and those plots owed much to the prescriptions of commercial moralism.[81]

The moralists, moreover, had influence beyond the molding of contemporary opinion about the justice of commercial behavior. Even if they were unsuccessful in guiding the actions of many antebellum bankrupts, as opposed to their public statements and rationalizations, their ideas increasingly found favor in conservative Protestant churches, fraternal organizations, and legislative halls. By the 1840s, for example, the Congregationalists of Chelsea, Vermont, had adopted a moral code that explicitly enjoined church members to "honestly provide for the Liquidation of debts to the extent of our ability." At roughly the same time, the Masonic Lodge of Jacksonville, Illinois, was demonstrating a willingness to expel members found guilty of "defrauding creditors," while several state legislatures enacted laws that prohibited preferential assignments. As of 1853, eleven states had statutory bans of some sort against these instruments. Perhaps most important, when the economic dislocations of the late 1830s and early 1840s created political pressures for revisions of debtor-creditor law, and especially for the adoption of a national bankruptcy system, the creed of "the church commercial" guided the labors of congressional draftsmen.[82]

American Jubilee

Let the bankrupt rejoice, for the Sheriff no more
Shall follow his coach as it rolls from the door—
His mansion—no more shall he hastily lock it
And skulk though the street with the key in his pocket,
But lightly his heart 'neath his ruffles shall beat,
While his racy old liquors shall soon sooth his retreat.
O, the beauties of the law.
—New Hampshire "Locofoco poet,"
  New York Herald, March 21, 1842

Fraud vitiates everything into which it enters. It is like the deadly and noxious simoom of arid and desert climes. It prostrates all before its contaminating touch, and leaves death only and destruction in its wake. No act, however solemn, no agreement, however sacred, can resist its all-destroying power.

All acts into which fraud enters are nullities.
—Argument of Mr. Day, Attorney for the Appellant,
  Commercial Bank of Manchester v. Buckner (1857)

Before the Civil War, the U.S. Congress launched two experiments in bankruptcy law, both of which quickly foundered on the rocks of localism. The first occurred in 1800, when a Federalist Congress enacted bankruptcy legislation as a means of supplying relief to numerous land speculators and seaport merchants who had been ruined in the aftermath of a 1797 commercial crisis. Explicitly modeling the 1800 Bankruptcy Act on British law, Federalist legislators provided only for involuntary petitions by creditors and furnished legal relief only to insolvent merchants who had racked up comparatively substantial debts. After Jeffersonians gained control of Congress in the election of 1800, they tolerated the statute for a time before repealing it in 1803 as a dangerous extension of centralized power and a brand of commercial regulation inappropriate for an agrarian republic.[1]

Nearly four decades later, in 1841, the Whig-dominated 27th Congress again created a federal bankruptcy system, largely in the hope of attracting the political support of thousands of Americans whose businesses had failed in the wake of the panics of 1837 and 1839. To curry favor with these voters, the Whigs made bankruptcy discharges available to all citizens and allowed debtors as well as creditors to initiate bankruptcy proceedings. Like the first federal bankruptcy act, the 1841 law remained on the books only briefly. Within eighteen months, complaints about expensive and inconvenient bankruptcy administration, excessively lenient treatment of failed debtors, and deleterious impacts on the supply of business credit fueled a successful Democratic campaign for repeal—though not before thousands of Americans received legal discharges through the auspices of the federal courts.

The history of the short-lived 1841 bankruptcy statute offers rich perspectives on the complex interactions between commercially minded debtors and creditors in antebellum America, including their contributions and responses to a changing legal environment. Numerous bankrupts and creditors strove to shape the bankruptcy legislation under consideration by the 27th Congress and to guide the federal bench in interpreting and applying the statute's ambiguities after its passage. Bankrupts won most of these political and legal battles. The 1841 act accordingly shifted the balance of legal power markedly in favor of insolvent debtors, with important implications for the tenor of private negotiations that often settled the terms of bankruptcies. In some respects, this shift endured long beyond the legislation's demise, as the law's incorporation of voluntary bankruptcy deepened commitment to the principle that in America, failed business owners generally deserved a fresh start, unencumbered by past obligations.

At the same time, the new bankruptcy system manifested a regulatory dimension, embodied in provisions that penalized failing debtors who did not treat their creditors equally. Drawn from the suggestions of bankruptcy reformers with ties to commercial moralism, these disciplinary elements reflected a coercive impulse born of frustration with the impact of moral suasion—much as calls for the prohibition of alcohol grew out of impatience among temperance advocates with the results of mere agitation. Even though the federal judiciary did not give the Bankruptcy Law's regulatory sections as much force as they might have, these stipulations nonetheless armed creditors with significant legal weapons in instances of failure, which the most savvy among them did not hesitate to exploit. Antebellum America's encounter with a federal bankruptcy process thus underlines the crucial importance of examining the role of litigants as well as legislators and judges in shaping American law.[2]

In addition, the implementation of the 1841 act reveals the substantial obstacles that confronted antebellum reformers who wished to use law as a means of refashioning commercial culture. The legislation only partially achieved its fundamental goal of mandating equal treatment of creditors in cases of bankruptcy. Diligent creditors continued to find ways to compel preferential payments, while many embarrassed debtors continued to place a high priority on shielding relatives and close business associates from the consequences of failure. Like most efforts at legal change, the second national bankruptcy system did not instantaneously transform long-standing conceptualizations of rights and duties, as numerous bankrupts and creditors retained values and expectations that clashed with the letter and spirit of the new law of bankruptcy.[3]

Premises of Bankruptcy Reform

Throughout the 1820s and 1830s, a number of prominent businessmen, politicians, and jurists sought to enshrine the tenets of the commercial moralists in national law through the establishment of a federal bankruptcy system. Chiefly identifying with the National Republicans, and in later years, the Whigs, these men included national leaders such as Daniel Webster, Henry Clay, and Supreme Court justice Joseph Story. By reconfiguring the legal treatment of insolvency, proponents of bankruptcy reform hoped to change the economic incentives and business culture that directed the actions of debtors and creditors. Their aims were several. A national bankruptcy system would thwart dishonest debtors, nullifying actions that defrauded legitimate creditors; it would limit the power of vengeful creditors, releasing the economic energies of honest debtors through legal discharges from past debts; and it would ensure that all creditors shared fairly in the distribution of a given bankrupt's property.[4]

Reformers additionally reasoned that a proper bankruptcy law would change the way that debtors and creditors treated one another in the normal course of business. If every debtor might go to bankruptcy court, reformers argued, creditors would think carefully before extending a loan. By the same token, if "hopelessly involved" debtors knew that bankruptcy discharges depended on honest and forthright behavior, they would prove far more likely to stop their business activities as soon as failure loomed. With a permanent bankruptcy system, reformers maintained, people in financial trouble would shy away from risky measures aimed at retrieving essentially hopeless financial situations. They would also eschew preferential payments to favored creditors or attempts to conceal property from creditors or bankruptcy officials.[5]

Finally, advocates for bankruptcy legislation insisted that a national system for dealing with business failures would greatly improve the certainty surrounding commercial transactions and significantly reduce their cost. Reformers ceaselessly observed that every state had its own set of laws governing the relationship between debtors and creditors, maintaining widely divergent court systems, providing creditors with various means of attacking their debtors' property, and granting debtors multifarious protection against their creditors. The legal context in any one state also changed regularly, as legislators tinkered with the law of debtor and creditor. In such an environment, businessmen who engaged in interstate commerce either spent substantial time and money keeping track of the basic ground rules of commercial exchange or, as was often the case, operated without a perfect understanding of those ground rules. A national bankruptcy law with uniform application from Maine to Louisiana would make the legal foundation of commerce and debt far more easily understood by creditor and debtor alike. Each would have a clear grasp of the legal risks posed by a given commercial transaction.[6]

Despite the best efforts of reformers, antebellum Congresses almost always shied away from bankruptcy legislation, even after the panic of 1819 and initially in the aftermath of the panics of 1837 and 1839. The reluctance to create a national bankruptcy code reflected enduring political opposition to the growth in federal power that such legislation would entail. However persuasively the arguments of commercial moralists might strike voters and politicians enamored of Henry Clay's "American System," they did not go over well with myriad Americans who supported the Democratic Party's commitment to "equal rights" and limited national authority, at least over matters of economic policy.[7]

Nonetheless, as the presidential election of 1840 approached, Whig leaders seized on bankruptcy reform as a leading issue for their campaign. The panics of 1837 and 1839 had produced legions of bankrupts, which several Whigs thought might reach into the hundreds of thousands. In a tight election, such a large block of voters could easily swing the outcome; and in 1840, the two parties saw themselves as relatively evenly matched. As a result, national politicians paid close attention to the thousands of citizens who petitioned Congress for bankruptcy relief between the fall of 1837 and the summer of 1840. Eager to persuade troubled debtors to join the Whig banner, the party assiduously linked criticism of Democratic economic policies with a call to provide relief for the victims of those policies. In the congressional session of 1840, Whigs pushed hard for bankruptcy legislation; during the 1840 presidential campaign, Whig orators strongly favored the passage of such a law. A bankruptcy statute, Whigs promised, would release insolvent debtors from the economic nightmare brought on by Andrew Jackson's war against the Second Bank of the United States.[8]

After winning both the presidency and a majority in both houses of Congress in the 1840 election, Whig leaders felt bound by their pledge to give the nation a bankruptcy system. Taking their cue from both the commercial moralists and the fervent demands of bankrupts, Whig leaders cobbled together a bill that gave all Americans the ability to petition for voluntary bankruptcy, while allowing the creditors of merchants and brokers to petition their debtors into bankruptcy involuntarily. Initially, party discipline was only firm enough to provide a majority in the Senate. But Whig leaders soon overcame their difficulties in the House through a classic exercise of political horse-trading. By promising to link bankruptcy legislation with passage of a bill to distribute the proceeds of land sales to the states, bankruptcy advocates mustered a bare majority in the House. On August 9, 1841, the bill cleared Congress. President Tyler signed it into law the next day.[9]

A Law for Debtors

Insolvent debtors throughout the United States welcomed the passage of the 1841 Bankruptcy Act, with good reason. In accordance with the pleas made by thousands of bankrupts in petitions to Congress, the legislation extended a legal means of relief to all Americans who could not meet their financial obligations. Under the statute's provisions, persons residing in the United States could put forward petitions declaring that they were "unable to meet their debts and engagements." Applications further had to set forth complete lists of creditors, including their residences and the amount of each debt, as well as full inventories of property held by applicants. So long as petitioners honored the statute's requirements, surrendered all of their property to the relevant bankruptcy assignee, and obeyed all court orders, they were entitled to legal discharges from their debts. All debtors, no matter how small or how large the total value of their indebtedness, could gain financial absolution unless they violated a specific statutory prohibition. Without such a violation, creditors were powerless to prevent a discharge, even if every creditor opposed a bankrupt's petition.[10]

This statute gave unprecedented power to insolvent debtors. There were previous examples of legislation empowering a debtor to initiate a bankruptcy process, both in state insolvency proceedings and in some nineteenth-century foreign bankruptcy laws. But in almost all of these bankruptcy or insolvency systems, voluntary applicants could not receive a discharge from past obligations unless some percentage of their creditors—typically over half in number, collectively holding over half of the total amount owed—explicitly agreed to the release. Several petitions from groups of merchants implored Congress to incorporate a similar process in any bankruptcy legislation, but to no avail.[11]

Juxtaposed alongside legislative innovations friendly to failed debtors, however, were a series of restraints on the conduct of financially troubled proprietors. Applicants were not entitled to a release from their debts if they offered insufficiently precise schedules of debts and assets. Discharges were also unavailable if petitioners included fictitious debts in their petition, concealed any property from the bankruptcy court, or fraudulently conveyed property to a third party in order to foil the legitimate claims of creditors. Petitioners who were merchants could not obtain a discharge if they had not kept proper books of accounts, nor could public officers if they had defaulted on their public obligations. If an individual had contracted debts in a fiduciary capacity, such as through service as a trustee or the administrator of an estate, those obligations were exempted from the operation of the law. The statute further adopted one of the most important precepts of the commercial moralists, denying discharges to anyone who made a preferential payment to a creditor in contemplation of bankruptcy.[12]

Under the Bankruptcy Act, any creditor of a voluntary applicant could oppose the petition on one or more of these grounds, filing objections at two stages in the bankruptcy process. The first opportunity came when petitioners moved that the court formally declare them to be bankrupts. Creditors could object here chiefly on grounds that the schedules of debts and assets were insufficient, either through the inclusion of fictitious debts or the exclusion of some assets. Even after an applicant had successfully received a bankruptcy decree, creditors might still file objections to the granting of discharges. These objections generally alleged fraudulent behavior under the terms of the act, such as making illegal preferences, conveying property with the intent to defraud lawful creditors, or owing debts contracted in a fiduciary capacity (that is, as the trustee of an estate, or as a public officer in charge of public funds). If an objecting creditor presented a compelling case at either stage in the bankruptcy proceedings, the federal judge with jurisdiction over the case could deny the bankruptcy applicant's motion, in the first instance for a bankruptcy decree, and in the second instance for a discharge from financial obligations.

The Act of 1841 further enabled creditors to force some debtors into bankruptcy, authorizing involuntary proceedings against merchants, traders, bankers, brokers, or insurers who owed more than $2,000, including more than $500 to the petitioning creditor, and who had committed any one of a number of specified acts of bankruptcy. These acts included absconding from one's place of residence or business in the hopes of defrauding creditors, concealing oneself from arrest for debt, hiding one's property to prevent attachment by creditors, willingly or fraudulently cooperating with the attempts of some creditors to attach property for debt or to sell the same on final execution, making any fraudulent conveyance of property in order to protect it from legal attack by creditors, and executing an assignment for the benefit of creditors that included preferential payments. Thus if a debtor broke the rules of appropriate behavior as defined by the commercial moralists, the Bankruptcy Act of 1841 gave creditors a means to arrest his financial career.[13]

There were limitations, however, to the ability of creditors to either oppose voluntary petitions or successfully instigate involuntary ones. As congressional opponents of the bankruptcy system pointed out repeatedly, the 1841 bankruptcy legislation did not require scrutiny of how a voluntary bankruptcy applicant had failed. The most reckless speculators or gamblers were entitled to a discharge if they followed the rules and regulations of the court and did not violate one of the law's prohibitions. In this respect, the 1841 law differed from nineteenth-century bankruptcy legislation in France, Russia, the German principalities, and China, which all provided for wide-ranging judicial examination of commercial behavior by bankrupts. Creditors, moreover, might never even find out about voluntary applications. The statute required that bankruptcy petitioners had to inform creditors of their action through the post, as well as place long-running notices in local newspapers.[14] But debtors who were not sure of creditors' addresses could still proceed in their petitions; and when individuals filed for bankruptcy far away from the scenes of their failures, as many did, creditors were extremely unlikely to see relevant newspaper notices.

Other restrictions curbed the ability of creditors to initiate bankruptcy proceedings against their debtors. Creditors could not file involuntary petitions against individuals who were not traders, bankers, or insurers. Equally important, the acts of bankruptcy that permitted legal action by creditors did not include nonpayment of maturing obligations. Merchants who could not pay their debts but did not conceal their property or commit another of the specified commercial sins remained immune from involuntary proceedings.

To the bankruptcy system's most vocal critics, these limitations ensured that the 1841 act would bring about the rankest injustices. Democratic senator Thomas Hart Benton of Missouri offered the most comprehensive indictment of the statute during a Senate debate in late December 1841, in support of an unsuccessful motion to repeal the Bankruptcy Act before it went into operation the following February. Benton castigated a mechanism of voluntary bankruptcy that reversed "the natural order of things," giving the debtor "full dominion" over the process. Debtors could file their petitions "any where that [they] please within the limits of the Union," moving far away from the scene of their insolvencies in order to make opposition difficult for creditors. Petitioners additionally had complete control over the timing of applications, which, the Missouri senator proclaimed, would usually occur not while "on the road to ruin," when debtors might still possess some assets, but rather "at the end of the road," when "everything was used up." The only real hope that objecting creditors had was to demonstrate out-and-out fraud; other "vicious" causes of bankruptcy, such as "the gaming table, the lottery wheel, the stock exchange, the house of ill fame, luxury, debauchery, foolish extravagance, and neglect of business," proved no obstacle to petitions. According to Benton, the 1841 act had as its major aim "the abolition of debts at the will of the debtor," regardless of the amount of property surrendered or the views of creditors.[15]

As Benton recognized, the new bankruptcy legislation vastly increased the negotiating leverage that insolvent debtors could bring to bear on their creditors. Almost immediately after the passage of the law, bankrupts pressed their creditors for comprehensive settlements that were often premised on payments that were only a fraction of the overall sums due. The alternative would be voluntary bankruptcy petitions, subjecting creditors to the uncertain outcome of an untried bankruptcy system. After the failure of attempts to repeal the bankruptcy statute before it was scheduled to go into effect, many creditors yielded to proposals for such compositions. In the early months of 1842, newspapers were filled with reports of widespread compromises settling the claims owed by bankrupts, resulting in "a savings of time, expense and feeling." Numerous creditors judged that a definite payment of five to thirty cents on the dollar would most likely surpass the dividends they would receive from a bankruptcy court, especially if other creditors were accepting an insolvent's proposal. On some occasions, insolvent debtors went so far as to file a bankruptcy petition in order to heighten pressure on their creditors. When this tactic led to general compositions or extensions of payment dates, applicants then withdrew their bankruptcy applications. The large number of private settlements, estimated by some observers in the thousands, lessened the crush of bankruptcy petitions once the new bankruptcy system began operation.[16] Even so, a steady stream of insolvent Americans took advantage of the law throughout 1842 and early 1843, filing applications, fulfilling their obligations under the Bankruptcy Law, and thus gaining legal releases from their pecuniary obligations.

A willingness to accept compositions after the new law's passage, although a crucial aspect of creditors' reaction to the new legal environment, by no means exhausted the range of their responses. Secured creditors remained essentially unmoved by the 1841 act, because it specifically preserved liens valid under state law unless debtors created them as a means of giving preferences in contemplation of bankruptcy. If creditors of defaulting debtors held mortgages on real estate or furniture, they could foreclose on the property; bankruptcy courts had no claim on such assets. Similarly, creditors who held collateral could sell it to satisfy their claims against bankrupts, while those who had gained property attachments and debt judgments before the filing of a bankruptcy petition could proceed to final execution, enforcing judicially mandated sales of a bankrupt's assets in state courts. Secured creditors rarely found themselves inconvenienced by the operation of the Bankruptcy Law. They simply took advantage of liens to satisfy their claims.[17]

In addition, a determined minority of unsecured creditors refused to accept the generous legal treatment of insolvent debtors seemingly mandated by the new bankruptcy system. Some of these creditors mounted a rearguard action to sustain the rights of diligent creditors, hoping to encourage judicial interpretation that would either void or modify the Whig experiment with a voluntary bankruptcy process. Still others sought to make the most of the new law's provisions for involuntary bankruptcy.

As voluntary bankruptcy petitions poured into the nation's federal courthouses during the winter and spring of 1842 and early 1843, a number of creditors and their lawyers cast about for legal strategies that might complicate the task of insolvent debtors who desired a federal bankruptcy discharge. Congressional opponents of the 1841 act presaged a legal tactic pursued by some creditors. Several Democratic lawmakers had insisted that the Whig measure was unconstitutional, at least insofar as it permitted voluntary bankruptcy, because the men who had drafted and ratified the Constitution had understood "bankruptcy" to mean the involuntary legal process then enshrined in English law, and later followed by the U.S. Congress in 1800. After the statute came into force, creditors in Louisiana, New York, and Missouri pressed federal judges to accept this line of reasoning. Missouri district judge Robert Wells found it so compelling that he refused to hear voluntary bankruptcy petitions. Wells's interpretation of the Constitution, however, proved to be idiosyncratic. No other district judge followed his lead, and his own ruling was overturned on appeal. For most federal judges, the 1841 act did not so clearly conflict with constitutional limitations as to compel the voiding of congressional legislation for only the second time since the Constitution's adoption in 1788.[18]

While some creditors tested the constitutionality of voluntary bankruptcy, others encouraged federal bankruptcy judges to apply the 1841 act in ways that would entangle insolvent debtors in interpretive and procedural thickets. Like all legislation, the Whig Bankruptcy Act contained substantial ambiguity, especially in its definitions of the various actions that would prevent insolvent debtors from obtaining discharges or make them subject to involuntary bankruptcy petitions. Nowhere did the statute specify how judges should distinguish between sufficient debt and asset schedules and insufficient ones; nowhere did it state how much leeway creditors might have in interrogating insolvent debtors through bankruptcy-related depositions; nowhere did it make clear what constituted a "concealment of property," a "fraudulent conveyance," or a preferential payment "in contemplation of bankruptcy." Creditors who chose to oppose voluntary applications or to file involuntary petitions wasted little time in suggesting that the judiciary clarify such obscurities with statutory construction favorable to their interests.[19]

In hundreds of cases heard while the 1841 act remained on the nation's statute books, creditors opposed voluntary bankruptcy applications or filed involuntary petitions of their own. Most commonly, objecting creditors maintained that voluntary applications were riddled with mistakes and omissions, or alleged that petitioners had committed some unspecified act of fraud, hoping to compel court-ordered depositions that would bring evidence of such commercial wrongdoing to light. Creditors who sought to force individuals into involuntary bankruptcy proceedings similarly tended to claim that their debtors were guilty of one or more of the acts of bankruptcy listed in the statute, without offering details.

These sorts of legal sallies were regularly rebuffed by the federal judiciary. As long as voluntary bankrupts swore that their debt and asset schedules were accurate according to their knowledge and belief, federal judges were willing to take them at their word. Supreme Court judge Joseph Story offered a typical ruling in one 1842 case while sitting on the Appeals Court for the First Circuit, which covered most of New England. Omission of a debt, according to Story, was no bar to a voluntary petition unless creditors could demonstrate that it was "intentional and fraudulent." Even when objecting creditors demonstrated a significant problem with debt or asset schedules, such as complete lack of detail about the transactions that had created financial obligations, bankruptcy judges almost always gave bankrupts the chance to amend their petitions. In the southern district of New York, for example, Judge Samuel R. Betts stood ready "to make every indulgence in cases of informality."[20]

A similar disposition guided the federal judiciary in circumstances in which a creditor's allegations were vague and unspecific, or in which a creditor wished to make objections but missed deadlines imposed by the court. Bankruptcy judges refused to entertain objections to a voluntary petition or sustain an involuntary petition unless a creditor offered specific claims of fact. Simply alleging that a petitioner had "concealed property" or "made fraudulent preferences" was not enough to gain court-mandated depositions before a bankruptcy commissioner. In the absence of a listing of the assets that an applicant had omitted from his petition or of the debts that were fictitious, or a description of alleged behavior that contravened express provisions of the 1841 act, judges would dismiss objections or involuntary petitions. Bankruptcy judges showed no more sympathy to creditors who filed objections after a court hearing on a bankrupt's motion for a decree or a discharge. As New Jersey district judge Philemon Dickerson informed lawyers for one objecting creditor in June 1842, he would not grant orders for the taking of depositions at an applicant's final hearing—creditors could not delay the granting of a discharge by waiting until the last minute to demand testimony relating to their objections.[21]

If creditors did provide detailed allegations of illegal behavior by insolvent debtors, federal judges would order a commissioner in bankruptcy—an official appointed by the judge in accordance with the 1841 statute—to take testimony relating to those specific claims. At least in southern New York, however, orders for depositions precluded investigations into matters not relevant to the specific claims of wrongdoing. Thus creditors could not use the bankruptcy process as a fishing expedition, objecting on general grounds and then grilling bankrupts about every aspect of their financial dealings.[22]

In addition, creditors who opposed voluntary applications discovered that they faced exacting legal standards. Claims of fraud against a debtor required, in the words of Vermont district judge Samuel Prentiss, "the strictest proof." For creditors to establish such allegations, they needed to bring forth "direct testimony, or . . . such facts as afford unequivocal circumstantial evidence." District judge Betts articulated a similar position in southern New York, explaining in one early case that for him to deny a motion for a discharge and certificate, "there must appear by indisputable evidence some act of fraud, wilful concealment of property, &c., or facts, from which such a deduction would be plain and palpable." In the second federal circuit, which encompassed Connecticut, Vermont, and New York, a persuasive showing that a bankrupt had concealed property at some time before the passage of the 1841 act still did not constitute a barrier to a discharge. According to Smith Thompson, justice of the U.S. Supreme Court and appellate judge for the circuit, only concealment of property at the time of a bankruptcy filing fell within the bounds of the 1841 act's prohibitions. If creditors proved that a merchant had fraudulently concealed property before such a filing but could not demonstrate that "he possessed or owned any property at the time his petition in Bankruptcy was presented," the applicant was entitled to his discharge.[23]

The tendency to protect debtors also found wide acceptance in the interpretation of what constituted an illegal preference or conveyance "in contemplation of bankruptcy." Federal judges in Maine, Rhode Island, the southern and northern districts of New York, the eastern district of Pennsylvania, Ohio, and Maryland, as well as the U.S. Supreme Court, all gave relatively narrow scope to these crucial terms. Representatives of the federal bench universally took pains to distinguish between struggling debtors who made payments to some creditors before others but who fully expected to make good on all maturing obligations, and insolvent debtors who knew that failure was imminent and who hoped to take care of relatives and friends. Only payments by the latter sort of debtor contravened the 1841 act. To rule otherwise, judges reasoned, would place all sorts of business transactions in doubt. Individuals and firms had the right to pay their debts in the order they wished, as long as they did not view themselves to be insolvent. Thus successful demonstrations of illegal preferences had to prove that payments embodied conscious attempts by hopeless insolvents to prefer one creditor over another.[24]

In some cases, federal judges did embrace statutory constructions that weakened the legal position of bankrupts. Members of the federal bench consistently exempted debts created by noncommercial civil judgments from the operation of the Bankruptcy Act. Bankruptcy petitions did not enable men who had fathered illegitimate children to escape their obligations to pay child support, nor did they allow individuals held in contempt of court to avoid the resulting fines. In a few jurisdictions, judges refused to grant bankruptcy decrees to any petitioner who had incurred debts in a fiduciary capacity. Several federal judges also denied habeas corpus motions from voluntary applicants who had been imprisoned for debt under state law, compelling them to bide their time in jail until they had obtained a bankruptcy decree.[25] Perhaps most importantly, in southern New York, wholly destitute applicants could not proceed with their petitions unless they could pay for newspaper notices and the fees of court officials. As a result of this ruling, several southern New York bankrupts languished for years before they scraped together the $30 or so necessary to clear their accounts with the court.[26] The occasional decision that improved the legal position of creditors, though, did not shift the basic orientation of the federal judiciary. In courthouses throughout the union, judges treated the Bankruptcy Act as a mechanism to provide relief to insolvent debtors.

Interpretive generosity toward bankrupts greatly eased the legal burdens for several petitioners under the 1841 act who had engaged in suspect financial practices, a consequence vividly illustrated by the bankruptcy application of John Bailey. A resident of the lower Hudson Valley village of Goshen, Bailey entered the business world in 1820 as a grocer. Over the next two decades, he attempted a wide variety of enterprises, including stints in dry goods dealing, butchering, and hotel keeping. None of these ventures brought prosperity, as Bailey found himself continually "straightened and embarrassed." By 1840, the weight of his obligations finally overwhelmed his resources. In that year, two creditors foreclosed on mortgages, divesting him of his remaining property, including a hotel in Goshen, a few parcels of local real estate, and considerable household furniture. At the resulting sheriff's sales, the parcels of real estate were purchased by one of Bailey's sons-in-law and the furniture was bought by another. This latter son-in-law, A. D. Jansen, also served as the attorney who handled the foreclosure suits for the individuals who held the mortgages against his wife's father.[27]

These arrangements suggested the possibility of collusion between Bailey and the individuals who held the mortgages against him, a characterization espoused by the two creditors who objected to Bailey's bankruptcy petition. The objecting creditors argued that the foreclosures served only to keep Bailey's property out of the hands of other claimants and under the control of the bankrupt or his relatives. This claim received some support from the fact that the furniture bought by the son-in-law at the sheriff's sale remained in Bailey's possession for a year after the auction. At the time that Bailey presented his bankruptcy petition, however, he did not have possession of the furniture, nor any other property. Moreover, the objecting creditors could not prove that the Bailey family had engineered the foreclosures and the resulting auctions so as to defraud other creditors. In ruling on the request to deny Bailey a bankruptcy decree, Judge Betts accepted that there were aspects of "the bankrupt's affairs, which might most naturally excite suspicions in the minds of his creditors." But in the absence of evidence that Bailey had intentionally sought to defraud his creditors, Betts refused to bar the bankrupt's progress toward a discharge.[28]

When creditors opposed bankruptcy petitions by individuals such as John Bailey, they hoped to maintain the legality of their claims and eventually to compel payment. To that end, they essentially insisted that the federal judiciary had to balance the 1841 act's purpose of extending relief to bankrupts against its regulatory injunctions. Seth Driggs, a New York City merchant who opposed the discharge of one voluntary petitioner on the grounds that he had engaged in repeated fraudulent misrepresentations, conveyances, and preferences, made this argument explicitly. By denying a discharge in this case, Judge Betts would help to purify American commerce. In Driggs's view, "the Bankrupt Law was made only for unfortunate, but honest men"; the petitioner in this case did not qualify. His various machinations should "remain a millstone around . . . [his] neck to remind him of his past conduct during his natural life." In addition to preventing future fraud by this particular entrepreneurial miscreant, such a millstone would serve as "a lasting monument and a warning to others."[29] Driggs's statement of objections offered a compelling interpretation of the Bankruptcy Act, placing it in the context of the commercial moralists' strictures on upright economic conduct.

Despite this argument's invocation of the central premises of antebellum bankruptcy reform, it did not move Judge Betts. In his ruling on the creditor's motion, he noted that all of Driggs's allegations concerned events that had occurred long before the Bankruptcy Act's passage. Betts further observed that the legal record neither showed that the petitioner had acted in contemplation of the passage of a national bankruptcy law nor proved that he possessed concealed property at the time he filed his application. Accordingly, he saw no legal bar to a discharge.[30]

Prevailing canons of statutory interpretation gave the antebellum federal judiciary ample opportunity to rule against the petitions of individuals like the debtor of Seth Driggs or John Bailey. In fixing the scope of commercial behavior that fell within the 1841 act's prohibited categories, for example, judges possessed the jurisprudential tools to adopt the implicit logic suggested by creditors such as Driggs. Members of the federal bench might have held that the statute's various elements had to harmonize with its overall structure and aims, which sought not only to provide relief to honest debtors, but also to check the frauds of dishonest ones. Such an approach would have fitted comfortably within the long-standing maxim that judges define ambiguous statutory "parts" so as to conform with the legislative "whole."[31]

Bankruptcy judges could have turned to still other commonly accepted principles of statutory construction had they wished to accord creditors more power in bankruptcy proceedings. Thus they might have argued that in light of the 1841 act's sweeping derogation of common-law rights regarding the collection of debts, bankrupts had to follow the legislation's procedural requirements rigorously. In a similar vein, they might have emphasized the need to read the statute's obscurities in light of the earlier Bankruptcy Act of 1800, which gave creditors substantially more control over legal process. Such a juxtaposition might have undergirded rulings that creditors deserved leeway in trying to bring possible commercial malfeasance to light.[32] Unwillingness on the part of federal judges to adopt these plausible interpretive strategies merits explanation.

The orientation of the country's most powerful creditor toward bankruptcy cases in which it was a potential litigant served as one crucial influence on interpretation of the 1841 act. Rather than attempting to nudge judicial interpretation in the directions suggested by creditors such as Seth Driggs, the U.S. government resolutely avoided becoming a party to bankruptcy proceedings. Viewing the statute as a Whig measure intended to provide relief to bankrupts and thus to curry political favor from them, the Tyler administration sent out a circular that strongly encouraged U.S. attorneys not to file objections against voluntary applications under the 1841 act.[33]

A number of federal judges whose political origins lay with National Republicanism or Whiggery similarly identified the Bankruptcy Law's chief purpose as relieving insolvent debtors. Supreme Court justice Joseph Story served as the most prominent judicial champion of the nation's bankrupts. One of America's most influential jurists, Story had helped to draft the 1841 act, including its voluntary provisions. He did so with the intention of giving failed business owners a new lease on life. In Kentucky, district judge Thomas Moore signaled his agreement with this approach to the 1841 statute by suggesting publicly that Congress remove the ability of creditors to oppose discharges. Judges who held such beliefs were not about to assail the legal position of insolvent debtors through creative interpretation. Other members of the federal bench, though not voicing approval of the 1841 statute as sensible public policy, nonetheless stressed that the economic crisis and political debate surrounding its passage made its overriding purpose clear. As Judge Samuel Betts maintained in one early 1842 bankruptcy opinion, "a reference to contemporaneous history" provided unmistakable evidence about the legislation's objective: "[I]t was made a prominent incident to the policy of this law, that it should apply relief to that oppressive condition of indebtedness then weighing upon the community."[34]

For some Democratic judges who harbored abiding skepticism about the wisdom of voluntary bankruptcy, political considerations may have dictated the avoidance of rulings that would seriously hamstring the ability of failed debtors to receive discharges under the Bankruptcy Law. In Georgia, for example, the Whig *Savannah Republican* issued complaints about the slow pace of bankruptcy hearings in district judge Nicholl's court. After a court session in September that ended with numerous petitioners receiving their discharges, a rival Democratic newspaper challenged the Savannah daily to "admit that Judge Nicholl will administer the law, though with not so much dispatch, [with] at least as much justice [as] has been done by some of the Whig Judges in other States, who have made a perfect quarter race of it, by discharging these applicants by the hundred in a few weeks time." In the minds of Georgia Democrats, a judicial policy of impeding the path to a bankruptcy certificate risked associating their party with a politically damaging reputation for unfeeling injustice. Rather than seek to limit the impact of the Bankruptcy Act through judicial obstruction, most Democrats preferred to work through legislative channels for its repeal.[35]

Exploding caseloads gave federal judges an additional reason not to grant legal indulgences to creditors. Within a few weeks of the 1841 act's coming into operation, federal dockets throughout the country bulged with bankruptcy cases. As these cases moved through the legal system, district judges had to hear every motion for a decree or a discharge, every request for a delay in proceedings, and every argument when someone objected to a petition, while continuing to preside over all other controversies in their courts. Members of the judiciary quickly found themselves overwhelmed by bankruptcy-related business. Faced with unending court calendars, judges came to look with particular disfavor on creditors who seemed intent on slowing down the progress of a bankruptcy case without good reason. Judge Betts again gave voice to judicial sentiment, linking his rigid rules about filing objections to the press of business in his court. When one objecting creditor's lawyer asked to revisit the granting of a bankruptcy decree because he had mistakenly left the court early the day before, Betts gave him a lecture. "There are over 700 petitions before the court," the judge intoned, "and the number will probably be doubled[;] . . . they can be disposed of only by prompt and decisive action."[36] Thus partisan political calculations, perceptions that the demands of bankrupts had provided crucial impetus to the Bankruptcy Law's passage, and administrative pressures all helped to persuade the federal judiciary to favor debtors when approaching most legal questions raised by that statute.

Negotiation in the Shadow of the Law

Despite the interpretive charity that federal judges extended toward bankrupts, debtors could not count on an automatic passage through the bankruptcy system. Creditors who petitioned to begin involuntary bankruptcy proceedings against a debtor generally succeeded when they produced strong evidence of a specified act of bankruptcy. Similarly, creditors who opposed a voluntary petition prevented the granting of decrees or discharges when they demonstrated that a debtor had violated one of the prohibitions in the 1841 act.

Bankrupts like Rufus Hoyt and John Quackenbos found that the bankruptcy system could dash the hopes and desires of insolvent debtors as well as assist them. Hoyt manufactured and sold carriages and sleighs in Fairfield County, Connecticut. By early June 1842, he lacked the funds to pay his debts and confronted insistent demands from one of his creditors, David Wakeman. The manufacturer's response, on June 15, was to execute mortgages and assignments to several family members in order to secure their legitimate claims against him. These mortgages and assignments embraced "all of his property, including the stock, tools, &c., in his carriage establishment." Wakeman sought to void these property transfers by filing an involuntary bankruptcy petition against Hoyt. After presenting clear evidence of the carriage maker's desperate financial position and the assignment of all his property, Wakeman succeeded in his aim. The United States Circuit Court for Connecticut declared Hoyt to be a bankrupt, thereby requiring him to deliver his assets to the Fairfield County bankruptcy assignee for liquidation and an equal distribution to creditors.[37]

While Rufus Hoyt was unable to fend off an involuntary petition against him, John Quackenbos failed in his attempt to gain a voluntary discharge. Quackenbos and two partners ran a New York City mercantile firm during the late 1830s. By the fall of 1840, the firm's members saw no way of extricating themselves from financial difficulties. In November and December of that year, Quackenbos made a number of payments to the firm's "confidential creditors," openly stating the intent of the partners to take advantage of a national bankruptcy law when Congress passed one. Given the uncontroverted testimony about Quackenbos's expectation that Congress would provide him with a means of getting free from his nonconfidential debts, Judge Betts ruled that the merchant had made preferences "in contemplation of bankruptcy." Quackenbos appealed the ruling but lost in a jury trial before circuit judge Thompson.[38]

During the period in which the 1841 act remained in force, federal judges accepted scores of involuntary petitions besides the one against Rufus Hoyt and rejected hundreds of voluntary applications in addition to that of John Quackenbos— about 3 percent of all voluntary petitions.[39] Although judges might easily have denied a higher percentage of bankruptcy applications, the new bankruptcy system still provided diligent creditors with means to exert considerable pressure on many debtors.

Involuntary bankruptcy petitions, for instance, could create serious problems for struggling businessmen. Since these petitions were proclaimed in newspaper notices, they essentially advertised that proprietors faced grave pecuniary difficulties.

Such publicity did not assist businessmen in gaining extensions or new credit. Debtors thus had good reason either to head off bankruptcy proceedings against them or to arrest those proceedings quickly after creditors had initiated them.

William Dolton and Lewis Requa, partners in a New York City dry goods firm, discovered the discomfort that an involuntary bankruptcy petition could elicit. By the late summer of 1842, Dolton and Requa's firm was struggling to pay its debts or to find new sources of credit. On September 21, two creditors of the partnership, James Struthers and George Scofield, filed a bankruptcy petition against Dolton and Requa in Judge Betts's court. Struthers and Scofield alleged that the dry goods dealers had obtained goods from them through knowingly false representations of solvency, that they had furnished forged securities as collateral, and that they had confessed a judgment to William Dolton's father in order to secure him a preference. As the sheriff's sale resulting from the judgment was due to take place on September 22, and as store goods worth over $3,000 were in the hands of the sheriff, the petitioners asked the bankruptcy court to grant an injunction against the impending sale.[40]

Dolton and Requa quickly responded to the threat posed by involuntary bankruptcy proceedings, immediately seeking to satisfy the petitioning creditors. On September 23, attorneys for Struthers and Scofield withdrew their petition and asked the bankruptcy court to cancel all public notices of the proceedings against Dolton and Requa. The lawyers explained in their motion that "the whole matter [had] been amicably settled and adjusted." While this wording does not divulge what consideration Struthers and Scofield received in order to discontinue their petition or from whom they received the consideration, it clearly indicates a settlement of some sort.[41]

The bankruptcy records for Dolton and Requa atypically provide explicit evidence of a payment to creditors in order to stop an involuntary bankruptcy petition. This case is by no means atypical, however, in its outcome. Involuntary petitions in Judge Betts's court usually did not result in a decree against the debtor. Creditors frequently withdrew their petitions or allowed cases to lapse for want of prosecution. Often the motions for withdrawals were accompanied by requests that the court cease newspaper publication of legal notices of canceled bankruptcy hearings. When petitioning creditors simply allowed deadlines for prosecution to pass, they probably reckoned that they would gain little by continuing with bankruptcy proceedings. But in other cases, petitioning creditors most likely received some kind of payment.[42]

Even though the grounds of objection to voluntary petitions were narrower than the federal judiciary might have allowed, and even though the standard proof required to sustain an objection was high, the ability to oppose a bankrupt's discharge also gave creditors a potentially powerful negotiating instrument. The travails of William Griggs and Micah Seabury demonstrate the leverage that object-ing creditors could exert. A partner of John Quackenbos, Griggs filed for bank-ruptcy in March 1842 and soon faced a challenge to his petition. One of his creditors alleged that he had given preferences in contemplation of bankruptcy, both before and after the passage of the Bankruptcy Act, and that he had concealed his possession of three promissory notes, each worth $6,000. Presumably this creditor had strong evidence; Griggs paid him $1,000 worth of goods in exchange for withdrawal of his objections. Seabury, a manufacturer of steel carriage springs who lived in the upstate New York town of Sangerfield, handled objections to his bankruptcy in a similar fashion. When confronted with well-documented allega-tions that he had illegally preferred some creditors in contemplation of bankruptcy, he arranged settlements with the two creditors who opposed his discharge. One of the objectors received a payment of $140; the other earned $100. In return, the creditors waived their legal opposition.[43]

There is no way to know how typical it was for voluntary applicants to deal with objections as William Griggs and Micah Seabury did. The pattern of withdrawals by objecting creditors in southern New York, however, suggests that compromises were fairly common. In Judge Betts's court, almost 17 percent of voluntary appli-cants faced objections; roughly one-third of these applicants faced objections from more than one creditor. When creditors opposed a voluntary application, they withdrew their objections 57 percent of the time.[44] Such withdrawals do not neces-sarily indicate a settlement. Occasionally they reflected the determination, after investigation, that a particular bankrupt had acted uprightly. Some objecting credi-tors may also have judged that the likelihood of coercing payments out of bankrupts or of having Judge Betts uphold their objections was slim. Anxious not to throw good money after bad, one Philadelphia mercantile firm explicitly instructed its attorneys to oppose a debtor's New York bankruptcy proceedings only so long as legal expenses remained under $50.[45] Nonetheless, the bankruptcy records of a number of southern New York petitioners suggest that removal of a creditor's objections frequently came with a price. In a few instances, removal of objections came *after* Judge Betts had denied discharges because of fraudulent behavior. In other cases, opposing creditors provided damning evidence about the actions of bankrupts but then withdrew their objections before the court could rule on them. In these contexts, there was almost certainly some kind of payment.[46]

A letter published by the New York *Journal of Commerce* in late 1842 gives credence to the supposition that settlements between bankrupts and objecting creditors were commonplace. In the course of advocating amendments to the 1841 act, the anonymous contributor suggested adoption of a provision that would void any security or other payment given to a creditor by a bankrupt in exchange for the former's withdrawal of objections, as well as a mandate that any creditor who accepted such security or payment should forfeit three times the amount to the bankruptcy court.[47] These recommendations reflect a perception that payments to objecting creditors were subverting the goals of the bankruptcy system, creating preferences that the legislation sought to prevent.

Campaign for Repeal

Although the complex legal tactics of assiduous creditors drew occasional commentary in newspaper columns or congressional debate, such maneuvering mostly remained outside of the limelight. Public discourse about the implementation of the 1841 act focused on two much more visible aspects of the new bankruptcy system—the ability of so many bankrupts to free themselves from past obligations, seemingly regardless of the circumstances surrounding their failures, and the rate of dividends paid to creditors of individuals who became bankrupts under the terms of the legislation, which struck many observers as unconscionably low. As Democrats revitalized their assaults on the bankruptcy statute toward the end of 1842, these characteristics of the federal bankruptcy process received most of their attention.

Even before the 1841 Bankruptcy Act went into operation, critics foresaw scoundrels and gamblers brazenly wiping off their debts while creditors received the barest fraction of payment; they further envisioned widespread fraud that would go unpunished, as creditors helplessly watched canny debtors consign their financial obligations to oblivion. One newspaper commentator encapsulated this viewpoint on the eve of the new bankruptcy system's inauguration, imagining a "Jubilee of the Bankrupts" that would emancipate thousands of rash debtors "who rushed so madly into wild speculations a few years since." After the federal courts began hearing bankruptcy petitions, these same critics eagerly sought out cases that would validate their predictions, a quest that did not require too much digging. Especially in commercial states such as New York, high-flying debtors who owed tens of thousands of dollars, and in a few cases millions, made their way through the bankruptcy process. Many of these bankrupts owed their failures to ill-judged speculation. Toward the end of 1842, the *New York Herald* published the bankruptcy schedules of some of the more notorious applicants, pairing the lists of assets and debts with editorial commentary about the ease with which one could obtain a federal discharge. James Gordon Bennett, the *Herald*'s editor, primarily chose individuals who had failed stupendously as the result of large-scale investments in real estate or other schemes. The lesson that Bennett drew from these examples was that the antebellum experiment with bankruptcy had primarily catered to "speculators, overtraders, and fictitious capitalists." Many other newspaper editors and Democratic politicians throughout the nation shared his sentiments.[48]

Political opponents of the 1841 act attacked its process of asset liquidation with similar venom. Once a federal court had granted a decree of bankruptcy, the law stipulated that almost all of the bankrupt's property legally passed to a court-appointed assignee. Bankrupts were allowed to keep $300 worth of possessions such as tools, furniture, and kitchen utensils, as well as necessary clothing for themselves and their families. Assignees were charged with converting assets into cash as quickly as possible, collecting debts owed to bankrupts and selling other property either through private sale or by public auction. They then had the task of distributing pro rata shares from the proceeds to all creditors of the bankrupt who had "proved their debt." Only creditors who officially documented their claims against bankrupts qualified for a dividend, which assignees would distribute only after all court officials had received their fees.[49] Before the bankruptcy system came into force, Democrats complained bitterly about these provisions, arguing that only creditors could choose assignees familiar with a given bankrupt's affairs and line of business, and thus capable of extracting the maximum amount of money out of his assets. With court officials in charge of bankruptcy estates, critics predicted that administrative fees would absorb any property that had survived the country's many economic failures. Senator Benton again took the lead in these attacks, maintaining that "a bankrupt's estate in the hands of assignees, is a lump of butter in a dog's mouth."[50]

The handling of bankruptcy estates under the 1841 act convinced its critics that the dogs had feasted on a steady diet of butter. In jurisdictions all over the country, the estates of most bankrupts generated *nothing* for their creditors. When the assets of a bankrupt did bring more than required to pay the fees of the assignee and court clerks, creditors still generally received minuscule payments. The jurisdiction with the best outcome for creditors was the northern district of New York. There creditors who proved their debts received an average payment of over thirteen cents on the dollar. No other jurisdiction with more than fifty bankrupts paid out above the rate of five cents on the dollar; in twenty-one of the thirty-three jurisdictions that reported statistics to the House of Representatives in 1846 and 1847, creditors who proved their debts garnered 1 percent or less of their claims.[51]

The ease with which debtors obtained discharges under the 1841 act and the meager dividends meted out to creditors under its provisions provided substantial ammunition for Democratic politicians who viewed the legislation as a leading example of the Whig penchant for overcentralized, meddling governance. By the summer of 1842, Democratic leaders once again sought to kill the new bankruptcy system. Their first tactic was to have several Democratic state legislatures send memorials to Congress, pleading for repeal on the grounds that the bankruptcy system greatly favored the interests of canny debtors and grasping court officials over those of creditors.[52] They then introduced legislation in the fall that would eliminate both voluntary and involuntary bankruptcy proceedings in the federal courts.

SCHEDULE *A*.

NAME OF CREDITOR.	RESIDENCE.	DEBT.	DIVIDEND.	REMARKS.
Neponset Bank	Massachusetts	521 02	5 76	
Hiram Marsh	New York	888 84	9 83	
Peter Morton	Brooklyn	349 05	3 86	
William Chauncey & Co	New York	498 85	5 52	
Hunking Winkley	do	242 80	2 68	
William Austin &	do	165 62	1 83	
Corlies Haydock & Co	do	102 79	1 14	
John W. Harris	do	565 72	6 26	
W. C. H. Waddell a/c	do	1076 21	11 90	
		$4410 93	48 78	

William W. Campbell

J. W. Metcalf

Auditors

PALTRY DIVIDENDS. An auditor's report on James Alden's bankruptcy estate shows typically low payments to creditors under the 1841 Bankruptcy Act—in this case barely more than one cent on the dollar (C-F 16, National Archives and Record Administration, Northeast Region, New York City).

Defenders of the bankruptcy system, mostly consisting of Whig editors and politicians, vigorously challenged Democratic characterizations of the 1841 act as an abject failure. Conceding that some discharges might have been obtained by scoundrels "who did not deserve to have them," Whig spokesmen insisted that the scrutiny of bankruptcy judges would in the future serve as a healthy "restraint upon unlicensed speculation." Whigs further maintained that the Bankruptcy Act had released thousands of worthy Americans from the clutches of unfeeling creditors.

Without this legislation, the *Journal of Commerce* argued, the victims of mercantile misfortune would have had nothing to look forward to but "bondage for life, and ruin and beggary for their families."[53] Advocates of a permanent bankruptcy system drew sustenance from reports that federal court officials sent to Congress in response to a fall 1842 circular asking for appraisals of the 1841 statute. Federal judges, court clerks, and district attorneys overwhelmingly reported that most voluntary applicants had not engaged in fraud and deserved relief. Joseph C. Potts, clerk for the district of New Jersey, informed the nation's lawmakers that for the vast majority of the applicants in his court, "all hope of being able to fulfill [their obligations] is at an end." Since these New Jerseyans were "hopelessly insolvent," the operation of the Bankruptcy Law was "merely the sponging out in form, what was, on all hands, held to be lost in fact, long since." Andrew Judson, district judge for Connecticut, offered a similar view, pointing out that the creditor "loses nothing when he parts with a phantom."[54]

The voluminous records left by debtors who passed through the bankruptcy system in southern New York confirm the assessments of these federal judges and court officials. Most voluntary applicants in Judge Betts's jurisdiction failed long before submitting their petitions, with well over half failing at least two years and almost three-fourths at least one year before they came into the bankruptcy court.[55] In the interim, their assets typically had been assailed through foreclosures, debt judgments, and state chancery proceedings, or liquidated as the result of a state insolvency process or a private assignment for the benefit of creditors. Such prior liquidation largely accounts for the extremely low dividends paid out by court-appointed bankruptcy assignees. By the time that most applicants reached federal bankruptcy court, the bulk of their assets had already been exhausted by the race of diligence among their creditors. In addition, the deflation of the late 1830s and early 1840s greatly depreciated whatever property had survived previous legal attacks.[56]

As Democratic and Whig editors and politicians offered sharply diverging judgments about the bankruptcy system, popular opinion ran solidly against it in many sections of the nation, a reality noted by several judges and court clerks. From New Hampshire, the northern and western parts of New York, Ohio, Kentucky, and Tennessee came reports of deep-seated opposition. Sympathetic court officials explained the "clamor" against the legislation as the result of ignorance, the injured feelings of some creditors, and widespread resentment against the exclusion of banks and other corporations from involuntary bankruptcy proceedings. As a result, court officials were confident that if Congress gave its statute a decent trial of five years, the people would eventually see the bankruptcy system's many virtues. At least some Americans did not need to wait that long. In late 1842 and early 1843, Congress received a number of petitions from merchants and city chambers of commerce that called for the retention of the 1841 act. These statements of support for the bankruptcy system boasted a greater number of signatures than correspond-ing petitions requesting the law's repeal.[57]

With public sentiment divided, the fate of the 1841 act lay with the shifting balance of political forces in Washington, D.C. By the middle of 1842, that balance was tipping away from the long-standing supporters of a federal bankruptcy law, as splits within the Whig congressional caucus greatly weakened the party's influence in both legislative houses. President Tyler's veto of a bill to recharter a national bank, the centerpiece of Henry Clay's legislative program, eventually rent the party in two—one faction castigated Tyler as an apostate; the other sided with him, intent upon maintaining influence over the distribution of federal patronage. With the Whig agenda in tatters, Democrats pressed their bankruptcy repeal bill, hoping to exacerbate Whig divisions and roll back those aspects of Clay's legislative program that had become law. By the end of 1842, several Whigs were disinclined to stand in the Democrats' way. Some Whig congressmen had favored only temporary relief for debtors in the first place, wishing to limit federal discharges to individuals brought down by the impact of Democratic financial policies. The commitment of other Whigs waned as expected political gains from passage of bankruptcy legislation did not materialize. State elections in Maine, New York, Pennsylvania, and Ohio brought a string of Whig defeats in 1842, despite the large number of bankrupts in these states.[58]

In the face of increasing party disarray, Whig legislators who remained fervently committed to a permanent federal bankruptcy process sought to stave off outright repeal by offering amendments to the 1841 act. Senator Berrien of Georgia, chair-man of the Senate Judiciary Committee, led this effort, proposing in February 1843 that Congress eliminate voluntary bankruptcy, allow discharges only with the con-sent of one-half of a bankrupt's creditors in number and amount of debt, and authorize creditors to select assignees.[59] In effect, Berrien sought to strip the pro-spective elements of the bankruptcy system—those focused on constraining future business activity in line with the vision of the commercial moralists—from its retrospective aspects, which had provided crucial political support for the 1841 stat-ute. Berrien's scheme fell considerably short of success. Once Democrats amended the repeal bill in late February to allow all pending bankruptcy cases to continue to their conclusion—a sticking point for several Whig legislators—both houses of Congress voted for the bill by large majorities; the House by 140 to 71; the Senate by 32 to 13. On March 3, 1843, President Tyler signed the bill into law, closing off the federal courts as a means of relief to American bankrupts and their creditors.[60]

The United States would not again boast a federal bankruptcy process for another generation, until the myriad financial catastrophes of the Civil War con-vinced a Republican Congress untroubled by absent southern Democrats to pass a third bankruptcy statute in 1867. In the intervening years, recollections of the 1841 act's shortcomings shaped the political calculations of many congressmen, while the prosperity unleashed by railroad expansion and the discovery of gold in California made bankruptcy legislation seem unnecessary even to several Whigs, and later Republicans. In 1854 and 1857, financial panics did bring forth renewed calls for a federal bankruptcy code. But with Pierce and then Buchanan in the White House, their fellow Democrats in control of the Senate, and national politics consumed by the question of slavery extension, such pleas from the northern mercantile community fell on deaf ears.[61]

The Resurrection of Canceled Obligations

During the thirteen months that Americans could file petitions under the 1841 act, well over 41,000 individuals, including roughly one in every hundred adult white men, came before federal bankruptcy courts as debtors, overwhelmingly as the result of voluntary applications. More than 33,000 of these Americans successfully negotiated the legal process set up by the 1841 statute, earning a certificate that constituted "a full and complete discharge" of all their "debts, contracts, and other engagements," which they could plead as a "full and complete bar to all suits brought in any court of judicature whatever." These bankruptcy certificates, in most cases, signified the death of the holder's past financial obligations. If creditors sued bankrupts on claims that predated the filing of bankruptcy petitions, bankrupts only needed to show their certificates of discharge in order to quash the suits.[62] There were ways, however, to disinter debts that bankruptcy proceedings had seemingly buried forever. As a result, the give and take between creditors and debtors did not necessarily end with final hearings in federal bankruptcy court.

Bankrupts themselves could resurrect discharged obligations by making a new promise to pay the canceled debt. In some cases, this sort of promise served as a means of persuading creditors either not to file objections to a bankrupt's petition or to withdraw objections already lodged with the court. Clearing the path to a bankruptcy discharge motivated the new promise that James L. Butler, a New York commission merchant, made to one of his creditors. Among his debts, Butler owed a total of $2,588 to Butler, Farnwell, & Co., a Utica mercantile firm. Since the commission merchant had incurred these obligations while acting as an agent for the Utica firm, his bankruptcy petition was vulnerable to the allegation that he owed a fiduciary debt. As Butler was "sensible" that the objection "would be an effective bar" to his discharge, he sought "to induce the members of the firm . . . to abstain from opposing in any way my obtaining a full discharge from all my other debts which are not of a fiduciary character." To that end, he provided the Utica merchants with a new acknowledgment of his indebtedness to them, promising to pay regardless of the bankruptcy discharge he hoped to obtain.[63]

In Bankruptcy.

At a **DISTRICT COURT** of the United States of America, held for the Southern District of New-York, at the City-Hall of the City of New-York, on *Wednesday* — the *twenty second* day of *June,* — in the year one thousand eight hundred and forty-two.

Present, SAMUEL R. BETTS, *District Judge.*

In the Matter of

Nicholas Haight,

a **Bankrupt.**

Nicholas Haight, of the City of New York, Merchant, a _____ Bankrupt, having filed a petition praying to be discharged in full from all his debts, and for a certificate of such discharge, pursuant to the act of Congress, entitled " An Act to establish a Uniform System of Bankruptcy throughout the United States," passed August 19, 1841.

And it appearing to the Court upon the said petition, and the report of the clerk and assignee accompanying the same, that the said Bankrupt has bona fide surrendered all his property, and rights of property, (with the exception of such articles as were designated and set apart by the assignee,) and that the said Bankrupt has fully complied with and obeyed all the orders and directions which have from time to time been passed by this Court _____

and has otherwise conformed to all the requisites of the said act, and that no written dissent to such discharge has been filed by a majority in number and value of his creditors who have proved their debts ; and no cause being now shown to the Court why the prayer of the petitioner be not granted, it is, therefore, by virtue of the act aforesaid, ordered, decreed and allowed by the Court, that the said *Nicholas Haight, of the City of New York, Merchant,* be, and he accordingly hereby is fully discharged of and from all his debts proveable under the said act, and owing by him at the time of the presentation of his petition to be declared a Bankrupt. And it is further ordered, that the clerk duly certify this decree, under the seal of this Court, and deliver the same to the said Bankrupt when demanded.

Sam R Betts

I, CHARLES D. BETTS, Clerk of the said Court, do certify, that the above order and decree was made by the Court, and duly entered in the docket of Bankrupt proceedings.

In Testimony whereof, I have caused the seal of the said Court to be hereunto affixed, at the City of New-York, in the Southern District of New-York, this *Twenty Second* day of *June,* — in the year of our Lord one thousand eight hundred and forty-two, and of the Independence of the United States the sixty *sixth.* _____

Chas D Betts

Clerk of the District Court of the United States,
for the Southern District of New-York.

CERTIFICATE OF ECONOMIC REBIRTH. Nicholas Haight's bankruptcy discharge (C-F 927, National Archives and Record Administration, Northeast Region, New York City).

Considerations other than the desire to placate objecting creditors also led bankrupts to offer new promises of payment. Bankrupts who wished to continue in their line of business sometimes found that acknowledging discharged debts aided them in gaining credit or otherwise reestablishing themselves. Other bankrupts wished to extinguish what they viewed as a moral obligation to make good on their earlier promises, with respect either to a few debts or to all of the claims against them. One upstate New York bankrupt made such a promise soon after earning a bankruptcy decree in April 1843. The bankrupt told the clerk of one of his creditors, a local mercantile firm, that although "he was unable to pay just then," the claim by the partnership "was a just and honorable debt and should be paid."[64]

Throughout the nation, such promises created new legal obligations enforceable in state courts, even if former bankrupts made them years after receiving a discharge. The evidence necessary to prove that a bankrupt had made a new promise varied from state to state, depending on the particulars of statutory law and judicial interpretation. In Mississippi, creditors had to show a written acknowledgment of a discharged debt in order to enforce the claim; in Pennsylvania, a verbal promise sufficed, so long as the bankrupt made the acknowledgment in the presence of a witness. Maine law required only a verbal promise before 1848, but in that year the legislature passed a statute requiring a written declaration. Whatever the legal test prevailing in a given state, creditors who could meet it had the right to enforce the old debt, notwithstanding the existence of a bankruptcy discharge.[65]

Even if bankrupts did not formally promise to pay the old claims against them, they occasionally set out to make good on discharged obligations. The commercial moralists strongly encouraged such behavior, arguing that there was a moral obligation to pay legally canceled debts. After gaining bankruptcy certificates or other releases from lawful debts, upright individuals should, as J. H. Allen told the members of Boston's Young Men's Christian Union, "nobly exert themselves to leave behind them an untarnished name."[66]

At least some recipients of bankruptcy discharges heeded these words. Joseph Brewster, the New York City hat maker and spokesman for Christian benevolence who failed as the result of disastrous real estate speculations, provides a case in point. On receiving his bankruptcy certificate toward the end of June 1842, Brewster endorsed the envelope in which it came. Despite his newly granted legal release, the hatter inscribed his intention to pay back the many creditors listed on his bankruptcy petition, declaring that he was: "Free legally, but not so morally." For the next nine years, until his death in 1851, Brewster struggled to extinguish the moral obligations that he believed still bound him. According to his eulogist, he managed to liquidate "a considerable amount" of these claims. *Hunt's Merchants' Magazine* delighted in reporting similar actions by onetime bankrupts, commending the demonstrations of "commercial honor" by individuals who had failed.

Throughout the 1840s and early 1850s, the commercial periodical continually reprinted stories chronicling examples of "mercantile integrity" from around the country.[67]

The great attention received by general repayments of legally canceled obligations, though, indicates that they were rare events. George Templeton Strong, the New York City lawyer and member of the city's social elite, astutely analyzed this public praise in an 1851 diary entry. Strong observed that former bankrupts who made good on all their discharged debts were "paragraphed in the papers as prodigies." The press treated such individuals as "interesting martyrs to a nice sense of honor," glorifying them "as if they had sacrificed all their earthly possessions in endowing hospitals and founding churches." The implication, for Strong, was that very few bankrupts acted in this fashion. Instead, the great majority of Americans who failed had lost sight of "the sanctity and religious force of a promise to pay money." Degraded, debased, and demoralized by "our wretched 'financial' system," most bankrupts "look men in the face whom they have ruined by breaking their promises, and have nothing to say but that it was a 'business transaction.'"[68] As the New York lawyer recognized, rapid commercial expansion weakened moral strictures concerning the payment of debts.

The New York City lawyer and diarist, however, overstated the impact of expanding market relationships on the moral commitments of debtors. One can see the continued influence of those commitments in instances where legally released bankrupts selectively made voluntary payments of discharged debts. Such payments were far more common than the actions that resulted in canonization by commercial publications.

When former insolvents made good on a selected number of old debts, they usually paid relatives or close business associates. Bankrupts saw the consequences of their failures for family members and friends far more readily than for more anonymous creditors, such as banks, insurance companies, or brokers who held promissory notes that had passed through several intermediaries. The latter group often represented the increasingly faceless national economy and the impersonal forces that often hastened individual financial crises.

Silas Stilwell's postfailure actions illustrate both the persistence of feelings of moral obligation after insolvency and the common limitation of those impulses to a narrow circle of creditors. Stilwell, a prominent New York attorney who led the legislative battle in 1831 to abolish imprisonment for debt in New York State, and who also lobbied tirelessly for the adoption of the 1841 act, failed through ill-fated real estate ventures. Soon after gaining his discharge in 1842, he made clear that he did not consider himself wholly free from his past debts. In a letter thanking a North Carolina senator for his vote in favor of the bankruptcy bill, Stilwell remarked that since he was now "free from legal restraint," he expected to "be able within a few years to discharge all my confidential debts, which must have forever remained unpaid without the effects of this law." This pledge reflected a commitment to the moral obligations imposed by relations of friendship and family, rather than those emphasized by commercial moralists. The claims of people close to the New York City lawyer, including those who had lent him money or provided endorsements as he struggled to avoid failure, would still receive attention. Other former creditors would not be so lucky.[69]

Bankruptcy discharges, then, did not cast the debts of bankrupts into an irretrievable oblivion. Possessors of bankruptcy discharges could conjure those obligations back into existence, either through explicit promise or unstated intention. Creditors of bankrupts also had the power, in some circumstances, to breath life into debts that bankruptcy proceedings had left moribund. In order to perform this act of revivification, creditors had to sue their ostensibly released debtors and then attack the legality of their federal bankruptcy certificates.

Senator Thomas Hart Benton, in his persistent opposition to the 1841 act, charted one course for antebellum creditors of discharged bankrupts who did not wish to accept the loss of their claims. In one of his many speeches against the legislation, Benton, after repeating his argument that the creation of voluntary bankruptcy was unconstitutional, called on state judges to treat bankruptcy certificates as irrelevant to cases that came before them. Some creditors took their cue from the Missouri senator. They sued bankrupts in state courts, and when the debtors pleaded their discharges as a bar to the suits, the creditors maintained that the 1841 act was unconstitutional, at least with respect to voluntary bankruptcy. On at least two occasions, this tactic worked. Judges in both the Cincinnati Court of Common Pleas and the state Circuit Court of Illinois ruled that the Bankruptcy Law was unconstitutional; as a result, they recognized the claims of creditors as still in force. Most state courts, however, upheld the authority of Congress to pass the 1841 act.[70]

Despite this sanction, creditors who wished to sidestep the impact of a debtor's bankruptcy certificate had two other legal avenues open to them. The first of these options was to argue that their claim was exempt from the operation of the Bankruptcy Law. Creditors who provided evidence that the debt resulted from either a judicially imposed fine or a breach of fiduciary responsibility generally found sympathy from state judges. Alternatively, creditors could try to impeach the discharge on the grounds of fraud. The 1841 statute explicitly created this possibility, stipulating that a bankruptcy certificate "shall be conclusive evidence of itself in favor of [a] bankrupt, unless the same shall be impeached for some fraud or wilful concealment by him of his property or rights of property, . . . contrary to the provisions of this act."[71] The significance of this clause depended, as with the rest of the Bankruptcy Law, on the interpretation and application of judges—though in this instance both federal and state judges, as each heard cases in which creditors attempted to impeach bankruptcy certificates.

Judicial interpretation of the impeachment clause followed the pattern set by the federal judiciary's treatment of the rest of the Bankruptcy Act. Creditors who sought to have a discharge set aside did not have the easiest of legal tasks. First of all, such creditors had to tread carefully while a debtor made his or her way through the federal bankruptcy process. The Bankruptcy Law declared that any creditor who proved a debt in the bankruptcy court "shall be deemed thereby to have waived all right of action and suit against such bankrupt." Antebellum judges read this clause as precluding creditors who intended to attack a discharge in the state courts from either opposing the bankrupt's petition in the federal bankruptcy court or taking part in the distribution of dividends from a bankrupt's estate. Both of these actions required creditors to prove their debts against a bankrupt, which, according to antebellum courts, automatically forfeited the rights of creditors to sue that debtor.[72]

Moreover, when creditors moved to impeach a bankruptcy discharge, the burden of proof fell on them. As with attempts to oppose a bankruptcy petition, creditors who hoped to void a debtor's discharge had to make specific allegations of fraud against the Bankruptcy Act and they had to back up those allegations with compelling evidence. In addition, claims that a bankrupt had not included debts, that he had excluded assets, or that he had given preferences by themselves did not constitute actions that nullified a discharge. Antebellum courts further required creditors to show that this behavior resulted from a "wilful" intent to defraud creditors. Without such evidence, a creditor had little chance of persuading a judge to disregard the Bankruptcy Act's declaration that a certificate constituted "conclusive evidence" of its holder's freedom from past debts.[73]

Despite these arduous legal burdens, antebellum state tribunals jealously upheld their legal authority to entertain motions to vacate federal bankruptcy discharges because of fraud. To do otherwise would have conceded exclusive jurisdiction over bankruptcy matters to the federal courts, something few state judges were inclined to allow. Although creditors had to prove their case against a bankrupt, they almost always received a hearing in state courts. And the judges presiding in those courts did vacate bankruptcy discharges when presented with clear evidence of fraud. State courts in Massachusetts and New York set aside bankruptcy certificates on the grounds that bankrupts had made illegal preferences, while state courts in Alabama and North Carolina vacated discharges for concealment of property.[74]

The possibility of impeaching discharges gave creditors a means of continuing the give-and-take of negotiation with bankrupts, even after the successful conclusion of bankruptcy applications. Claimants could sue bankrupts on the basis of ostensibly discharged debts, alleging fraud in bankruptcy proceedings, or they could merely threaten to do so. Defendants of such actions might consider settlements whether or not they felt their creditors had strong cases; legal process meant the expenditure of time and money, as well as at least some risk of adverse judgments.

Given the legal avenue of impeaching a bankruptcy discharge, some creditors tenaciously held on to the prospect of collecting debts that the bankruptcy court had canceled. John Jones, a resident of Utica, New York, and a creditor to William Roberts, who had gained a discharge under the 1841 act, demonstrated such tenacity. Early in 1844, Jones wrote to his lawyer to find out whether Roberts had agreed to make good on his discharged debt. If no settlement had occurred, the Utica creditor instructed his legal counsel either to "coaks [sic] him to it or fright him." Jones suggested that the attorney "try [to] terrify him" by making him believe "he has Done something very wrong in his proceedings." Once Roberts thought that his discharge was in jeopardy, Jones reasoned, he would surely pay to avoid "a great deal of trouble and of shame and [having to] pay all of his debt worst of all." A few weeks later, the creditor gleefully informed his legal representative about evidence that Roberts had concealed property from the bankruptcy court—an action that threw the validity of his bankruptcy certificate into doubt. The Utica client empowered the attorney to give Roberts a choice—a lawsuit attacking the validity of his discharge, or payment of Jones's claim. By adopting the latter alternative, Jones pointed out, Roberts would ensure that his fraud would remain "unknown" to his other creditors.[75]

John Jones's persistence did not typify antebellum creditors, the great majority of whom responded to bankruptcy proceedings by writing off discharged debts in their account books. The ability to void bankruptcy discharges, however, did provide creditors with a meaningful legal tool. As with successful collections made by the many secured creditors of bankrupts, settlements that dissolved the objections of creditors to bankruptcy petitions, and new promises to pay old debts, attempts to impeach bankruptcy certificates belied the political attacks on the 1841 act. This legislation, however friendly to debtors when compared with the bankruptcy systems of Europe, did not leave all creditors of bankrupts bereft of payment for their claims, the unwitting victims of a general repudiation of debts.

Taming the Credit System

Antebellum proponents of bankruptcy reform touted the 1841 Bankruptcy Act as a means to reshape the culture of the marketplace. This legislation, its supporters averred, would inject principles of equal treatment into credit relationships and heighten the incentives for prudence on the part of both debtors and creditors. In some respects, the statute lived up to these aspirations. The 1841 act, for example, seems to have restricted the impulse on the part of bankrupts to prefer creditors. In reports to Congress on the operation of the Bankruptcy Law, several federal court officials claimed that the legislation had curbed the tendency of bankrupts to take care of a selected number of claims against them. District judges from Connecticut, eastern Pennsylvania, Indiana, and middle Tennessee, as well as the U.S. district attorney in Michigan, all maintained that the law's involuntary provisions had greatly decreased the frequency of preferences granted by bankrupts to "some relative or favored creditor." Justice Joseph Story further asserted that the Bankruptcy Act had restrained the use of accommodation paper in the jurisdictions over which he presided, since the individuals who granted such credit could no longer count on priority in repayment. With the decrease in accommodations, Story also reported a significant reduction in the number of bankrupts who engaged in "delusive struggles" to salvage an impossible financial position. Unable to attract the credit necessary for most desperate schemes, failing debtors in New England accepted their fate more readily than before the passage of the Bankruptcy Act.[76]

Such observations gain credence from the kinds of private assignments executed by failing debtors after the bankruptcy system came into operation. The Bankruptcy Act's sanctions against the voluntary granting of preferential payments essentially stopped the practice of making assignments for the benefit of creditors that included preferred classes of debts. Many insolvents still executed private assignments after the legislation came into effect, hoping to exert more control over the disposition of their assets than they would be able to if they simply petitioned for bankruptcy relief and surrendered their assets to the bankruptcy assignee; but most of these bankrupts took care to treat all of their creditors alike in their assignments, preferring none over others.[77]

The 1841 Bankruptcy Law further may have served to slow down the pace of the credit system. Commercial moralists portrayed a permanent system of bankruptcy as a means of curbing the periodic excesses of the American economy. If creditors knew that their customers might easily apply for bankruptcy relief, moralists had promised, then they would grant loans and advances with greater care. Similarly, if debtors knew that a wrong step could lead to an involuntary bankruptcy petition, they would mind the niceties of mercantile integrity. The result would be a slower but more stable growth of trade and industry.

Gauging the impact of bankruptcy legislation on the everyday business decisions of the nation's many economic actors is fraught with difficulty, particularly in light of the short life of the 1841 act and the generally dull economic conditions that prevailed throughout 1842 and early 1843. Appraisals of the bankruptcy system by the advocates of the statute's repeal nonetheless offer a clue in this regard. Several supporters of repeal attacked the bankruptcy system in part because of its debilitating impact on commerce. These politicians repeatedly portrayed the law as having a chilling effect on the extension of credit.

The word that the opponents of the 1841 act turned to again and again was "confidence." The ability of debtors to wipe off their obligations, according to critics of the bankruptcy system, had badly shaken the confidence of the nation's creditors. Representatives like Kenneth Rayner of North Carolina and Henry Wise of Virginia sketched a picture of American investors with "hidden and hoarded" capital, unwilling to take any chance because of the threat that voluntary bankruptcy posed. The Bankruptcy Act, these legislators continued, served as a "damper" on commerce, just as they had predicted in the bankruptcy debates of 1840 and 1841. Only by repealing this affront to the sanctity of contracts would American capitalists once again look to make profitable use of their resources.[78] Insofar as these political opponents of bankruptcy correctly measured the response of those Americans who possessed capital, their attacks on the statute suggest that the legislation did help to slow down the pace of American commerce.

Still, antebellum America's short-lived bankruptcy system by no means stifled the long-standing proclivities of creditors to seek preferential treatment in the wake of financial failure, or of debtors to grant such preferential treatment. Diligence by creditors continued to bestow priority in the distribution of insolvents' assets. By recognizing liens that were valid under state law, the 1841 act continued to reward creditors who gained judgments against petitioners before they petitioned for bankruptcy or who had demanded security before extending credit. Settlements between bankrupts and creditors who initiated involuntary proceedings against them, who objected to the granting of a bankruptcy certificate, or who threatened to impeach a discharge also conferred preferential status on the persistent creditor. New promises to meet canceled obligations similarly led to de facto preferences, since discharged bankrupts tended to limit such promises to "confidential creditors," those individuals whose claims rested on close, personal relationships. Deeply entrenched throughout antebellum American society, among both middling proprietors and elites, the culture of preference fostered attitudes that stubbornly resisted the grand designs of reform.

"Jubilee of the Bankrupts"—so one critic had derisively termed the 1841 Federal Bankruptcy Act, and in hindsight, with considerable justification. In light of the legislation's expeditious repeal, there is a strong temptation to deem it an ephemeral showering of legal releases upon one generation of ruined proprietors, very much akin to a biblical cancellation of debts. And yet this mechanism for sponging out financial obligations produced reverberations that lasted long after the 27th Congress discontinued the United States' second trial with a national system of bankruptcy administration.

By embracing voluntary bankruptcy proceedings open to all free Americans, this

Congress set a powerful precedent about the contours of federal bankruptcy policy, which the federal courts ratified through their interpretive generosity toward bankrupts. The 1841 act stood for the propositions that business failures often resulted from circumstances beyond the control of individual proprietors, and that, as a result, most ruined business owners should not remain perpetually beholden to their creditors in law. When later Congresses revisited the question of creating a uniform system of bankruptcy in the decades after the Civil War, large majorities of representatives accepted both propositions as axioms of political economy. If the United States was going to have a federal bankruptcy process, as the Bankruptcy Acts of 1867 and 1898 eventually mandated, it would include discharges for voluntary applicants.[79]

In the shorter term, one must not lose sight of the tens of thousands of Americans for whom the 1841 law signified freedom from the bonds of insolvency, through either federal bankruptcy certificates or private settlements with creditors. Their second chances in the marketplace would inject considerable vitality into the development of American capitalism. Even before America's discharged debtors had a chance to rejoin the world of commerce, moreover, the 1841 act unleashed a different kind of economic energy. The federal bankruptcy system created abundant opportunities for those individuals with the knowledge, connections, and desire to cash in on the business of economic failure. Contemporaries referred to these individuals as "wreckers"—people who either worked for the bankruptcy court or found some other way to profit from the legal disposition of failed Americans and their remaining assets. Before we investigate the economic and social implications of the antebellum fresh start, the business of wrecking merits its own examination.

Chapter 5

The Art of Wrecking

Mortality is Fatal
Gentility is fine
Rascality heroic
Insolvency Sublime
—Emily Dickinson, "Valentine,"
    Springfield Daily Republican, February 20, 1852

When antebellum ships foundered on the rocks of the Florida Keys, as several dozen did every year, local boats rushed to take possession of the salvageable cargo still on board the wrecked vessels. In accordance with the regulations of maritime law, the owners of these salvage boats then scrupulously placed the rescued goods in the possession of the Key West admiralty court, acquiring legal title to the cargo at a court-mandated public sale. As the Key West mercantile community was extremely small, merchants arranged not to bid against one another, ensuring rock-bottom prices. After the conclusion of admiralty auctions, Florida wreckers shipped their newly bought merchandise to nearby American and Cuban ports, reaping excellent profits for their troubles. Alongside the wreckers, local attorneys gained handsome fees for superintending legal procedures required by the American law of salvage.[1]

Like shipwrecks off the Florida coast, antebellum bankruptcies created means of profiting from economic calamity. Throughout the first six decades of the nineteenth century, scores of Americans made a living from financial failures. Private assignees and receivers appointed by either state chancery or insolvency courts earned compensation for their management of the property that bankrupts placed in their care. In every county of the nation, sheriffs and auctioneers received fees and commissions for carrying out foreclosures or other court-ordered sales. The country's newspapers regularly published legal notices that announced private assignments for the benefit of creditors, the attachments by creditors against the property of absconding debtors, and court-mandated auctions of assets owned by insolvents. Sharp-eyed individuals who possessed cash or credit frequented these auctions, looking to pick up valuable property at bargain prices. American lawyers, moreover, owed a considerable proportion of their income to the collection of debts, from both solvent and insolvent debtors.

While assignees, sheriffs, newspaper publishers, and lawyers received work as the result of specific financial failures, and while speculators busied themselves at the ensuing forced sales of property, antebellum writers capitalized on a more general fascination with bankruptcy. Fiction writers and the authors of advice literature returned to the subject again and again, supplying America's reading public with a steady diet of commentary about economic failure. This public discourse included fantastic stories about grand commercial schemes and spectacular collapses, more mundane morality plays that emphasized the evils of speculation, extravagance, and overtrading, and nonfictional counsel about how to avoid pecuniary embarrassment.[2] Throughout the antebellum decades, bankruptcy put dinner on a great many tables.

The emergence of "wrecking" as an entrenched part of America's economy serves as a telling marker in the evolution of American capitalism. By the early 1840s, financial salvage increasingly became the work of individuals who specialized in profiting from economic distress—a development hastened by the operation of the 1841 Bankruptcy Act, despite its short life.[3] The creation of economic niches relating to insolvency suggests the extent to which capitalist rhythms had come, in at least some quarters of American society, to structure assumptions about economic life. Deepening market relations led some Americans to recognize business failure as a characteristic feature of capitalism, signifying not only capitulation to competition or depression but also a means to earn a living. In the rise of wrecking as a career, or to use a more biological metaphor, in the emergence of human vultures who fed off the economic carcasses around them, one sees the capacity of America's capitalist culture to extend the entrepreneurial impulse— to find, even in the very occurrence of commercial catastrophe, the raw materials for profit.

The path of the would-be vulture capitalist, however, was not an easy one. As the history of the 1841 Bankruptcy Act demonstrates, gleaning profits from business failures generally required more than the identification of insolvency as a potential source of income. Successful wrecking also depended on low-cost access to information—whether about legal change, credit histories, or the value of assets entrusted to bankruptcy estates. Without access to this kind of "intelligence," attempts to benefit from the financial misfortune of others could easily miscarry. In antebellum America, the individuals best placed to garner such information were insiders to the world of bankruptcy—people who had tasted the bitter fruit of insolvency themselves or who regularly dealt with the legal and financial tangles produced by the nation's many business collapses. These Americans most commonly recognized the possibility of profiting from bankruptcy and possessed the contacts and knowledge to transform entrepreneurial possibility into remunerative investment.

Equally important, Americans did not necessarily embrace vulture capitalism as a testament to the innovative potential of the entrepreneurial ethos. Initial cultural commentary on wrecking was almost uniformly negative, even from writers who equated social progress with commercial growth and lauded the "self-made man" as the chief agent of civilization. Before 1850, antebellum commentators typically portrayed wreckers as disreputable characters whose income was tainted by unscrupulous methods and sordid dependence on the misfortunes of others. After midcentury, more positive views toward wrecking appeared in commercial discourse, reflecting diminished anxiety about the frequent occurrence of insolvency in America. As commercial writers became more and more familiar with the workings of a volatile market economy, the wrecker took on a different symbolic significance, suggesting business savvy and instructive internalization of capitalist values. This cultural shift, prompted largely by an accumulation of experience with bankruptcy and wrecking, indicates the extent to which commercially inclined Americans were beginning to perceive even the most complex aspects of a capitalist economy as consonant with nature.[4]

Court Costs, Legal Fees, and the Beginnings of a Bankruptcy Bar

Congressional critics of the 1841 Bankruptcy Act were quick to highlight the most obvious beneficiaries of financial failure in antebellum America. Even before the bankruptcy bill became law, Democratic opponents such as New York congressman Victory Birdseye predicted that it would benefit court officials, newspapers, and the legal fraternity far more than it would creditors or the economy generally. In considering the likely impact of the proposed legislation, Birdseye envisioned bankruptcy estates that produced funds sufficient only to pay "the expenses of litigations, agencies, fees, and commissions." Placemen and attorneys would prosper; creditors would get next to nothing. Several newspapers made similar claims, both on the eve of the bankruptcy system's inauguration in February 1842 and throughout the system's brief existence. Editors paid close attention to the windfall that the act gave to court officials, lawyers, and those newspapers fortunate enough to have secured selection as publishers of bankruptcy notices in a given federal district. The 1841 act, in the words of one New York paper, meant a "golden harvest" to those anointed as superintendents of failure.[5]

These characterizations of the bankruptcy system did not exaggerate. The 1841 law directly placed over $1 million in the pockets of those people responsible for making the bankruptcy process work. In some federal districts, such as Vermont and the eastern and western districts of Virginia, creditors received less money from dividends than clerks, newspapers, and other bankruptcy placemen earned from fees. Elsewhere in the country, such as in Massachusetts and the eastern district of Louisiana, payments to creditors were more substantial. On the whole, though, court officials earned almost as much as creditors from the funds that bankruptcy courts distributed as a result of the 1841 act.[6]

The nature of bankruptcy-related court costs in southern New York gives an indication of how the 1841 act created sinecures throughout the country. In order to gain a voluntary bankruptcy discharge from the Empire State's southern federal district, an applicant had to make a bevy of payments. In routine cases, where creditors offered no opposition and petitioners owned little or no property beyond that exempted by the Bankruptcy Act, costs were relatively low. Even in such instances, though, clerks of the court received fees for drawing up court orders, copying documents, entering items onto docket books, and filing papers; a commissioner in bankruptcy received payments for taking the applicant's oath that the petition was true to his or her knowledge; the bankruptcy assignee and his assistants earned remuneration for cataloging the petitioner's assets and determining how much property the applicant could retain; and the *Morning Courier and New York Enquirer* gained ninety days worth of guaranteed advertising, as the applicant had to publish twenty days worth of notices for a hearing to be decreed a bankrupt, and another seventy days worth of notices for the hearing on a final discharge. Finally, after a successful motion for a discharge, a petitioner had to pay the costs of printing a bankruptcy certificate and drawing up a court order that legally released the applicant from past debts.[7]

The total court costs of such routine bankruptcy cases varied from district to district, depending on the fees set by presiding judges. In Judge Betts's jurisdiction, a straightforward bankruptcy proceeding required about $50 from the voluntary applicant. Other districts managed to make the process cheaper. New Hampshire's average costs came to only $15 per applicant; most petitioners in Connecticut paid no more than $25; and the typical voluntary bankrupt in Georgia incurred charges of around $39.[8] When a bankruptcy case involved complexities, however, court costs mushroomed. Opposition by creditors occasionally led to the taking of depositions, which could lead to substantial fees. If creditors or bankrupts spent several weeks gathering evidence, the resulting costs could reach into the hundreds of dollars.[9]

Administration of bankruptcy estates with a fair amount of property similarly entailed significant expense. In such instances, the U.S. marshal and his deputies received payments for taking charge of bankrupts' assets and transporting them to the assignee. Fees also went to the assignee and his clerks for cataloging and storing assets, collecting any debts due to bankrupts, and any other work required in the management of the bankruptcy estate. Both the assignee and his appointed auctioneer additionally received commissions on liquidation sales, usually 5 percent each.[10]

If a bankruptcy estate yielded a surplus over and above the foregoing costs, the assignee then had the task of supervising the distribution of the fund to creditors who proved their debts. This process generated yet more court costs. Bankruptcy commissioners received payment for verifying proofs of debt and serving as auditors who checked the accounts of the assignee; newspapers gained more business, as the assignee had to advertise impending dividends; and the assignee's time in calculating and distributing dividends merited additional compensation. The money to pay these asset-related court costs came out of the funds raised through the sale of a bankrupt's property, often leaving little or nothing for creditors.[11]

Thus the bankruptcy system provided hundreds of court officials and dozens of newspapers with substantial income. Every district court appointed numerous bankruptcy commissioners and assignees to carry out the work of the 1841 act, usually one per county, with a greater number of commissioners in large cities like New York or Boston. Senior court officials and official newspapers received the most handsome direct payments. In southern New York, the general assignee, William Coventry H. Waddell, received the largest compensation. Waddell's office had the task of superintending all bankruptcy estates in Manhattan and Brooklyn, a task that brought fees in excess of $40,000. The *Morning Courier and New York Enquirer* received over $20,000 in advertising revenues, and the U.S. marshal earned around $10,000. (Both the general assignee and the marshal had to share some of their proceeds with deputies and assistants.) Commissioners earned between $700 and $2,500, with city commissioners at the higher end of the range, and court clerks could count on income of more than $1,000, roughly akin to the salaries of antebellum corporate officers. The one group of federal officials who did not receive monetary payment for bankruptcy work was federal judges, who, despite exploding caseloads, earned not a penny more than they would have if the legislation had never gone into effect.[12]

Judges nonetheless profited indirectly from the 1841 act. The remuneration attached to most of the offices in the bankruptcy system made them highly sought after positions, creating opportunities for federal judges to create patronage networks. Positions frequently went to a judge's family member. Judge Betts's son Charles served as his clerk; in Boston, district judge Sprague appointed the son of Supreme Court justice Joseph Story as a bankruptcy commissioner; and Alfred Conkling, the federal judge in New York's northern district, appointed a young relative as a deputy clerk. Other bankruptcy officials, like Jacob Radcliff, a New York City bankruptcy commissioner, gained their appointments by seeking favors from an "old friend"— in Radcliff's case Supreme Court justice Smith Thompson.[13]

Bankrupts themselves often secured a place within the bankruptcy system. These individuals benefited doubly from the 1841 act, simultaneously freeing themselves of past debts and obtaining a well-paying position. Judge Betts employed one such bankrupt, William W. Campbell, as a commissioner in New York City; another, Silas M. Stilwell, as federal marshal; and a third, James Watson Webb, as the official publisher of the district's bankruptcy notices. Campbell had the pleasure of presiding over his own bankruptcy application, proving debts against himself. Stilwell and Webb gained far more notoriety, since they each earned more than $10,000 from the operation of the 1841 act, even as that legislation erased their previous financial obligations.[14]

Like bankruptcy placemen and newspaper publishers, lawyers gained handsomely from the Bankruptcy Act. Although some petitioners eschewed legal representation, most sought it out, both to prepare asset and debt schedules and to attend court proceedings. A large majority of objecting or petitioning creditors also turned to attorneys to transact their business in bankruptcy court. As with the payment of court costs, straightforward bankruptcy cases required only limited legal fees. In instances where bankrupts possessed little in the way of property and faced no legal opposition, lawyers' bills rarely exceeded $25.[15]

Whenever a legal counselor had to prepare lengthy and complicated bankruptcy schedules, or attend depositions, or make legal arguments against an objecting creditor, costs increased rapidly. In the bankruptcies of Jonathon Amory and Henry Leeds, the two New York City commission merchants accused by their creditors of fraud, all three of these contingencies applied. Their case began with the preparation of extremely complicated schedules of assets and debts, led to the taking of myriad depositions, which took several weeks, and culminated in a number of arguments before both the district and circuit courts. The lawyers for Amory and Leeds and those representing the creditors who opposed their application each earned $2.50 for every day they attended the taking of testimony, $5 for every day spent arguing the case before Judge Betts, and $8 for every day spent arguing before Judge Thompson. By the end of proceedings, the lawyers for both sides were owed several hundred dollars.[16]

Thousands of antebellum attorneys gained business from the bankruptcy system, representing either voluntary applicants, objecting or petitioning creditors, or creditors who wished to file proofs of debt in a given bankruptcy proceeding. Hundreds of lawyers, for example, made at least one appearance in a southern New York bankruptcy case; Judge Betts's clerks entered nearly half as many different attorneys as bankrupts onto the bankruptcy dockets. Thus the benefits that the 1841 act conferred on the legal fraternity were widely spread, with the overwhelming majority of lawyers representing only a few bankrupts or creditors. Bankruptcy work for most antebellum attorneys simply represented an extension of their most basic stock-in-trade—debt collection and the handling of matters related to real estate.[17]

Some lawyers, however, viewed the opportunities presented by the 1841 bankruptcy statute as sufficient to justify specialization in bankruptcy practice. A few attorneys, like John Romeyn, from the Hudson River town of Kingston, and partners James N. Reynolds, Obadiah Platt, and Salem Dutcher, of New York City, went so far as to advertise their services in newspapers. The entrepreneurial efforts of these lawyers paid excellent dividends. Both Romeyn and the firm of Reynolds, Platt, & Dutcher attracted a steady stream of bankruptcy clients, primarily from voluntary applicants, but also from the occasional creditor who wished either to oppose a bankrupt's petition or to file an involuntary petition of his own.[18]

Other attorneys who built up bankruptcy practices eschewed the advertising sections of local papers, relying on previous client bases, reputation, connections, and word of mouth to secure business. The New York City lawyer Charles Stuart cultivated bankruptcy work in this fashion. Stuart ended up representing several bankrupts who were linked through either business dealings or kinship, indicating a trail of recommendations. A handful of legal counselors based in rural towns, such as C. W. Swift, Virgil Bonesteel, and William Wilkinson, all of Poughkeepsie, similarly drew on their local standing and contacts to attract bankruptcy work from residents of surrounding areas. These three attorneys took on the great majority of bankruptcy cases in Dutchess County despite the existence of seventeen other law offices in Poughkeepsie. Wilkinson almost certainly owed much of his bankruptcy work to the fact that his partner, William J. Street, was bankruptcy commissioner for the county. C. W. Swift similarly had a professional advantage in gaining bankruptcy clients, as he was a master in chancery for the state of New York and thus had extensive experience with lawsuits arising from insolvency.[19]

Within the circle of southern New York bankruptcy attorneys, a handful became even more specialized, particularly by concentrating on the representation of creditors who wished to oppose the voluntary petition of a bankrupt. Foremost among these lawyers was Philip J. Joachmissen. Joachmissen obtained appointments as counsel for opposing creditors in three early cases. Each case presented new questions of law, led to several public arguments before Judges Betts and Thompson, and received considerable coverage in the New York City papers. Although Judge Betts eventually overruled Joachmissen's objections in all three instances, the exposure received by the attorney laid the foundation for a thriving bankruptcy practice, one largely devoted to the representation of objecting creditors.[20]

The band of southern New York lawyers who grasped the professional opening created by the 1841 act shared one important characteristic with the individuals who had secured positions as bankruptcy officials—like the group of placemen, the bankruptcy bar attracted a number of bankrupts. Some of these attorneys were among the most successful practitioners of bankruptcy law, none more so than Peter Clark. A Brooklyn resident, Clark owed his failure to land speculations during the 1830s, which left him owing debts worth over $500,000. The Bankruptcy Law threw him a pair of lifelines, at once releasing him from his obligations and giving him a steady income. Dozens of voluntary petitioners came to the attorney's office seeking legal counsel, as did several creditors of bankrupts. When Clark traveled to Judge Betts's chambers to represent his clients, he mingled with several lawyers who, like him, enjoyed a doubly beneficial relationship with the 1841 act.[21]

Having to navigate the bankruptcy system on their own behalf even gave some attorneys a professional advantage in gaining clients. Such was the case with Charlemagne Tower, the distiller and liquor merchant from Oneida County who failed largely as a result of disastrous price declines in the early 1840s. Along with his brother and partner, Julius, Charlemagne had made a range of preferential payments just before they landed on the bankruptcy docket, including a mortgage on one gristmill given to another brother and the outright conveyance of a second mill to the family's matriarch. Tower knew that the granting of the mortgage might constitute a voluntary preference in contemplation of bankruptcy, having discussed the matter with his endorsers before executing the deed. The brothers had also converted trust funds to their own use, since they borrowed almost $10,000 from their father's estate to keep the firm's distilleries running. Finally, the pair had doctored the business's account books in a vain attempt to keep their shenanigans from coming to light. Sixteen of the Towers' many creditors opposed the pair's motion for a bankruptcy discharge, laying out almost every conceivable objection under the 1841 act, most of which were substantiated by a voluminous record of depositions and exhibits.[22]

Confronted with such damning evidence of frauds against the Bankruptcy Act, the Towers would appear to have had little chance of obtaining certificates. Charlemagne Tower, however, quickly demonstrated great skill in navigating the bankruptcy system. After collecting information about the law of bankruptcy and how it related to his predicament, Charlemagne set out to play his creditors off one another. His first moves were to demand delays wherever possible and to require endless depositions, which dramatically increased court costs. He then filed a proof of debt on the part of his father's estate, as the distilleries had borrowed a substantial sum from the estate. These two maneuvers greatly increased the Towers' bargaining power. So long as creditors stood in the way of the two brothers' discharges, the bankruptcy estate would continue to go to legal fees and court costs. But if objecting creditors were to forgo their opposition, Charlemagne offered to scale back the claim of his father's estate against the failed firm of Reuben Tower's Sons, increasing the share that other creditors would receive from the bankruptcy assignee. Tower also offered the objecting creditors additional payments. By late 1842, these tactics had made almost all the opposing creditors "fearful of more expenses and willing to make [a] settlement." One creditor, though, continued his opposition in the hope of "worrying something" out of the Towers or their "friends." Charlemagne was able to overcome this last obstacle by exploiting a legal technicality, which resulted in Judge Conkling's dismissal of the holdout's objections.[23]

As Tower fended off his creditors throughout 1842, he became familiar with the intricacies of the bankruptcy system and honed legal skills left dormant after his earlier training at Harvard Law School. As he explained in June, "[S]ince my disaster I have turned to the practice of my profession. . . . I believe I am in the midst of legal questions that will give me experience and practice enough for a start." Tower's analysis proved to be prescient, as he soon found himself representing a range of bankrupts and creditors from both Oneida County and other parts of upstate New York.[24]

The 1841 act hastened the development of specialized bankruptcy practices well beyond the boundaries of New York State. In Boston and Philadelphia, a number of attorneys represented several different bankruptcy clients in oral arguments before federal judges. Often these attorneys either had previous experience with the law of insolvency, had secured positions within the bankruptcy system, or both. Similarly, several law firms in central Illinois devoted their attention exclusively to bankruptcy work, aggressively advertising their services in local newspapers and making periodic trips through the countryside to solicit business.[25]

The legal proceedings spawned by the 1841 Bankruptcy Law, then, supported hundreds of antebellum families, especially those headed by men who recognized the potential payoff to individuals who helped to make the bankruptcy system work. But the economic impact of the bankruptcy system went beyond the direct payments to court officials, newspapers, and lawyers that so angered the system's critics. An additional source of profit beckoned to Americans who could provide various guides to the new legislation and the legal actions it spawned. For the brief period of the 1841 act's life, a small industry grew up to meet the growing demand for such explanations.

The Demand for Legal Knowledge

Bankrupts, their creditors, and the attorneys who hoped to secure bankruptcy work all relished information about the new bankruptcy system once President Tyler signed the bankruptcy bill into law on August 19, 1841. Demand for legal treatises, reports of judicial opinions, and more simplified guides relating to the law of debtor and creditor were nothing new; throughout the antebellum years, treatise writers and court reporters had found a ready market for their efforts.[26] The 1841 Bankruptcy Law, however, created a wholly new means of dealing with insolvent debtors, one that required bankrupts, creditors, and lawyers to learn about novel legal procedures, definitions, and standards.

The most obvious needs of participants in bankruptcy cases were the actual text of the bankruptcy law and the rules and regulations drawn up by the federal judge in their district. Without a copy of the 1841 act and the regulations governing bankruptcy cases in a given jurisdiction, parties to bankruptcy proceedings would have had little sense of how to make or oppose a bankruptcy application. Newspapers throughout the country provided the text of the law for the benefit of their readers, and a number of legal stationers published the law in pamphlet form. These same stationers often printed the bankruptcy rules of the local federal district court, along with blank forms that attorneys or bankrupts might use in lieu of writing out the prescribed text of petitions or motions. Attorneys, bankrupts who intended to file for bankruptcy relief without the benefit of legal counsel, and creditors who similarly wished to avoid legal fees had a particular need for these sorts of legal aids.[27]

Other quick-thinking legal entrepreneurs offered additional guides to the 1841 act, seeking to provide authoritative constructions of the bankruptcy statute's manifold ambiguities. Even before the bankruptcy system began to function in early February 1842, three eastern attorneys published commentaries on the 1841 act, seeking to clarify statutory obscurities and offering additional suggestions to individuals who had to take part in bankruptcy proceedings. A fourth eastern lawyer published a similar guide a few months after the law came into effect. These pamphlets offered extended discussions of each section in the act and set forth step-by-step instructions for bankrupts who wished to petition for relief. They also provided answers to such questions as what distinguished legal from illegal preferences or when attachments on a bankrupt's property constituted a lien that secured the creditor a preference over other claimants. One lawyer engaged in more extensive work, crafting a full-length treatise on the law of bankruptcy. Lacking direction from the decisions of sitting federal judges, since the bankruptcy courts either had yet to begin operation or had just begun to function, these legal entrepreneurs had to fall back on precedents from America's first experiment with bankruptcy, as well as English bankruptcy law.[28]

Once federal judges began to rule on actual bankruptcy cases, the early commentaries quickly lost currency. Bankruptcy attorneys required intelligence about the sitting judiciary's interpretation of the new legislation, which counted far more than discussions of English precedents or the cases resulting from the very different American Bankruptcy Act of 1800. The first responses to this demand came from newspapers such as the *Cayuga Patriot* and *Morning Courier and New York Enquirer*. These publications were located in the same town or city as federal district courts and attempted to boost their circulation by offering regular reports of bank-ruptcy proceedings in those courts, as well as occasional opinions from judges in other parts of the country.[29]

Newspapers by no means cornered the market in bankruptcy reports. Several legal periodicals also cashed in on the demand for bankruptcy coverage. Four such journals—the *Law Reporter*, published in Boston, the *New York Legal Observer*, based in New York City, the *Pennsylvania Law Journal*, produced in Philadel-phia, and the *Western Law Journal*, compiled in Cincinnati—devoted considerable space to bankruptcy decisions. Editors of these publications realized, in the words of the *Law Reporter*, that "there is no subject of greater interest to the profession throughout the country, at the present time, than the late act of congress establish-ing a uniform system of bankruptcy." The reach of this statute was so broad that "every [bankruptcy] decision . . . is eagerly sought for by the community in general, as well as by the legal profession."[30] All four law journals did their best to satisfy the thirst for bankruptcy intelligence, with the seaboard periodicals allocating over half of their pages to bankruptcy opinions through 1842 and much of 1843 and covering northeastern cases with particular comprehensiveness.

In all of these attempts to answer the demand for guides to bankruptcy law, insiders to the bankruptcy process predominated. Newspapers such as the *Cayuga Patriot* and the *Morning Courier and New York Enquirer* already had a close relationship with the bankruptcy court because they published notices of petitions, auctions, and dividends. In Philadelphia, the *Pennsylvania Law Journal* bought the first rights to the work of the official court reporter, John W. Wallace. Moreover, two of the treatises written on the 1841 act were authored by editors of an eastern legal periodical, both of whom doubled as bankruptcy lawyers. Peleg Chandler had founded the *Law Reporter* in 1838 and continued at its helm throughout the early 1840s, juggling editorial duties, pamphlet writing, and work as a bankruptcy com-missioner and attorney. In 1842, Samuel Owen established the *New York Legal Observer*, relying on the reputation of his recently published bankruptcy treatise, a close relationship with Judge Betts, and an earlier career as a bankruptcy attorney in England to bolster the fortunes of his new publication.[31]

The role of bankruptcy participants in the business of disseminating information about the operation of the 1841 act should come as no surprise. Whether as editors of newspapers that published bankruptcy notices, officers of the bankruptcy court, or bankruptcy attorneys, these individuals had especially good access to bank-ruptcy news, and so enjoyed entrepreneurial opportunities not readily available to other Americans. Placement within the legal world of bankruptcy nurtured per-sonal relationships with federal judges and court officials, connections that made it possible for someone like Peleg Chandler to secure copies of judicial opinions before anyone else. These sorts of relationships were not essential preconditions to making money from the provision of bankruptcy news. The *New York Herald*, for example, offered reports of bankruptcy decisions that rivaled those of the *Morning Courier*, despite the *Herald*'s lack of connections to federal court officials in southern New York. But inside contacts made it much easier to get the latest word on developments in bankruptcy law, and hence to package that information for public consumption.

Bankruptcy and the Rise of Credit Reporting

In addition to boosting demand for guides to bankruptcy law, the 1841 Bankruptcy Act, along with the disastrous economic conditions of the late 1830s and early 1840s, whetted appetites for knowledge about debtors. Participants in antebellum commerce increasingly craved information about the economic standing of the people with whom they transacted business. In an economy predicated on the extension of long-term credit, importers and manufacturers constantly found themselves assessing the creditworthiness of jobbers, who in turn had to judge how much leeway to grant urban retailers and country merchants. At the same time, retail merchants constantly appraised the likelihood that customers would make good on their promises to pay for credit purchases.

As the American economy grew more dynamic and complex in the early nineteenth century, old mercantile habits of relying on personal connections to evaluate the creditworthiness of customers or suppliers became less and less satisfactory. Merchants and manufacturers found themselves regularly doing business with strangers; businessmen additionally confronted a rapidly changing economy, in which their suppliers and customers might be excellent credit risks one month and bankrupts the next. In such circumstances, a number of eastern merchants looked to new means of estimating the risks associated with granting credit. One method used by urban wholesalers was to require letters of recommendation that attested to a country merchant's good character. Other businessmen in eastern cities developed business relationships with attorneys throughout the country, at once asking for credit assessments of local merchants and providing collection work when circumstances required such action. By the 1820s, some New York City merchants adopted a different strategy, employing a traveling agent to collect reports on the economic condition of their customers in particular regions of the country.[32]

While each of these mechanisms retained some currency throughout the antebellum decades, they did not fill the growing need for reliable credit assessments. In 1835, three New York City lawyers developed a more comprehensive plan for credit reporting. The firm of Griffen, Cleaveland, & Campbell created a network of attorneys throughout the city's expansive economic hinterland. These correspondents provided regular evaluations of local businesses that bought their stock in

New York City. After paying an annual subscription fee, any merchant in New York who wished to consult these reports could do so as often as he wished. The reporting attorneys received fees for their work, as well as the prospect of additional retainers, since Griffen, Cleaveland, & Campbell promised to forward any requests for collection of outstanding debts. The agency treated all information as strictly confidential and kept the identities of its reporters secret.[33]

This initial foray into credit reporting proved short-lived. The heady economic boom of the mid-1830s reduced the caution of many merchants, and hence their willingness to pay for information about potential customers. In addition, one of the partners in the new business suffered substantial losses from his own real estate speculations, placing additional financial pressure on the agency. By 1841, however, the well-known merchant, philanthropist, and abolitionist Lewis Tappan had re-solved to make a second attempt at developing a credit-reporting agency, drawing heavily on the earlier scheme of Griffen, Cleaveland, & Campbell. Tappan enjoyed better timing than the three lawyers. He began the Mercantile Agency after the crises of the late 1830s, which reminded businessmen throughout the country that the credit system presented great dangers as well as great opportunities. Although the enterprise faced several obstacles, including the refusal of southern attorneys to have anything to do with an abolitionist, squabbling between Tappan and some of his partners, resentments about the "spying" of credit reporters, and several libel suits by proprietors who alleged that the dissemination of false information had materially damaged their concerns, the Mercantile Agency and its later incarnations prospered. By 1857, the business had fifteen branches throughout the United States, as well as offices in Montreal and London.[34]

In setting up the Mercantile Agency, Tappan hoped to accomplish more than the creation of a profitable business. He further wished to tame the American credit system. The philanthropist reasoned that reliable information about the economic position of businesses would improve mercantile relations in two ways. Reckless businesses that overtraded on a limited capital base would lose the ability to pur-chase goods on credit, as suppliers would discover the high risks associated with their mode of operation. While the overtraders found themselves tethered by a short economic leash, credit reports would aid the business of prudent firms. Once hardworking, solvent merchants had received a favorable credit report, they would more readily forge business relationships and obtain loans—so long as they main-tained prudent business operations. Soon after launching his new agency, Tappan summed up these hoped-for effects of credit reporting, remarking that it "checks knavery, & purifies the mercantile air."[35]

Historians of nineteenth-century credit reporting have emphasized Lewis Tap-pan's personal acquaintance with failure as a crucial element in his drive to establish the Mercantile Agency and "purify" the credit system. As a partner with his brother

Arthur, Lewis was forced to suspend payments to his creditors during the 1837 panic, when hundreds of debtors defaulted on their obligations to the Tappans' firm. The latter Tappan also was deeply affected by Arthur's personal financial woes, which were brought on by an ill-fated willingness to back a friend's real estate speculations, and which led to a bankruptcy petition in 1842.[36]

The Tappans' brushes with failure, though, were not the only links between antebellum insolvency and the rise of credit reporting. The Mercantile Agency's successes quickly encouraged emulation, with several competitors also entering the field after first-hand experiences with bankruptcy. One such competitor was Sheldon P. Church, an early traveling agent for New York mercantile firms, including Arthur Tappan & Co. Church failed as a Brooklyn saddler after the 1837 panic, after which he resumed work as a traveling credit reporter. In 1842, he received a bankruptcy discharge and carved out his own niche as a provider of commercial intelligence. The former saddler undertook regular journeys throughout the South, where the abolitionist Lewis Tappan had difficulty signing up reporters, and gathered information on businessmen who bought their goods in New York City. He then sent reports back to a group of New York merchants, who collectively paid for his services. Church continued this arrangement throughout the 1840s, on at least one occasion publishing a collection of reports for the use of New York jobbers and wholesalers.[37]

Other emulators of the Mercantile Agency similarly began their operations after encounters with insolvency. William Coxe Dusenberry failed in a number of southern New York businesses before founding the Commercial Agency with a partner in 1843. This New York City business copied Tappan's methods and specialized in the coverage of southern firms. And John Bradstreet, the Mercantile Agency's most effective rival throughout the nineteenth century, began his enterprise after serving as the private assignee of a complicated bankruptcy estate in Cincinnati during 1848.[38] The route to many early ventures in credit reporting ran through the world of bankruptcy.

The 1841 Bankruptcy Act, moreover, prompted innovation in the provision of information about credit risks wholly separate from the consolidation and growth of credit-reporting agencies. By creating court dockets and legal notices that detailed the names, occupations, and residences of thousands of insolvent debtors, the statute made it possible to publish lists of bankrupts. A New York City merchant writing to the *New York Herald* signaled the likely demand for such registers as the bankruptcy courts opened for business in February 1842. The businessman noted that "New York merchants find themselves interested in almost every village, town, and city of the United States," making it "just as necessary for them to know who become bankrupts in other places as in their own city." He further observed that for years a London periodical, *Perry's London Bankrupt Gazette*, had maintained a comfortable circulation by publishing the names of all bankrupts and insolvents in the United Kingdom and Ireland. The merchant then called on the *Herald* to produce a similar gazette, which he predicted would receive "great patronage every where in this country, as well as in Europe." James Gordon Bennett, the *Herald*'s editor, indicated that he would "seriously" consider this suggestion, but his paper confined itself to compiling the names of bankrupts in southern New York.[39]

Publications with greater contacts to the bankruptcy courts led the way in preparing bankruptcy rolls. Newspapers that served as official publishers of bankruptcy notices and legal journals that specialized in bankruptcy reports were particularly active in this endeavor. Soon after bankruptcy proceedings got under way, James Watson Webb's *Morning Courier and New York Enquirer* announced an intention to publish the name of every bankrupt in the United States. Throughout the early months of the 1841 act's operation, Webb tried to make good on his promise, regularly including lists of bankrupts from federal districts all over the country. But since the paper lacked close connections to court officials outside New York, it soon found the costs of amassing comprehensive registers prohibitive. As a result, Webb eventually concentrated on providing rosters of bankrupts in the Empire State. In Boston, the *Law Reporter* relied on its contacts to compile similar lists. Peleg Chandler collected the names and residences of bankrupts in every New England state except Vermont, also publishing bankruptcy rolls for southern New York and Illinois.[40]

After the repeal of the 1841 statute, law stationers in New York City, Philadelphia, and Pittsburgh went one step further than newspapers and legal periodicals. These printers compiled a register of every bankrupt in their respective federal districts, publishing an alphabetized listing in pamphlet form. The pamphlets offered creditors an easy-to-use reference guide to hundreds of bankrupts in their regions.[41]

The collection and dissemination of bankrupt lists differed in a number of respects from Tappan's scheme. The Mercantile Agency depended on the exertions of myriad reporters and clerks and presupposed an ongoing evaluation of antebellum businesses. Putting out a register of bankrupts, by contrast, was a much simpler and less costly affair. One merely compiled the names, residences, and occupations of bankrupts from the court records or newspaper notices of a given federal district and then published the resulting register of failure. Bankrupt lists, while easier to prepare and much less costly to buy, provided much less information than the Mercantile Agency's credit reports. The latter gave its subscribers periodic, calibrated assessments of creditworthiness for its subjects, indicating whether a business was reliable for any conceivable engagement, reasonably strong, only good for a limited amount of credit, doubtful, or so suspect that one should only

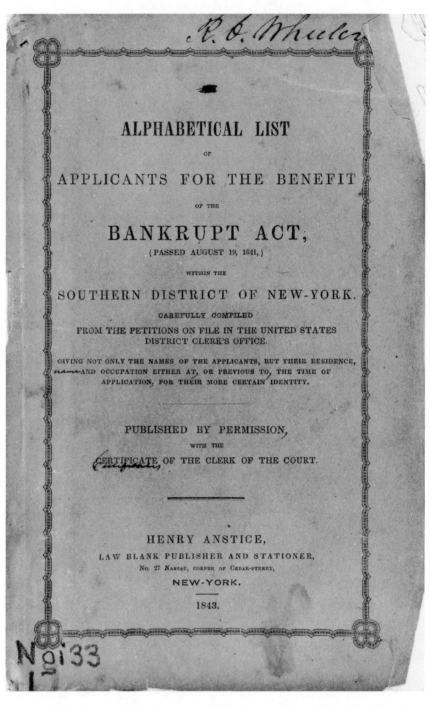

ALPHABETICAL LIST

OF

APPLICANTS FOR THE BENEFIT

OF THE

BANKRUPT ACT,

(PASSED AUGUST 19, 1841,)

WITHIN THE

SOUTHERN DISTRICT OF NEW-YORK.

CAREFULLY COMPILED

FROM THE PETITIONS ON FILE IN THE UNITED STATES
DISTRICT CLERK'S OFFICE.

GIVING NOT ONLY THE NAMES OF THE APPLICANTS, BUT THEIR RESIDENCE,
AND OCCUPATION EITHER AT, OR PREVIOUS TO, THE TIME OF
APPLICATION, FOR THEIR MORE CERTAIN IDENTITY.

PUBLISHED BY PERMISSION,

WITH THE

CERTIFICATE OF THE CLERK OF THE COURT.

HENRY ANSTICE,

LAW BLANK PUBLISHER AND STATIONER,

No. 27 NASSAU, CORNER OF CEDAR-STREET,

NEW-YORK.

1843.

N9i33

MEETING THE DEMAND FOR CREDIT HISTORIES. This 1843 pamplet supplied residential and occupational information about bankrupts, extracted from their bankruptcy papers, "for their more certain identity" (Mudd Library, Yale University).

transact business in cash. The former communicated only one message—that the individuals on the list had found themselves in federal bankruptcy court during the life of the 1841 act.

Relying on the bankruptcy registers as guides to the provision of credit had several additional shortcomings. Although the lists usually made distinctions between voluntary and involuntary bankrupts, they did not indicate whether courts had actually decreed individuals to be bankrupts. Thus voluntary petitioners who withdrew or did not pursue their applications took their place alongside their counterparts who received a discharge; and debtors who faced an involuntary petition but who arranged a settlement endured the same publicity as involuntary bankrupts who were compelled to give up their assets for court-supervised liquidation. Even more important, bankruptcy rolls presented problems of identity. Knowing that Samuel Smith of New York City had filed a voluntary bankruptcy petition did not necessarily pin down the individual whose financial troubles had led him to Judge Betts's court. By the same token, bankrupts frequently moved away from the scene of their failures, increasing the difficulty of connecting people and their calamitous financial pasts.[42]

Despite these limitations, there is good reason to think that bankruptcy lists would have flourished if Congress had not repealed the 1841 act. In Massachusetts, the state insolvency courts resumed operation as soon as the national legislature had stricken its bankruptcy law from the statute books. The *Law Reporter* continued its work of naming names, publishing monthly lists of Massachusetts insolvents from 1843 into the 1860s. Imperfect credit information was better than no information at all.[43]

Wrecking in the Bankruptcy Court

Of all the economic opportunities created by the 1841 Bankruptcy Law, those with the greatest potential lay with the property relinquished by bankrupts. The amount of property surrendered under this legislation was limited by its retrospective operation and the recognition that the statute gave to liens. Thousands of applicants under the 1841 act had previously turned over their assets to state insolvency courts, private assignees, or debt-collecting local sheriffs, and a significant proportion of other assets were exempted from the operation of the bankruptcy system because creditors had gained a lien over them prior to the filing of a bankruptcy petition. Nonetheless, agents of the short-lived antebellum bankruptcy system received an avalanche of tangible and intangible property. Under the 1841 act, federal marshals and assignees took possession of essentially every kind of movable property known to antebellum America—household furniture and kitchenware; artisanal tools and farm implements; lots of crockery, cloth, and hardware; family stores such as barrels of flour and salted meat; silver plate, jewelry, and paintings; Bibles, schoolbooks, histories, and romances; instruments for surveying land and navigating the oceans; carriages, wagons, and boats; firearms and farm animals; and in the South, slaves. Bankrupts also surrendered thousands of deeds to real estate, mostly heavily mortgaged, and extensive inventories of intangible property. These latter assets consisted of book-account debts owed by the customers of bankrupts, as well as corporate stock, patent rights, promissory notes, bills of exchange, mortgages, and other commercial instruments.

The 1841 act permitted bankrupts to keep up to $300 worth of "necessaries," such as clothing, household furniture and kitchenware, and tools. Assignees had the responsibility of converting the rest of a bankrupt's property into cash, which first paid the costs of managing the assignment, and then, if the bankruptcy estate produced sufficient funds, provided dividends to creditors who proved their debt against the bankrupt concerned. The legislation granted assignees a reasonable degree of flexibility in carrying out their duties. They could sell a bankrupt's property privately or at public auction; they possessed the authority to redeem mortgages on a bankrupt's property in order to facilitate a sale; and they were able to reach settlements with the individuals and firms who owed debts to a bankrupt. Each of these actions, however, required the sanction of the district judge. While the statute gave assignees discretion over how to liquidate assets, it also mandated a "speedy settlement" of bankruptcy estates, instructing assignees to close the proceedings in each case within two years after the court had issued a bankruptcy decree.[44]

Sales made under the auspices of the 1841 act gave purchasers the chance to make hugely successful speculations. Bankruptcy auctions and private sales primarily occurred between the spring of 1842 and the end of 1844; in the first eighteen months of this period, commodity prices, real estate values, and stock and bond markets remained moribund, still weighed down by the economic slowdown following the financial crises of the late 1830s. In addition, bankruptcy assignees generally required cash payments for a bankrupt's assets. As a result of the prevailing economic conditions and the terms of sale, a speculator with cash reserves could make purchases from the bankruptcy court at extremely low prices.[45]

The vast majority of the assets surrendered by bankrupts, though, were of uncertain value. Tangible goods such as furniture, jewelry, or consignments of cloth commanded ready markets, as a potential buyer could gauge the value of such items on the basis of a first-hand inspection. But most of the property sold by the nation's bankruptcy courts lacked such easily judged market value. Both the real estate and the intangible property of bankrupts were often completely worthless.

Several characteristics of the real estate owned by bankrupts made it a precarious investment. First of all, bankrupts frequently owned land that was located hundreds of miles away from the place where they petitioned for bankruptcy and surrendered their assets. Potential buyers of these properties often had no way to evaluate their quality without incurring substantial expense. Purchasers of land claims also had to consider the legal strength of bankrupts' asserted rights to given pieces of property. Bankruptcy assignees only received the same legal title to real estate as the bankrupt possessed. Thus when they sold a bankrupt's land, they did so on the basis of a quitclaim deed, conveying only the rights that the bankrupt enjoyed and providing no guarantee that the title to the land would stand up against legal challenges. If someone else had a better title—a common occurrence in antebellum America—the purchaser of the bankrupt's deed gained nothing more than a worthless scrap of paper. Finally, most real estate surrendered by bankrupts was heavily mortgaged, giving the mortgagor a lien against the property. Unless the buyer of a mortgaged property was willing to redeem the mortgage, the holder of the bond could fore-close on the farm, town lot, or plot of wilderness, obliterating any legal claim of the bankrupt or a subsequent purchaser.[46]

Intangible assets presented analogous conundrums. An account book filled with columns of unpaid debts, a pile of promissory notes, or a stack of bills of exchange might have had a combined face value of several thousand dollars. But the individuals who owed these debts might have been insolvent or dead, or they might have moved to parts unknown. Even when the location of a bankrupt's debtors were known, collection might not have been the most straightforward affair, possibly re-quiring additional investment of time and money. Similarly, corporate stock owned by a bankrupt often represented equity in marginal companies with uncertain futures, or was mortgaged to secure one of the bankrupt's debts. And a bankrupt's claim to a patent right might have been disputed, or might have only signified exclu-sive ownership of a useless invention. In short, the commercial value of the property that bankrupts relinquished under the 1841 act was often extremely doubtful.

Successful scavenging among this wreckage required solid intelligence. Without reliable information about a bankrupt's assets and a clear idea of how to turn them into money, buyers had little or no chance of realizing gains from the bankruptcy sales. Blessed with such information, a purchaser could make handsome profits, discriminating between the few assets with current or potential market value and the many that possessed no value at all.

For obvious reasons, no one knew more about the property in many bankruptcy estates than bankrupts themselves. A person engaged in a particular business gener-ally knew which of his debtors might eventually make good on their obligations or whether a patent right was likely to become lucrative. The same advantages occa-sionally obtained in instances where bankrupts had engaged in speculations of one sort or another. While many recipients of relief under the 1841 act had thrown away money on ill-considered schemes about which they knew little, others had intimate knowledge of their investments and recognized their continuing potential. Thus bankrupts and the people in whom they confided often possessed an edge over other would-be buyers when their property came up for sale.

In New York City and Brooklyn, bankrupts regularly took advantage of their inside information, buying back the assets surrendered to the bankruptcy court.[47] Many of these purchases reflected sentiment rather than an attempt to salvage businesses or speculations gone awry. Dozens of bankrupts successfully redeemed a watch, some furniture, a few pieces of jewelry, a church pew, or a painting. In at least thirty-five instances, however, bankrupts sought to reclaim a portion of previous enterprises or investments. These recipients of relief under the 1841 act believed that they could at least partially reverse their previous misfortune, so long as they were able to retrieve some particularly promising assets.

A few southern New York bankrupts bought assets like formerly owned store stock, store leases, machine tools, and business sites. These bankrupts, like Judson Gilbert, an iron founder from Peekskill, in Westchester County, sought to return to their previous line of trade. At a New York City bankruptcy auction on July 13, 1843, Gilbert repurchased the site of his foundry in Peekskill and a complete set of forging tools—all for $60.[48]

More commonly, bankrupts sought to salvage money from the remains of their failures rather than to restart a failed business. A handful of bankrupts pursued this more limited goal through the purchase of book-account debts owed by former customers. Bankrupts possessed substantial advantages over other potential buyers of such claims. To most people a list of book-account debts would have been utterly worthless, as the time and expense required to locate debtors and compel payment would almost certainly exceed the resulting proceeds. As a result, there was scant interest in the debts owed to most bankrupt businesses. The former proprietors of those concerns, by contrast, usually possessed detailed information about their debtors and the most effective means of collecting from them. Able to regain legal title to their overdue accounts for a fraction of their face value, bankrupts stood a reasonable chance of turning a profit. Other bankrupts were certain that old speculations, which had turned terribly sour during the depression of the late 1830s and early 1840s, would eventually prove to be wise investments. These released debtors retrieved claims to real estate, corporate stock, and patent rights, almost always for a pittance.[49]

Bankrupts were not the only people who relied on intelligence to guide them in making purchases from the bankruptcy court. Relatives and lawyers of bankrupts also made their presence known at bankruptcy sales, as did their creditors. These individuals often knew a good deal about the affairs of a bankrupt, and thus had an advantage in recognizing assets that were worth purchasing.[50]

Scattered evidence suggests that outside of Judge Betts's jurisdiction, bankrupts and people familiar with their affairs were just as likely to buy formerly owned assets from bankruptcy courts. A bankrupt from Chautauqua County, New York, re-purchased his interest in a large tract of upstate land from his bankruptcy assignee in 1844. Several additional parcels of upstate land were sold by the Oneida County bankruptcy assignee to a bankrupt's mother. Farther to the south, in Washington, D.C., the sister of a bankrupt purchased his claim against the Mexican government for the illegal seizure of a vessel's cargo. And in central Illinois, a failed land developer and a discharged bankruptcy attorney both managed to reacquire most of their assets through purchases at bankruptcy auctions.[51]

Although bankrupts and individuals who were either close to them or knew about their business dealings regularly purchased the assets of southern New York bankruptcy estates, these individuals did not dominate the bankruptcy auctions and private arrangements overseen by William Coventry H. Waddell. That distinc-tion went to a group of roughly twenty men who quickly specialized in wrecking among the assets of bankrupts from New York City or Brooklyn. These New Yorkers made it their business to attend most of the bankruptcy auctions under Waddell's authority and bought a substantial percentage of the goods on offer. There were dozens of individuals who showed up at one auction or another, buying a lot of furniture here or a mortgaged tract of wilderness there. But a relatively small band of purchasers made their presence known regularly at the bankruptcy sales, attending several auctions and consistently buying large amounts of property.[52]

Two of these bargain hunters were bankrupts themselves. Both Lucius Field, a Brooklyn resident who had failed as a merchant, and Elisha Bloomer, a New York City hatter, emulated their fellow bankrupts who had found employment as bank-ruptcy officials or bankruptcy attorneys. The pair recognized the opportunities open to individuals who were willing to devote time and energy to scavenging among the assets held by the bankruptcy assignee; each actively participated in most of the bankruptcy auctions that took place in New York City. Bloomer clearly found this newfound career to his liking. Even after the liquidation mandated by the 1841 Bankruptcy Act had run its course, he continued to make a living by speculat-ing in real estate sold at New York City sheriff's sales.[53]

In the case of most wreckers, the strategies used to distinguish attractive bank-ruptcy assets from those best left alone remain opaque. Asset buyers such as Field and Bloomer did not leave behind accounts of how they identified property worth pursuing. One can infer, however, the operations of the two most active purchasers of property surrendered to William Coventry H. Waddell. Jonathon D. Clute and Gordon Burnham bought more of these assets than anyone else, often making dozens of purchases at public auctions and constantly arranging private sales with

Waddell. Each of these speculators enjoyed unparalleled access to information about the property of southern New York bankrupts. Clute served as Waddell's secretary, while Burnham earned a salary as one of the assignee's appraisers.[54]

The positions that Clute and Burnham secured within the office of the bankruptcy assignee allowed them to pinpoint assets that merited a speculative investment. From March 1842, when applicants first gained bankruptcy decrees, through most of the next two years, these two men oversaw hundreds of bankruptcy estates. They cataloged assets as they came into the possession of the assignee's office; they aided Waddell in determining which assets were exempt from the operation of the bankruptcy process; and they maintained regular communications with bankrupts about the liquidation of their property. No one was better placed to gauge the potential value of the claims for sale in the southern district of New York.

In the bankruptcy system's first year, the pair of officials maintained a low profile, buying only occasionally and usually through private arrangements with their employer, Waddell. Sometime in the fall of 1843, though, Burnham resigned his position and turned his attentions fully to wrecking. By late 1843, Clute and Burnham dominated New York City bankruptcy auctions, often making the highest bids for more than one-third of the property up for sale and sometimes purchasing assets from other wreckers after the auction. Their purchases during a May 1844 auction were typical. For $255, Burnham walked away with claims to town lots and city houses in New York City, Brooklyn, upstate New York, New Jersey, Indiana, and Missouri; larger tracts of rural land in upstate New York, New Hampshire, Illinois, Michigan, and Tennessee; a steam sawmill in Michigan; shares in a Mississippi bank; and one-third interest in the commercial debts owed to a New York City mercantile firm. Clute acquired a similar range of assets for his combined payments of $205, buying the interest that bankrupts possessed in town lots on Long Island and in Utica, New York; rural tracts in upstate New York, New Jersey, Illinois, Mississippi, Tennessee, and Missouri; a Brooklyn distillery; shares in a New York railroad; and a mortgage valued at $6,000.[55] By 1845, Clute and Burnham had amassed large portfolios of bankruptcy assets, each owning claims to real estate all over the country, vast collections of book-account debts and commercial paper, and stock in numerous corporations.

Buying so extensively from bankruptcy estates by no means assured eventual profits. But the information collected by Clute and Burnham significantly increased their chance of realizing gains from their speculations. The payoffs from such investments, moreover, could be substantial, as demonstrated by a purchase that Burnham made of William Haskins's claim to a plot of land near Chicago. The former appraiser bought the plot at a July 1845 auction for $5. At the time, the land was heavily mortgaged and worth far less than its encumbrances. But as the Chicago economy boomed after the discovery of gold in California, the parcel rapidly increased in value. In 1856, Burnham was able to sell his interest in the property for $2,000, even though $29,000 was still required to pay off the mortgage.[56] With returns such as this one, and with the low prices that Burnham and Clute almost always paid for their investments, the pair could afford to have many of their purchases result in losses.

Clute and Burnham found yet another way to profit from the bankruptcy process, one involving less risk, though also smaller returns. Their offices made them privy to information about the ongoing liquidation of bankruptcy estates, including the likelihood that a given estate would lead to the distribution of a dividend to creditors and the probable size of the dividend. Armed with this knowledge, both men periodically bought up the claims of creditors against a bankrupt. Since the creditors often did not know whether a dividend was in the offing or how large the payment from the bankruptcy assignee would be, Burnham and Clute were able to purchase such obligations at a considerable discount. They then proved their debt as a bona fide creditor of the bankrupt and collected their share of the dividend.[57]

The wrecking by Burnham and Clute made each man wealthy by the 1850s. Mercantile Agency credit assessments indicate that Burnham was worth several hundred thousand dollars by 1855, while Clute owned property valued at around $150,000. Their employer, William Coventry H. Waddell, shared similar good fortune. Credit reports on Waddell suggest that he had profited handsomely from real estate bought in the bankruptcy court.[58] Although Waddell did not directly make purchases from bankruptcy estates, he may have arranged to do so through agents. Like his employees, Waddell possessed detailed knowledge of the property under his care; instructing a surrogate to buy selected assets for him would not have been difficult.

Wreckers, Respectability, and Conceptions of Economic "Nature"

As with wrecking on the Florida Keys, seizing the opportunities created by antebellum financial calamity depended on connections, expertise, and "local knowledge." The right contacts secured positions within the bankruptcy courts and contracts to publish bankruptcy notices, as well as bankruptcy clients for many attorneys. Familiarity with the law of creditor and debtor gave professional advantages both to bankruptcy lawyers and to the legal writers who interpreted the ambiguities of bankruptcy for a larger audience. And intelligence about the property that bankrupts had surrendered to the nation's assignees was a crucial precondition to profiting from bankruptcy sales or speculations in the debts owed by bankrupts. Equally indispensable for exploiting some "markets in failure" was a recognition that information about bankruptcy itself constituted a marketable commodity. In a commercial society where bankruptcies touched the lives of most people, one could count on strong demand for information about the law of bankruptcy, as well as the identity of bankrupts.

The characteristics of individuals who profited from the 1841 Bankruptcy Act were usually those of insiders—either to the workings of the bankruptcy system in a given place, or to the particular circumstances of individual bankruptcies. Moreover, the greatest beneficiaries of the short-lived experiment with federal bankruptcy legislation, like Peleg Chandler, William Coventry H. Waddell, Gordon Burnham, and Jonathon D. Clute, all took maximum advantage of their connections and position. Peleg Chandler used the office of bankruptcy commissioner as a base from which to pen a guide to the bankruptcy law, collect bankruptcy opinions, bankruptcy lists, and other news for the *Law Reporter*, and solicit business as an attorney. Waddell and his two assistants even more brazenly used the information gleaned in their supervision of bankruptcy estates to amass fortunes.[59]

In greatly favoring insiders, the world of bankruptcy resembled other sectors within the antebellum economy, such as banking and the distribution of public lands. The era's New England banks operated primarily to service the business dealings of its directors and influential shareholders, providing them with easy access to long-term capital and short-term credit. Similarly, federal land officers and surveyors found a multitude of ways to profit from their offices. Superintendents of the public domain appointed relatives and friends to subordinate positions, used funds deposited in land offices to finance local banking schemes, and acted as private land agents in addition to performing their public duties. Some of these federal officers additionally used information about the quality of public land as a basis for private speculation, or simply appropriated thousands of dollars of land office receipts for their own use.[60] In antebellum America, taking advantage of position and local knowledge was a common way to make money.

These actions of insiders did not go unnoticed or uncriticized by contemporaries. State bank commissioners in New England frequently complained about the cozy relationship that bank directors enjoyed with the institutions they served; the acceleration in the granting of state bank charters largely reflected efforts to widen access to credit beyond the narrow confines provided by many older banks. By the same token, congressional debates on the public lands regularly turned to the exposure of some malfeasance or excessive profit making by land officers.[61] Thus antebellum political culture did place some limits on the economic activities of individuals who ostensibly acted as trustees for the public good. Concern about these limits probably led to Gordon Burnham's resignation of his position as appraiser before he became an active buyer of bankruptcy assets. By quitting his official post, Burnham most likely sidestepped accusations of wrongdoing or impropriety. Despite such constraints, the workings of the bankruptcy system, like those of antebellum banks or land offices, provided substantial room for "operators" to maneuver.

The activities of these operators demonstrates the adaptability of at least some Americans to the unpleasant by-products of an economic order increasingly based on credit and commerce. Perhaps the greatest flexibility resided in those bankrupts who responded to their failures by seeking out the opportunities within the world of bankruptcy. Initially shackled by bad debts, falling prices, or ill-considered speculation, men such as William W. Campbell, Peter Clark, and Elisha Bloomer relied on the bankruptcy system as a means to reestablish solvency and social position. These men rebounded from failure by studying it, exploiting it, and making a business out of it. Their efforts both embodied and contributed to the complex evolution of American capitalism, which created entrepreneurial openings in the very process of bringing ruin to thousands and thousands of business ventures.

Yet in the first half of the nineteenth century, social commentators who turned their attention to this relationship between economic misfortune and economic opportunity generally did not celebrate the inventiveness of wreckers, choosing instead to portray them unsympathetically. William Gouge, the Jacksonian economic theorist, offered typical assessments in his widely read 1833 work, *A Short History of Paper Money and Banking in the United States*. As part of his attack on what he considered to be America's excessive reliance on credit and its oversupply of banking facilities, Gouge argued that the "forced extension of the credit system" inevitably caused cyclical economic fluctuations, which periodically broke thousands of sturdy farmers, mechanics, and merchants. This state of affairs, the Democratic political economist maintained, benefited only "that kind of trade in which sheriffs, constables, and assignees are the active agents." "Multitudes become bankrupt," allowing "a few successful speculators to get possession of the savings and earnings of many of their frugal and industrious neighbors." These speculators then rose "to wealth on the ruin" of their fellow citizens.[62]

The reproving image of the wrecker demonstrated considerable staying power. Through the 1840s, characters in antebellum fiction who engaged in wrecking invariably had names like Mr. Gouge or Mr. McScrew, and served as villainous foils to virtuous protagonists who pursued far more reputable livelihoods before falling on hard times.[63] The individuals who sought profit from business failures fared no better in the pages of *Hunt's Merchants' Magazine*, the most influential commercial periodical of the era, a vigorous supporter of Whig and later Republican proposals for governmental aids to commercial development, and a journal committed to setting standards of mercantile rectitude. According to the *Merchants' Magazine*, wreckers were among the most contemptible members of the commercial classes. "This class of men," in the estimation of editor Freeman Hunt, was "to the mercantile world what the filthy carrion-fowl are to the animal creation." Always willing to attack business confidence by spreading rumors of impending difficulties for a given firm or the economy at large, these scavengers feasted upon the commercial "death of others." As "land pirates of trade," such men "reared their fortunes from the wrecks of the times, from the fallen estates of their betters, from the overthrown houses, the dilapidated and forsaken homes of neighbors." To Hunt, the nation's speculators in distress only cheapened the marts of trade.[64]

Social commentators occasionally infused critiques of profiting from bankruptcy with gendered imagery, suggesting that the impulse to take advantage of misfortune manifested unseemly, "womanly" behavior. An 1857 cartoon in *Harper's Weekly*, prompted by that year's financial panic, offers a particularly stark demonstration of this tendency. The cartoon depicts female urban shoppers as scavenging, sharp-beaked "lady-birds" who swoop down on insolvent dry goods houses, availing themselves of liquidation sales mandated by the firms' creditors.[65]

Disdainful views of wrecking reflected long-standing premises about economic morality. Despite their substantial political differences, for example, William Gouge and Freeman Hunt both embraced the traditional, Protestant distinction between productive, socially useful callings, such as farming, manufacturing, and perform-ing the basic functions of commercial exchange, and dangerous, immoral occupa-tions, like financiering or speculation. The former pursuits created value through honest toil; the latter merely appropriated it through the unscrupulous manipula-tion of financial instruments and commercial markets. In this moral taxonomy of economic behavior, the wrecker more closely resembled a parasitic, gambling spec-ulator than a prudent, hardworking producer or merchant. Similarly, although both Gouge and Hunt accepted the need for extensive credit to finance America's legitimate business enterprises, each feared excessive reliance on the credit system, desiring to curb both the supply of and the demand for credit. To both thinkers, America's periodic financial crises and ever-present bankruptcies were symptoms of economic disease. These symptoms called for urgent measures to eliminate the evils of easy access to borrowed money and widespread "haste to be rich," not opportunistic strategies of money-getting.[66]

By midcentury, however, a number of commercial commentators began to reject the conceptual linkage between wrecking and unproductive commercial chicanery. For the novelist John Beauchamp Jones and Edwin T. Freedley, a well-known Philadelphia-based dispenser of financial advice, bankruptcies were simply a fact of life in a society driven by risk taking and market exchange. As a result, prof-iting from someone else's economic difficulties was a perfectly honorable way to make money.

Jones, in his 1851 novel, *The City Merchant; or, The Mysterious Failure*, ap-provingly chronicled the savvy schemes of a Philadelphia merchant, Edgar Saxon,

Descent of the Lady-Birds on the fallen Dry Goods Stores.

WRECKING AS WOMANLY SCAVENGING. As this lampoon of panic-induced liquidation sales indicates, disdain for wrecking by no means disappeared in the face of more sympathetic assessments (*Harper's Weekly*, Nov. 7, 1857, Rare Book, Manuscript, and Special Collections Library, Duke University).

who sells all of his assets just before the panic of 1837 and then builds a fortune after the panic by purchasing the property of bankrupt firms at depressed prices. These actions are not a matter of chance. Saxon is guided by an explicit set of instructions in his father's commercial diary. After failing himself in the panic of 1819, the elder Saxon came to the realization that capitalist economies are prone to cycles of boom and bust. He then penned his journal in order to prepare his son not only to navigate safely through times of general financial crisis but also to grasp the great opportunities they presented.[67]

Freedley offered an analogous perspective in his 1852 *A Practical Treatise on Business*. Seekers of wealth, Freedley counseled, would do well to keep an eye on "that fated circle whose business and expenditures are of the dazzling, magnificent kind." Inside this circle lived "the demon of bankruptcy," who would eventually bring about "downward progress" and utter "ruin." Once such men were overwhelmed by outright insolvency, Freedley continued, "there will be excellent opportunities to improve our fortunes, by picking up the pieces of the wreck at our own prices."[68]

Jones's and Freedley's interpretations of wrecking were part of a larger cultural trend in which many American economists, religious thinkers, and popular writers began to conceive of America's tumultuous capitalism as part of nature. In the 1850s, panics and financial revulsions increasingly appeared to these commentators as akin to a spate of terrific thunderstorms or the occurrence of a hurricane—periodic, terrifying events, but not evidence of divine retribution or impending economic apocalypse.[69] In the same vein, bankruptcies were little different from auctions, customs duties, or federal land sales—each was a standard feature of the American marketplace. By extension, individuals who discovered ways to profit from bankruptcies did not deserve characterization as despicable, "filthy carrion"; rather, these individuals merited admiration and even emulation.[70]

The reconceptualization of wrecking as sensible and perfectly consistent with progress signaled a growing self-consciousness and self-confidence about the social and economic consequences of market expansion in the nineteenth-century United States. In any capitalist society, bankruptcies and people who profit from them are routine elements of the economy. But people who encounter a rapid extension of commercially oriented production and exchange, such as the inhabitants of antebellum America, do not necessarily grasp this fact intuitively, nor instinctively seek to take advantage of it, nor immediately accept it without ambivalence or criticism. Several decades of experience with business failures underlay both the establishment of wrecking as a specialized economic pursuit and its public characterization as a legitimate activity.[71] This process, in many ways spearheaded by individuals personally educated in the school of bankruptcy, simultaneously aided and reflected the development of modern, capitalist mores and expectations. Through the growth of vulture capitalism, many commercially minded Americans found a means of coming to terms with some of the harsher aspects of a market economy. To these Americans, individual business collapses and general depressions were just part of the price for long-term economic growth and material abundance; and even those collapses created markets that entrepreneurs could profitably exploit.[72]

Part 3

The Promise of Economic Rebirth

The best energies of the country have been paralyzed; the brightest visions of gain have disappeared; and the wisest and most prudent schemes, uniting public improvement with individual interest, have perished as if by magic, in the universal revulsion that has desolated the country. This bill proposes to cast the mantle of oblivion over the past conduct of the debtor, over his acts which may have been compelled, or the preferences which may have been extorted, in his vain struggles to prolong his existence in the marts of trade.

—Speech of Senator Wall, May 12, 1840

It [the Bankrupt System] will also, in time, draw the line between respectability and infamy, in the business affairs of life—and operate as a moral check upon that class of society who acknowledge no other law, either human or divine. By and by no man will trust, credit, or associate with any person, however respectable in mere appearance, without first consulting the bankrupt lists.

—*New York Herald*, Oct. 10, 1842

Chapter 6

Fresh Starts

> After surrendering their property . . . under a bankrupt law, many will not be able to
> command sufficient capital to commence business anew on the spot which was the
> scene of their misfortunes, but, by the aid of friends will be enabled to gather up a
> moderate amount to commence the world again in that region [the West], where
> small means become great, by the manner in which nature has provided a reward
> for intelligence, industry, and enterprise.
>
> —Speech of Senator Tallmadge, July 24, 1841

> Just twenty-three years of age was Harry Melville, when he shrank back from his ad-
> vanced position in the business and social world, a bankrupt, his name a word of
> reproach or contempt on hundreds of lips, and sought a hiding-place with his help-
> less wife in the house of his father, whose predictions had been too speedily
> fulfilled.
>
> —T. S. Arthur, "Shattered by the First Storm," *Godey's Lady's Book* (1858)

In addition to taming the credit system, antebellum bankruptcy reformers hoped to
give insolvent debtors a second chance. With unpayable obligations hanging over
their heads, the reformers argued, American debtors faced bleak futures. The absence of a uniform bankruptcy law consigned insolvent debtors to sleepless nights
and anxiety-filled days. It further placed unacceptable burdens on the American
economy, as the "mental and physical energies" of failed proprietors lay dormant,
while their communities bore the onus of supporting them and their families.[1]

In discussing the plight of bankrupts, commercial moralists and their political
allies emulated the rhetorical strategies of most antebellum reform movements. Like
temperance activists, evangelical Christians, early feminists, representatives of the
nascent labor movement, and abolitionists, bankruptcy reformers turned again and
again to the conceptual opposition of slavery and freedom. The obligations owed
by insolvent debtors, according to the proponents of a national bankruptcy system,
were shackles as oppressive as those fastened around the limbs of America's black

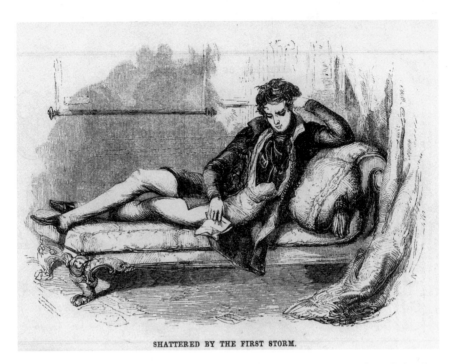

SHATTERED BY THE FIRST STORM.

FAILURE'S POTENTIALLY TRAUMATIC IMPACT. This lithograph of one of T. S. Arthur's fictional characters conveys the despondency that often followed insolvency (*Godey's Lady's Book* [1858], Sterling Library, Yale University).

slaves. In the language of one pamphlet writer, an individual who could not make good on his debts conveyed "his privileges as a freeman." With creditors continually looking to pounce on any form of property earned by the unfortunate debtor, he faced the equivalent of "perpetual bondage," since his creditors, rather than he and his family, retained legal claims on all "the products of [his] future efforts."[2]

During congressional debates on bankruptcy legislation, some politicians went so far as to suggest that insolvent debtors confronted hardships that surpassed those endured by chattel slaves. According to Representative James Roosevelt, a New York Democrat who supported legislative relief for bankrupts, the cruelties associated with plantation slavery paled in comparison to "the bondage of the mind and the heart." No matter how deplorable "the physical chains and shackles" on southern farms and plantations, these devices did less damage than the "chains of the soul" that insolvency draped around its victims. Slaves, Roosevelt continued, might still experience the "joys of freedom" in spite of their myriad disabilities, so long as they kept their "spirit . . . free." White bankrupts, by contrast, possessed all sorts of technical freedom. Yet their minds remained "slave[s] . . . to debt" and the unceasing worries caused by pecuniary embarrassment.[3]

Such assessments were obviously fatuous. In the nineteenth-century United States, bankruptcy did not transform individuals into systematically dishonored human chattels, bound by law to provide hard labor without compensation, vulnerable to the harshest physical coercion and to sale at a moment's notice. When southern slaveowners failed, their slaves went onto the auction block, not they or their children. Indeed, legal actions for debt may have accounted for as many as one-half of all antebellum slave sales. Antebellum bankrupts, by contrast, often managed to negotiate their way into legal releases from their obligations in return for payments of pennies on the dollar.[4]

Characterization of insolvency as a type of slavery nonetheless came readily to antebellum politicians and social commentators. Well versed in the Old Testament, these individuals knew that unpaid debts in the ancient world often led to enslavement. Steeped in the language and premises of republicanism, they also inherited intense fears of economic dependence, viewing it as a formidable barrier to autonomous evaluation of public matters or manly participation in public debate. To be overwhelmed by debt meant, at a minimum, to lose one's capacity for self-direction and become dependent on the indulgence of others. In the early 1840s, it further meant imprisonment for some Americans, as several states had not yet abolished debtors' prisons.[5]

While bondage served as the dominant motif for descriptions of antebellum bankrupts in the absence of a bankruptcy law, the concept of emancipation supplied commercial moralists with a vision of how the lives of insolvent Americans would be transformed by the passage of such legislation. A national bankruptcy system would put an end to the ability of "heartless creditors" to "imprison a man's energies." Bankruptcy discharges would, in the words of one Georgia congressman, "redeem the enthralled, . . . strike off the fetters of servitude, and restore the bondsman to the life and light of liberty." Once possessed of a bankruptcy discharge, reformers confidently intoned, insolvents would no longer lay "prostrate" and "paralyzed." Instead they would return to the world of commerce, unhindered by the weight of past debts and hopeful of regaining lost property and social position.[6]

In a purely legal sense, the 1841 Bankruptcy Act achieved the goals set out by commercial moralists and opportunistic Whig politicians. Certificates granted under the act, unless successfully impeached on the grounds of fraud, freed petitioners from the legal obligation to pay outstanding claims against them. The Whig bankruptcy statute literally created new legal persons. In so doing, this legislation reflected one of the leading aims of antebellum political economy—to "release the economic energies" of America's prototypical citizens, adult white males. Taking its place alongside other legislative initiatives and legal doctrines that explicitly sought to expand entrepreneurial opportunities, such as the embrace of general incorporation statutes and the curbing of vested property rights, especially in the context of transportation improvements, the 1841 Bankruptcy Law removed major impediments to enterprise for tens of thousands of overwhelmed debtors.[7]

Americans who negotiated the bankruptcy process frequently viewed it in this light, characterizing discharges as documents of personal liberation. After successfully "passing through the fiery trial of bankruptcy," one upstate New York bankrupt confidently brushed aside the significance of his losses from ill-judged endorsements and a disastrous fire, which amounted to "upwards of $100,000, the earnings of 17 years." To this Lockport miller, such misfortune merited only the comment, "[N]o matter—I can try again." Freed from debt, he declared that his "health and spirits are as good as new." Charlemagne Tower, the Oneida County distiller whose bankruptcy led him to return to the legal profession, offered analogous sentiments upon receiving a bankruptcy certificate. After beating off legal challenges by his creditors, Tower crowed that he was "free as air." No longer confined by the grasping efforts of creditors, Tower proudly maintained that he had "come out at last, as I always knew I should, triumphant as a Phoenix bird."[8] Such expressions of deliverance would not likely have emanated from the pens of contemporaneous Russian bankrupts, who were regularly banished to Siberia, nor those of failed Chinese businessmen, who often faced disgrace and severe physical punishment, nor of absconding German merchants, whose insolvencies were commemorated with mock public funerals.[9]

Attainment of legal releases, of course, did not efface all memory of past insolvency. Bankruptcy discharges could not truly "cast the mantle of oblivion" over its recipients, as Senator Garret Wall suggested in an 1840 congressional speech that advocated a legal process of voluntary bankruptcy. Commercial biographies that included chapters of failure did not constitute the most compelling advertisements for future business dealings. As the rise of credit reporting demonstrates, antebellum Americans usually assumed that there was a link between previous financial difficulties and future economic prospects, viewing a history of failure as a reason to think twice before entering into business agreements. As a result, many failed debtors placed a premium on arranging private settlements with creditors, even when they could pursue discharges through public court proceedings. Compromises achieved the same result as bankruptcy discharges—legal releases from obligations to pay past debts—without requiring public airing of failure. One New York City lawyer tried to cash in on this perception, advertising his services in negotiating compositions that would "avoid the . . . publicity of applying to the courts."[10]

An additional measure of bankruptcy's enduring legacy rested in the back pages of the *Morning Courier and New York Enquirer*'s 1842 weekly editions. There readers encountered two lists, lying side by side—one of rates of discount for the nation's bewildering variety of banknotes, including descriptions of counterfeit bills in circulation; and one of bankruptcy applicants under the 1841 act. Prudent

F. A. LOHSE, No. 65 Liberty street, offers for sale
  6 cases French gum elastic-Suspenders, assorted quali-
  4 do Percussion Caps, plain and ribbed and split [ties
  2 do Buffalo Dressing and Twist Combs
  4 do Bone Suspender Buttons and Moulds
  4 do Accordions, plain and semi-tones
Also, a handsome assortment of silk and gum Guards, ivory
and bone Tooth Brushes, Hair Brushes, Hooks and Eyes, gilt
Jewelry, ebony and marble Clocks, bronze Candelabras and
Candlesticks, fancy Soap, gentlemen's Dressing Cases, ladies'
Work Boxes, Mosaicks, silver Knives and Forks, Music Boxes,
3, 4, 6, 8 and 12 tunes, Opera Glasses, Silk Purses, Silver Snuff
Boxes, &c. Many of the above goods are entitled to deben-
ure.   s17

IN BANKRUPTCY

*Names of Applicants throughout the United States for the
Benefit of the Bankrupt Law, other than in the Southern
District of New York*

NORTHERN DISTRICT OF NEW YORK.

To be declared Bankrupt, Feb. 5th—Nelson Rowe, of Ellington;
Daniel Stilson, of Villanova; Caleb Souls, of Charlotte; John H.
Briggs, of Brutus; Wm. Fosmire, of Parma; Artemas W. Whiting,
of Arcadia; Samuel W. Wotkyns, of Rochester; Elias Richard-
son, of Newark; George L. Fisher, of Tioga; George Coryell, of
Nichols; Stephen Covert, of Le Roy; Joseph Allen, of Oxford;
Edward Webb of Lansingburgh; Daniel F. Curtis, of Fort Plain;
Hiram Shuart, of Clarkson; Samuel G. Bartlett, of Sweden; Geo.
W. Worden, of Clarkson; James P. Benedict of Auburn; Jared
T. Benton, of Pultney; Meredith Mallory, of Urbana; Benjamin
Isaacs, of Oswego; Isaac S. Isaacs, of do.; Job Taylor, of Utica;
Isaac N. Eldridge, of Clarendon; Henry Evard, of Amsterdam;
Jacob Klock, of St. Johnsville; Lyman Tobey, of Naples; Robert
Forsyth, of Oswegatchie; James Lane, of Massena; Wm. Martin,
of Edwards; Hiram Delong, of Hammond; Ephraim Whitney, of
Groton; Horatio N. Washbon, of Butternuts, Baldwin Woodruff,
of Pamelia; Chauncey W. Ivens, of Murray; Jacob M. Eldridge,
of Clarendon; Douglas I. Fouquet, of Plattsburg; Henry Good-
child, of Galen; Nathaniel Davis, of do.; Hiram Fisk, of do.; An-
drew Gross, of Root; Thomas H. Locke, of Milo; Cornelius Ash-
ton, of Shelby; Hugh Hubbard, of Batavia; Francis L. Taylor, of
Royalton; Ethan Cotes, of Tinsdale; Cyrus Hunter, of Mentz;
Talbot P. Powers, of Rochester; Horace T. Crofoot, of Mendon;
Sherman Newberry, of Bolton; Wm. M'Cord, of Warrensburgh;
Rensselaer Murdock, of do.; Andrew Robinson, of Chester; John
Darcy, of Johnsburgh; Curtis Gallup, of Athol; Wm. C. West, of
Johnsburgh; Lumau Andrews, of Chester; Levi B. Andrews, of
do.; Charles A. Stevenson, of Chesterfield; David A. Sherman,
of Lockport; Benj. Colegrove, of Jerusalem; Cary Carr, of do.;
Socrates Ayres, of Penn Yan; John Ostrom, Jr. of Tompkins;
Wm. R. Anthony, of Little Falls; Wm. H. Moore, and Saml. W.
D. Moore, of Rochester; Daniel M. Brown, of Franklin; James
H. P. Wagner, of Canajoharie. 13th—John Rowling, Jr. of Man-
lius. 20th—Edward Hall, of Ithaca; Wm. Betts, Jr. of Franklin;
Orson Warner, of Lima; Olney Gould, of Le Roy; Aaron P. Stow-
ers, of Bangor; Edwin Smith, of Whitestown; Benj. F. Burr, of
Stockton; Albert S. Clark, of Burlington; Lucius Thatcher, of
Pembroke; Jeremiah Ruland, of Batavia; Nathan Lyman, of
Rochester; Wm. V. Caswell, of Bainbridge; John P. Wind, of
Camillus; Leonard Olney, of Cato; Wm. E. Stagg, of Geneva;
Robert Lane, of Phelps; George G. Hill, of Rome; John Peck, of
St. Johnsville; Abraham Wessle, of Root; Perse Morgan, of

BANK NOTE TABLE.
Corrected Weekly for the Morning Courier & Enquirer,
By Drew, Robinson & Co. No. 40 Wall street.

New-York Notes.	Dis.	New-Jersey Notes	Dis.
New-York City Notes	par	Rahway, under $10	
Long Island Bank	par	Newark Insurance, un. $5	
Lansingburgh Bank		Farmers' & Mechanics' Bank,	
Dutchess Co. Bank	par	New Brunswick,	
Tanners' Bank, Catskill	par	Princeton Bank	
West Chester Co. Bank	par	Union Bank, Dover	
Poughkeepsie Bank		Paterson Bank	no sale
Commercial Bank, Albany		People's Bank	
Canal Bank	do	Commercial Bank	
Mechanics' & Farmers' Bank		Manuf. B. Belville	no sale
Farmers' Bank, Troy	par	Elizabethtown Bk under $5	
Bank of Troy		Sussex Bank, under $10	
Newburgh Bank	par	Mount Holly Bank	
Catskill Bank	par	Belvidere Bank, under $10	
Hudson River Bank	par	All other current notes	
Ulster County Bank	par	Pennsylvania Notes	
Kingston Bank	par	Bank U. S. & Branches	50
Livingston County Bank		Banks in Philadelphia	
Saratoga County Bank		Banks of Penn Township	
Albany Bank		Bank in Chester Co.	
New York State Bank		Bank in Delaware Co.	
Merchants' & Mechanics B.		Farmers' Bank, Lancaster	
Mohawk Bank		Harrisburgh Bank	9
Orange County Bank		Middletown Bank	8
Utica Bank		Easton Bank	par
Utica Branch Bank		Miner's Bank, Pottsville	9
Ontario Bank		Germantown Bank	
Ontario Branch Bank		Berks Co. B'k Reading	80
Geneva Bank		Northampton Bank	35
Auburn Bank		Lancaster Co. Bank	
Central Bank		Bank of Honesdale	
Chenango Bank		Lumbermen's Bank	
Jefferson County Bank		Monongahela Bank	5
Steuben County Bank		Farmers' & Drover's Bank	12
Rochester Bank		Columbia Bridge Co.	2
Bank of Monroe		Lewiston Bank	22
Bank of Ithaca		Erie Bank	6
Newburgh Branch, Ithaca	par	Farmers' Bank, Bucks Co.	
Highland B. Newburgh	par	York Bank	8
Ogdensburgh Bank		Gettysburgh Bank	8
Lewis Co. Bank		Chambersburgh Bank	8
Bank of Whitehall		Carlisle Bank	8
Wayne County Bank		Bank of Pittsburgh	1
Bank of Geneseo		Reading Bank	2
Lockport Bank		Brownsville Bank	5
Onondaga County Bank		All other current notes	
Otsego County Bank		Relief Notes	12 a 15
Chautauque County Bank		N. Hope Del. Bridge	50
Bank of Salina		Delaware Notes.	
Bank of Rome		Commercial Bk. & Bran	
Bank of Lyons	40	Delaware Bank	
Clinton Co. Bank	40	Farmers' Bk. & Branches	
Commercial Bk, Oswego	35	Bank at Wilmington	
Commercial Bk, Buffalo	26	All other current notes	1
Bank of Buffalo	1	Maryland Notes.	
Connecticut Notes.		Baltimore Banks	
Hartford Banks		Farmers' Bk. & Branches	1
New Haven Banks		Frederick County Bank	3
East Haddam, Windham, and		Hagerstown Bank	1

DISCOUNTING BANKNOTES, DISCOUNTING BANKRUPTS. Business readers of this newspaper found
a register of prevailing currency discounts right next to the latest bankruptcy notices (*Morning
Courier and New York Enquirer*, Feb. 4, 1843, courtesy of the New York State Library, Albany,
N.Y.).

Americans, the newspaper suggested with this juxtaposition, should evaluate potential partners, customers, and suppliers with the same care that they examined
paper currency offered to them in the course of daily trade. In both cases, a suspect
pedigree warranted outright rejection or considerable discount.

Most discharged bankrupts further lacked a crucial prerequisite for business
ventures—capital. As a Georgia newspaper noted in an August 1842 squib, the
answer to the question "Why is a bankrupt's property like a riddle that no one can
solve?" was simply, "because it is given up."[11] Insolvency, whether it led to a private
assignment for the benefit of creditors or a court-mandated liquidation, ostensibly
left bankrupts without property. Bereft of a stake to finance new enterprises and
burdened with the reputation of economic losers, failed debtors faced important
obstacles in rejoining the antebellum business world.

For numerous onetime bankrupts, however, these obstacles were not insurmountable. Antebellum Americans routinely emerged from insolvency to reenter the world of commerce on their own responsibility, sometimes in fields far removed from their earlier endeavors and often far away from the locations in which they had failed. In doing so, they demonstrated notable adaptability to the increasingly protean world of market exchange. Yet not all bankrupts possessed the same chances of regaining the status of proprietorship. Individuals who could count on influential social connections or highly demanded skills enjoyed the greatest likelihood of being able to reestablish an independent place within America's commercial economy.

Bankrupts in Motion

Throughout the nineteenth century, one of the most common American responses to pecuniary embarrassment was to skip town. Sometimes prompted by an attempt to escape the clutches of creditors, especially when debtors could not cajole or compel legal releases from their obligations, this course of action more commonly followed calculations that opportunities would prove greater in places where neighbors and potential business associates would not harbor recollections of failure. The search for anonymity led tens of thousands of bankrupts to move west, seeking their futures in fast-growing rural and urban settlements. This impulse shaped popular culture throughout the first half of the nineteenth century. During the hard times that followed the War of 1812, residents of western Massachusetts began to use the name "Shirkshire Road" to refer to the thoroughfare that traversed the Berkshire region of the state, as countless debtors used the byway to head into upstate New York. Two decades later, the propensity of heavily indebted southerners to leave for Texas became so great that novelists and short-story writers regularly packed characters off to the southwestern republic when they could not meet their financial obligations. The acronym "G.T.T." eventually emerged as a shorthand means of conveying the actions of many insolvent debtors; unable to pay, these individuals had "Gone to Texas."[12]

While myriad American bankrupts attempted to escape their pasts in the West, countless others sought sanctuary within the nation's growing eastern entrepôts. Bankrupts streamed into eastern cities like New York during the "dull times" of the late 1830s and early 1840s. Many of these migrants had failed in the immediate hinterland of the metropolis and so only moved a relatively short distance from nearby market towns or villages.[13] Other bankrupts who sought a discharge in Manhattan or Kings County came from much farther afield. New York City and Brooklyn attracted scores of individuals who had failed in upstate New York, in New England, or in the Middle Atlantic states. Bankrupts also migrated to the seat of American commerce after failing in towns and cities throughout the South and the

Old Northwest. From all over the country, Americans who could not pay their debts moved to New York City and its sister city across the East River.[14] Newspaper notices for bankrupts residing in Boston, Providence, Albany, New York, and Savannah, Georgia, suggest similar migrations to these centers of trade. Most predictably, individuals who failed in the towns of rural New England flocked to Boston and Providence, while insolvents from the Erie Canal corridor and the Hudson River valley moved to Albany, and those from the eastern Georgia countryside headed to Savannah. Each of these commercial hubs, however, also attracted failed debtors from much greater distances, including other regions of the republic.[15]

To a great extent, bankrupts were attracted to eastern cities for the same reasons that led so many other Americans to move there. These urban areas offered myriad economic opportunities in the antebellum years, especially compared to many rural counties or small towns. For people running away from an unsuccessful past, the city possessed yet another advantage—it was a place where enterprising persons might hide from their pasts and reinvent themselves. Meteoric growth during the first half of the nineteenth century rendered America's largest commercial centers far more conducive to the maintenance of anonymity. By the 1830s, these places had ceased to be "walking cities" in which inhabitants were familiar with most streets and a significant proportion of their fellow city-dwellers. Explosive increases in population, tremendous demographic turnover, and rapid physical expansion made American cities into "worlds of strangers," where anonymous crowds dominated public spaces.[16]

The very size of New York City, Boston, or Philadelphia offered protection to individuals with biographies that might not thrill the hearts of would-be employers, creditors, or partners. These cities were home to thousands of businessmen, professionals, artisans, and clerks, many of whom had recently arrived themselves. In such an environment, tracing the past of every potential customer, employee, or agent presented serious difficulties. Business deals frequently turned on the acceptance of appearances rather than detailed knowledge of the person with whom one was dealing. As a result, onetime bankrupts who migrated to a large city often had ample opportunity to recommence business or find promising employment, especially if they had mastered the art of selling themselves.

Antebellum bankruptcy records vividly testify to the frequency of geographic mobility among insolvent proprietors. The documents created by the 1841 Bankruptcy Act teem with references to partners, business associates, and debtors who had failed and moved on to parts known or unknown. These same records offer a rare opportunity to quantify the willingness of financially troubled Americans to pull up stakes. Bankruptcy petitions systematically reveal the migration of applicants either through explicit reference or circumstantial evidence, such as the place where bankrupts faced suits for debt, executed assignments for the benefit of creditors, or went through state insolvency processes. In southern New York, roughly 30 percent of bankruptcy petitioners failed somewhere else before moving to the place where they filed for relief; at least an additional 3 percent moved away from their residence soon after the initiation of bankruptcy proceedings.[17] Elsewhere in America, geographic mobility among bankrupts may have been even more pronounced. According to the federal court clerk in Illinois, over half of the 1,592 individuals who appeared on Illinois's bankruptcy dockets as a result of the 1841 act "were insolvent before they came to the State." In a society where migration was commonplace, bankrupts were especially likely to try their luck in a new locale.[18]

If thousands of antebellum Americans who experienced insolvency took the path of flight, one must not lose sight of the thousands more who eschewed that option. For bankrupts such as James Van Duzer, simple poverty made a move difficult. Van Duzer, an Orange County farmer, petitioned for bankruptcy in January 1843, owing almost $4,600 to local merchants, and possessing only basic clothing. This agriculturalist was unable to complete his bankruptcy petition for over three years because he could not afford the $30 to $50 necessary to pay the costs of processing a discharge. In this instance, limited access to resources diminished a bankrupt's ability to set out for a new home.[19]

Economic constraints, though, probably kept only some bankrupts from leaving the setting of their financial difficulties. Travel costs declined throughout the antebellum decades as improvements in transportation made even long journeys relatively affordable. For less than the amount of money needed to obtain a bankruptcy discharge under the 1841 act, an American could travel from Detroit to Boston or from Louisville to New Orleans. For slightly more than the cost of a discharge, one could get from Decatur, Alabama, all the way to New York City. Shorter trips entailed proportionally less expenditure. An 1843 journey from Memphis to Decatur, which covered roughly 200 miles, cost $12, and a trip from New York City to Albany in the same year required less than $3.[20] These sums were not insignificant; especially in the case of longer journeys, the cost of travel equalled or exceeded the average monthly income of a skilled artisan. Furthermore, once mobile bankrupts arrived at their destinations, they almost certainly faced additional expenses before finding work or reentering the business world. But many failed Americans were able either to rely on financial resources that they had concealed from creditors or to borrow travel funds from relatives or business associates. As a result of these tactics, antebellum bankrupts, like poor Americans generally, displayed remarkable transiency throughout the period.[21]

Age also influenced the decision of antebellum bankrupts to seek a new home or to stick with an old one. In the case of bankrupts such as Joseph Brewster, advanced years militated against a move. For many decades a leading New York City hatter and temperance advocate, Brewster had long made New York City home. Fifty-four years old when he failed in 1841, the hatter was an unlikely candidate for migration. By contrast, younger bankrupts demonstrated a greater willingness to respond to insolvency by moving.[22]

While economic resources and age each played a role in determining whether or not bankrupts remained in the communities where they had endured pecuniary embarrassment, perceptions of opportunity most powerfully shaped this decision. The nation's network of roads, rivers and lakes, canals, and railroads could transport failed debtors away from collective memories of broken contracts and unpaid debts. But geographic mobility frequently meant that such individuals turned their backs on family, friends, and familiar business environments. In weighing these considerations, many bankrupts judged that the benefits of staying close to home, combined with the uncertainties of a new life elsewhere, outweighed the gain that escape from a checkered financial past might offer.

Helping Hands

Whether or not failed debtors in antebellum America sought to improve their opportunities through migration, they had to come to grips with two restraints on future entrepreneurial activity—lost capital and tarnished credit. The latter consequence of insolvency could dog Americans for years. Credit reporters frequently noted ten or even fifteen years after the fact that individuals had previously failed, usually linking this observation to calls for "caution." Even a move across the country did not guarantee escape from general awareness of past financial difficulties, especially for individuals who aspired to return to the nation's marts of trade. Relocation from New York City to St. Louis in 1843, for instance, did not enable Nicolas Berthoud to shake reports of his failure as a merchant before the move. Dependent on commercial relations with a host of eastern businesses, Berthoud had little chance of skirting his prior financial record.[23]

With the right family connections, though, pecuniary embarrassment might compel only a temporary break from independent proprietorship. Marriage and inheritance provided two means of rekindling previously dampened economic ambitions, giving bankrupts such as Charles Ring and Edward and Henry Heyer the oxygen of capital so vital to many business ventures. Some years after failing in New York City as a druggist and receiving a federal bankruptcy discharge, Ring "married a small fortune." This injection of funds enabled him to buy out a retail drug business with cash in the late 1840s. For the Heyers, a funeral rather than wedding nuptials paved the way to a new start. After gaining bankruptcy discharges toward the end of 1842, these two brothers and New York City hardware wholesalers confronted an uncertain future. A matter of months later, however, their father died, leaving his sons a considerable fortune. Had this windfall preceded their bankruptcy application, the money would have gone to the assignee in bankruptcy for distribution to the pair's creditors; since their father's demise occurred after the hardware merchants had become, in a legal sense, new economic men, they were entitled to keep their inheritance. Once again possessed of capital, the Heyers were able to return to their line of business. Family aid to bankrupts who wished to restart a business also took other forms, as relatives frequently took on failed debtors as partners, extended them credit or capital for use in new ventures, or passed along operating businesses.[24]

Assistance from business "friends" similarly enabled some bankrupts to regain their footing as independent businessmen. The experience of Andrew Near and William Teller, who each failed as tanners in different Hudson River towns, suggests the crucial role that a single patron could play in this regard. After their respective failures in the late 1830s, Near and Teller went to work as journeyman tanners in Kingston, employed by A. H. Bruyn. In 1846, Bruyn retired, selling his tannery to the two former bankrupts in return for long-term notes. Without their employer's willingness to extend favorable terms of credit, Near and Teller would have remained journeymen. In other instances, creditors accepted settlement terms that left failed businessmen with sufficient capital to begin modest new ventures.[25]

Hopes for financial support from family members or business associates loomed so large in the calculations of many antebellum bankrupts that they frequently guided their destinations when they chose the path of migration. Within two months of failing as a distiller in the upstate New York village of Waterville, Julius Tower had settled in Albany, where a business associate, the flour merchant Benjamin P. Jones, had offered him board and employment as a clerk, with the "prospect of something better hereafter." Over the course of the next several months, the connection with Jones allowed Julius to "get a little initiated into the business" of New York's capital city.[26] Some insolvent businessmen, like Edward Kellogg, sought refuge in the houses of their parents or in-laws. After faltering as a Binghamton, New York, dry goods dealer and real estate speculator in the wake of the panic of 1837, Kellogg owned little property beyond clothing, farming tools, some livestock, and a library of books. Without other compelling options, Kellogg and his family moved in with his wife's parents in the lower Hudson Valley town of New Canaan. This sort of retreat was sufficiently common in the antebellum Old Southwest that Joseph Baldwin reported large numbers of ruined Virginians "limp[ing] back" to "the old stamping ground" of family homesteads, "with feathers moulted and crestfallen . . . , carrying the returned Californian's fortune of ten thousand dollars—six bits in money, the balance in experience."[27]

On occasion, the attractions of kith and kin could even persuade bankrupts to migrate to the place where most of their creditors resided. Temple Hall, for example, failed as a merchant tailor in New Orleans in 1836, owing most of his debts to suppliers in Newark and New York City. After executing an assignment for the benefit of creditors, Hall continued to ply his trade in New Orleans through 1839, despite the old debts owed to eastern suppliers. Soon thereafter, he left behind the memories that the people of New Orleans had of his pecuniary difficulties; but he traveled to New York City, placing himself where his principal creditors might see him on the street and, more importantly, limit his future prospects. Hall made this move because he was able to obtain employment and board with a relative.[28]

The motives of parents, siblings, and other relatives in extending a helping hand to antebellum bankrupts seems clear enough—family ties dictated the sharing of resources. Financial assistance offered to failed debtors by successful businessmen such as A. H. Bruyn or Benjamin P. Jones, though, had a less obvious rationale. Such patronage reflected more than just idiosyncrasy or unusual faith in a few employees. Merchants and manufacturers in antebellum America recognized the frequency with which business owners failed. Many of them resolved to aid their fellows in the event of bankruptcy, at least in principle. This impulse constituted a class-based scheme of mutual insurance.

William Sullivan, a Boston merchant, made these ideas explicit in an address to the Boston Mercantile Association in 1832. So long as a businessman's failure had resulted from "innocent misfortune," Sullivan argued, other members of the business class should "declare to the world, that an unfortunate man has not forfeited his rank." Rather than forsaking the bankrupt, successful proprietors should "pour a precious balm on his wounded spirit, and carry sympathy and consolation to the innocent hearts of the wife and of the children, who must be partners in his sorrows." Even more importantly, solvent businessmen should extend at least a moderate sum of capital to a bankrupt, so as to "lay . . . a new foundation for his fortunes." Such assistance, Sullivan stressed, was not only just and charitable; it also constituted a sensible means of limiting the "hazards necessarily involved in commercial life." No matter how well-off a businessman might be, reverses were common enough to justify a communal spirit of liberality to the unfortunate. The prosperous merchants or manufacturers of today might themselves require assistance tomorrow, or next year.[29]

Sullivan's distinction between upright and shady bankrupts was central to the worldview of the commercial moralists. Echoing a transatlantic concept of brotherhood created by shared exposure to risk that dated back to eighteenth-century British commercial commentary, antebellum spokespersons for mercantile rectitude uniformly counseled charity toward proprietors who failed honestly and disdain for those who had not. On occasion, commercial moralists even insisted that "when a man fails honestly and can demonstrate that fact to his creditors, there is an almost universal disposition in the latter rather to support than oppress him." In such a cultural climate, honorable commercial conduct was crucial not only because justice and God demanded it, but also because such behavior, or at least the reputation for such behavior, made assistance far more likely in the event of bankruptcy.[30]

Credit reporters shared the tendency to differentiate among bankrupts, placing especially great significance on the causes of failures and the manner in which broken proprietors handled insolvency. Individuals who failed as a result of endorsements usually received kinder treatment in credit assessments than businessmen whose bankruptcy resulted from speculation, overtrading, or other forms of mismanagement. By the same token, reporters normally moderated criticism of bankrupts who forthrightly gave up all of their property in the attempt to satisfy the claims of their creditors or who attempted to make good on debts from which they had earned legal releases.[31]

Antebellum bankrupts understood the consequences of a widespread perception that a failure involved suspect financial practices. Several applicants in southern New York sought to preempt criticisms of their previous actions by offering the court unsolicited explanations of their failures. These bankruptcy petitioners invariably sought to portray themselves as unfortunate or misguided, but scrupulously honest. One particularly trenchant effort at self-indemnification came from Granville Sharp Pattison, a physician who lost over $40,000 during the 1830s as a result of stock and real estate speculations in Philadelphia. Pattison explained that his misfortunes were the result of being "entirely unacquainted with business" and "excited by the spirit of speculation," which led him to believe the grand promises of brokers and land agents from whom he bought stock and real estate. He further claimed that he could have avoided his failure, since he had sold his various properties to "English capitalists" at a handsome profit, only to find out later that the real estate was essentially worthless. Unwilling to maintain his own solvency at the expense of the people to whom he had sold the valueless land, Pattison unilaterally "released . . . the English purchasers from their obligations." He did so because he preferred "to be a Bankrupt in fortune than that the shadow of a suspicion should rest upon the uprightness and rectitude of his character."[32]

Similarly, bankrupts who faced unflattering public characterizations of their failures generally did not hesitate to defend their mercantile reputations. The most common means of rejoinder were through the pens of friendly newspaper editors, privately published pamphlets, or libel suits. Failed debtors recognized all too well that attacks on their past commercial behavior impaired their ability to attract backing for new ventures.[33]

Points of Reentry

However crucial financial support from relatives or patrons proved for scores of discharged bankrupts, it was not an indispensable prerequisite for individuals who wished to reclaim their place as proprietors. Several niches within the antebellum marketplace beckoned to failed Americans because of their limited barriers to entry and minimal initial capital requirements. In some cases, individuals who had experienced insolvency continued to possess skills or talents in short supply, and thus readily attracted new credit despite their previous commercial predicaments. Finally, despite the considerable dangers associated with a tainted commercial reputation, numerous antebellum bankrupts managed to resume entrepreneurial activity by engaging in deceptive financial or commercial practices, including outright fraud.

For bankrupts who possessed professional training, continued pursuit of their craft often posed few problems. So long as these individuals could attract clients, their past misfortunes did not stand in the way of transacting business. Many professionals who had failed in the 1830s or early 1840s as the result of speculation in land and stocks never stopped practicing their occupation. Others who possessed a professional pedigree but who failed in commerce forsook the world of trade for the less risky avenues of tending the sick or advising those in need of legal advice. Martin K. Bridges, for example, found his way into financial difficulties as a Brooklyn lumber merchant; he walked away from the southern New York bankruptcy court as a dentist. Edmund Porter underwent a similar occupational transformation. Porter failed in 1839 as a furniture dealer. By the time he received his bankruptcy discharge, he was earning a living as a lawyer.[34]

The nature of the antebellum economy, moreover, provided several openings to individuals with business sense and contacts, but no real stake on which to base a substantial operation. Former bankrupts who were willing to peddle or operate small retail stands, beginning with very small stocks, could usually find a merchant who would sell them goods on credit, especially if they accepted stringent terms. Other onetime bankrupts attracted more substantial amounts of credit into new commercial endeavors because they could sweet-talk people into investing in their schemes. William F. Voorhies exemplified this kind of operator. Voorhies failed in 1837 as the result of speculation in "wild lands, or anything else that might have a show of value." Sometime in the mid-1840s, this New York City operator convinced two men with capital that he was rich and well versed in the dry goods trade. Their resources gave Voorhies the means to become a dry goods jobber.[35]

Various financial services also provided entrepreneurial opportunities for onetime bankrupts. Over the course of the antebellum decades, auction houses and brokerage firms increasingly avoided the buying and selling of goods on their own accounts. Auction houses merely sold goods or property deposited with them and took a commission; brokers simply found buyers for sellers, or vice versa, taking a fee in return. Thus many auction houses and brokers required essentially no capital and incurred only minimal overhead, such as office rent and the placing of newspaper advertisements. Success in these kinds of endeavors required business intelligence, salesmanship, and reputation for good service, not reserves of capital or records of long-standing solvency. Many antebellum bankrupts recognized the opening that auctioneering or brokerage offered them. In New York City, dozens of applicants under the 1841 act turned to these activities as a way to maintain self-employment.[36]

Within the world of antebellum handicrafts and manufacturing, a modicum of knowledge enabled at least some artisans and small-scale manufacturers to shake off the debilitating impact of bankruptcy and retain the status of business ownership. The provisions of the 1841 act protected a workman's tools from the bankruptcy assignee, like the debtor-exemption laws of many states. With the necessary tools and the ability to attract customers, bankrupt artisans or manufacturers might also lure enough credit to resume a small-scale operation, especially in one of the trades increasingly characterized by subcontracting.[37]

John Stevens, a New York City match manufacturer, demonstrated such resilience. Conflicts over patent rights and ill-fated accommodation loans to business associates led to Stevens's failure in 1841 and his bankruptcy application the following year. In accordance with the bankruptcy statute, he surrendered all his property. By October 1842, however, he had convinced a machinist to build him a press, dipping machines, splint machines, a rack, a scoring machine, and a cutting machine—everything necessary for match production. These machines cost $190; the machinist agreed to receive payment after Stevens had begun production. The matchmaker then leased a small space for his new manufactory, moved his family into a corner of it in order to save on rent, and rehired the people who had previously worked for him. Soon thereafter he and his employees were once again churning out Locofoco matches.[38] Stevens had extensive knowledge about this business, having pursued it for six years previous to his failure. This background may have persuaded his new supplier that he was a reasonable credit risk.

Technical skills could lead to far grander extensions of credit to proprietors who had gone through the bankruptcy courts, as illustrated by the experience of Richard and Robert Hoe, the acclaimed New York City manufacturers of printing presses and circular saws whose 1842 failure resulted from an insupportable load of bad debts. Insolvency did not diminish the engineering talents and manufacturing experience of these two brothers, nor the willingness of the firm's primary creditor to finance their operations, albeit on the basis of greater security than previously. After the Hoes filed for bankruptcy in December 1842, their factory remained closed for only one week. Ownership of their machinery passed to one of the firm's creditors, who held a mortgage on it. This creditor then extended the concern additional loans so that they could resume production. R. Hoe & Co. regularly developed patentable innovations in manufacturing processes and made the best circular saws and printing presses in the United States. As a result, bankruptcy had essentially no impact on demand for their goods and only limited implications for their ability to arrange credit. A week after the machinists submitted their bankruptcy applications, their clerks were busy filling orders from customers far and wide. When the Hoes' bankruptcy notices appeared in New York City papers, they shared space with large advertisements heralding a reduction in the prices charged by the company for its presses and saws.[39]

In addition to professional education, the willingness to pursue a line of business that required very little capital, or mechanical genius, chicanery provided a route back into the antebellum marketplace. The most common form of duplicity involved the conveyance of assets to wives, other relatives, or friendly creditors on the eve of business suspensions. If failed debtors who pursued this strategy obtained legal releases from their debts, either through private settlements, state insolvency processes, or the short-lived federal bankruptcy system created by the 1841 act, they then took back their property and once again had a capital stake with which to begin anew. Should bankruptcy certificates or private compromises prove not to be available, failed debtors simply continued in business as the agents of their confederates. Alternatively, financially pressed businessmen sometimes suspended debt payments and, concealing the extent of their property, negotiated settlements in which the proportionate disbursements to creditors did not exhaust their secreted assets.

Calculating the frequency of such financial maneuvers is greatly complicated by their illicit nature, but bankruptcy records and R. G. Dun credit assessments suggest that they were by no means rare. Several southern New York applicants under the 1841 Bankruptcy Act initially sought to continue their business operations by assigning property to friendly trustees for the benefit of creditors and then acting as their agents. One Manhattan bankrupt similarly laid the groundwork for a relaunch of a failed boardinghouse by arranging to have a friend buy her furniture at a distraint sale. In later decades, this path to financial resurrection persisted as a stratagem of North American business owners. Studies of nineteenth-century commercial culture in San Francisco, Poughkeepsie, New York, and Hamilton, Ontario, have all found that insolvent proprietors commonly adopted analogous strategies.[40]

Reinvigorating business careers in this fashion, of course, carried great risks, particularly when the property in question exceeded the costs of lawsuits. Property conveyed by failing business owners remained vulnerable to legal attack, even after the receipt of legal releases; and in situations where creditors could not prove illegal transfers of assets, suspicions of such actions significantly hurt later assessments of one of the late firm of Keefe & King, for his discharge and certificate as Bankrupt, Thursday, May 25, 1843, 11 A. M. (fe17 70t)

WILLIAM W. EDWARDS, of Hunter, Greene County, N. Y., Tanner, (and as one of the late firms of S Chichester & Company, and Bradley, Andrews & Company,) for his discharge and certificate as Bankrupt, Thursday, May 25, 1843, 11 A. M. (fe17 70t)

JOSIAH F. JIMMERSON, of the city of New York, Clerk, for his discharge and certificate as Bankrupt, Thursday, May 25, 1843, 11 A. M. (fe20 70t)

WILLIAM HENRY BROWN, for his discharge and certificate as Bankrupt, Thursday, May 25, 1843 11 A. M. (fe20 70t)

AARON SWARTS, of the city of New York, Grocer, for his discharge and certificate as Bankrupt, Thursday, May 25, 1843, 11 A. M. (fe20 70t)

ADDISON REED, of the city of New York, for his discharge and certificate as Bankrupt, Thursday, June 1, 1843, 11 A. M. (fe20 70t)

ORRIN HOFFMAN CROSBY, of the city of New York, for his discharge and certificate as Bankrupt, Thursday, June 1, 1843, 11 A. M. (fe20 70t)

HENRY JOHN SEAMAN, Junior, for his discharge and certificate as Bankrupt, Thursday, June 1, 1843, 11 A. M. (fe20 70t)

WILLIAM NIXON, of the city of New York, Clerk, (late of New Orleans,) for his discharge and certificate as Bankrupt, Thursday, June 1, 1843, 11 A. M. (fe20 70t)

JAMES HOWARD LONGBOTHAM, of the city of Brooklyn, for his discharge and certificate as Bankrupt, Thursday, June 1, 1843, 11 A. M. (fe20 ot)

JOHN B. SNOOK, of the city of New York, Carpenter, (and as one of the late firms of Beer & Snook, and Beer, Snook & Co.,) for his discharge and certificate as Bankrupt, Thursday, June 1, 1843, 11 A. M. (fe20 70t)

DANIEL CRANE, Junior, of the city of New York, Clerk, (and as one of the late firms of Crane, Dickinson & Co. and Peck, Crane & Co.,) for his discharge and certificate as Bankrupt, Thursday, June 1, 1843, 11 A. M. (fe20 70t)

ISAAC H. MEAD, of the city of New York, (and as one of th late firm of Mead & Dempsey,) for his discharge and certificate as Bankrupt, Thursday, June 1, 1843, 11 A. M. (fe20 70t)

HENRY W. SCOTT, of Brooklyn, Kings County, N. Y., Agent, (and as one of the late firm of Brittan & Scott,) for his discharge and certificate as Bankrupt, Thursday, June 1, 1843, 11 A. M. (fe20 70t)

CHARLES BOUTON MERRITT, of Rye, Westchester County, N. Y., Tailor, (and as one of the late firms of Pierson & Merritt,) for his discharge and certificate as Bankrupt, Thursday, May 25, 1843, 11 A. M. (fe20 70t)

EDWARD PURDY, of Rye, Westchester County, N. Y., Clerk for his discharge and certificate as Bankrupt, Thursday, May 25, 1843, 11 A. M. (fe20 70t)

JOHN C. CLARK, of the city of New York, for his discharge and certificate as Bankrupt, Thursday, June 1, 1843, 11 A. M. ...

ROBERT HOE, of the city of New York, Machinist, (and as one of the late firm of R. Hoe & Co. and also as survivor of Sereno Newton and Matthew Smith,) for his discharge and certificate as Bankrupt, Thursday, June 15, 1843, 11 A. M. (mh9 70t)

HORATIO A. CARTER, of the city of New York, Auctioneer (and as one of the late firm of Carter & Co.) for his discharge and certificate as Bankrupt, Thursday, June 15, 1843, 11 A. M. (mh9 70t)

THOMAS WHITE, of the city of New York, Mason, (and as one of the late firm of Kidder & White,) for his discharge and certificate as Bankrupt, Thursday, June 15, 1843, 11 A. M. (mh9 70t)

AUSTIN DAVIS MOORE, of the city of Brooklyn, late Merchant, for his discharge and certificate as Bankrupt, Thursday, June 8, 1843, 11 A. M. (mh9 70t)

JOHN McGREGOR, of Brooklyn, Kings County, P. Y., Merchant, for his discharge and certificate as Bankrupt, Thursday, June 15, 1843, 11 A. M. (mh9 70t)

DAVID TUTHILL, Junior, of Riverhead, Suffolk County, N. Y., late Merchant, for his discharge and certificate as Bankrupt, Thursday, June 15, 1843, 11 A. M. (mh9 70t)

ROBERT DYSON, of the city of New York, for his discharge and certificate as Bankrupt, Thursday, June 15, 1843, 11 A. M. (mh10 70t)

JOHN REID, of the city of New York, Baker, for his discharge and certificate as Bankrupt, Thursday, June 22, 1843, 11 A. M. (mh10 70t)

FREDERICK THOMAS, of the city of New York, for his discharge and certificate as Bankrupt, Thursday, June 22, 1849, 11 A. M. (mh10 70t)

LEWIS HUNTER, of the city of New York, (and as one of the late firms of I. Hunter & Co. and I. Hunter & Son,) for his discharge and certificate as Bankrupt, Thursday, June 22, 1843, 11 A. M. (mh10 70t)

EDWARD N. ROGERS, of the city of New York, late Merchant, (and as one of the late firm of Rogers & Brother,) for his discharge and certificate as Bankrupt, Thursday, June 22, 1843, 11 A. M. (mh10 70t)

SAMUEL C. MOTT, of the city of New York, (and as one of th late firm of Reve C. Hance & Co.) for his discharge and certificate as Bankrupt, Thursday, June 22, 1843 11 A. M. (mh10 70t)

ANDREW H. HOGEB, of the city of Brooklyn, County of Kings, and State of N. Y., Victualler, for his discharge and certificate as Bankrupt, Thursday, June 22, 1843, 11 A. M. (mh10 70t)

LATHROP W. CHAPIN, of Brooklyn, Kings County, New York, for his discharge and certificate as Bankrupt, Thursday, June 22, 1843, 11 A. M. (mh11 70t)

CHARLES H. RING, of the city of New York, Druggist, for his discharge and certificate as Bankrupt, Thursday, June 22, 1843, 11 A. M. (mh11 70t)

WILLIAM E. HYATT, of the city of New York, Butcher, for his discharge and certificate as Bankrupt, Thursday, June 22, 1843 ...

creditworthiness.[41] In the eyes of those Americans who embraced such tactics, however, such costs were offset by their continued ability to conduct independent business ventures.

Thus for many antebellum bankrupts, failure did not foreclose a return to proprietorship. Capital and credit might come from relatives, patrons, or friends; bankrupts might be able to convince potential investors or suppliers that their talents justified new ventures; or cloaked transfers of property might enable failed proprietors to continue conducting business under their own names or through commercial fronts. Alternatively, bankrupts might pursue a vocation that did not require much capital at the start, nor reliance on credit once the business was in operation.

Even in the absence of a federal bankruptcy statute or a state insolvency law, broken businessmen frequently found a way to reestablish independent enterprises. Throughout the antebellum decades, failed Americans arranged compromises with their creditors, paying a percentage of what they owed in exchange for legal releases from remaining obligations. Other bankrupts simply ran away from their debts. After such actions, American merchants and artisans were free to pursue the same kinds of strategies as individuals who possessed certificates of discharge from a bankruptcy or insolvency court.

The ability of these Americans to resume entrepreneurial pursuits is nowhere better exemplified than through the commercial vicissitudes of Edgar Jenkins. After failing as a New Orleans merchant in 1832, Jenkins migrated to New York City, set up shop as an auctioneer and real estate speculator, and sustained a second bankruptcy in the midst of the "general prostration of business" that followed the panic of 1837. Presumably undaunted by this latest financial collapse, he left New York City for Buffalo, spending the next two years taking part in the Lake Erie fish trade. Jenkins did not fail outright in Buffalo, but he did not prosper sufficiently to stay in western New York. By the spring of 1840, he had moved to Fort Gratiot, Michigan, where, along with a partner, he operated a steam sawmill and ran a store frequented by local soldiers. This venture fared little better than his previous ones. In mid-1842, the peripatetic businessman returned to New York City and recommenced the business of auctioneering. A few months later, he petitioned for bank-

Opposite: AN EXPEDITIOUS SOMERSET. For bankrupts with financial backers who retained confidence in their future prospects, like Robert Hoe, insolvency might mean only a brief hiatus from independent proprietorship. This newspaper page carried both Hoe's bankruptcy notice and an advertisement from his already reorganized firm (*Morning Courier and New York Enquirer*, May 5, 1843, courtesy of the New York State Library, Albany, N.Y.).

ruptcy, successfully wiping off debts created by four businesses in three different states. Although few nineteenth-century insolvents could match Jenkins's record of failure, geographic mobility, and entrepreneurial rebirth, several dozen southern New York bankruptcy applicants had managed to fail on more than one occasion.[42]

Clearly, then, thousands of antebellum American bankrupts realized the aspiration of Lyman Spalding and found a way to "try again." The Swedish traveler Frederika Bremer noted as much during her 1850 visit to the United States. Reflecting on the great faith that innumerable "Yankees" had in themselves, Bremer observed that if a business owner failed, "he immediately gets up again and says, 'No matter!' If he is unsuccessful he says 'Go Ahead' and he begins over again, undertaking something else until he succeeds."[43] But did "trying again" ineluctably, or even usually, lead to success? For an answer to that question, one must follow the careers of former bankrupts beyond the point at which they found a route back into the fray of the antebellum world of commerce.

Chapter 7

Return to Proprietorship

Bankruptcy and repudiation are the springboards from which
much of our civilization vaults and turns its somersets.

—Henry David Thoreau, *Walden* (1854)

On July 19, 1845, fire swept through Manhattan's commercial district, destroying dozens of buildings and warehouses. A mere three weeks later, construction crews were already raising new stores on the ashes of the blaze. This burst of energy prompted Philip Hone, elder spokesman of the city's mercantile elite, to reflect on the recuperative powers of his country's men of commerce. "Throw down our merchants ever so flat," Hone remarked in his diary, "[and] they roll over once and spring to their feet again. Knock the stairs out from under them, and they will make a ladder of the fragments, and remount." To Hone, as to Frederika Bremer, a defining characteristic of American businessmen was their resilience, their ability to overcome financial ruin and once again scale the heights of the marketplace.[1]

Hone's comment encapsulates an important characteristic of the mid-nineteenth-century American economy. Businessmen of that era often established thriving enterprises after absorbing the jolt of insolvency. The most well known emulators of Hone's ladder climbers include Roland H. Macy and P. T. Barnum. For fifteen years in the 1840s and 1850s, Macy pursued a series of unsuccessful mercantile ventures in Massachusetts, California, and Wisconsin. At least one of these enterprises ended in outright insolvency, as he eventually compromised with the creditors of a Massachusetts dry goods establishment for twenty-five cents on the dollar. This setback remained a blot on his credit reports for over a decade, but did not prevent him from founding one of New York City's leading department stores or, in the process, helping to reconstruct the contours of urban retailing in the United States. Barnum's failure in 1855, the result of endorsements for a heavily indebted clock manufacturing company in his hometown of Bridgeport, Connecticut, consumed his attention for several years. But once protracted negotiations led to settlements with most creditors, he resumed his leading role in the marketing of American entertainment. By the early 1860s, he had attained a dramatic return to profitability as the reestablished owner of the American Museum in New York City and as a property developer in Bridgeport, laying the economic foundation for his later success with traveling circuses.[2]

Less spectacular reversals of fortune recur throughout the ledgers of credit reports compiled by R. G. Dun & Company. Of 108 southern New York applicants for relief under the 1841 Bankruptcy Act whose later enterprises attracted the attention of Dun credit reporters, over two-fifths eventually prospered, maintaining profitable concerns and accumulating significant assets, often estimated to exceed $25,000, and in 16 instances, $75,000. These bankrupts nurtured lucrative businesses in fields as various as tanning, the manufacturing of printing presses and hats, auctioneering, brokerage, land and stock speculation, and dealing in dry goods, coal, and flour.[3]

At the same time, Philip Hone's observation disregarded the regularity with which failure was followed by years of economic difficulties or additional bouts with hopeless indebtedness. Success in finding new partners, uncovering new sources of credit, or embracing economic niches that required little capital by no means guaranteed that onetime insolvents would eventually "remount the ladder" of commercial prosperity. Among the sample of southern New York bankrupts whose later business ventures received evaluations from R. G. Dun, roughly one in six struggled throughout their later careers to maintain solvency, at no point gaining more than the most guarded credit assessments or amassing much of any wealth. Just under two in five careened once more into financial disaster and either ended their entrepreneurial pursuits as bankrupts or managed to refloat businesses yet again, but without establishing profitable concerns. Failure, like success, came in many guises. Onetime bankrupts failed in all sorts of enterprises, from mercantile ventures in liquor and hardware, to textile manufacturing, to speculation in real estate and corporate stock. As in the period before the adoption of the 1841 Bankruptcy Act, the decades after it demonstrated that Americans were fully capable of suffering pecuniary embarrassment on more than one occasion.[4]

Business ventures in Philip Hone's America, then, frequently took entrepreneurs on an oscillating financial journey, alternatively raising up fortunes and tearing them down. Some bankrupts managed to rise from the financial ashes to notably high positions on America's economic ladder; others made such a recovery only to fall once again, or never ascended more than a rung or two. These findings help to explain the pervasive mid-nineteenth-century characterizations of America as a land of substantial social flux, a place in which, in Alexis de Tocqueville's words, "it is not uncommon for the same man in the course of his life to rise and sink again through all the grades that lead from opulence to poverty."[5] Despite considerable financial stability among the wealthiest inhabitants of urban antebellum America— those elites tended to come from wealthy families and to maintain their wealth over time—proprietors who did not count among the most affluent city dwellers experienced substantial economic volatility. Even if the richest American families largely preserved their hefty portfolios of stock and real estate, it simply was not rare for antebellum merchants, artisans, or manufacturers to win and lose considerable financial stakes over the course of their lives, sometimes on more than one occasion.[6]

The variability of outcomes among former bankrupts who reestablished themselves as business owners calls out for explanation. As with the failures that brought so many Americans into the nation's bankruptcy courts during 1842 and 1843, the later economic fates of proprietors who populated the lists of bankrupts in those years turned both on the structure of nineteenth-century capitalism and on patterns of individual agency. The business cycle, shifting trends in manufacturing and marketing, and the resulting pressures of competition all played their part, but so too did reservoirs of mercantile or technical acumen, the varying lessons that former bankrupts drew from their respective financial collapses, and the degree of assistance upon which they could draw from relatives or business associates.

Cyclical Rhythms and Structural Faults

In the decades after the panics of 1837 and 1839 drove thousands of businesses to the wall, cyclical economic fluctuations continued to shape the fortunes of once-ruined business owners. Like most of their compatriots, former bankrupts benefited from flush times in mid-nineteenth-century America. In similar fashion, they felt the pinch when economic activity dulled.

Several onetime bankrupts who became wealthy did so by taking advantage of opportunities created by economic booms. Francis Amidon serves as a case in point. A New York City hatter, Amidon struggled along for almost two decades after receiving his bankruptcy discharge, keeping his concern afloat, but not making much in the way of profits. During the Civil War, however, Amidon's business mushroomed along with the general northern economy. Success in the war years allowed the hatter to expand, opening a branch of his business in Chicago. By 1869, he was reputedly worth $150,000.[7]

As the heady days of vibrant economic growth carried some former insolvents to an easy retirement, panics and depressions left others facing the all-too-familiar demands of insistent creditors. Among the ranks of onetime southern New York bankrupts who returned to the business world on their own account, postdischarge failures clustered around periods of financial crisis. Sharp economic downturns in 1854, 1857, 1861, and 1873 brought bankruptcy to many Americans for the second or even third time.

Alongside the pressures of the business cycle, numerous onetime insolvents

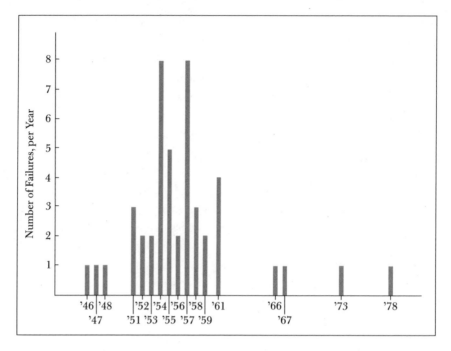

FIGURE 1. Timing of Later Failures by a Group of Individuals Discharged under the 1841 Bankruptcy Act in Southern New York, 1846–1878 (N = 43). In the mid-nineteenth century, postbankruptcy failures tended to coincide with economywide financial crisis.

continued to face daunting competition in their chosen field of endeavor. Artisans, small-scale manufacturers, and petty retailers often faced especially difficult market conditions. The same low start-up costs that enabled them to regain their footing as independent proprietors attracted plentiful competitors. As a result, these entrepreneurs encountered both constraints on prices and strong pressure to provide generous credit terms to customers.

William Kehlbeck's travails illustrate the exacting economic environment confronting many petty producers who hoped to overcome past failures. Once in possession of a federal bankruptcy discharge, Kehlbeck returned to his trade as a Brooklyn boot- and shoemaker, spending the next thirty years at "work on the bench." Over that period, credit reporters repeatedly noted that this German artisan was a skilled craftsman who pursued a relatively safe line of business. He only made custom footwear and did repair work, so his requirements of working capital were far lower than shoe manufacturers who turned out ready-made products for a mass market, especially after the industry began to mechanize in the 1860s. In addition, Kehlbeck did "g[oo]d work" and boasted a reputation for being "extremely honest." Despite these advantages, he faced chronic problems with cash flow. Lacking sufficient capital reserves, he constantly found himself struggling to

SUCCESSFUL FORMER BANK-
RUPT: Richard M. Hoe,
(*National Cyclopedia of
American Biography*, Lilly
Library, Duke University).

obtain payments from his customers in time to meet his obligations to suppliers. A
lifetime's toil was insufficient to get clear of financial difficulties, which plagued the
shoemaker from the 1840s through the early 1870s. Without enough working capital, even highly skilled craftsmen remained prone to liquidity problems after they
relaunched business careers in the wake of initial failures. Similar vulnerability
beset discharged bankrupts who sought to reestablish themselves in highly competitive areas of retail trade, such as grocery or liquor dealing.[8]

By contrast, several onetime insolvents prospered in part by developing specialized economic niches, often made possible by comparatively rare technical
skills. The business careers of Richard and Robert Hoe typified this pattern. After
attracting sufficient credit extensions to resume their operations in the fall of 1842,
these manufacturers of peerless circular saws and printing presses continued to sell
their wares aggressively throughout North America. As general economic conditions improved, so did both the firm's orders and its collection rates. By the
mid-1850s, the Hoes once again owned their factory and machinery; twenty years
later, the two brothers were wealthy.[9]

The business cycle and the degree of competition within given economic sectors, however, do not exhaustively account for the relative successes of some former
bankrupts and the relative failures of others. Not all profitable ventures by these
individuals occurred in boom times, and not every failure took place during a
depression. By the same token, neither economic specialization nor undoubted
commercial or technological acumen guaranteed individual prosperity; nor did

dogged commitment to artisanal modes of production or to especially competitive markets make renewed defaults inevitable.[10] A full accounting of the return to proprietorship requires closer attention to entrepreneurial attitudes, habits, and decision making, as well as to the nature of commercial supports provided by kith and kin.

Bankruptcy as a Mercantile School

The teachings of the commercial moralists point the way toward one set of personal traits that contributed to prosperity after failure. In sermons, lectures, and particularly fiction, the moralists portrayed financial ruin as an invaluable test of character. Some bankrupts would only "become disheartened by such reverses, . . . spend[ing] the remaining portion of their lives as shiftless drones and wandering loafers." Others would sink into "uncontrolled passion," seeking to "forget their sorrows in the inspiration of the wine cup."[11] But for many bankrupts, moralists consistently predicted, pecuniary embarrassments would teach vital lessons that would pave the way for later success.

Before actually enduring the trials of bankruptcy, commercial moralists reasoned, many Americans closed their ears to advice about the need for a cautious approach to the changeable nineteenth-century marketplace. Eager to attain prosperity as independent proprietors, they plunged headlong into business, all too often ending up well beyond their depths. The experience of being dragged down by unpayable debts made Americans more receptive to warnings about the dangers of extravagant consumption, speculation, or overtrading. After a failure or two in the business world, the moralists predicted, individuals were much more likely to adopt prudent mercantile habits and a patient attitude toward the accumulation of wealth.

This viewpoint most commonly received expression in the form of fictional stories. Throughout the 1840s and 1850s, writers such as T. S. Arthur and Sarah Hale penned tales about bankruptcies that reformed the habits of businessmen and their families, with wondrous results for later commercial performance. Most of these stories have remarkably similar plots. Unsatisfied with the earnings and social status of an employee, a young man rushes into the business world with limited experience and capital, but a hankering for riches and social standing. Initially, the venture seems to go well and the protagonist's wife happily spends money on jewelry, fancy furnishings, and a larger house. Within a few years, though, the debts owed by the young man's business overwhelm his assets. Failure destroys the confident visions of a bountiful future, and the stylish possessions are taken by the sheriff or the bankruptcy assignee. At this moment of crisis, the bankrupt teeters on the brink of despair. But with the emotional support of his wife, who pledges to give up her finery and to economize, the young man resolves to face the world with newfound determination. Some years later, a new business opportunity beckons, and the former bankrupt, wiser for his past mistakes, pursues the second enterprise far more prudently and with substantial success. Looking back on his early failure, the older man reflects on both the follies of youth and the crucial insights provided by the experience of bankruptcy. One of T. S. Arthur's characters offers a typical moral, declaring that his initial "reverses were blessings in disguise. They were sent as correctors of evil."[12]

Whether or not failed antebellum proprietors or their wives read these fictional tales, some applicants under the 1841 Bankruptcy Act acted as if they had internalized their message. These individuals responded to insolvency by quelling the urge to become rich quickly. They adopted far more cautious approaches to business, seeking to constrain risk at the cost of forgoing potential profits. In several instances, such conservative business practices laid the foundation for considerable fortunes.

Most commonly, former bankrupts who adopted a less chancy mode of operation tried to escape from the uncertainties associated with entanglement in complex webs of credit. Buying and selling on credit, as so many bankrupts discovered in the late 1830s and early 1840s, exposed one to all kinds of commercial misfortunes—general economic downturns, declines in particular markets, and the inability or unwillingness of debtors to meet their obligations, to name but a few. If one had a sufficient reserve of capital, the risks posed by the credit system lessened; but few antebellum bankrupts were able to resume independent business with a large capital stake.

Former bankrupts who lacked reserves of capital and who wished to reduce their vulnerability to the vicissitudes of trade usually sought to follow the impulse articulated by a failing Mississippi merchant in April 1839. "I am getting tiered [*sic*] of this credit system," the Mississippian noted in his diary, "and I think I shall change my plan of doing business—neither credit nor be credited."[13] For many onetime bankrupts who continued to buy and sell goods, such a resolve meant that customers would no longer be able to transact business on a store account or, in the case of wholesalers, through promissory notes or book debts. Instead, sales would be predicated on immediate payment in cash. Preference for cash modified buying practices as well, leading these businessmen to purchase their goods outright or to ask only very short credit terms, such as one or two months, of their suppliers.

Other previously insolvent businessmen who adopted a conservative commercial philosophy turned away from trade altogether. Instead of concentrating on the distribution of goods, these individuals offered commercial services, like auctioneering, brokerage, or storage, or pursued a career such as schoolteaching or writing.

Such businesses often did not depend on significant extensions of credit, especially if proprietors were able to pay for advertisements, rent, and other overhead costs with cash.

Commercial ventures of this ilk minimized risk. Proprietors of such businesses might not prosper, but they were unlikely to find themselves inundated with unpayable debts. At the same time, businesses founded on cash or on the provision of services did not present easy roads to wealth and riches. Retailers who rejected credit sales often restricted the amount of merchandise they could move and thus limited potential profits. Selling someone else's goods for a commission, introducing landlords to tenants for a fee, or running an academy for young women similarly did not present anything like the opportunities for gain in credit-based mercantile operations.

Over a sufficiently long period, though, cautious business practices could lead to substantial wealth. The patient enterprise of bankrupts such as Frederick J. Conant and Joseph H. Lester might have served as models for the commercial moralists. Conant's 1842 failure as a clothing merchant, which resulted from an accumulation of bad debts and protested discounts, shaped his approach to business for the next quarter century. Sometime in the mid-1840s, he formed a partnership with Jesse N. Bolles, whose father provided the capital for the firm to begin its operations. After reentering the clothing trade, Conant scrupulously limited his financial exposure, ensuring that he had a sufficient fund of working capital. Although the new business did not eschew credit entirely, the two partners took care to limit the annual amount of their business to twice the value of their capital. Wherever possible, they transacted business in cash. These policies reflected the former bankrupt's determination "to go along safely," and they ensured an excellent reputation for paying debts. From the late 1840s through the Civil War, Conant & Bolles received laudatory evaluations from credit reporters, who approvingly noted that the firm did "a sm[all] bus[iness] & this is what makes them so secure." Prudence also eventually led to remarkable profits. By the end of the Civil War, during which Conant & Bolles garnered several war contracts, R. G. Dun & Co. valued the business at $150,000.[14]

Joseph Lester adopted an even more cautious approach to the nineteenth-century marketplace. Lester had failed twice before petitioning for bankruptcy under the provisions of the 1841 act—in 1834, as a merchant in Norwich, Connecticut, and in 1840, as a tallow chandler in Buffalo. By the early 1850s, this expert in failure had found an economic niche that almost completely insulated him from the credit system. Along with four other men, including another former bankrupt, Lester ran a business that inspected and stored pot and pearl ash for New York City dealers in these commodities. The venture required minimal overhead, chiefly consisting of rent and wages for cartmen; it also involved no extension of credit, as the group of ash inspectors demanded cash payments for their services. For the next twenty-eight years, the firm maintained the same basic structure, skirting any reliance on credit and providing steady if unspectacular returns. By 1871, two decades as an inspector had allowed Joseph Lester to accumulate assets valued at $15,000. Another decade brought continued good business and increasingly strong credit ratings.[15]

For men like Frederick Conant and Joseph Lester, encounters with bankruptcy led to successful redirection of entrepreneurial endeavors. Having learned the bitter consequences of transacting more business than warranted by one's capital, they trimmed their mercantile sails and abandoned the pursuit of quick riches. Over the years, patience and prudence paid them good dividends.[16]

The Lure of Riches

Commercial moralists were not the only Americans who offered predictions about the impact of a bankruptcy law on the later behavior of bankrupts. Political opponents of the 1841 act prophesied that a system of voluntary bankruptcy would unleash the worst kind of scheming from a dangerous class of sharpsters. These critics feared that an easy route to legal discharges would hardly chasten bankrupts or tame speculative impulses. Instead, once provided with a means to wipe off obligations created by reckless ventures of the past, "gamblers" of every description would infer that they might expect future relief as well. Freed from their contractual obligations, the practitioners of "rascality and knavery" would once again swoop down "upon society in droves and swarms like the locusts of Egypt." As with the pests who plagued the ancient world, America's roguish bankrupts would do great damage, "destroying and eating up the substance of all honest men."[17]

The view that a bankruptcy discharge would encourage some recipients to return to risky enterprises, like the opposite faith that a legal release would tame commercial practices, accurately foretold the later behavior of some bankrupts. Grandiose visions by no means perished with every antebellum failure. For a number of bankrupts, the experience of insolvency constituted merely a temporary setback, not a warning to adopt more modest goals. Rather than turning to the cautious strategies advocated by the commercial moralists, these individuals continued to harbor dreams of riches, which they intended to attain through aggressive pursuit of whatever alluring ventures presented themselves.

Real estate development and stock deals particularly occupied speculatively inclined former bankrupts, though wholesale businesses, commodity markets, lottery policies, and mining ventures also attracted attention as potential paths to new wealth. The postbankruptcy activities of Samuel Throckmorton typified the willingness to pursue such strategies in the hope of overturning previous misfortunes. A New York City dry goods merchant in the 1830s, Throckmorton failed as a result of losses from real estate purchases. Along with his partner, Peter Roach, Throckmorton had cannily bought up dozens of New York City and Brooklyn lots after the panic of 1837. But the pair had insufficient reserves to weather the financial downturn that beset American markets a mere two years later. Collapsing property values after the panic of 1839 left the two merchants unable to pay their many creditors. After further economic setbacks in the mid-1840s, Throckmorton left for San Francisco, where he became convinced that no other place "affords the opportunity of getting up quickly." In accordance with his optimistic estimations of the local economy, the onetime bankrupt plunged once again into real estate investments. Relying primarily on credit, he spent several years buying up large tracts in and around the booming California seaport.[18]

Ventures of this sort required substantial commitments of capital and exposed their principals to high levels of debt. The potential for profits was considerable; but so too was the financial danger if market conditions became unfavorable. Former bankrupts who embraced such chancy enterprises did not mind hazarding their solvency once again, calculating that the opportunities associated with them justified the risks.

Such optimism, as the postbankruptcy experiences of James Lorimar Graham and Elisha Bloomer suggest, could lead to remarkable prosperity. Undeterred by failed real estate and stock schemes in the 1830s that left him with almost $400,000 in debts, Graham continued to take part in stock and property deals after receiving a legal release from his obligations. By the late 1860s, these investments, along with work as a legal counselor, provided the foundation for a fortune that credit reporters estimated at $150,000. Bloomer, the former New York City hatter who turned to "wrecking" after a variety of schemes left him with well over $100,000 in unpayable obligations, initially confined his speculations to New York City real estate that came available at sheriff's sales. In the 1850s, he expanded his horizons, buying patent rights to machines used in woodworking and mining. Secretive about his various undertakings and known to "take advantage" of contractual ambiguities, he developed a reputation as a "tricky," "unreliable" operator, of whom "all say they would not trust him a dollar." Despite a series of credit assessments urging great caution, this speculator was able to retire from active business by the end of the Civil War, his various enterprises leaving him the owner of considerable property. Such furtiveness and talent for hard bargaining—traits that partly reflected experience with negotiations prompted by bankruptcy—characterized other failed businessmen who managed to accumulate significant assets through speculation.[19]

Good fortune, however, was not the norm for onetime bankrupts who tried their luck with risky enterprises. Most commonly, the plunge into real estate deals, stock operations, or other hazardous ventures sent former bankrupts on a financial path to failure. Sometimes the road to an accumulation of unpayable debts was quick and direct, with this mode of operation constituting "a through ticket to speedy bankruptcy."[20] In other instances, a return to speculative undertakings initiated a more circuitous journey to insolvency. Samuel Throckmorton's California property ventures serve as a case in point. In the mid-1850s, Throckmorton's various investments had made him a seemingly wealthy man, as land values in San Francisco continued to move upward. But in the wake of the panic of 1857, he found himself unable to sell any of his property except at a huge sacrifice. At the same time, his creditors demanded payment. The combination of a depressed real estate market and heavy obligations once again made him a bankrupt.[21]

The collapse of Samuel Throckmorton's San Francisco property empire illustrates a crucial shortcoming in the speculative schemes of many former bankrupts. Even if these enterprises prospered at first, they were extremely vulnerable to fluctuations in the wider economy. Unless investments were backed by sufficient capital, economic downturns could rapidly transform apparent fortunes into assets held by an assignee, and then into dividends distributed to creditors.

Despite the dangers, numerous former bankrupts acted on the belief that somehow they would avoid the pitfalls that turned so many speculations into failures. The siren call of quick profits could even entice a man like Frederick Conant, who had spent over twenty years taking care to "go along slowly." Despite his long-standing determination to protect himself from the vagaries of the capitalist marketplace, Conant eventually turned to one of the riskiest businesses in postbellum America. In 1865, Conant entered into a new partnership with his son-in-law and began to buy and sell cotton in the New York market. For a time, the former clothing merchant prospered; R. G. Dun & Co. estimated his worth at over $400,000 toward the end of 1868. Within just a few years, however, a sharp decline in cotton prices caught him unawares and almost brought on a second failure. By 1871, he had cut his losses and left the brokerage business. Conant avoided insolvency in 1871 because over two decades of slow growth had deepened his pockets; other onetime insolvents who pursued similar ventures had less capacity to withstand reverses.[22]

Commercial Supports

In looking for auguries of the future that lay in store for antebellum bankrupts, the commercial moralists and the opponents of easily obtained bankruptcy discharges pursued a similar method. They each placed an emphasis on the kind of enterprise that former bankrupts would pursue and on the business habits that would govern their business strategies and decision making. Moralists foresaw the widespread adoption of prudence and caution; opponents of bankruptcy reform worried about continued or even intensified speculation. Neither group of soothsayers paid much attention to the sustained assistance that a bankrupt could expect from family members or business associates. Such assistance, often crucial in providing bankrupts with a means to return to the business world as independent proprietors, also constituted an essential contributor to later economic success, regardless of whether former bankrupts took care to limit their financial vulnerability or once again embraced substantial risk.[23]

Family members and mercantile or political associates often promoted the interest of bankrupts by throwing business in their direction. Thus one New York City lawyer earned a steady postbankruptcy income by managing the assets of his wealthy mother and one of her friends. Another southern New York applicant under the 1841 Bankruptcy Act made profitable use of connections to the Democratic Party. After toiling for over a decade in the New York City clothing trade without much success, sometimes as a cutter and sometimes as an independent subcontractor, this tailor used partisan contacts to gain an 1855 clothing contract with the U.S. Navy. Once positioned within the system of military procurement, he obtained steady and remunerative business, garnering annual orders in excess of $70,000 for the next decade. In the case of a third former bankrupt, an Irishman who had emigrated in the 1820s, long-standing relationships with Irish linen producers sustained postfailure endeavors. Despite two bouts with insolvency in the 1830s, including a colossal failure prompted by ill-timed ventures in cotton speculation, this New Yorker retained the confidence of his correspondents in Ireland, who almost immediately resumed their shipments of linens to him after he had received a federal discharge. For the next twenty-eight years, until his death, he reaped steady profits as a commission merchant.[24]

In addition to directing business toward former bankrupts, relatives and friends also extended periodic infusions of capital and offered generous terms as suppliers of raw materials or finished goods. Capital injections enabled some formerly bankrupt wholesalers to overcome persistent liquidity problems, creating sufficient reserves to make the discounting of customers' promissory notes unnecessary. Once able to meet maturing debts without relying on short-term borrowing, these merchants enjoyed healthier profit margins and strengthened credit. Indulgence from friendly suppliers, as in the case of Francis Amidon, the New York City hatter whose business eventually took off during the Civil War, could similarly limit borrowing costs. Throughout the late 1840s and early 1850s, Amidon bought his raw materials "almost wholly" from one mercantile firm—Haight, Halsey, & Co. This arrangement allowed Amidon to maintain a supply of wool, felt, and other materials without facing immediate pressures for payment. After slowly building up his business for over a decade, Amidon accumulated sufficient capital to dispense with reliance on credit. The turn to a cash trade protected Amidon from the panic of 1857. Emerging from that financial crisis unscathed and with excellent credit,

Amidon was well positioned to take advantage of the opportunities created by a war economy. But none of this later success would have been possible without the earlier willingness of Haight, Halsey, & Co. to offer the hatter lenient terms.[25]

Other proprietors who overcame a legacy of pecuniary embarrassment regained a mercantile foothold through endorsements from established patrons. The post-bankruptcy experiences of Effingham Cock suggest the potential importance of this kind of commercial support. Cock came from a well-respected Quaker family in New York City. His father, once an eminent merchant, had failed during the War of 1812, and then again some years later in a farming venture. Without a family business to take over, Effingham migrated in the mid-1830s to Alton, Illinois, where he opened a general store along with a partner. The pair had insufficient resources to withstand the financial pressures brought on by the panic of 1837, finding it impossible either to collect from their customers or to make payments to their eastern suppliers. Cock "returned to New York poor," gained his bankruptcy discharge in 1842, and then started up a small-scale dry goods business along with his brother William. Lacking capital, the Cocks were able to buy goods cheaply in Boston because of endorsements provided by a New York City patron, the dry goods merchant Joseph Lawrence. This arrangement continued for a number of years, allowing E. & W. Cock to expand its operations in a manner that would have been impossible without the loan of its benefactor's credit. By the latter part of the 1840s, the firm had become "independent" of its reliance on Lawrence and aggressively pursued a cash business. As with Francis Amidon, the prudence of avoiding credit relationships insulated the Cocks from the financial crises of the 1850s. Their firm's trade grew steadily into the 1860s, making its proprietors each worth more than $100,000. Also as in Amidon's case, the assistance provided by a patron served a crucial precondition to later expansion.[26]

Some onetime bankrupts, like Andrew Near and William Teller, the two Ulster County tanners who gained ownership of a Kingston tannery in 1846 when their previous employer, A. H. Bruyn, sold it to them on generous terms, benefited from all these sources of mercantile assistance. In essence, Bruyn gave his employees the capital they needed to begin independent production. But his generosity did not end with the transfer of the keys to the tannery. Possessing "unlimited confidence in [Near's] moral integrity and business capacity," the retired tanner introduced his two protégés to merchants in New York City, vouched for their responsibility, and provided endorsements "for as long as they needed assistance." Near and Teller relied on the commercial scaffolding offered by Bruyn for several years, slowly nurturing their enterprise. In 1856, a credit reporter estimated the value of the tannery as more than $5,000, with each partner individually worth an additional $4,000. By the start of the Civil War, the two tanners were well placed to expand production. With "leather in demand at good prices," Near and Teller prospered.

Their business was worth $50,000 in 1865 and $75,000 in 1871, when Near retired. Again, however, success depended on the willingness of a mercantile backer to extend assistance during the early years of postbankruptcy enterprise.[27]

In his brief portrayal of mercantile resurrection, Philip Hone implicitly characterized American bankrupts as atomistic individuals, disconnected from relationships to relatives, friends, associates, and fellow members of a business class. The dense familial and social networks that surrounded these souls of misfortune made no appearance in his commentary. Rather, flattened merchants "spring to their feet," using the "broken fragments" of their former enterprises to "make a ladder and remount." In Hone's rendering, there were no metaphoric hands reaching out from a parent, a close friend, or a patron, extending the capital that allowed many well-placed bankrupts to stand up amid the financial debris and begin a new commercial ascent. Nor did the retired New York City merchant sketch an image of the same palms reaching down from higher and more stable rungs on the economic ladder, offering information, business recommendations, and endorsements that eased the journey upwards.

Credit reporters, whose work often exposed the familial and social connections that buttressed postfailure endeavors, could also obscure those relationships. In the 1840s, for example, the Mercantile Agency's reporters emphasized the dependence of E. & W. Cock on endorsements from their patron. A decade later, this vital contribution to the firm's healthy balance sheet no longer merited notice. During the fall of 1857, as the firm continued to do well amid hard times, a reporter gushed that the Cock brothers had "risen to th[ei]r present position by th[ei]r own exertion." Three months later, commercial recall again slipped, as an assessment proclaimed that the Cocks were "self made, as to means, having done a successful cash bus[iness] from the beginning."[28] Sustained profitability could not just rebut the presumed need for caution generated by prior failure, but efface communal memory of it altogether. Yet in spite of the impulse of contemporaries to equate success with self-reliance, onetime bankrupts rarely overcame unfortunate financial pasts or the presumptions associated with them by themselves.

Aid provided by family members, business associates, or commercial benefactors, of course, did not ensure postfailure success. Not infrequently such assistance took the form of an entrepreneurial shell game, in which former bankrupts shifted the pecuniary responsibility of their businesses to relatives or close friends in response to renewed financial difficulties. This tactic frequently complicated the legal prosecution of debt suits by creditors, especially when available assets were neither extensive nor easily liquidated. On occasion, such maneuvers provided crucial breathing space for firms, which were able ultimately to reestablish profitable operations. This approach to financial troubles, though, almost always curtailed future access to credit—one R. G. Dun report characterized this sort of arrangement as "a cat's paw to cover property from execution"—and thus circumscribed growth prospects. The transferal of technical ownership often merely prolonged the life of marginal businesses.[29]

Reliance on personal business circles, moreover, carried risks of its own. This kind of dependence rendered former bankrupts vulnerable to any pecuniary entanglements besetting their backers. Under such circumstances, recipients of loaned capital or informal credit subsidization typically lost the financial supports they had heretofore enjoyed. They might further confront insistent pleas for payments or requests to return previously granted favors, especially by providing endorsements. These developments could quickly weaken a firm's financial position.[30]

The challenge, as seen by at least some bankrupts, was to maximize access to sorely needed capital through the mutuality of business networks, while limiting exposure to reciprocal obligations. As the postfailure career of Charlemagne Tower indicates, a combination of careful calculation and skillful use of commercial rhetoric could achieve this delicate balance. In the decades following Tower's failure, the Oneida County distiller who transformed himself initially into a bankruptcy attorney expressed strong commitment to the advancement of those within his business circle, particularly his several brothers. He further voiced ready acceptance of the need for business associates and family members to prop up one another financially, and he did not hesitate to draw on accommodation loans at moments when various schemes of his in real estate speculation and mining required a timely injection of capital. Yet Tower also proved extremely adroit at fending off similar requests if he judged that they might threaten his ability to meet his own engagements. Especially in times of general economic crisis, he would either agree to grant assistance when asked, but then delay actual transfer of funds for as long as possible, or beg off more directly, gently explaining that he was "disappointed" in collections, "pretty short myself," "mighty dry for money," or unwilling to draw upon his "reserve fund." Such tactful refusals safeguarded his postdischarge solvency, as four of his brothers flirted with pecuniary embarrassment during the 1850s and 1860s, with three actually failing.[31]

Even in the absence of financial pressures that arose from the interlinked obligations of personal business circles, discharged bankrupts who received substantial financial aid sometimes failed again, especially if they lacked commercial skills or embraced risky enterprises. Three New York City brothers, Jacob, Jordan, and Samuel Mott, discovered this bitter lesson in the 1850s. Heirs to their mother's local real estate holdings, which were valued at over $500,000, the Motts faced little difficulty in returning to the business world after they had separately gone through bankruptcy proceedings under the 1841 act. Yet even though they routinely received endorsements from their mother, the Mott brothers' various enterprises did poorly. Jacob Mott joined the rush of Americans to California in the early 1850s, without success. He returned to New York City and took a place in his brothers' jewelry business, which also struggled. Despite maternal guarantees that should have calmed the nerves of any potential creditor, the Mott brothers often had difficulties raising credit and meeting their obligations. Judgments from R. G. Dun credit reporters were unequivocal; the Motts "aren't g[oo]d bus[iness] men." In 1854, a series of financial "operations" outside the regular business of the firm left these former bankrupts with debts totaling six figures. The next year, the brothers Mott found themselves once again insolvent and assigned their property to a trustee for the benefit of their creditors. Other onetime bankrupts with impressive connections and financial backing similarly failed on more than one occasion, usually because of a penchant for hazardous investments.[32]

By contrast, credit evaluations of bankrupts who enjoyed considerable backing and whose businesses eventually flourished make clear that these individuals also possessed ample business "virtues." They worked industriously, maintained prudent business strategies, and offered their customers quality goods and services. Effingham Cock, for example, earned plaudits for being "shrewd," "enterprizing," "frugal," and "cautious." Andrew Near and William Teller similarly received mercantile compliments, as credit reporters judged them "careful, prud[en]t, . . . hon[es]t, hardw[o]r[ki]ng men." A combination of financial assistance, commercial skills, and a cautious approach to the American economy by no means constituted the only recipe for success after bankruptcy. That admixture, however, served as the most effective formula for achieving postinsolvency prosperity, for taking advantage of flush times and warding off general economic downturns.

Failure and the Entrepreneurial Ethos

In addition to resuscitating the entrepreneurial exertions of myriad antebellum bankrupts and fostering considerable social flux, general releases from debt contributed to the mutability and dynamism of the nineteenth-century economy. Along with the culture of privately negotiated compromises, antebellum bankruptcy discharges increased the pool of entrepreneurs who actively sought to make their fortune by extending the reach of commercial exchange, inventing new products, or developing new marketing techniques. These businessmen were driven, in the words of one nineteenth-century commentator, "to break the bondage of antiquated habit, and inaugurate a revolution in trade." Debt relief furnished by legislation such as the 1841 Bankruptcy Act thus facilitated the perpetual search for profitable innovation that constitutes a defining characteristic of modern capitalism.[33] The emergence of systematized wrecking provides one expression of this linkage, as discharged bankrupts played a crucial role in devising businesses structured to profit from insolvency. Other illustrations abound, perhaps none more striking than instances in which commercial endeavors after bankruptcy strove to remold corners of the American marketplace, yet ended ultimately in disappointment. Two instructive examples in this regard are provided by the checkered careers of George North, a Kingston, New York, merchant and property developer, and Lewis Feuchtwanger, a New York City chemist.

After failing in the early 1840s as a storekeeper, George North emerged from bankruptcy in 1842 with expansive visions of real estate development in Kingston and the neighboring settlement of Rondout. Throughout the 1840s and 1850s, he gobbled up local lots, built docks and riverfront stores, and branched out into lumbering and the local milk trade. Though his various initiatives did well, he continually overstretched himself. With "the spirit of enterprise and speculation . . . restless within him," North consistently extended his many businesses, incurring large debts as a means of financing expansion. General financial stringency following the panic of 1857 weakened his position, forcing him to liquidate many assets in order to meet his obligations. These actions kept the Kingston entrepreneur solvent for a few more years, but the economic dislocations brought on by southern secession crippled his cash flow. In April 1861, North made his second assignment for the benefit of creditors. At the end of the Civil War, North found the money to invest in a southern plantation, hoping to rebuild his wealth by turning the homestead into a hotel. As with the investments of numerous northerners who hoped to cash in on southern reintegration into the national economy, this scheme too was unsuccessful.[34]

Lewis Feuchtwanger's entrepreneurial preoccupations lay with the world of chemicals and medicines rather than the commercial development of particular localities, though they also reflected a decades-long commitment to reconfiguring nooks of the nineteenth-century American economy. A German immigrant whose range of pesticides and elixirs found insufficient demand to stave off a bankruptcy application in 1842, Feuchtwanger remained convinced after his failure that acumen in the laboratory would eventually translate into remunerative products. For over thirty years after his insolvency, he plowed whatever capital came his way—including an inheritance received by his wife and numerous high interest loans—into chemical experimentation. Like other patent medicine manufacturers, he aggressively advertised his wares, touting their remarkable properties. Toward the end of the 1850s, he published books detailing the properties of gems and various novel processes for manufacturing chemicals, in the hopes of buttressing his professional and commercial standing. All of this technical investigation and puffery, though, did little for the chemist's personal assets or credit. Though Feuchtwanger avoided a second failure, he never achieved more than the most guarded evaluation from credit reporters, who regularly cautioned that the financial drain of his research made him a substantial risk.[35]

The projects and plans of former bankrupts such as George North and Lewis Feuchtwanger receive scant attention from historians of American business, who remain focused primarily on profitable enterprises. Their careers nonetheless offer intriguing insights into the culture of nineteenth-century American capitalism, much like the fruitless efforts of so many boosters to transform their towns into commercial emporiums and manufacturing centers. The ranks of nineteenth-century Americans who unsuccessfully chased dreams of reconstructed commercial channels and revamped ways of doing business far outnumbered those business owners and promoters who realized such designs. Such enduring commitment to remaking the world of business, despite recurring setbacks and eventual failure, powerfully illustrates the prevalence of entrepreneurial impulses in nineteenth-century American life, as well as the widespread if sharply contested equation of "progress" with ongoing commercial metamorphosis.[36]

These broad implications are most readily apparent in the postbankruptcy careers of proprietors who embraced a speculative, adventuresome business style; but they also follow in less dramatic fashion from the strategies of former bankrupts who shied away from especially risky ventures.[37] By carving out business niches that limited competition, these proprietors accelerated the trend toward specialization within the nineteenth-century American economy. Adoption of cautious business practices by individuals who had endured failure also assisted a crucial transformation in the organization of trade—the replacement of "credit" with "cash" in mid-nineteenth-century America's economic distribution network. As several scholars have noted, during the 1850s merchants increasingly adopted a "cash basis" for their business, in places as diverse as western Massachusetts, New York's Hudson Valley, and central Illinois, often with profound implications for local exchange culture. This shift depended crucially on dramatic augmentation of the nation's money supply in the 1840s and 1850s, which in turn was fostered by mining discoveries in California and Nevada, explosive growth in the country's banking facilities, and sustained periods of general economic prosperity. Without sufficient currency in circulation, few proprietors could enforce a "no credit" policy. Yet monetary expansion by itself did not compel the turn away from selling "on time." Widespread experience of the commercial headaches that often culminated in insolvency—uncollectible debts from customers, anxious bouts of shinning, ever intensifying pressure from creditors—constituted a major impetus for the general tendency to rest trade on a foundation of cash. Former bankrupts, moreover, were in the forefront of this trend, often, as in the cases of Frederic Conant and Effingham Cock, turning away from the credit system years before it became common mercantile practice.[38]

Bankruptcy discharges, of course, did not ineluctably generate aggressive risk taking or the formulation of novel business strategies. Especially in the case of failed artisans who recommenced their trades, tradition frequently remained a touchstone of commercial practice. Credit reporters often launched biting critiques of individuals who exhibited such behavior. Even if they scrupulously made good on their obligations and managed to build up some savings, reporters characterized these producers as "rusting out" and "completely behind the age."[39] Within the households of other former bankrupts, the experience of asset liquidation prompted careful thinking about available legal mechanisms to protect at least some holdings from the clutches of future creditors. Placement of familial property—especially homes and furnishings—under the names of wives was commonplace among one-time insolvents.[40]

For still other failed proprietors, encounters with insolvency led them away from business ownership altogether. In ruminating on the patterns and significance of entrepreneurial resurrection, commentators such as Frederika Bremer, Philip Hone, and Henry David Thoreau all neglected a substantial class of bankrupts who either could not resume independent business careers or chose not to accept the risks associated with doing so. As T. S. Arthur's *Home Magazine* noted in 1855, of the numerous Americans who "venture . . . upon the sea of trade" each year only to become "engulphed" by "reverses of fortune," "hundreds" would not return "to the troubled waters" of proprietorship.[41] Many of these individuals walked away from the scenes of ongoing financial wreckage, seeking a different and less hazardous means of securing a living. Cognizant of the dangers that confronted all commercially oriented proprietors, they searched for careers that limited their dependence on unpredictable markets. Their efforts link the experience of antebellum bankruptcy to the rise of a salaried urban middle class.

Chapter 8

Sidestepping the Credit System

The moment I relinquish my salary, and go round begging for credit, I shall lose the glorious feeling of independence that I now enjoy. . . . It's a dog's life to live—this running from store to store to scrape together money enough to keep your concern in a decent credit, and from tumbling down in a crash all about your ears. Better be a day-laborer, hand-cartman, hod-carrier, or a plantation negro, than lead such a miserable, truckling, dependent, precarious existence.

—E. M. Gibson, "Going into Business," *Ballou's Magazine* (1855)

If ever there was an advertisement for the salaried middle class in nineteenth-century America, E. M. Gibson's 1855 short story, "Going into Business," qualifies. Published for a Boston women's magazine that reached a national audience, Gibson's tale turns on the career decisions of two young brothers-in-law, Edgar Sargent and Rufus Granger. Residents of "a well known city," both men initially hold clerkships in "a large mercantile establishment" and each earns a "liberal salary" of $1,000 a year. But while Edgar Sargent remains satisfied with his lot and religiously saves "a considerable sum" from his annual earnings, Rufus cannot resist the temptation to enter the marketplace as an independent merchant. Rufus tries to convince his brother-in-law to join him in the venture five months after its launch, but Edgar demurs. Where Rufus sees a future of easy profits, showy possessions, and high social station, Edgar anticipates only troubles and difficulties. The latter character would much prefer the security of his salary to "all the hazards and perplexities of trying to become a merchant without capital."

Confronted with Rufus's insistent requests that Edgar forsake his clerkship to enter the antebellum commercial sweepstakes, the satisfied clerk and his wife, Emma, furnish a comprehensive defense of sticking to a salary. Both these characters stress the dangers lurking within the credit system—the vulnerability created by reliance on credit purchases, the difficulties of enticing customers to pay promptly, and the fearful consequences of outright bankruptcy. Observing that "the chances would be against me, where nine out of ten have failed," Edgar argues that the undercapitalized business owner constitutes "a mere cipher in the sum of business relations—the veriest slave of every one he owes, and of those from whom he wished to borrow."

While Edgar and Emma disdain the anxieties and embarrassments that would almost certainly confront them if he were to take the mercantile plunge with Rufus, they laud the advantages of their current financial position. Emma may have to toil without the assistance of domestic servants and Edgar may have to reconcile himself to laboring for the pecuniary benefit of his employer. But both husband and wife rest easy in the knowledge that they do not owe anyone a cent. Content with "enough to eat, drink and . . . wear," the couple caution Rufus that his ambitions are likely to leave him utterly dependent on his creditors, who will be unlikely to offer him a shred of mercy when he fails to meet his notes. A plunge into retailing, Edgar envisions, would eventually lead him to "tremble at the very *creak* of a wholesale merchant's shoes." Simply contemplating the possibility makes the satisfied clerk "feel nervous." Predictably, Rufus shrugs off all of these admonitions and quickly finds himself bankrupt, a victim of inexperience, extravagant consumption, and limited capital resources.[1]

In contrasting the "miserable, truckling, dependent, precarious existence" of many merchants with the "glorious feeling of independence" created by a secure salary, E. M. Gibson offered an increasingly common commentary on the American economy. During the 1840s and 1850s, a number of fiction writers, dispensers of advice to youths, and contributors to the commercial press discovered the virtues of salaried, white-collar employment. These authors emphasized the ways in which salaried employees were insulated from the potential terrors of the credit system. Clerks, bookkeepers, and the holders of similar jobs could count on reasonable compensation, social respectability, and the opportunity to save for the future. Although these individuals remained employees, answerable to the demands of a boss, they avoided both the anxieties of trying to sustain a fragile credit and the humiliating dependencies created by struggles to meet looming obligations. As "the clerk" waxed in the estimation of these social commentators, "the business owner," and especially the business owner operating on a small base of capital, waned. This latter person could look forward primarily to indignant letters from creditors, protested notes, and court judgments.[2]

By linking salaried occupations to the republican ideal of independence, social commentators such as E. M. Gibson executed a striking reversal of cultural meaning. Throughout the first eight decades of American independence, political discourse in the new nation glorified proprietorship as an essential precondition of republican liberty. Farm-owning agriculturalists, workshop-owning artisans, and masters of countinghouses stood as exemplars of republican citizenship. These proprietors did not cower under the arrogance of landlords or employers. Instead, they made their own way in the world, deciding what crops to plant, how to go about their craft, and when to pursue opportunities in the marketplace. In the minds of politicians and social commentators alike, the absence of degrading personal subordination and the widespread experience of economic self-direction combined to produce a large class of independent citizens. This group of Americans possessed sufficient freedom and political acumen to underpin the new nation's experiment with republican government.[3]

The growth of market relationships, however, greatly complicated the equation of proprietorship with either political citizenship or personal independence. Economic developments during the first half of the nineteenth century left a steadily increasing proportion of adult white men in dependent economic positions, as tenants or employees. The bastardization of industrial crafts, the rise of textile factories, the early stages of agricultural mechanization, and the integration of regional and then national markets all narrowed the opportunities for self-employment while simultaneously fostering expansive demand for wage and salaried work. Yet the growing numbers of "dependent" employees in the antebellum decades did not shy away from asserting their rights as citizens, generally taking advantage of the suffrage's extension to almost all adult white men.[4]

As the collective biographies of antebellum bankrupts make abundantly clear, transformations in the American economy simultaneously heightened the risks inherent in market production or distribution. Complex networks of credit, intensified competition, and a more impersonal basis of trade all played their part in enlarging the perils that confronted farmers, mechanics, and merchants. Increasingly, supposedly "independent" participants in the market found themselves to be exceedingly "dependent," on both the indulgence of creditors and the fluctuations in faraway markets. When proprietorship meant "running from store to store to scrape together money enough to keep your concern in a decent credit, and from tumbling down in a crash all about your ears," the juxtaposition of business owners and "plantation negros" took on unexpected salience.[5]

Not surprisingly, the growing perplexities associated with mercantile trade prompted the authors of northern agricultural journals and almanacs to make strident pleas for local sons not to forsake "the hard work of the farm" for the imagined dash and glamour of urban countinghouses. Farmboys who took the latter path invariably found themselves, in the words of one 1854 editorial, "compelled to look anxiously at the prices current of cotton and railroad stocks, in order to learn each morning, whether [they were] bankrupt or not." The fate of these would-be "gentlemen" almost always was "to fail, and compromise with . . . creditors and . . . conscience, and sigh for . . . native hills."[6] From this perspective, the wreckage strewn about the American marketplace called for renewed dedication to republican ideals of manly citizenship based on widespread ownership of productive agricultural land.

That urban commentators could draw such different lessons from the increasingly common experience of bankruptcy suggests both the universal attraction of "independence" as a cultural ideal in antebellum America and the malleability of that concept. By construing occupations such as "clerk" and "bookkeeper" as desirable havens from mercantile uncertainties, writers such as E. M. Gibson charted a course for white-collar employees to see themselves as heirs to America's republican legacies, rather than as dependent outsiders who lacked the respect owed to the self-employed. Plotting such cultural redefinitions, however, required dramatic shifts in focus—magnification of proprietorship's risks and minimization of the indignities and psychological limitations associated with long-term employment.[7]

This interpretation of business failure played a crucial, mediating role in the evolution of middle-class values, especially concerning the relative importance of economic stability and security, as well as the formulation of strategies to attain such priorities amid the tumultuous environment of mid-nineteenth-century American capitalism. The process was an uneven one, both in cultural discourse and in economic decision making. At no point did paeans to the respectability of salary displace celebrations of the go-getting, risk-taking entrepreneur. Similarly, independent proprietorship remained a fundamental aspiration for myriad Americans, including large numbers of individuals whose names had graced the nation's bankruptcy lists. The regular occurrence of insolvency nonetheless encouraged urban Americans of the middling sort to pay greater attention to the risks inherent in proprietary enterprise and to seek out ways of protecting themselves and their families from ever more chaotic swings of commercial confidence. Former bankrupts played key roles in this aspect of middle-class formation. As a result of both limited options and newfound respect for the hazards of entrepreneurship, failed business owners frequently adopted career strategies that conformed remarkably closely to the business philosophy of the fictional Edgar Sargent.

Retreat to Employment

In the immediate aftermath of failure, most bankrupts had little choice but to join the ranks of the employed. Without a legal release from past obligations, new business ventures were usually impossible, even in sectors of the economy that did not require significant inputs of capital. Some insolvents could rely on the separate property of wives or the assets of parents to provide sustenance for themselves and their families.[8] More typically, failed business owners had to find work in order to make ends meet. The opportunities they found within the labor market varied greatly, depending on their business skills and personal networks.

For individuals with particularly good connections, bankruptcy might prompt appointments to corporate office. Throughout the antebellum decades, the nation's business elite reserved the executive positions of insurance companies, banks, and transportation corporations for members of their circle who had suffered financial reverses. Posts of "president" and "secretary" in the new corporations offered substantial salaries, typically exceeding $1,500 a year, and often required minimal work. The career move of Benjamin Cox exemplifies this kind of assistance. Cox failed as a New York City leather dealer in 1839, along with a Boston partner. Soon thereafter, he obtained employment as the secretary of the New York & Harlem Railroad.[9] Relatively few bankrupts, however, were able to wrangle such appointments.

Greater numbers of failed proprietors relied on political networks to provide them with remunerative employment. Government at all levels provided potential places to Americans who had been unsuccessful in the commercial world. The national government, despite its small size in the decades prior to the Civil War, still needed thousands of men to serve in post offices, customhouses, and the federal judicial system. State and local governments had far more positions to fill, including openings for street cleaners, court officials, policemen, and inspectors of meat and other goods.

Bankrupts sought out these positions in large numbers. According to an 1840 petition that pleaded for congressional adoption of a federal bankruptcy system, "of the thousands who are seeking to obtain the emoluments of office, more than three-fifths are forced to become applicants because they have been unfortunate in business." This supplication almost certainly exaggerated the proportion of bankrupts among antebellum office seekers, but there is no question that failed businessmen regularly pursued "the smallest ministerial office in the gift of the appointing power."[10] Many of these bankrupts were successful in their quest.

In southern New York, dozens of bankrupts had either obtained a public office at the time of their bankruptcy application or secured such a position soon after their discharge. New York bankrupts held a range of offices, including places as inspectors, measurers, postmasters, deputy sheriffs, customhouse officials, and prison keepers. Several New York City bankrupts even managed to gain places under the bankruptcy system created by the 1841 act. A smaller number of bankrupts sought out public election rather than appointment, running for offices such as assistant alderman, tax assessor, or town clerk.[11]

In order to secure a patronage job or to win a party nomination for elective office, antebellum bankrupts had to pay their political dues. Attendance at party meetings, the cultivation of political patrons, and a willingness to press one's case unceasingly were often essential preconditions to gaining public office.[12] Even when political activity led to the desired outcome, the position of publicly employed bankrupts remained precarious. If the political party to which such individuals belonged lost at the polls or if their status within the party shifted, appointments might quickly come to an end. Soon after Charles Cooper and Joseph Francis Lippit received their bankruptcy discharges, each of these bankrupts discovered the perils that confronted political appointees. At the time of their bankruptcy petitions, each man was an inspector of beef and pork under the auspices of the State of New York. In 1843, though, the Democrats won back the governorship from the Whigs. By March of that year, both Cooper and Lippit had lost their jobs to Democratic replacements. On the same day, Jessie West, a Democratic bankrupt, took over one of the positions as inspector of beef and pork. Antebellum rotation in office fre- quently meant rotation of bankrupts.[13]

Although office seeking took place more commonly among bankrupts than a move into the largely honorific positions in the nascent corporate world, neither form of employment predominated among Americans who had recently suffered insolvency. After failing, most individuals who found employment did so with private noncorporate employers and most secured either salaried white-collar positions or manual wage work. Bankrupts who had experience in the world of commerce typically returned to the former kind of employment. In southern New York, the second most common occupation given by bankruptcy applicants was that of "clerk." Of over 2,200 bankrupts who listed an occupation on their petition, almost 20 percent characterized themselves as earning a living in this fashion. This figure almost certainly underrepresents bankruptcy applicants in clerical positions, as many petitioners described themselves with reference to the businesses in which they had failed rather than their present occupations.[14]

Clerkships by no means accounted for all the noncorporate and nongovernmental work taken up by antebellum Americans who had recently failed. Bankrupts in southern New York also took up a range of jobs in transportation and manufacturing. Some of these positions, such as stagecoach driver, steamboat captain, or sawmill foreman, tended to provide comparatively secure tenure and remunerative salaries. In other instances, postfailure employment left bankrupts in a more vulnerable situation. Many bankrupts were able to obtain only wage work, as mariners, journeymen artisans, cartmen, or farm laborers. These positions brought comparatively small earnings and likely exposure to periodic unemployment.[15]

In addition to taking on salaried positions or less well-paid wage work, antebellum bankrupts flocked into the growing ranks of commercial agents. As the American economy became more integrated, and as large firms and corporations with far-flung business interests became more and more common, the demand for commercial representatives burgeoned. Manufacturers and merchants who sold their wares to customers throughout the country found a range of uses for mercantile emissaries. Such agents often provided essential services for the home office, such as ferreting out business intelligence, collecting debts, making payments, and negotiating sales.

The term "agent" encompassed a wide spectrum of economic functions in nineteenth-century America. In some cases, a mercantile representative performed services for a principal, such as debt collection or the management of a station on a transportation route, and received a salary in return. Other agents operated on a commission basis, with their earnings pegged in part or whole to the amount of business they transacted. Traveling salesmen, freight agents, land agents, and the local representatives of insurance companies tended to work on this basis, as did many commercial correspondents for distant corporations or mercantile firms.[16]

Bankrupts frequently possessed commercial skills and experience that made them well suited for these kinds of positions. Even if onetime merchants and manufacturers had run their own enterprises into the ground, they nonetheless often had learned a great deal about how to drum up business, evaluate credit risks, or coax debtors to fulfill their obligations. Bankrupts typically also had cultivated a range of mercantile "connections" that aided the gathering of commercial news. Agencies, in turn, could offer attractive terms of service for individuals whose failure precluded independent business activity. Agents who received salaries could count on a relatively secure source of income. In many instances, they also retained a significant degree of self-direction in work. Principals provided broad guidelines and directions but generally left day-to-day decision making up to their representatives. The most basic premise of agency was that mercantile emissaries had authority to act on behalf of principals, using their own judgment, within limits. For agents who received commissions, the prospect of potentially greater economic returns also beckoned. If these individuals were successful in attracting customers, such as shippers to a steamboat service or policyholders to insurance agreements, they stood to make a good income—in some cases over a thousand dollars a year.

At the same time, agents normally did not incur financial responsibility for the contracts that they arranged. They acted for principals, who were legally responsible for all contracts arranged by agents and legally entitled to resulting profits, less any relevant commissions. Principals, whether mercantile partnerships, manufacturing firms, or corporations, shouldered all financial risk, so long as their agents expressly transacted business in their principals' names, stayed within the bounds of delegated authority, and conformed to legal standards of diligence. Many principals additionally paid for part or all of the expenses that representatives incurred in carrying out their directives. Agency, then, provided bankrupts with a means to remain in the thick of the antebellum marketplace, and even to retain the possibility of substantial economic returns, without requiring capital investment or access to credit. To serve as a commercial agent was to pursue a middle course between the hazards of independent proprietorship and the subservience of closely directed employment.[17]

In southern New York, scores of bankrupts pursued this middle course before receiving a discharge under the 1841 act. Forty applicants in New York's southern district actually listed "agent" as their occupation on their bankruptcy petition; but as in the case of bankrupts who accepted employment as clerks, this number does not include many individuals who were working as agents at the time they applied for bankruptcy relief, yet listed the occupation in which they failed, or did not list an occupation at all. Henry Ogden, for example, listed himself as a "boatman" on his bankruptcy petition, suggesting employment as a deckhand. At the time of his application, however, he served as the Poughkeepsie agent of the New Paltz Ferry Company.[18]

Southern New Yorkers who responded to failure in this fashion fulfilled a wide range of commercial needs, usually in sectors of the economy related to their previous lines of trade. While Henry Ogden supervised the running of ferries across the Hudson River from Poughkeepsie to New Paltz, Israel Kinsman earned his keep by acting as the New York City agent for a Philadelphia pipe manufacturer. A mechanic and inventor, Kinsman had failed in Philadelphia during 1841, largely as a result of disastrous investments in a blast furnace outside Philadelphia and a plantation in Georgia. His experience gave him excellent credentials for work as a manufacturer's representative. James Webster Hale and Lyman Taylor similarly drew on commercial knowledge gained from past business ventures in securing employment as agents. Hale had failed as a publisher in West Bedford, Massachusetts, before moving to New York City and becoming a literary agent. Taylor, a New York City dealer in timber before his failure in the wake of the panic of 1837, found employment as an agent for lumber wholesalers.[19]

The great frequency with which antebellum bankrupts sought out employment immediately following their failures, of course, does not demonstrate newfound distaste for the responsibilities of business ownership. For many antebellum bankrupts, entry into the labor market was something that their misfortunes had forced upon them and that they showed every intention of overcoming, rather than accepting. As one bankrupt explained while seeking a patronage job from Governor Seward in 1840, "[U]nder other circumstances I should not have become an applicant for office—but the law of necessity compels me to solicit."[20] In addition, broad support for federal bankruptcy reform in the antebellum decades reflected both the desire among reformers to give bankrupts the chance to return to independent enterprise and the political demand by bankrupts for such an opportunity. To gauge the extent to which pecuniary embarrassment reshaped social aspirations, one has to consider the economic strategies adopted by bankrupts *after* they received legal releases from their debts, whether gained through private negotiations or through court-supervised insolvency or bankruptcy processes.

Respite, Sojourn, Career

In light of the central place accorded to economic individualism within antebellum culture, one might reasonably expect that even ruined business owners who had accepted some form of paid work would generally retain fervent desires to re-establish themselves as proprietors. The advice of writers such as E. M. Gibson, after all, served only as a counterpoint to more dominant themes of self-reliance, self-direction, and individual uplift. Alongside stories such as "Going into Business," readers of antebellum periodicals found sundry paeans to self-made men who rose from obscurity to affluence, as well as numerous approving references to failed businessmen who remained convinced that the future would offer avenues to profitable enterprise. At political meetings and in newspaper editorials, moreover, antebellum voters encountered a steady stream of rhetoric that emphasized the ability of Americans to improve their economic standing and attain the status of self-employment. Right up to the Civil War, Republican orators emphasized the transient status of most Americans who worked for wages or salaries.[21]

Even in the publications of authors who urged salaried workers to avoid the risks of setting out on their own, one often finds recurrent admiration for entrepreneurial drive. Freeman Hunt typified this ambivalence. In both the *Merchants' Magazine* and his other writings, Hunt repeatedly called on clerks to stick with their salary, noting again and again that failure rates in mercantile trade were extremely high. Yet he regularly carried celebratory biographies of leading businessmen in his magazine, which he eventually compiled in a multivolume *Lives of American Merchants*. Similarly, his 1855 collection of mercantile homilies, *Worth and Wealth*, included both stern warnings about rash entries into business *and* tributes to the aggressive, resolute entrepreneur. In the latter book, scorn for "the haste of the young man to be master, instead of clerk" shared space with praise for "the straightforward, fearless, enterprising man for business—one who is worth a dozen of those who, when anything is to be done, stop, falter, and hesitate, and are never ready to take a decided stand." Despite his recognition of the hazards confronting most business ventures, Hunt continued to esteem the businessman who refused to cower before the possibility of financial reverses.[22]

The postdischarge occupational experiences of applicants under the 1841 Bankruptcy Act suggest that personal priorities often meshed with such valorization of self-directed market participation. Numerous former bankrupts who retreated to salaried employment did so only temporarily, returning expeditiously to independent proprietorship. Of a sample of thirty-five New York City and Brooklyn bankrupts who identified their occupation as "clerk" on their bankruptcy petitions, over two in five were listed in an 1845 city directory as business owners. Agents who had previously failed showed a comparable desire to see their names displayed over storefronts or workshops. Thus acceptance of a salary or an agency often represented only a momentary respite in the ranks of the employed, a way station to the preferable status of a business owner.[23]

Eagerness to resume entrepreneurial endeavors, however, was not a universal predilection among antebellum insolvents. The willingness to accept employment frequently persisted well beyond the date when court papers or private releases emancipated the era's bankrupts from their previous embarrassments. After brushes with business failure, many former proprietors tended to shy away from economic ventures on their own responsibility, instead building careers that were premised on doing someone else's bidding.

For years and even decades after their failures, some former bankrupts in southern New York worked as clerks, bookkeepers, public servants, or agents. After one such individual failed as a storekeeper in Troy, New York, he moved to Manhattan and secured a position as a bookkeeper in a large mercantile firm, which he kept for at least sixteen years. Another bankruptcy petitioner from the Dutchess County town of Rhinebeck failed in the mid-1830s as a dry goods dealer. Before receiving his bankruptcy discharge, he earned a salary from a New York City countinghouse; afterward, he obtained a place as Rhinebeck postmaster, which he held for over two decades.[24] One can find similar paths in the later careers of ruined businessmen who obtained relief under the 1841 Bankruptcy Act in Georgia or Illinois, or under the Massachusetts Insolvency Act during the mid-1840s.[25]

In the absence of direct evidence about the consciousness of salaried former bankrupts, the motivations behind their economic decision making remain subject to conjecture. Some of these individuals may have remained in white-collar employment less because of prudence born of past failure and more as a result of constrained prospects for new business ventures. Occasionally, though, one can infer specific attitudes and habits of mind with a degree of confidence. The career choices of Edward Kent provide such an opportunity. An inkmaker and chemist who failed in 1841 as the result of endorsements for friends and slow payments from customers, Kent had reestablished a business on his own account by the mid-1840s and maintained a good credit rating through the first half of the next decade. In 1855, however, he secured a salaried position as a gold refiner in the U.S. Assay Office. For the next quarter of a century, Kent plied his craft in this position, content with a salary in four figures. In this instance, caution probably dictated occupational choice. Possessing an excellent reputation as a chemist, Kent faced few obstacles in pursuing an independent line of business; but he preferred the security of a substantial salary.[26]

Even when failed proprietors continued to view salaried positions or agencies as stepping-stones to self-employment, the experience of bankruptcy could prompt re-conceptualization of paid work as a transitional phase in the occupational life cycle. Antebellum writers who extolled "salary" in light of the great dangers that confronted antebellum businesses invariably engaged in such rethinking. The favorably treated characters in E. M. Gibson's or T. S. Arthur's tales of mercantile life do not wholly forsake the ambition to join the ranks of business owners. In "Going into Business," for example, Edgar Sargent does not reject the goal of becoming a merchant. But cognizant of his limited capital and limited experience, he refuses to leave his employment and strike out on his own responsibility. Instead, Edgar hopes that his employer will one day recognize his long-standing contribution to the firm and ask him to join the business as a partner. After his brother-in-law Rufus's failure, Edgar's prudence is rewarded. The story ends with Edgar's promotion and his hiring of Rufus as a clerk. Freeman Hunt offered similar advice when he was not glorifying the fearless merchant prince. Rather than hurtle into almost certain insolvency, white-collar employees should, in Hunt's estimation, "enjoy the ease and comfort attendant upon a salary prudently and safely managed," waiting patiently for an offer of partnership "with those he has faithfully served."[27]

Antebellum calls for patience from white-collar workers have attracted scholarly attention primarily as nostalgic attempts to recreate the paternalistic commercial world of the early nineteenth century—a world in which well-established merchants took in young men from respectable families, put them through a long and rigorous apprenticeship as clerks, and then, assuming sufficient development in business capacity and personal character, extended offers of partnership. Historians such as John Cawelti and Allen Horlick have depicted T. S. Arthur's and Freeman Hunt's advice to clerks as prompted by alarm over the aggressiveness with which so many aspiring businessmen sought wealth and social advancement, and as largely out of step with social realities. At midcentury, Cawelti and Horlick argue, such guidance struck increasing numbers of ambitious young men as hopelessly outdated. Amid the bustle of antebellum America's growing economy, clerks and salesmen honed their skills at moving merchandise and regularly shifted from employer to employer, seeking higher salaries and more responsibility. They also manifested great impatience at remaining "dependent" employees, anxious, in the words of one clerk's diary, not to be "kept down by those who would feign to be my superiors."[28]

Although Cawelti and Horlick appropriately stress both widespread ambivalence in mid-nineteenth-century America toward moralistic assaults on grasping individualism and the continuing draw of proprietorship for numerous white-collar workers, their interpretations slight the trenchant focus of writers like Gibson, Hunt, and Arthur on the incidence of business failure in America. High rates of bankruptcy made pleas for circumspection in relinquishing salaried posts more than just wishful pining for a simpler, more stable, bygone era. While many clerks and salesmen brushed off such advice, others heeded aspects of it, though they might not have simply bided their time in the hope that employers or other patrons would anoint them as partners.

One indication of growing trepidation about exchanging white-collar positions for independent enterprises lies with the development of a mercantile practice in which employees, rather than setting out on their own, loaned savings to their employers. In the two decades after the panic of 1857, employers in San Francisco and other cities frequently advertised salaried positions in their countinghouses, shops, and manufactories but required applicants to loan them money as a condition of employment. Retail merchants were particularly likely to place these sorts of notices. Would-be clerks, foremen, and superintendents also advertised a desire to take up such jobs, offering to place capital at the disposal of prospective employers as an added enticement.[29]

Such "job-loan trades" partially reflected imperfect capital markets and a glutted supply of labor, especially in a city like San Francisco. Banks in the quickly growing California city shied away from granting loans to many small businesses, and especially to retailers. These businessmen typically lacked large reserves of capital and experienced high rates of business failure. Unable to arrange credit from the city's early banks, San Francisco's less established entrepreneurs turned to other sources of financial intermediation. White-collar employees obliged the capital needs of these businessmen in part because of a tight labor market. With "large numbers of well-educated migrants" arriving from the eastern parts of the United States each year, job applicants offered loans in order to distinguish themselves from competitors.[30]

This mercantile practice additionally suggests the level of concern that a class of salaried workers harbored about the risks of proprietorship. Rather than using their savings to go into business themselves, some clerks and superintendents loaned their savings as a means of gaining a stake in the marketplace without taking on much exposure to losses. Loans granted by job applicants typically were secured, and since employees would generally learn of impending financial difficulties before other creditors, they had ample opportunity to protect their capital should their employers face looming insolvency. Extensions of credit on these terms, moreover, may have occurred most frequently between proprietors and salaried workers who had long been in their employ. Such loans were common enough to receive the approval of one commercial editor in New York City, who encouraged dry goods clerks to advance their savings to their employers as a matter of financial policy, rather than trying to start out on their own.[31]

Salaried workers who had previously endured insolvency were especially likely to tread warily before once again embarking on mercantile ventures. The career of

John Dayton, the New York City dry goods merchant whose 1841 experiment in transacting business without capital had so quickly careened into bankruptcy, illustrates this receptivity to a model of upward mobility premised on long-term service in white-collar employment. After obtaining a federal discharge, Dayton returned to work as a clerk for his former employer. He remained in this position for over a decade, gleaning considerable experience in dry goods wholesaling, building up a network of trade connections, and saving several thousand dollars. In 1853, with a much more solid foundation of capital and mercantile knowledge, he entered into a wholesale dry goods partnership with two seasoned businessmen, each of whom had more than $10,000 at his command. From then until the mid-1880s, Dayton pursued extremely cautious commercial practices, buying only with cash or on short-term credit and carefully assessing the creditworthiness of his customers. He quickly established sterling credit ratings, though southern secession forced him to negotiate extensions in 1861, as his firm had sold heavily to southern storekeepers. At the end of his career, his careful approach to reestablishing himself in business allowed him not only to negotiate the nation's recurrent financial crises, but also to accumulate assets well in excess of six figures.[32]

John Dayton's patience was by no means emulated by every bankrupt who had to turn to paid work as a means of support, much less by every salaried employee or entrant into the mid-nineteenth-century business world. But salaried positions and agencies continued to serve as occupational fallbacks for failed businessmen throughout the middle decades of the nineteenth century. Credit reports from the era are filled with references to individuals who accepted white-collar jobs after their businesses had collapsed. Applicants for posts in the federal government frequently explained that failures in business had induced them to seek places as public servants. In Chicago, the throng of commercial drummers sent out by postbellum lumber dealers included numerous individuals who had gone bust in the trade. Such patterns became sufficiently commonplace that they came to serve as tropes in nineteenth-century fiction. Characters who failed in the period's novels and short stories routinely ended up as corporate secretaries, governmental officials, bank tellers, clerks, or agents.[33]

Bankruptcy and the American Middle Class

By transforming so many lives and career paths, bankruptcy powerfully shaped the development of the urban middle class in the United States—that constellation of mostly native-born professionals, small-scale entrepreneurs, and white-collar employees who, along with their spouses and children, increasingly lived apart from the families of manual wage workers or urban elites, belonged to separate churches and voluntary organizations, and pursued distinctive strategies of social reproduction.[34] Most directly, brushes with insolvency prompted many antebellum Americans of the middling sort to change their approach to the world of commerce. Failure convinced numerous individuals to restructure the way they conducted business as independent proprietors, limiting reliance on credit and eschewing the transaction of business that increased the risk of financial embarrassment. These business owners, already singed once by the marketplace, accepted a ceiling on profits in order to prevent a repeat of pecuniary difficulties. In other cases, former bankrupts turned their backs on independent business ventures altogether, opting for positions either as mercantile agents or as salaried white-collar employees. For both types of bankrupts, failure heightened the value placed on economic security.

The social and cultural ramifications of business failure, moreover, extended far beyond its tendency to guide large numbers of bankrupts into middle-class occupations and encourage their adoption of stability as a financial beacon. In antebellum fiction and social commentary, the recurring figure of the bankrupt served as a vivid reminder that the credit system could ruin people even as it provided the finance to clear farms, build canals and cities, and send all manner of commodities back and forth across the continent. Anxiety about insolvency spurred a reshaping of cultural ideals about social mobility in America, indicated not only in the revamped advice to aspirant businessmen, but also in cultural models of success for young women.

By the 1830s, novelists and short-story writers had begun to stress that females in America had to pay attention to the specter of bankruptcy at every stage in their life. Fiction writers encouraged women contemplating marriage to look for a mate who would eschew the reckless business methods of a Rufus Granger, while instructing already wedded housekeepers about the importance of rigorous domestic economy. In both the choice of a suitable spouse and the maintenance of a frugal lifestyle, women had the opportunity to safeguard their own social status and reduce the overall rate of failure in the marketplace. These messages typically occurred in fictional accounts of bankruptcies that result from a wife's expensive tastes and desire to be part of high society, or in comparisons between sensible female characters who choose level-headed husbands and thus maintain at least material comfort, and foolhardy ones who marry highfliers and so invariably endure insolvency. The theme of redemption through failure runs throughout this fiction, as encounters with bankruptcy lead profligate female protagonists to mend their ways.[35]

In light of the volatility of antebellum commerce, antebellum authors of fiction further cautioned that no daughter, wife, or mother, no matter how discerning in marriage or thrifty in consumption, could assume her family to be safe from bankruptcy. As a result, these writers insisted that thorough education was essential for antebellum women. In addition to inculcating the habits and skills associated with effective motherhood, appropriate education enabled women to enter the commercial world if the businesses of husbands or fathers failed. Without the ability to earn income, once "genteel" women could easily find themselves with no alternative to the almshouse. With that ability, especially in a socially respectable field such as teaching, women would be able to avoid the most dependent forms of poverty, even in the event of the most severe financial crisis. They would also have the capacity to aid their bankrupt husbands' attempts to regain economic footing.[36] The experience of several women married to bankruptcy petitioners under the 1841 act underscores the relevance of such advice, as they became their families' main source of support after the collapse of their spouses' enterprises.[37]

Neither this fictional discourse about bankruptcy and women nor the attempts to recast models of career advancement for middle-class men rejected aspirations of rising in the business world or reaching higher social circles. But the authors who explored these themes counseled Americans to temper their dreams in the face of an economy that treated inexperience and a lack of capital harshly. In a world where the credit system ruined so many businesses, caution and prudence constituted crucial virtues for both men and women. Families had to learn to live within their means. Women had to be able to earn income in the event of a husband's failure or death. And men had to accept that a steady salary had substantial advantages over an uncertain business venture, especially when such employment offered the possibility of promotion within an already established firm.

These messages likely gained careful consideration from numerous readers of antebellum fiction and advice literature. Bankruptcy occurred with sufficient frequency in the mid-nineteenth-century United States that almost everyone was touched by it sooner or later. Even if family members did not personally experience the pain of watching sheriffs remove their household possessions in order to satisfy the claims of creditors, they probably had relatives or friends who had endured this fate. In a society where perhaps as many as one in two business ventures ended with insolvency notices, Americans had ample reason to ponder the consequences of being unable to pay one's debts.[38]

Such a high incidence of business failure almost certainly influenced the evolution of familial economic strategies and attitudes that historians have persuasively associated with the mid-nineteenth-century middle class. Delayed entry into the marketplace by sons, provision of as much education as possible to children, postponement of marriage and conception, and a preference for caution over the pursuit of riches all made sense to numerous Americans caught in the midst of a fluctuating and hazardous economy. On the one hand, these strategies increased the chances of success if family heads or their children entered into business as independent proprietors. On the other hand, such approaches left open the option of salaried, white-collar employment should individuals wish to limit exposure to the risks inherent in a capitalist economy.[39]

The prevalence of insolvency additionally helps to explain why, in the middle decades of the nineteenth century, Americans increasingly accepted lifelong careers as white-collar subordinates. By the 1860s and 1870s, substantial numbers of native-born urban Americans had begun to forgo independent ventures into the marketplace, choosing instead to pursue careers within business organizations. If these individuals experienced upward mobility, it was movement from "clerk" to "bookkeeper," "salesman," or "agent." Recognition of the hazards inherent in independent business helped to persuade the growing ranks of nonmanual workers to remain content with limited occupational horizons.[40]

In an incisive examination of one segment of the postbellum class of white-collar workers—employees of the federal government—historian Cindy Aron portrays the first generation of Americans who experienced an essentially permanent status of salaried subordination as "reluctant pioneers." Aron notes that when men pursued postbellum clerical positions in the civil service, their letters of application overwhelmingly expressed preference for self-employment and often apologetically characterized their place-seeking as regrettable, necessitated by misfortune, and only temporary in nature. These entrants into "a new white-collar world" gained "regular monthly paychecks" that provided decent if unspectacular income, comparative job stability, and, as a result, the ability to obtain consumer credit and plan for the future. They traded "autonomy for security" but, in Aron's judgment, remained "less than proud of their choice."[41] The collective biographies of antebellum bankrupts largely corroborate this emphasis on aversion to dependence in the workplace. On the whole, failed proprietors demonstrated a strong impulse to reestablish themselves as business owners, even when they initially responded to insolvency with extended sojourns as paid workers. In addition, former bankrupts who eventually turned away from proprietorship tended to gravitate toward positions as agents, which minimized day-to-day supervision.

Still, the shift from business ownership to employment on salary or commission—both for former bankrupts and for growing numbers of Americans who never entered business on their own account—may have been eased by the cultural redefinitions so dramatically on display in E. M. Gibson's story "Going into Business." This occupational transition generally entailed that members of the middle class lower their sights, reject grand commercial schemes, and settle for circumscribed positions predicated on subordination. Holders of white-collar jobs, though, could take a large measure of solace in the philosophy articulated by fictional characters such as Edgar and Emma Sargent. In the middle decades of the nineteenth century, America's white-collar employees often earned sufficient income to live in "respectable" neighborhoods and rent tolerably well-furnished accommodations. They could supply a limited number of children with considerable education, as well as purchase household amenities such as books, ornaments, and in some cases, those crucial markers of middle-class status, pianos. In addition, they remained able to contrast the genteel surroundings and nonmanual character of their work with the laboring conditions faced by factory operatives, journeymen, or manual laborers.[42]

Thus the burgeoning class of clerks, bookkeepers, and agents could not only take consolation in their enjoyment of relative economic stability but also lay claim to a version of republican independence—one in which the most fundamental "autonomy" rested not on the responsibilities of self-employment, but on freedom from both the most severe forms of subservience and the degrading precariousness of irretrievable indebtedness. Even if growing numbers of middle-class heads of households no longer counted themselves among the ranks of independent pro-prietors, they nonetheless had skirted the plight of exploited "wage-slaves." Even if they answered to a boss, they did not lead the "dog's life" of so many nineteenth-century business owners—who "trembled at the very creak" of a creditor's shoes, who sank day after day under the anxious burden of ever more pressing obligations, who lost sleep night after night to nightmares of bankruptcy.[43]

Individual Bankruptcy and the
Rise of American Big Business

Have you insurance on your life, for the benefit of a surviving family, relatives, or friends? Are they fully protected by insurance on your life from the many evils that may arise from your unexpected death, at a moment of embarrassment, perhaps of utter insolvency?

—Advertisement of the United States Life Insurance Company, *The Independent*,
   May 24, 1854

Sometime during the first few months of 1852, a seventeen-year-old resident of New York City asked a former teacher for advice about what kind of business career he should pursue. A native of the Hudson River valley town of Catskill, the youth had spent the previous year clerking in a dry goods establishment and now contemplated a future in either private banking or wholesaling. In reply, the teacher declared that "the Banking houses and Mercantile houses that you have been speaking of, will all pass away. You may enter them and rise to such position as will suit you and only live to see all your future hopes darkened by unforeseen circumstances which you yourself would be unable to prevent." This mentor advised his onetime student that instead of courting almost certain disaster in such commercial or financial pursuits, he should "[g]o into Life Insurance . . . ; you will find it certain and sure." The youth took this suggestion very much to heart. Within the year he accepted a salaried position with a leading New York City insurance company; over the rest of his life, he never sought employment in any other kind of business.[1]

This vignette underscores the resonance that particular narratives of failure could have across the generations in mid-nineteenth-century America. The youth's father and the teacher to whom he looked for guidance both became insolvent after the financial crises of the late 1830s. The father, Henry Hazen Hyde, failed in 1842 as a Catskill dry goods merchant, largely as a result of his guarantee on a business associate's ill-fated real estate deal. The teacher, John C. Johnston, encountered disappointment in several commercial endeavors—as a Catskill cooper in the early

1830s, as a grower of mulberry trees outside Mobile, Alabama, during 1837, and as a partner in a window sash factory back in Catskill two years later. Both men received bankruptcy discharges under the 1841 Federal Bankruptcy Act. Their checkered commercial experiences undoubtedly helped to convince the young Henry Baldwin Hyde to eschew independent business ventures.[2]

The episode of the younger Hyde's career choice further opens a vantage point on a more profound and far-reaching consequence of individual bankruptcy in nineteenth-century America—facilitation of the growth of big business. In considering the causal relationship between the emergence of large-scale firms and the failure of relatively small-scale ones, the most familiar impulse is to view the arrival of commercial behemoths as hastening the demise of far less well capitalized competitors. One thinks of antebellum New England textile factories that squeezed out weavers, or of postbellum midwestern meatpackers that used refrigerated railroad cars to put pressure on the nation's urban butchers, or of the late-nineteenth-century mail-order distributors that cut so deeply into the business of myriad rural storekeepers. Nonetheless, in three crucial ways endemic business failure among proprietors and partnerships contributed to consolidation in the American economy. Widespread insolvency increasingly channeled entrepreneurial ambitions into corporate enterprises, where individual liability was limited and the possibilities for growth were extensive; it assisted some fast-growing businesses in constructing effective sales pitches for their products; and it substantially increased the supply of white-collar labor indispensable to the functioning of sizable, complex firms that wished to distribute goods and services to an integrated, national market. One can see all of these processes at work in the industry that Henry Baldwin Hyde joined in 1852—life insurance.

It was not until the 1840s and 1850s that the business of insuring lives took off in the United States. During this time, several newly incorporated mutual insurance companies instituted aggressive sales techniques that depended on personal solicitation by agents and that sought to overcome deep-seated cultural aversion to life insurance, either as a form of socially disruptive gambling or a sacrilegious means of tempting providence. Former bankrupts had leading roles in several of these financial institutions, serving as corporate founders and early company officers who directed the industry's rapid expansion. Mutual life companies attracted the attention of failed businessmen largely because these enterprises required minimal capital outlay, so long as one could obtain a legislative charter and conjure up enough early policyholders to create a sufficient reserve fund out of premiums. Promoters could launch mutual insurance businesses with remarkably small stakes.[3]

These early insurance boosters included Henry Hazen Hyde, John C. Johnston, and Hyde's son Henry Baldwin. The elder Hyde served as the first "general agent" of the Mutual Life Insurance Company of New York, building a far-flung network of agents that enabled the company to become the largest in the country by 1860. Johnston quickly became the Mutual Life's most successful salesman during the late 1840s and early 1850s, accumulating sufficient influence to force a reorganization of company management in 1853. A few years later he moved to the Old Northwest, where he founded the Mutual Life Insurance Company of Wisconsin, now known as Northwestern Mutual Life. Henry Baldwin Hyde's career selection of life insurance as a haven from business failure eventually had even greater implications for the industry's growth. After working for seven years as a clerk and cashier for New York's Mutual Life, in 1859 he founded the Equitable Life Assurance Company, which he then managed for the next forty years. Through savvy marketing campaigns, persistent driving of his agency force, and the regular introduction of popular new investment vehicles, such as deferred dividend policies, Hyde made Equitable into the largest life insurance company in the world, with over one billion dollars of insurance in force at the time of his death in 1899.[4]

While either personal legacies of business failure or fear of it led some entrepreneurially minded Americans to pursue managerial careers in life insurance, the widespread incidence of bankruptcy served as a primary reference point in company advertisements and pamphlets, as well as in the direct appeals made by agents. Again and again in the 1850s and 1860s, industry literature stressed that insolvency was all too common in America, and that a policy on a breadwinner's life would "shield him against business reverses," allowing him and his family to "get peace of mind." Financial panics and ensuing economic downturns throughout the century prompted insurance managers to make such arguments with even greater insistence. As the American economy settled into prolonged stagnation during the spring of 1874, for example, Henry Baldwin Hyde spent the better part of April drafting scores of lengthy personal letters to his corps of agents around the country. In all of these missives, he characterized "the unsettled state of trade" and "the many failures in business" brought on by the previous year's great panic as "strong points in favor of the Life Insurance canvasser." Amid such economic circumstances, Hyde instructed, men were "most readily convinced of the *intrinsic value* of Life Insurance." Even if many potential customers were "not in a condition to pay a single premium, their promise to insure *as soon as things turn*, lays a foundation for an enormous business as soon as flush times come."[5]

Insurance companies further emphasized that several industrial states had adopted legislation that exempted most life insurance payments to widows from the claims of their deceased husbands' creditors. These statutes, like other early grants of independent property rights to married women, had the goal of extending financial protection to the entrepreneurial classes, allowing the families of businessmen to create reserve funds insulated from the consequences of bankruptcy. All of the insurance acts placed a ceiling on the amount of coverage shielded from a deceased bankrupt's creditors, generally restricting such protection to policies that carried premiums under $300 a year. In the 1850s and 1860s, this limitation still left widows of bankrupts free to claim as much as $10,000 in insurance—enough to provide an annual income of $600 when conservatively invested—regardless of their dead spouses' indebtedness. Insurance companies invariably portrayed these statutory exemptions as means to lessen the risks associated with entrepreneurship. Industry pamphlets even suggested that the exemptions promoted healthy risk taking, enabling businessmen, in the words of one such publication, "safely to apply all [their] present income in furthering any desirable scheme which may be presented to [them]"—a course of action that they "could not possibly entertain were the future not secured."[6]

As one might expect, these various attempts to use the specter of insolvency as a means of selling life insurance had their greatest impact on the urban, commercially oriented middle class. The families of merchants, manufacturers, professionals, and ambitious clerks were especially attuned to the dangers of bankruptcy in the mid-nineteenth-century United States. Such individuals were also especially inclined to reject the argument that insuring lives usurped divine prerogatives, and especially able to afford annual premiums, which for each $1,000 of insurance on someone aged thirty could cost several weeks wages for journeymen or day laborers. Up through the 1860s, the urban middle class constituted the most remunerative market for life insurers, with numerous policies taken out by married women on the lives of their husbands, in order to take advantage of statutory protection against any assault by creditors.[7]

A final link between individual bankruptcy and the rapid development of life insurance lies with the recruitment of people to sell the industry's stock-in-trade. During the nineteenth century, volume business in the insurance of lives was heavily dependent on vigorous face-to-face marketing. Advertising copy, no matter how compelling, simply did not move large numbers of people to take out policies on their lives. Neither did early systems of agency, which depended on "respectable" citizens who were disinclined to expend much time or effort in convincing the residents of their communities to take out policies. The most persistent and persuasive agents, by contrast, could coax Americans to insure by the hundreds. Unfortunately for the executives of life insurance companies, convincing individuals with such attributes to accept positions as sales representatives proved to be a trying endeavor. Even though popular distrust of life insurance dissipated considerably around midcentury, in no small measure because of successful industrywide efforts to depict policies as required by the Christian duty to provide for one's dependents, antipathy toward life insurance agents remained strong. Despite vigorous attempts to portray themselves as missionaries who preached an altruistic gospel of protecting the weak and vulnerable, sellers of life policies continued to confront three stigmas—that of dependents who had to defer to the guidelines and rulings of distant, corporate masters; that of tricky dealers prone to misrepresentation; and that of "dirty workers" who profited, like undertakers, from the profane world of death. Credit reporters typically characterized even the most successful agents in extremely unflattering terms—as "oily tongued," "uncertain," and "not strictly reliable." Such low public standing made most nineteenth-century Americans unwilling to consider this sort of work.[8]

Not surprisingly, the ranks of nineteenth-century life insurance agents tended to be comprised of persons who had been unsuccessful in other occupations, including numerous bankrupts. The occupational odyssey of James W. Judd conveys the typical pattern. Judd first failed in the 1830s as a Hartford, Connecticut, book publisher. After receiving a bankruptcy discharge in New York City, he resumed business there as a book dealer, only to fail again amid the general economic turbulence of 1854. At this juncture, he secured an appointment as a New York City agent of a Maine life insurance company, retaining this position for the next quarter of a century.[9]

On occasion, postbellum life insurance executives candidly admitted that failure served almost as a precondition to acceptance of sales positions in their businesses. One company president remarked that agencies in the industry had long constituted "an asylum" for the "refuse of every calling"; another recalled toward the end of the century that "there was a time when the life insurance agent's name was anathema, when men after making failures in other lines started out to solicit for ours." Perhaps because both his father and mentor had come to life insurance through the same route, Henry Baldwin Hyde maintained a less critical perspective on the disappointments that had led many of his agents to look to Equitable for employment. As Hyde explained to a Chicago agent in 1874, he had nothing but contempt for "the man who calmly sits down and folds his hands in despair because his previous efforts have failed to place him on the topmost rung of the ladder." But to the man who "endeavor[s] to discover where and how he made his mistakes and the best means of avoiding them in the future"; who "gather[s] renewed courage from repeated failures," since he benefits from "wisdom gained by experience"; and who "in the strength and might of his manhood press[es] forward in the accomplishment of his purpose in spite of all difficulties and all obstacles that may beset him"—to that individual, Hyde was more than ready to extend the opportunities associated with selling life insurance. Regardless of whether company managers viewed their agents' financial pasts with distaste or understanding, they all relied on failure to provide them with the labor force that made industry expansion possible.[10]

High rates of individual bankruptcy, of course, did not constitute the sole impetus behind the growth of American life insurance into one of the country's most important mechanisms of finance. Shifting religious mores greatly assisted the industry, as most Protestant denominations came to endorse greater individual agency in preparing for the eventuality of death; so too did the promise of direct economic rewards, most tangibly embodied in the escalating dividends offered by mutual companies over the course of the century. The most dramatic increases in life insurance coverage, moreover, occurred from the 1870s onward, when some companies began to target working-class customers through inexpensive policies that promised to cover only funeral expenses, when others began to market their products vigorously overseas, and when almost every company developed products that combined insurance with various investment vehicles, many of which were highly speculative in nature.[11] Business failure—both actual and imagined—nonetheless provided crucial boosts to the industry in its early decades of expansion, furnishing leading companies with some of their most effective executives, marketing strategies, and salesmen.

Individual bankruptcy had analogous reverberations in other parts of the nineteenth-century American economy, though perhaps not with the same degree of force as in life insurance. Most importantly, the willingness of so many nineteenth-century bankrupts to turn to salaried employment or agency assisted numerous large businesses in finding the skilled white-collar employees who were so vital to volume-based marketing in a national economy. Such labor was not always easy to attract in a society that tended to lionize individuals who worked for themselves and to question the manliness of men who sought long-term careers in white-collar occupations.[12]

Thus when a New York City dry goods magnate like Alexander T. Stewart sought out salaried employees to oversee aspects of his operations, recent bankrupts constituted prime recruits. The owner of America's largest wholesaler and retailer of dry goods from the mid-1830s though the early 1870s, Stewart made it essentially a rule to offer handsomely paid positions to well-regarded but insolvent merchants. Once this policy became generally known in commercial circles, failed businessmen from both New York and urban centers farther afield came to his Marble Palace in search of employment. These former bankrupts, one writer observed in 1862, "turn[ed] their energies into that mighty channel which flows into [A. T. Stewart & Co.'s] treasury." As buyers or the heads of the business's various departments, they were to New York's greatest "merchant prince" as "his marshals were to Napoleon." An "Autocrat of Trade," Stewart had attained a status comparable to that of the French conqueror, "enthroned in the insulated majesty of mercantile greatness." He owed this position in no small measure to his ability to harness the talents of ruined businessmen. To this author of capsule biographies on leading figures in American life, Stewart's savvy employment of broken traders conferred great benefits both to them and to society generally. The "refuge" he afforded to "the weak" offered "a better condition than the one from which they have been driven," while contributing to the economic efficiency associated with "centraliza-tion of trade."[13]

This remarkable commentary, which lauded A. T. Stewart as an "Autocrat of Trade" even as Union troops sought to redeem American democracy through the defeat of a southern confederacy led by autocratic slaveholders, suggests a fur-ther connection between individual bankruptcy and the rise of big business in America. The emergence of dominant firms like A. T. Stewart & Co., run by powerful and in many ways unaccountable businessmen, did not always graft easily onto a democratic culture premised on widely dispersed opportunities for indepen-dent economic decision making. Commercial autocracy did not look so threaten-ing, though, if it reflected heroic striving in an unforgiving marketplace that drove most businesses to the wall. That autocracy might even take on the aura of philan-thropy if it provided entrepreneurial losers with productive places in the newly dominant business organizations.[14]

In the tales of insolvents turned life insurance pioneers and dry goods emporium managers, one sees two common approaches to navigating failure in nineteenth-century America—renewed commitment to entrepreneurial undertakings, and heightened appreciation of economic security. These opposing impulses encour-aged very different postbankruptcy career strategies, which in turn produced diver-gent social and economic consequences, alternately invigorating capitalist innova-tion and enlarging the proportion of the urban middle class that demonstrated a willingness to let someone else bear the anxieties associated with proprietary re-sponsibility. Despite the substantial contrast between these responses to personal legacies of insolvency, they worked together to help usher in a new economic order structured around large, bureaucratic companies, rather than small-scale producers and purveyors of goods and services. In part, postbellum America's world of trusts and tycoons rested on a foundation of pervasive individual failure.

My study of the court records created by the operation of the 1841 Bankruptcy Act in the United States District Court for the Southern District of New York merits some explanation of research strategy. Aside from a few instances in which I used a straightforward method of sampling in order to ascertain simple percentages, as when calculating the percentage of bankrupts who represented themselves in bankruptcy court, I eschewed an approach governed by the rigorous precepts of statistically minded social science. I did so largely because those precepts require that scholars choose their cases randomly, and I quickly discovered that making full use of the bankruptcy records required me to choose many bankrupts for study precisely because they were linked to other petitioners for relief.

In my initial examination of southern New York bankruptcy records, I did apply a crude form of stratified sampling so as to ensure a rough degree of representativeness in my survey of archival materials. I could engage in such an enterprise because of the alphabetical list of southern New York bankrupts published in 1843.[1] This pamphlet, which served as an early form of credit reporting, provided its readers with a register of every bankrupt who appeared on the federal bankruptcy dockets in southern New York under the 1841 act. It included the residences of bankrupts, and either the occupation in which they had failed or the occupation they had adopted since failing. The list also indicated whether a bankrupt had filed for relief voluntarily, or whether the bankrupt's creditors had filed an involuntary petition.

Using the bankruptcy list as a guide, I surveyed about twenty case-files of bankrupt farmers, approximately twenty-five case-files of bankrupt merchants, a similar number of case-files for bankrupts who identified themselves as clerks, or as brokers or agents, another fifty to provide evidence about bankrupt manufacturers, artisans, and laborers, an additional fifteen who listed occupations as public servants, a smaller number who described themselves as "gentlemen," and about fifteen who were involuntary, rather than voluntary bankrupts. I also read the bankruptcy records of all nine southern New York bankrupts who were women, as well as the case-files of all but one of the forty-six bankrupts who resided in Ulster County at the time that bankruptcy proceedings began. I chose Ulster County bankrupts for particularly comprehensive analysis because it included both rural areas and the large Hudson River town of Kingston; the experiences of bankrupts from both the countryside and the river town, I assumed, would provide useful comparisons to the experiences of bankrupts from New York City and Brooklyn. Finally, I singled out the bankruptcy records of individuals whose previous or later careers had made them important historical figures, such as Arthur Tappan, James Watson Webb, and Silas M. Stilwell, and the case-files of persons for whom I was able to locate collections of archival papers.

While these categories provided me with a place to start, my analysis of particular bankruptcies soon led me to examine the records of scores of other southern New York bankrupts. Applicants frequently had relatives, partners, endorsers, and business associates who had also failed, and who had also petitioned for bankruptcy relief under the 1841 act. By investigating the bankruptcy case-files of family members and business associates, I was able to reconstruct the dense networks of trade, investment, and finance that permeated the antebellum economy and that provided the conduits through which financial difficulties often spread. As my research progressed, additional leads directed my attention to still other case-files. I soon discovered that some attorneys or court officials who worked in the bankruptcy system created by the 1841 act were themselves bankrupts; the case-files of these men deserved a look. After examination of the records relating to the administration and sale of assets held by bankrupts, I inspected the case-files of several bankrupts who had atypically surrendered meaningful assets to the court-appointed assignee or who repeatedly took part in liquidation auctions.

Two further sources led me to investigate still other southern New York bankruptcies. The first of these were reports of legal decisions relating to the 1841 Bankruptcy Act, either in federal court or in the state courts after Congress had repealed the act in 1843. (State courts had jurisdiction to rule on a number of disputes resulting from the federal bankruptcy legislation, such as attempts by creditors to impeach a discharge on the grounds of fraud.) Judicial opinions in law magazines and federal and state law reports, and newspaper accounts of the day's happenings in Judge Betts's court steered me to the case-files of approximately forty bankrupts, many of which teemed with creditors' objections, depositions of witnesses, exhibits, and memoranda of legal arguments.

Evidence about the postbankruptcy careers of individuals on the bankruptcy dockets further guided my research choices. Local histories published in the nineteenth century about places such as Dutchess and Greene Counties provided short biographies of several individuals who appeared on the bankruptcy register that supplied details about their postdischarge lives. With this evidence in hand, I went back to the record of their failures. Similarly, partnership notices and business advertisements in the New York City papers during 1843 often included the names of people who appeared on the bankruptcy dockets. These notices indicated that some bankrupts had little difficulty reentering the business world after obtaining legal releases, and led me back to the evidence about their previous difficulties. Most importantly, the R. G. Dun & Co. credit reports for the nineteenth century directed me to dozens of case-files. By perusing the New York City index of the Dun reports, I noted scores of potential matches with applicants under the 1841 act. After scrutinizing the credit reports for these individuals, I was able to distinguish businessmen who might be the same persons as the ones listed on the southern New York bankruptcy register from those who clearly were not applicants for federal bankruptcy relief in 1842 or 1843. A return to the bankruptcy case-files usually cleared up any remaining confusion. My use of the Dun archives also went in the other direction. If I had already examined the case-file of a southern New York bankrupt, I checked the Dun records to see if he or she had received later attention from credit reporters.

I should add a word about the manner in which I approached the task of record linkage, since much of my work rests on the tracing of bankrupts over time, using unrelated sources of evidence. Record linkage, as social historians have long noted, presupposes that when historians use two different sources to compile information about a particular individual, both sources convey information about the same person. With many sources, such as cumulative editions of city directories or cumulative census returns, the potential for ambiguity in record linkage is great. These sources provide limited information, and thus offer researchers a restricted basis on which to gauge whether the John Smith in one city directory or census was the same individual as the John Smith in the next.[2] Nineteenth-century bankruptcy records and credit reports provide a much stronger basis for making positive identifications of historical subjects. Each of these sources offers a host of details about the individuals concerned, and thus eases the task of determining whether bankruptcy petitions and later credit reports described the same persons. An example should make this point clear.

The register of bankrupts who appeared in the United States District Court for the Southern District of New York under the 1841 act includes Dwight Bishop, a New York City agent. The R. G. Dun & Co. credit ledgers for nineteenth-century New York City also include reports on a person named Dwight Bishop. In the Dun records, Bishop is described as a furniture dealer. On the basis of this information, one cannot be certain that the two sources describe one person and not two. Together, however, bankruptcy records and the credit reports offer solid evidence that the bankrupt and the like-named person described in the Dun ledgers are one and the same. One of Bishop's first Dun entries, on July 15, 1851, recounts an earlier partnership in furniture manufacturing with a man named Breckels, which had ended badly. Bishop's 1842 bankruptcy application offers copious details about the $11,944 in debts that Bishop and Breckels owed jointly as the result of their partnership.[3] In over 150 instances, I was able to find similarly strong evidentiary links between bankrupts under the 1841 act and subjects of later R. G. Dun credit reports.

Notes

Abbreviations Used in the Notes

ACG   *Appendix to the Congressional Globe*

BV   Bound Volume

C-F   Case-file, Entry 117, Bankruptcy Records, Act of 1841, United States District Court for the Southern Federal District of New York, National Archives and Record Administration, Northeast Region, New York City

CTP   Charlemagne Tower Papers, Columbia University Rare Book and Manuscript Library, New York City

CG   *Congressional Globe*

DBR   *De Bow's Review*

Dun   R. G. Dun & Co. Collection, Nineteenth-Century Credit Ledgers, Baker Library, Harvard Business School, Boston, Mass.

GLB   *Godey's Lady's Book*

GM   *Graham's Magazine*

HMM   *Hunt's Merchants' Magazine*

LMLM   *Livingston's Monthly Law Magazine*

LR   *Law Reporter*

MCNYE   *Morning Courier and New York Enquirer*

NAR   *North American Review*

NWR   *Niles' Weekly Register*

NYH   *New York Herald*

N-YHS   The New-York Historical Society, New York City

NYLO   *New York Legal Observer*

PLJ   *Pennsylvania Law Journal*

S-B   Record of Sales (Sales Book), Entry 127, Bankruptcy Records, Act of 1841, United States District Court for the Southern Federal District of New York, National Archives and Record Administration, Northeast Region, New York City

WLJ   *Western Law Journal*

Note: When published legal decisions appeared in newspapers or periodicals, I have cited these decisions in the same manner as cases published in law reports, essentially treating the newspaper or periodical as a volume of law reports. Where possible, I have indicated the court in which the case occurred. "CC Mass." refers to the United States Circuit Court for the District of Massachusetts; "DC ED Pa." refers to the United States District Court for the Eastern District of Pennsylvania; "Supreme Court Mass." refers to the Massachusetts State Supreme Court; and so on.

Introduction

1. For a description of the bankruptcy system's first day of operation in New York City, see *Brooklyn Daily Eagle*, Feb. 4, 1842.

2. The exact number of bankruptcy applications filed under the 1841 act remains uncertain. According to statistics compiled by the secretary of state from thirty-three federal districts, 41,108 individuals found their way onto the nation's bankruptcy dockets in 1842 and 1843. These statistics exclude eight districts that did not send tallies to the secretary of state—Delaware, North Carolina, Georgia, Indiana, the eastern district of Tennessee, the northern district of Mississippi, Missouri, and the western district of Louisiana (*Letter . . . Relative to the . . . Bankrupt Law*; *Letter . . . Showing Proceedings under the Bankrupt Act*).

3. Unless the specific context requires reference to technical distinctions in nineteenth-century American law, I follow the lead of Webster's 1853 *American Dictionary of the English Language*, and so use "bankrupt" and "insolvent" interchangeably, just as nineteenth-century Americans did in their everyday speech. Each term refers to individuals who could not pay their just debts, whose creditors would not grant extensions in the time of payment, and who, as a result, had to stop the transaction of business on their own responsibility. I similarly use the terms "bankruptcy," "insolvency," and "failure" to mean essentially the same thing.

4. "Why Some Succeed and Others Fail in Business," *HMM* 42 (1860): 650. For typical antebellum estimates of failure rates, see speeches of Reps. Milton Brown and Barnard, *ACG*, 27th Cong., 1st sess. (1841), 482, 498; "Risk of Mercantile Life," *Brooklyn Daily Eagle*, July 18, 1842; "The Late Bankrupt Law," *PLJ* 3 (1844): 15; "Chances of Success in Mercantile Life," *HMM* 15 (1846): 476–77; "A Citizen of Boston," 20–21; "The Value of a Clerkship in New York," *HMM* 20 (1849): 570; "Fluctuations of Mercantile Life," *DBR* 8 (1850): 78; Freedley, *Practical Treatise on Business*, 117; J. T. Hendricks, "A Sermon of Commerce," *HMM* 28 (1853): 679; J. H. Allen, "The True Mercantile Character," *HMM* 34 (1856): 61; "Money-Getting—Causes of Failure in Business," *HMM* 35 (1856): 774; and "Why Merchants Fail," *HMM* 41 (1859): 521. On postbellum expressions of this rule of thumb, see Kirkland, *Dream and Thought*, 8; Hilkey, *Character Is Capital*, 132; and Sandage, "Deadbeats, Drunkards, and Dreamers," 47–48.

5. Blumin, *Emergence of the Middle Class*, 115; Freyer, *Producers versus Capitalists*, 65; Clark, *Roots of Rural Capitalism*, 217; Decker, *Fortunes and Failures*, 92. These scholars primarily worked with credit assessments compiled by the Mercantile Agency and its later incarnation, the R. G. Dun & Co. Blumin's survey of mercantile establishments in New York registered the lowest failure rate, 25 percent, while Decker's sample of San Francisco firms resulted in the highest, around 67 percent. The other studies report incidences of insolvency between 40 and 50 percent. Dun generally did not furnish assessments for especially marginal businesses that were most likely to fail, since these firms rarely sought credit outside their communities and thus did not command the attention of the wholesalers who constituted Dun's primary customers. As a result, calculations based on Dun credit ledgers may understate actual bankruptcy rates. For additional discussions of the frequency of bankruptcy in various economic sectors, see Wallace, *Rockdale*, 21–22; Wilentz, *Chants Democratic*, 119–42; Griffen and Griffen, *Natives and Newcomers*, 104–92; and Blumin, *Urban Threshold*, 207–11.

6. Greene, *Perils of Pearl Street*, 5.

7. Doerflinger, *Vigorous Spirit*, 141–42. Since 1857, R. G. Dun & Co. and its corporate successor, Dun & Bradstreet, have compiled national statistics on business failures among firms that sought formal commercial credit. Annual commercial bankruptcy rates have typically hovered around 1 percent, with the exception of the period from 1935 through 1980, when the average annual incidence of business failure fell to around 0.5 percent. Over

time, of course, the chances of a given venture in any era encountering a failure went up significantly. In addition, several analyses have shown that new concerns have always been at especially great risk of bankruptcy. In the late 1970s, for example, one-half of new American businesses failed within the first five years of operation (Hutchinson et al., "Study in Business Mortality"; U.S Department of Commerce, Bureau of the Census, *Historical Statistics*, Series V: 20–30; Sullivan et al., *As We Forgive Our Debtors*, 108–27, 288, 330; Dun & Bradstreet, *Business Failure Record*, 1–2). Any capitalist society, and especially one undergoing rapid commercialization, is likely to experience significant insolvency rates. For a discussion of a comparably high incidence of business failure in eighteenth-century London, see Hoppit, *Risk and Failure*, 66–67.

8. Bushman, "Markets and Composite Farms"; Lamoreaux, "Accounting for Capitalism." For leading statements of the "market revolution" thesis, see Sellers, *Market Revolution*, and the essays in Stokes and Conway, eds., *Market Revolution in America*, both of which provide citations to an extensive literature.

9. The sample comprises just under one-fifth of all southern New York bankrupts. In terms of the number of failures experienced by applicants, the timing of failures, the place of residence at the time of entry onto the bankruptcy docket and at the time of failure, occupation at the time of failure, and amount of debt owed, the bankruptcy records created as a result of the 1841 act lend themselves to statistical measurement. A bankrupt's schedules of assets and debts offer clear indications about each of these issues in the great majority of instances. Depositions taken in contested cases and unsolicited personal statements also furnish information about these matters. The bankruptcy records further provide substantial evidence about age, place of birth, marital and parental status, religion, and political affiliation, though in a far less systematic fashion. For a discussion of the bases on which southern New York bankrupts became selected for the sample, see the Note on Research Method.

10. Several nonmigratory bankrupts in the sample also were partners in enterprises that operated outside southern New York. The court records of these individuals usually furnish details about the failures of such businesses.

11. *Act to Establish a Uniform System of Bankruptcy.*

12. For useful contemporaneous discussions of nineteenth-century European bankruptcy laws, see "Bankrupt Laws," *NAR* 7 (1818): 35–36; "Bankrupt and Insolvent Laws," *American Jurist* 3 (1830): 219–34; Charles Clark, "The Russian Insolvency Laws," *HMM* 6 (1842): 419–25; "The Law of Attachment in the Several States of the United States," *Bankers' Magazine* 12 (1857): 193–95; and Richard Brown, "Comparative Legislation in Bankruptcy." Historical treatments of nineteenth-century European bankruptcy are generally lacking in English-language scholarship, except with regard to English law. See in particular Lester, *Victorian Insolvency*, and Duffy, "Bankruptcy and Insolvency in London."

13. Holcombe, *Law of Debtor and Creditor*; "Law of Each State Relative to the Collection of Debts," *LMLM* 2 (1854): 3–19; "Household and Homestead Exemption Laws of the Different States," *LMLM* 2 (1854): 99–118; Warren, *Bankruptcy in United States History*, 87–92; Bauer, "Movement against Imprisonment for Debt"; Hartz, *Economic Policy*, 219–35; Rothbard, *Panic of 1819*; Coleman, *Debtors and Creditors in America*.

14. Warren, *Bankruptcy in United States History*, 90–91; Coleman, *Debtors and Creditors in America*; Angell, *Practical Summary of the Law of Assignments*; Burrill, *Treatise on the Law*.

15. Tocqueville, *Democracy in America*, 2:249. For similar views, see Martineau, *Society in America*, 364–66; Chevalier, *Society, Manners, and Politics*, 449–50; and Evans, *History of the Commercial Crisis*, 34.

16. For particularly influential treatments of the "household economy" that prevailed in isolated rural regions of antebellum America, see Merrill, "Cash Is Good to Eat"; Henretta, "Families and Farms"; Hahn, *Roots of Southern Populism*; Hahn and Prude, eds., *Coun-*

tryside in the Age of Capitalist Transformation; Clark, *Roots of Rural Capitalism*; Kulikoff, *Agrarian Origins of American Capitalism*; and Sellers, *Market Revolution*. Leading discussions of independence-minded artisans and journeymen include Faler, *Mechanics and Manufacturers*; Laurie, *Working People of Philadelphia*; and Wilentz, *Chants Democratic*.

17. As Part III demonstrates, reentry into the business world by no means translated ineluctably into postfailure success.

18. An immense range of scholarship has examined the development of market capitalism and impersonal market relationships in the nineteenth-century United States. Among the most important contributions are Taylor, *Transportation Revolution*; Hurst, *Law and the Conditions of Freedom*, 3–32; Porter and Livesay, *Merchants and Manufacturers*; Lindstrom, *Economic Development in the Philadelphia Region*; Freyer, *Forums of Order*, 1–52; Alfred Chandler, *Visible Hand*; Wilentz, *Chants Democratic*, 107–42; Halttunen, *Confidence Men*, 1–32; Lamoreaux, *Insider Lending*; Clark, *Roots of Rural Capitalism*; and Sellers, *Market Revolution*.

19. For especially instructive analyses of social and familial networks in the antebellum economy, see Wallace, *Rockdale*; Griffen and Griffen, *Natives and Newcomers*; Decker, *Fortunes and Failures*; Lamoreaux, "Banks, Kinship, and Economic Development"; and Adler, "Capital and Entrepreneurship." These sorts of business networks, of course, did not only convey benefits. As Part I makes clear, many antebellum insolvencies had their origins in loans and endorsements to family members or commercial associates who failed themselves. In addition, as Part III demonstrates, useful familial and other connections by no means ensured either a return to independent proprietorship or postfailure success.

20. On the relationship between nineteenth-century law and the "release of economic energies," see Hurst, *Law and the Conditions of Freedom*.

21. On the concept of "creative destruction," see Schumpeter, *Capitalism, Socialism, and Democracy*, 81–86, and Kutler, *Privilege and Creative Destruction*, esp. 4–5, 160–62.

22. On the westward migration of insolvent farmers, see Wiebe, *Opening of American Society*, 147, and Hammond, *Banks and Politics*, 282. On Alcott's financial struggles, economic theorizing, and commitment to Fruitlands, see Rose, *Transcendentalism as a Social Movement*, 117–30. Horace Greeley, the influential New York City newspaper editor, Whig and later Republican political kingpin, and eventual Democratic presidential candidate in 1872, recalled in his autobiography that so many antebellum socialist communities did not succeed financially because they generally attracted leaders and participants who had a personal record of business failure (*Recollections of a Busy Life*, 154). For discussions of the relationship between commercial failure in the Smith family and the construction of Mormon belief systems, see Bushman, *Joseph Smith*, 27–78, and Sellers, *Market Revolution*, 219–27. Robert Matthews, otherwise known as the Prophet Matthias, underwent a spiritual rebirth similar to that of Joseph Smith after failing as a storekeeper in upstate New York (Johnson and Wilentz, *Kingdom of Matthias*).

23. Remini, *Andrew Jackson*, 36–37; Sellers, *Market Revolution*, 177, 291. Amos Kendall, one of Jackson's closest advisers, was similarly shaken early in life by the insolvency of his brother and brother-in-law, who each lost a Vermont farm to the insistent demands of creditors (Hammond, *Banks and Politics*, 281–82).

24. For presentations of this interpretation, see Schlesinger, *Age of Jackson*; Wilentz, *Chants Democratic*; Ashworth, *"Agrarians" and "Aristocrats"*; Watson, *Liberty and Power*; and Sellers, *Market Revolution*. The antebellum Democratic Party, of course, also attracted numerous entrepreneurs who chafed at the commercial dominance of entrenched elites and who found in Jacksonian policies a means of opening up access to both credit and political power. See Hofstadter, *American Political Tradition*, and Hammond, *Banks and Politics*. Democratic bankrupts discussed in this book generally belonged to the party's entrepreneurial wing.

1. Brooke, *Debt*, 3–6. See also "Imprisonment for Debt," *NAR* 32 (1831): 502; "The Gains of a Losing Business," *American Monthly Magazine*, n.s., 5 (1838): 247–51; J. N. Bellows, "Morals of Trade," *HMM* 6 (1842): 253; Arthur, *Two Merchants*; and Mrs. C. H. Butler, "The Bankrupt's Daughters: A Tale of New York," *GM* 25 (1844): 34–39, 54–59.

2. Cary, *Dependence of the Fine Arts*, 11. For similar views, see "Existing Commercial Embarrassments," *Christian Examiner* 22 (1837): 392–406; "The Moral of the Crisis," *Democratic Review* 1 (1837): 108–16; Freedley, *Practical Treatise on Business*, 200–202; "Commercial Chronicle and Review," *HMM* 29 (1853): 587–88; and Logan McKnight, "Insolvency amongst Merchants," *DBR* 16 (1854): 311. The basic outlines of this dispute were present early in the century, as evidenced by an 1810 debate between the New York City debt reformer Joseph Fay and his opponent, "Diogenes, Jr." See Ciment, "In Light of Failure," 106. For a discussion of Puritan and republican sensibilities toward insolvency, see Clark, *Roots of Rural Capitalism*, 208–9. Scott Sandage has usefully characterized this strand of nineteenth-century discourse about the causes of bankruptcy as a collection of "moral masterplots"—overarching narratives of failure that focused attention on the short-comings of individual bankrupts and "that circulated endlessly in antebellum prescriptive and commercial literature" (Sandage, "Deadbeats, Drunkards, and Dreamers," esp. 50–99).

3. Extracting the "causes" of failure from bankruptcy case-files presents analytical challenges. For most southern New York bankrupts, the evidence bearing on their insolvencies is limited to their asset and debt schedules. These two schedules provide a great deal of information about economic position at the time of application, since the 1841 Bankruptcy Act required petitioners to list: all debts owed, including the names and occupations of original creditors, dates of origin, and, in the case of obligations not yet due, dates of maturity; what debts were for, otherwise know as their "consideration"; and, if applicable, to whom the original holders of debts had transferred them. The act further required applicants to make a complete listing of all assets, both tangible and intangible (*Act to Establish a Uniform System of Bankruptcy*, sec. 1). By no means, however, did every petitioner follow these instructions to the letter. In such instances, infering the reasons for a particular failure becomes extremely difficult. And even with relatively complete asset and debt schedules, one sees only snapshots of bankrupts' economic situations, which may indicate nothing about such crucial issues as their initial capital base or the roots of their pecuniary difficulties.

Nonetheless, many debt and asset schedules provide evidence about such issues. Furthermore, in 17 percent of the bankruptcy petitions processed by Judge Betts's court, creditors objected to the proceedings, asking the judge not to grant discharges. In these instances, creditors regularly subpoenaed depositions from bankrupts, their employees, and their business associates, while applicants frequently responded by calling witnesses of their own. This testimony provides a wealth of additional evidence about the roots of failure. Finally, documentation in other archives, such as account books, diaries, and correspondence, occasionally enriches incomplete narratives of failure in the court records. Together, these sources allow a reconstruction of the major patterns of economic ruin among southern New York applicants.

4. The pace and timing of America's emergence as a market society remains a matter of considerable debate among historians. Scholars like James Henretta, Michael Merrill, and Christopher Clark argue that in substantial parts of the rural United States, farmers pursued a precapitalist household economy well into the nineteenth century, engaging in relatively self-sufficient production and consumption, and placing primary emphasis on the provision of land for offspring, which would enable them to pursue their own household economy when they reached maturity. These historians readily concede that rural households were not economic islands and often oriented some of their production toward networks of long-

distance trade. But they contend that farm families generally tried to subordinate their market relationships to the demands of the household economy, eschewing capital accumulation for its own sake and the values of capitalist exchange. Clark further suggests that many rural Americans embraced market capitalism only gradually, as demographic pressures made land difficult to obtain and as the desire for store-bought goods became more widespread (Henretta, "Families and Farms"; Merrill, "Cash Is Good to Eat"; Clark, *Roots of Rural Capitalism*). Charles Sellers (*Market Revolution*) extends these arguments, contending that the major political conflicts in Jacksonian America stemmed from the resistance of hundreds of thousands of Americans to the developing market society around them.

The opposite analytical ground is occupied by historians such as Winifred Rothenberg, Joyce Appleby, and Gordon Wood. These scholars argue that by the late colonial period, most householders, including most farmers, were eagerly seeking out commercial opportunities, and that the American Revolution unleashed additional capitalist impulses throughout American society. By the 1790s, they insist, market values and aspirations had becoming clearly dominant in both town and countryside (Rothenberg, *From Market-Places*; Appleby, *Capitalism and a New Social Order*; Wood, *Radicalism of the American Revolution*). Despite their sharp interpretive disagreements, historians on both sides of the debate grant that by the 1830s processes of commercialization and market integration were in full swing—particularly in the Northeast, the Middle Atlantic states, the Ohio River valley, much of the Mississippi River valley, and significant portions of the Old Northwest.

5. Precise calculations of annual increases in per capita gross national product are difficult before 1860 and next to impossible before 1840, largely as a result of limited information in census and customs records. The best estimates suggest a growth rate of between 0.5 and 1 percent throughout the 1820s and early 1830s, with an average annual growth rate of slightly over 1 percent between 1820 and 1860 (David, "Growth of Real Product"; Lindstrom, "American Economic Growth before 1840"). Calculations of merchandise imports and Erie Canal trade provide the best statistical measures of antebellum increases in market-based consumption. Imports grew from around $74 million in 1820 to over $353 million in 1860; westward canal shipments, which included domestic manufactures, rose even more explosively, from $10 million in 1836 to $94 million in 1853 (Taylor, *Transportation Revolution*, 161, 444–45).

6. For incisive discussions of the workings and scope of the antebellum credit system, see Albion, *Rise of New York Port*, 260–86; Atherton, "Problem of Credit Rating," 534–56; Atherton, *Frontier Merchant*; Gates, *Farmer's Age*, 398–416; Temin, *Jacksonian Economy*, 29–37; Woodman, *King Cotton*, 1–195; Porter and Livesay, *Merchants and Manufacturers*, 13–78; Wallace, *Rockdale*, 160–63; Alfred Chandler, *Visible Hand*, 19–28; Freyer, *Forums of Order*, 3–7; and Wiebe, *Opening of American Society*, 150–54, 256–64.

7. Debt Schedules, C-Fs 399, 897. Numerous other southern New York bankrupts also required loans to launch independent ventures, including farmers as well as merchants, artisans, and manufacturers. For examples, see bankruptcy records of David Huggins, a Greene County farmer; Jonathon Amory and Henry Leeds, New York City commission merchants; and Francis Baldwin and Daniel Merritt, New York City tailors (C-Fs 1106, 30, 89). Borrowed start-up capital was particularly important in antebellum farm making, among both market-oriented farmers and agriculturalists who hoped to recreate a household economy. Most settlers of trans-Appalachian farmsteads bought their land on credit, either from the U.S. government, state governments, or speculators who had bought up tracts at government auctions (Hammond, *Banks and Politics*, 279–83; Woodman, *King Cotton*, 134–38; Swierenga, *Pioneers and Profits*, 117, 146–52, 162–72, 213–16; Kulikoff, *Agrarian Origins*, 44).

8. The great majority of southern New York bankrupts owed debts for these kinds of

expenditures. Bankrupts who owed substantial amounts of unpaid wages were usually manufacturers. For examples, see the records of the Westchester lumber and marble manufacturer Samuel F. Halsey and the New York City match manufacturer John H. Stevens (C-Fs 947, 2120).

9. For overviews of specialization in antebellum commerce, see Buck, *Development of the Organization of Anglo-American Trade*; Alfred Chandler, *Visible Hand*, 15–49; and Blumin, *Emergence of the Middle Class*, 78–83.

10. Debt Schedule, Depositions of Adolphus Lissak, Mark Samuels, C-F 2 1/2. The magnitude of Abrahams's debts in current dollars would be somewhere in the region of $50,000, as prices have increased by a factor of about sixteen since 1840. This multiplier provides only the roughest measure of the present-day value of debt amounts in the 1830s or early 1840s, as the dramatic changes in the nature of the American economy make precise comparisons impossible. For several measures of price rises over time in the United States, see U.S. Department of Commerce, Bureau of the Census, *Historical Statistics*, Series E: 1–214.

11. C-F 1779. By 1842, Martin Pond lived in New York City.

12. C-F 1021. The only areas of the country where Heyer & Heyer did not trade extensively were in the immediate hinterlands of other large American entrepôts, such as Boston, Philadelphia, and Baltimore.

13. C-Fs 283, 2376; Grund, *Americans in Their Moral, Social, and Political Relations*, 292. For an example of a manufacturer's reliance on credit from suppliers, see the bankruptcy records of John Mason, a Brooklyn machinist who failed while running a Belleville, New Jersey, textile mill in 1832 (C-F 1500).

14. C-F 502. For an extremely useful analysis of the discounting of both notes and bills of exchange in the antebellum economy, see Temin, *Jacksonian Economy*, 29–37. Temin's analysis concentrates on the role of banks as discounters, emphasizing the relationship between the financing of commercial transactions over long distances and the creation of a circulating medium through the issuance of banknotes. For discussions of the usual time granted by antebellum wholesalers to rural storekeepers, and of interest rates charged by note brokers, see Porter and Livesay, *Merchants and Manufacturers*, 31, 74. Bills of exchange and promissory notes drawn in the normal course of trade were "negotiable" in antebellum America—they could be transferred from person to person, and in case of default, a holder could seek payment from any of the individuals who had passed along the note (Freyer, *Forums of Order*, 36–48).

15. One important exception involved the loans that many antebellum banks made to their stockholders and directors. The era's Northeastern banks frequently aimed not so much to make an institutional profit as to provide capital to insiders (Lamoreaux, "Banks, Kinship, and Economic Development"). Southern New York bankrupts who could call on such connections did not hesitate to do so. For examples, see the bankruptcy records of two New York City merchants, Charles Oakley and Daniel Pomeroy (Jun. C-Fs 1663, 1775). A second exception encompassed certain kinds of accommodation loans, discussed in Chapter 3.

16. For a typical mortgage arrangement, see bankruptcy records of the New York City resident Mary Ann Harrington (C-F 975). For a typical arrangement using collateral, see the records for the New York City tailors Alfred and John Kershaw (C-Fs 1238, 1239).

17. For examples of southern New York bankrupts who provided endorsements to business friends and received them in turn, see the records of the merchants Warren P. Alden and Squire P. Dewey, the butcher Andrew Wheeler, and the druggist Nicholas Wheeler Badeau, all of New York City (C-Fs 17, 642, 2398, 70). For an illustration of endorsements for a partner, see the records of Edmund Elmendorf, a New York City attorney (C-F 719). Bankrupts who had a high percentage of debts resulting from family endorsements included

Charles Cooper, a New York City inspector; Stiles Curtis, a Fishkill, Dutchess County, gentleman; and Oliver Hewlett, a farmer from Huntington, Long Island (C-Fs 519, 584, 1020). See also Balleisen, "Navigating Failure," 54–59.

18. For particularly useful treatments of the antebellum transformation in transport, see Taylor, *Transportation Revolution*, and Sheriff, *Artificial River*.

19. "Address of the Albany General Republican Committee," *NWR*, July 22, 1837. This paean to the wonders of commercial credit has particular salience, since it reflected a defense of credit relationships in the aftermath of the panic of 1837.

20. The business cycle in antebellum America largely follows the pattern described by Joseph Schumpeter in his *Theory of Economic Development*, even though Schumpeter's analysis is primarily concerned with more thoroughly industrial societies. As in later eras, the opening up of promising new areas of economic activity before the Civil War attracted investments away from existing commercial channels, providing the spark for an inflationary boom and setting the basic dynamic of the business cycle in motion.

21. For treatments of nineteenth-century American panics and depressions, see Rezneck, "Depression of 1819–1822"; Rezneck, "Social History of an American Depression"; Rezneck, "Influence of Depression upon American Opinion"; Van Vleck, *Panic of 1857*; Taylor, *Transportation Revolution*, 334–51; Hammond, *Banks and Politics*; Rothbard, *Panic of 1819*; North, *Economic Growth*, 177–215; and Fabian, "Speculation on Distress."

22. Temin, *Jacksonian Economy*, 84–86, 100–112; R. C. O. Matthews, *Study in Trade-Cycle History*, 28–42, 49–55, 88–91, 134–36; Macesich, "Sources of Monetary Disturbances," 413.

23. On the financing of internal improvements, see Taylor, *Transportation Revolution*, 372–78. On the financing of land speculation, see McGrane, *Panic of 1837*, 43–69, and Rohrbough, *Land Office Business*, 177–98. On the huge rise in American imports, see U.S. Department of Commerce, Bureau of the Census, *Historical Statistics*, Series U: 190–96, and Hammond, *Banks and Politics*, 451–53. On specie inflow and the expansion of bank credit, see Temin, *Jacksonian Economy*, 64–90, and Rockoff, "Money, Prices, and Banks," 451–56. As Temin demonstrates, a shift in Chinese commercial practice also contributed to the rise in American monetary reserves. In the 1830s, Chinese exporters began to accept bills of exchange drawn by American importers on London banks, instead of demanding payment in hard currency, as they had previously. This change led to a significant decline in American shipments of silver to Asia.

24. "Commercial Chronicle and Review," *HMM* 17 (1847): 404–45; Hammond, *Banks and Politics*, 457; R. C. O. Matthews, *Study in Trade-Cycle History*, 57–58. The following discussion draws heavily on Peter Temin's *Jacksonian Economy*. Temin's account of economic fluctuations in Jacksonian America persuasively refutes several generations of scholarship that interpreted the economic woes of the 1830s and early 1840s as centrally related to Andrew Jackson's slaying of the Second Bank of the United States. As a result, the argument here does not spend time investigating the Bank War, the specie circular, or the distribution of federal monies to the states. For an argument that the Bank War indirectly caused the panic of 1837 by decreasing public confidence in the banking system, which led to an increase in the amount of specie held by the public, and thus monetary contraction, see Sushka, "Antebellum Money Market."

25. Temin, *Jacksonian Economy*, 136–39; Hammond, *Banks and Politics*, 458–59; R. C. O. Matthews, *Study in Trade-Cycle History*, 58–59.

26. Temin, *Jacksonian Economy*, 141–43; Hammond, *Banks and Politics*, 459; Woodman, *King Cotton*, 162–63. For weekly reports on the progress of commercial troubles in the Southwest, see *NWR*, Feb.–Apr. 1837.

27. C-F 1210.

28. Hone, *Diary of Philip Hone*, 1:248.

29. *Fragile Empires*, 39.

30. Hone, *Diary of Philip Hone*, 1:253.

31. For detailed coverage of the intensifying commercial pressure and eventual bank suspensions, see *NWR*, Mar.–May 1837. See also Hammond, *Banks and Politics*, 465–66.

32. The report of the New York paper was reprinted in *NWR*, Apr. 15, 1837. For representative failures by large firms in the midst of the panic, see the bankruptcy records of Nicholas Stuyvesant, a New York City cotton and rice broker, and Edward M. Morgan, a New York City note broker and bank agent (C-Fs 2145, 1583). For examples of less colossal insolvencies during the crisis, see the records of Oliver Hull, a New York City drug wholesaler; Agricola Wilkins, a merchant with a stake in a New York City and a Mobile, Alabama, firm; and the hatter Elisha Bloomer, the architect and builder Seth Geer, and the merchant Asa Deming Van Schaik, all of New York City (C-Fs 1111, 2435, 203, 838, 2304). For a useful analysis of the manner in which financial crisis moved from the nation's mercantile centers to its rural hinterlands, see Clark, *Roots of Rural Capitalism*, 199–203.

33. Philip Hone discussed the restorative impacts of bank suspension as early as May 9, one day after suspension began in New York City (*Diary of Philip Hone*, 1:256–58). See also Hammond, *Banks and Politics*, 478–79, and Macesich, "Sources of Monetary Disturbances," 422.

34. Temin, *Jacksonian Economy*, 148–51; Taylor, *Transportation Revolution*, 344–45; Hammond, *Banks and Politics*, 478–79; R. C. O. Matthews, *Study in Trade-Cycle History*, 58–61.

35. Temin, *Jacksonian Economy*, 152–55; R. C. O. Matthews, *Study in Trade-Cycle History*, 37–41, 65–68, 137–41. Southern New York bankrupts who owed their failure in large measure to the crisis of late 1839 included the New York City house carpenter Samuel Atkinson; the New York City broker and former merchant Samuel Bromberg; the Clarkstown, Rockland County, clothier Isaac Hewlett; the former Toledo, Ohio, merchant Charles G. McKnight; the New York City jewelers Jacob and Jordan Mott; and the Fishkill dry goods merchant Alfred Phillips (C-Fs 53, 269, 1018, 1441, 1602, 1603, 1746).

36. Temin, *Jacksonian Economy*, 154–55; Taylor, *Transportation Revolution*, 375–76. For contemporary analyses of American defaults and the response of British and other European creditors, see "State Debts," *NAR* 51 (1840): 316–36; "State Debts," *Southern Quarterly Review* 3 (1843): 142–66; "Debts of the States," *NAR* 58 (1844): 109–57; "The State Debts," *Democratic Review* 14 (1844): 3–15.

37. The quotation is from Joseph N. Balestier's *Annals of Chicago*, 26. Balestier was a Chicago lawyer who failed during the crisis of late 1839; by 1842 he had moved to New York, where he petitioned for bankruptcy.

38. Taylor, *Transportation Revolution*, 345–46; Blackmar, *Manhattan for Rent*, 202–5, 273.

39. Temin, *Jacksonian Economy*, 155–59; Taylor, *Transportation Revolution*, 345–46; U.S. Department of Commerce, Bureau of the Census, *Historical Statistics*, Series E: 52.

40. Julius Tower Deposition, Sept. 15, 1842, Bankruptcy Papers of Julius and Charlemagne Tower, 34–37, box 27, and Charlemagne Tower to Jonas Tower, June 1, 1841, Letterbook, 1837–44, CTP. Since the Tower brothers resided in Oneida County, New York, their bankruptcy case took place in the U.S. District Court for Northern New York State, under the jurisdiction of federal district judge Alfred Conkling.

41. Julius Tower Deposition, Oct. 12, 1842, Bankruptcy Papers of Julius and Charlemagne Tower, 51–58; Garrett & Co to Reuben Tower's Sons, Mar. 18, 1842, enclosed with Jonas P. Harris to Charlemagne Tower, Mar. 22, 1842; and Jonas P. Harris to Charlemagne Tower, Apr. 7, 1842, CTP. On the decline of whiskey prices, see U.S. Department of Commerce, Bureau of the Census, *Historical Statistics*, Series E: 62. Some southern New York bankrupts suffered financial losses as a direct result of the virtual halt in work on internal

improvements; see the records for the Mount Hope, Orange County, railroad contractor David Dodge; the New York City iron rail manufacturer James Jubb; the Yorkville railroad contractor John Rutter; and the Brooklyn farmer and former railroad engineer James F. Smith (C-Fs 654, 1213, 1913, 2045). Other bankruptcies that resulted in large measure because of dull markets included those of the New York City tailors Francis Baldwin and Daniel Merritt; the Tarry Town, Westchester County, shoe manufacturer George Ferguson; and the New York City cabinetmaker William T. Palmer (C-Fs 89, 747, 1704). For a discussion of the relationship between falling agricultural prices in the late 1830s and farm failures, see Clark, *Roots of Rural Capitalism*, 280–81.

42. This difficulty especially afflicted southern merchants, whose customers paid in local banknotes that were increasingly spurned by eastern creditors after the 1839 panic (Woodman, *King Cotton*, 108). Aaron Abrahams, the New York City peddler, also encountered currency woes. As Abrahams traveled through the South, he often received local banknotes in exchange for his goods; many of these banknotes traded at huge discounts along the eastern seaboard. (Abrahams's insolvency, if his testimony is to be credited, was prompted by the loss of his wallet in Philadelphia during his return to New York City. Even without this loss of banknotes, he would have struggled to pay his creditors, since the southern notes had depreciated by as much as 85 percent [C-F 2 1/2]).

43. C-Fs 1052, 1053; Stephen Tucker, "History of R. Hoe & Company" (New York, 1913); Letterbooks, Mar. 27–Nov. 11, 1837; Dec. 11, 1839–Feb. 15, 1841, R. Hoe & Co. Papers, Columbia University Rare Book and Manuscript Library, especially letters of May 9, 1837, to Castro Frasquierin & Co. of Havana; May 20, 1837, to Alexander Jones of New Orleans; June 24, 1837, to Duff Green of Baltimore; Aug. 8, 1837, to T. W. Harvey of Poughkeepsie; Sept. 21, 1837, to Snow & Fisk of Detroit; Dec. 20, 1839, to Hogan & Thompson of Philadelphia; Apr. 15, 1840, to Delaware Coal Co.; Nov. 30, 1840, to J. S. Silliman & Co. of Troy; and Dec. 1, 1840, to D. & L. Ames of Springfield, Massachusetts. Scores of southern New York bankrupts who failed in the early 1840s listed extensive debts owed to them among their assets. For representative cases, see the records of Antoine Boutete, a New York City cigar maker; Benjamin Cox, a New York City leather dealer; George Gunn, a New York City agent and former Louisville lumber dealer; Mack Oakley, a New York City carpenter; and Eliza Ann Russell, a New York City boardinghouse keeper (C-Fs 228, 534, 918, 1665, 1904). See also the failure of a firm of respected Amherst carriage makers described in Clark, *Roots of Rural Capitalism*, 243.

44. New York City *Plaindealer*, May 20, 1837, reprinted in Leggett, *Democratick Editorials*, 139–40.

45. For an overview of antebellum transformations in the nation's trades, see Laurie, *Artisans into Workers*. For more detailed accounts of the changing scale, marketing structure, and labor organization of particular trades or manufacturing sectors in the antebellum decades, see Dawley, *Class and Community*; Prude, *Coming of Industrial Order*; and Wilentz, *Chants Democratic*. For the deleterious impact of these changes on artisans in small towns, see Clark, *Roots of Rural Capitalism*, 248, and Barron, *Those Who Stayed Behind*, 73–74. On the competitive dynamics of grain production, see Gates, *Farmer's Age*, 156–78.

46. Debt and Asset Schedules, Report of Commissioner William W. Campbell on Private Assignee John Higgins, C-F 37. For a detailed discussion of antebellum competition in the New York City men's clothing trade, see Wilentz, *Chants Democratic*, 119–24.

47. On the extensive representation of these occupations among southern New York bankrupts, see *Alphabetical List of Applicants*. On competition in the shoe-making, furniture-making, and building trades, see Wilentz, *Chants Democratic*, 124–34. For contemporary reflections on mercantile competition, see "Mercantile Drumming," *Atkinson's Casket* 8 (1833): 405–6; G. B., "Bankruptcy-Banking," *HMM* 22 (1850): 311–12; and Boardman, *Bible*

in the Countinghouse, 108–9. The marketing of southern cotton provides another example of a trade that boasted particularly stiff competition. See Woodman, *King Cotton*, 64, 94–95, 184–85.

48. For trenchant analysis of antebellum manufacturers' problems with finance, see Porter and Livesay, *Merchants and Manufacturers*, 69–77. For an incisive contemporaneous treatment of similar difficulties besetting antebellum retailers, see *Shinning It*.

49. Debt and Asset Schedules, Deposition of John Dayton, C-F 610. For the similar failure of a western Massachusetts wagon maker, see Clark, *Roots of Rural Capitalism*, 127–28.

50. C-F 502. Other southern New York bankrupts who failed before the onset of panic and deflation and who encountered significant numbers of bad debts included Augustus Alleoud, a New York City clerk and onetime dry goods dealer who failed in 1832; James Jones, a New York City shoemaker who failed in Fairfield County, Connecticut, in 1830; and Epenetus Wheeler, a New York City grocer and later Hamburg, South Carolina, merchant who failed initially in 1836 (C-Fs 24, 1204, 2399).

51. Edmund B. Smith, a Smithtown, Long Island, farmer who owed $2,120, suffered relatively heavy losses as the result of a half-ownership in the schooner *Allure*, which wrecked off the Florida coast in February 1838. Epenetus Wheeler and the Kingston laborer Uriah Saunders each sustained significant losses as the result of floods. Wheeler had a stock of merchandise destroyed by a spring freshet in 1841 while he was operating a store in Hamburg, South Carolina; Saunders fell victim to a winter flood in 1839, losing 650 cords of wood that he had stored on a Kingston dock. Bankrupts ravaged by fire included Joseph and John Kirk, two Dutchess County woolen manufacturers, and William H. Jones, a Philadelphia auctioneer (C-Fs 2033, 2399, 1936, 1275, 1207).

52. For a compilation of newspaper accounts of the blaze, see "The Late Awful Conflagration in New York," *Atkinson's Casket* 11 (1836): 38–41. The characterization of aid after the fire as only delaying financial reckoning for many businesses is from "Suspension of Specie Payments," *NWR*, Nov. 9, 1839. Among the victims of the fire who eventually ended up on the southern New York bankruptcy docket were dry goods dealer David Comstock and silk merchant/evangelical reformer Arthur Tappan (C-Fs 499, 2171).

53. Debt and Asset Schedules, Deposition of William Hillyer, Deposition of Charles Stuart, C-F 1041. See also the bankruptcy records of the New York City dry goods jobber David Mellen Farnum, whose partner left New York in the fall of 1836 in order to collect the firm's debts but who never returned with the proceeds; and of the Kingston laborer Uriah Saunders, who, in addition to suffering flood damage, lost $800 when a former partner in a public works contracting business absconded with "the monies of the firm" (C-Fs 739, 1936).

54. C-F 749; *MCNYE*, May 31, June 18, 1842; Dun, New York, 224:58. For discussions of the early failures in the railroad supply industry, see Porter and Livesay, *Merchants and Manufacturers*, 88–89.

55. On unanticipated price fluctuations and market movements as a cause of bankruptcies among southern planters and cotton marketers and northern farmers and crop wholesalers, see Woodman, *King Cotton*, 183–84; Clark, *Roots of Rural Capitalism*, 280–81; and Cronon, *Nature's Metropolis*, 105. The same kind of difficulties afflicted merchants who specialized in the California trade during the 1850s. Because of poor communication networks within the territory and the time lag between the receipt of information about market conditions in San Francisco and the arrival of new shipments from Atlantic seaports, eastern merchants frequently sent off what they presumed to be items in great demand, only to discover several months later that their goods had simply added to a glut in the California market (Decker, *Fortunes and Failures*, 37–44).

Chapter Two

1. The commentary from labor leader William Heighton is quoted in Laurie, *Artisans into Workers*, 69. Over the past three decades, historians have lavished attention on the relationships among political liberty, economic independence, and nineteenth-century culture. For broad overviews of these relationships, see Foner, *Free Soil, Free Labor, Free Men*; McCoy, *Elusive Republic*; and Oakes, *Ruling Race*. For influential discussions of antebellum Americans who viewed the growing market society as a threat to economic autonomy, see Laurie, *Working People of Philadelphia*; Wilentz, *Chants Democratic*; Hahn, *Roots of Southern Populism*; Ford, *Origins of Southern Radicalism*; and Sellers, *Market Revolution*.

2. Greeley, *Recollections of a Busy Life*, 84–91.

3. Hunt, ed., *Worth and Wealth*, 315–17. For similar sentiments, see Greene, *Perils of Pearl Street*, 95–130; Judge Joseph Hopkinson, "Lecture on Commercial Integrity," *HMM* 1 (1839): 373–74; *Shinning It*; Griffith, *Two Defaulters*, 128–29; T. S. Arthur, "Don't Be Discouraged," *GLB* 27 (1843): 121–24, "Jacob Jones; or, The Man Who Couldn't Get Along in the World," *GLB* 32 (1848): 193–96, and "Taking Boarders," *GLB* 42 (1851): 13–20, 81–87, 160–67; Freedley, *Practical Treatise on Business*, 207; and J. H. Allen, "The True Mercantile Character," *HMM* 34 (1856): 59.

4. C-F 610; Greeley, *Recollections of a Busy Life*, 92–96. Greeley also struggled in his second venture, again because of limited capital. For representative antebellum failures by young proprietors, see the bankruptcy records of the New York City tailors Francis Baldwin and Daniel Merritt; the former Alton, Illinois, storekeeper Effingham Cock; the former Nashua, New Hampshire, mechanic Wingate Linscott; and the New York City merchants Robert Ogden, John Scudder, and Edwin Wilcox (C-Fs 89, 476, 1364, 1675). For illustrations of insolvency that resulted in part from older proprietors' pursuit of business about which they had scant knowledge, see the records of the New York City author and failed merchant Charles F. Briggs, and the New York City clerk, former jeweler, and former lime manufacturer William C. Dusenberry (C-Fs 259, 695).

5. Hunt, ed., *Worth and Wealth*, 176–78. See also Hopkinson, "Lecture on Commercial Integrity," 373; Frost, *Young Merchant*, 196; "Analysis of Bookkeeping," *HMM* 7 (1842): 526; Stowe, *Uncle Tom's Cabin*, 372; and "Was It for That He Failed?" *HMM* 32 (1855): 649.

6. Asset and Debt Schedules, Deposition of James Alden, Report of General Assignee Waddell, C-F 16.

7. For a telling lament about the poor state of general accounting knowledge among men of business, see "Analysis of Bookkeeping," 526. The first accounting primers aimed at a broad market included Thomas Jones, *Principles and Practice of Book-Keeping*, and Foster, *Practical System of Book-keeping*. For discussions of early commercial academies, see Sampson, "American Accounting Education," 463, and Griffen and Griffen, *Natives and Newcomers*, 10.

8. Creditors' Petition, Depositions of Alexander Cole, William Shaw, Peter D. Hasbrouck, Report of Assignee Hasbrouck, C-F 984. Other southern New York bankrupts who described poor accounting practices included the New York City boardinghouse keeper Angeline Brown; the New York City deputy sheriff and former merchant Abraham Hillyer; the Poughkeepsie saddle and harness maker Harvey Pettit; and the New York City undertaker and porterhouse keeper David Saffen (C-Fs 283, 1040, 1745, 1919). See also the account of several western Massachusetts bankruptcies during the 1830s in Clark, *Roots of Rural Capitalism*, 280–81. A Northampton man described the farmers who underwent these failures as "men who did not examine their affairs and would not believe they were going to ruin, but expected to come out well by some haphazard."

9. Gouge, *Short History of Paper Money*, 2:173; Cary, *Dependence of the Fine Arts*, 13–21. See also John Sargeant, "Mercantile Character," *HMM* 3 (1840): 20–21; Arthur, *Making*

Haste to Be Rich; "A Citizen of Boston," *Experimental Knowledge*, 16–19; and Freedley, *Practical Treatise on Business*, 215–16.

10. Cary, *Dependence of the Fine Arts*, 13–21. Among the myriad similar attacks on speculation as a major font of bankruptcy are J. H. P., "The Ends of Business Life," *Christian Examiner* 23 (1838): 327–33; "The Poor Debtor," *GM* 15 (1839): 244–45; Hannah Brown, *Farmer Housten and the Speculator*; Sawyer, *Merchant's Widow*; Cooper, *Autobiography of a Pocket Handkerchief*; "The Revulsion," *Democratic Review* 26 (1850): 422–23; "Money-Getting—Causes of Failure in Business," *HMM* 35 (1856): 774–75; and "Why Merchants Are Liable to Fail," *HMM* 38 (1858): 61–64, reprinted from the *Prairie Farmer*.

11. There is a large literature on speculation in the nineteenth century. For a thorough examination of speculative housing construction in antebellum New York City, see Blackmar, *Manhattan for Rent*. On the speculative impulse that created antebellum America's urban west, see Wade, *Urban Frontier*, 1–35; Faragher, *Sugar Creek*, 173–90; and Cronon, *Nature's Metropolis*, 24–93. For good introductions to the history of speculation in rural lands, see Rohrbough, *Land Office Business*, and Swierenga, *Pioneers and Profits*.

12. "Rural Tales and Sketches of Long Island: The Kushow Property," *Knickerbocker* 12 (1838): 190. For similar sentiments, see the compilation of newspaper reports in "Speculation!-Speculation!!-Speculation!!!" *NWR*, May 9, 1835; L. E. Penhallow, "The Failure: A Peep into Futurity," *GLB* 16 (1838): 41; "Suspension of Species Payments," *NWR*, Nov. 9, 1839; Balestier, *Annals of Chicago*, 26–27; and "The Revulsion," 422–23.

13. As Edward Pessen notes, in antebellum northeastern cities, less than one percent of the population typically possessed assets worth more than $50,000 (*Riches, Class, and Power*, 30–45). On the incomes earned by the era's skilled urban artisans, white-collar workers, and small-scale retailers, see Blumin, *Emergence of the Middle Class*, 109–16.

14. C-Fs 2139, 462. For additional examples of large-scale speculators who failed, see the bankruptcy records of the New York City dry goods jobber David Comstock; the Staten Island architect and builder Seth Geer; the New York City attorney James Lorimar Graham; the Williamsburgh merchant John S. McKibbin; and the New York City attorney and former mayor Silas M. Stilwell (C-Fs 499, 838, 881, 1438, 2125).

15. C-F 1231. Southern New York bankrupts who failed as the result of more modest speculations included the New York City agent Asahel Adams; the New York City crockery dealer Squire P. Dewey; the New York City broker Elisha Greely; the New York City shoe dealer James Jarvis; the former Newark house carpenter Stephen Munson; and the former New York City furniture dealer Edmund Porter (C-Fs 7, 642, 889, 1172, 1612, 1780).

16. C-Fs 2398, 255, 256, 2103. Wilentz discusses each of these individuals, and particularly Joseph Brewster, in *Chants Democratic*, 147–49, 171, 277, 280–81.

17. Wilentz, *Chants Democratic*, 145–50, 277–86. See also the eulogy for Joseph Brewster in Asa Smith, *Guileless Israelite*.

18. C-F 2398.

19. C-F 2103.

20. C-F 2431; Reverend Theron Baldwin, "A Sketch of the Late Marcus Wilbur," *New York Evangelist*, Sept. 9, 1852; C-F 2171. For an exhaustive discussion of the Tappans's role in antebellum reform, see Wyatt-Brown, *Lewis Tappan*. The bankruptcy of Thomas W. Dyott, a Philadelphia glass manufacturer and private banker, provides another example of a reformer ruined by speculative schemes. Dyott created a school with the goal of turning poor young boys into reliable glassworkers and opened a savings bank in 1836 in order to teach working-class Philadelphians the value of thrift. But he did not put sufficient capital into the bank and then used its deposits to finance real estate purchases. These maneuvers led to his failure in the wake of the panic of 1837, when he could not meet a run on the bank. See Dyott, *Exposition of the System of Moral and Mental Labor*; "Fraudulent Bankruptcy," *HMM* 1 (1839): 425–28; "Manual Labor Banker," *NWR*, Mar. 16, 1839; "Dyott's Manual Labor

Bank," *NWR*, July 6, 1839; "Case of T. W. Dyott," *NWR*, Aug. 17, 1839; "The Case of Dr. Dyott," *NWR*, Sept. 7, 1839; and *Highly Interesting and Important Trial of Dr. T. W. Dyott*.

21. Martineau, *Society in America*, 350–52.

22. G. B., "Bankruptcy-Banking," *HMM* 22 (1850): 313. Similar treatments of overtrading include: Hopkinson, "Lecture on Commercial Integrity," 375; T. S. Arthur, "Is She Rich," *GLB* 25 (1842): 2–6; Cary, *Dependence of the Fine Arts*, 16–21; Freedley, *Practical Treatise on Business*, 214–15; "Dangers of a Too Rapid Extension of Business," *HMM* 34 (1856): 765–66; and "Why Merchants Fail," *HMM* 41 (1859): 521–22.

23. Debt and Asset Schedules, Depositions of Jonathon Amory, Thomas Austin, William Davison, John Haslett, Report of Creditors Committee, Sept. 25, 1840, C-F 30; C-F 1352.

24. A wealth of evidence concerning the failure of Amory & Leeds makes a determination of overtrading easy. The records of other bankrupts suggest similar commercial excesses but do not provide crucial details—such as the amount of start-up capital—that would allow an unambiguous evaluation of their business practices. Among probable mercantile overtraders were the Saugerteis, Ulster County, freighter William Adams; the former Pawtucket, Rhode Island, merchant Hugh Macfarlane; and the Kingston merchant Henry H. Reynolds (C-Fs 11, 1458, 1836). For examples of southern New York manufacturers and artisans who lacked sufficient capitalization, see the bankruptcy records of the former Kinderhook cotton manufacturer David Buffum; the former East Greenwich, Rhode Island, manufacturer Daniel Greene; the Peekskill, Westchester County, iron founder Judson Gilbert; the Olive, Ulster County, cooper Minnar Hyatt; and the New York City cabinetmaker William T. Palmer (C-Fs 326, 897, 848, 1136, 1704). For an account of the low capital reserves typically held by antebellum cotton manufacturers, see Wallace, *Rockdale*, 73–123. On undercapitalization and overextension by northern farmers and southern planters, see Faragher, *Sugar Creek*, 181–84; Clark, *Roots of Rural Capitalism*, 281; Stampp, *Peculiar Institution*, 391–92; Woodman, *King Cotton*, 131–36; and Oakes, *Ruling Race*, 125–26. Town developers also failed with great regularity as a result of extending their businesses and investments well beyond the capacity of their capital to carry the strain of interest payments. For a telling illustration of such a failure in rural Ohio, see Wohl, "Henry Noble Day."

25. Blackmar, *Manhattan for Rent*, 196–204.

26. "A Citizen of Boston," *Experimental Knowledge*, 18–19; "The Failures in America," reprinted in Evans, *Commercial Crisis*, 123.

27. Henry W. Bellows, "The Influence of the Trading Spirit upon the Social and Moral Life of America," *American Whig Review* 1 (1845): 95; Cary, *Dependence of the Fine Arts*, 12.

28. Albion, *Rise of New York Port*; Taylor, *Transportation Revolution*; Atherton, *Frontier Merchant*; Clark, *Roots of Rural Capitalism*, 139–91; Blumin, *Emergence of the Middle Class*, 138–91.

29. Republican fears of "luxury" as a threat to self-government were particularly strong in the revolutionary era, though they continued well into the antebellum period. See Kerber, *Women of the Republic*, 36–44; McCoy, *Elusive Republic*; Barbara Matthews, " 'Forgive Us Our Debts,' " 69–73; and Kellow, "Duties Are Ours," 160–64, 192–93.

30. *GLB* 25 (1842): 2–6. Also see T. S. Arthur's "Shattered by the First Storm," *GLB* 57 (1858): 152–54; Cooper, *Autobiography of a Pocket Handkerchief*; Catherine Elizabeth, "Reverse of Fortune the Test of Character," *GM* 39 (1851): 289–95; and E. M. Gibson, "Going into Business," *Ballou's Magazine* 1 (1855): 37–41.

31. This attack on "living beyond income" was reprinted in Tuthill, *Success in Life*, 185–88, and Freedley, *Practical Treatise on Business*, 210–11. Similar assaults on extravagance permeated *Hunt's Merchants' Magazine*. See Sargeant, "Mercantile Character," 9–11; "Abuses of the Credit System," *HMM* 24 (1851): 133; and "Why Merchants Fail," 521.

32. This conclusion seems to hold as well for southern slaveholders. Despite the occasional planter who, like Thomas Jefferson, had his financial resources bled by an unwilling-

ness to curtail the consumption that marked a southern gentleman, slaveowners were more likely to deprive themselves and their families of "comforts" in order to buy more land and slaves. Insolvency appears to have resulted more frequently from the latter pursuit than the former. On Jefferson's losing battle with debt, see Sloan, *Principle & Interest*; on the expensive tastes of some planters, see Stampp, *Peculiar Institution*, 391. On the financial priorities of most slaveowners, see Oakes, *Ruling Race*, 81–87. For some bankrupts there may have been a symbiotic relationship between risky commercial behavior and a penchant for the high life. Several antebellum writers maintained either that initial successes in speculation encouraged freewheeling consumption or that financial difficulties caused by personal expenditure encouraged speculation as a means of sustaining a threatened lifestyle. See, for example, Gouge, *Short History of Paper Money*, 1:38–39, and Tuthill, *Success in Life*, 184.

33. Westbrook Diary, Jan. 1, Sept. 5, Dec. 15, 1840, New York Public Library.

34. Ibid., Jan. 1, Dec. 31, 1841; Jan. 1, Dec. 31, 1842. Westbrook's obsession with calculating expenses recalls that of Thomas Jefferson, who kept extraordinarily rigorous track of his worsening financial position over several decades. See Sloan, *Principle & Interest*.

35. Westbrook Diary, Jan. 1, Feb. 8, Apr., June 7–10, Sept. 9, 1840; Apr., Dec. 11, Dec. 31, 1841; Jan. 1, 1842, New York Public Library.

36. Ibid., July 2, 1842.

37. Ibid., Jan. 29, 1840. Another case of "pecuniary embarrassments" caused by excessive "domestic expenditures" became a celebrated example for antebellum moralists. John Webster, a Boston physician and Harvard Medical School professor, faced a heavy load of debt in late 1849 that was largely the result of maintaining a higher style of living than his income warranted. Webster was convicted of killing his most insistent creditor, Dr. George Parkman, ostensibly to avoid further harassment about his debt. Although Webster's guilt remains a matter of dispute, antebellum commentators did not shy away from recalling his supposed perfidy while entreating readers to practice economy in household expenditure. For a representative treatment, see the Reverend T. Shephard, "To Young Men in Mercantile Life," *The Happy Home* 1 (1855): 295. For a thought-provoking inquiry into both the Webster case and the nature of historical truth, see Schama, *Dead Certainties*.

38. C-F 8. Antebellum temperance activists argued that there was a strong link between dependence on alcohol and business failures. Reliance on "demon rum," the activists maintained, led to indolence, diminished business judgment, and often reckless speculation. See "The Ruined Family," *Atkinson's Casket* 11 (1836): 46–47, and T. S. Arthur, "The Broken Merchant," in his *Temperance Tales*, 1–44.

39. Crouthamel, *James Watson Webb*, 69, 80–81; C-F 2378. For another example of a large-scale speculator whose financial problems were compounded by expensive tastes, see the bankruptcy records of Anthony Dey, a New York City lawyer and real estate developer (C-F 644), and the criticism of Dey's bankruptcy application in *NYH*, Dec. 2, 1842. These instances make clear that in spite of the frequent contemporaneous association of "extravagance" with women's consumption, antebellum men were perfectly capable of pursuing a lifestyle beyond their means. For a similar conclusion based on analyses of credit reports in the 1840s and 1850s, see Sandage, "Deadbeats, Drunkards, and Dreamers," 318–19.

40. Freedley, *Practical Treatise on Business*, 202–4.

41. Thus in eighteenth-century England or late-twentieth-century America, the interplay between structural economic dangers and vulnerabilities of individual businesses look fairly similar. See Hoppit, *Risk and Failure*, and Sullivan et al., *As We Forgive Our Debtors*, 108–27.

42. A large body of scholarship examines the dynamics of antebellum industrialization and the expansion of permanent wage workers. See in particular Laurie, *Artisans into Workers*, 3–112, and Wilentz, *Chants Democratic*, 104–42.

Chapter Three

1. Legal complexity created strong demand among merchants, manufacturers, and especially lawyers for information about the current state of debtor-creditor law. Antebellum treatise writers strove to meet that demand, including Angell, *Practical Summary of the Law of Assignments*; Edwards, *On Receivers in Chancery*; Moore, *Laws of Trade*; Holcombe, *Law of Debtor and Creditor*; and Burrill, *Treatise on the Law*. Periodicals such as *Hunt's Merchants' Magazine* and the Cincinnati-based *Western Law Journal* sought to disseminate similar legal knowledge, publishing articles on the law of debtor and creditor in the several states. For an exhaustive treatment of nineteenth-century debtor-creditor legislation in fourteen eastern seaboard states, see Coleman, *Debtors and Creditors in America*.

2. For discussions of the socioeconomic background, intellectual assumptions, and sweeping cultural agenda of this group, as well as the parallels between their goals and tactics and those of Whig politicians, see Richard Weiss, *American Myth of Success*, 16–47; Cawelti, *Apostles of the Self-Made Man*, 39–75; Welter, *Mind of America*, 141–50; Howe, *Political Culture of the American Whigs*, esp. 32–42, 150–80; Halttunen, *Confidence Men*; and Kohl, *Politics of Individualism*, 63–99. One can see the interconnections of the various concerns of the moralists in Thomas Cary's 1845 address, *Dependence of the Fine Arts*, in which the Boston merchant linked his analysis of the causes of bankruptcy with pleas for mercantile morality and philanthropic support for appropriate forms of art.

3. "Mercantile Character," *HMM* 3 (1840): 18. See also Frost, *Young Merchant*, 198–99; Joseph Hopkinson, "Lecture on Commercial Integrity," *HMM* 1 (1839): 377; J. N. Bellows, "Morals of Trade: Number Two," *HMM* 6 (1842): 22–27; Beecher, *Seven Lectures to Young Men*, 55–59; Cary, *Dependence of the Fine Arts*, 15–16; Boardman, *Bible in the Countinghouse*, 195–97; Freedley, *Practical Treatise on Business*, 219–20; J. H. Allen, "The True Mercantile Character," *HMM* 34 (1856): 61; and Hunt, ed., *Worth and Wealth*, 78–80.

4. Allen, "True Mercantile Character," 61; Sara Hale, "The Broken Merchant," *Atkinson's Casket* 10 (1835): 85–89; Jackson, *Victim of Chancery*; J. N. Bellows, "The Morals of Trade: Number Six," *HMM* 7 (1842): 183; Arthur, *Two Merchants*; Beecher, *Seven Lectures to Young Men*, 58–59; "The Unfortunate and the Criminal Creditor," *HMM* 19 (1848): 569; Freedley, *Practical Treatise on Business*, 221; Boardman, *Bible in the Countinghouse*, 87–90, 119, 195, 204; "Commercial Chronicle and Review," *HMM* 31 (1854): 589–91; Hunt, ed., *Worth and Wealth*, 311–14.

5. Defoe outlined nearly every precept urged by America's moralists (*Complete English Tradesman*, 1:70–78, 163–83). For the significance of these standards in British commercial life and bankruptcy law between 1726 and 1847, see Evans, *Commercial Crisis*, i–lxxxviii; Evans, *History of the Commercial Crisis*, i–ccxli; Hoppit, *Risk and Failure*, 29–41; Weisberg, "Commercial Morality," 29–55; and Lester, *Victorian Insolvency*, 1–122.

6. Bellows, "Morals of Trade: Number Six," 182, emphasis in the original; Beecher, *Seven Lectures to Young Men*, 58–59. See also Frost, *Young Merchant*, 233–38; Cary, *Dependence of the Fine Arts*, 23; Boardman, *Bible in the Countinghouse*, esp. 85; and Hunt, ed., *Worth and Wealth*, 312. For an example of explicit reliance on a British commercial moralist, see the excerpts of Jonathon Dymond's 1828 *Essays on the Principles of Morality* in "Morality for Merchants," *HMM* 12 (1845): 351–56. The moralists' construction of "manliness" essentially sought to merge what E. Anthony Rotundo has identified as two distinct middle-class ideals—that of the "Masculine Achiever" and the "Christian Gentleman." See his "Learning about Manhood."

7. Frost, *Young Merchant*, 195, 199; Hopkinson, "Lecture on Commercial Integrity," 377; John Brown, *Constance*; Bellows, "Morals of Trade: Number Six," 183; Arthur, *Debtor and Creditor*; Hunt, ed., *Worth and Wealth*, 111–13.

8. Tappan, *Life of Arthur Tappan*, 281–82.

9. For an example of a failing debtor trading on his bank connections to obtain loans throughout the 1830s, see the records of the New York merchant Charles Oakley (C-F 1663). Identifying loans to bankrupts from private moneylenders is not an easy task, since bankrupts tended not to use the term when listing their creditors. New York architect Seth Geer probably owed money to moneylenders. See C-F 838.

10. Greene, *Perils of Pearl Street*, 124–27. See also the discussion of Joseph Fay's 1811 work, *A Disquisition on Imprisonment for Debt*, in Ciment, "In Light of Failure," 234–35; *Shinning It*, 28; and "The Poetry of Trade: A Song of the Street," *HMM* 37 (1857): 641. Harriet Beecher Stowe characterized the practice through a more rural simile in *Uncle Tom's Cabin*, 372. Consumed by indebtedness, the slaveowning character Mr. Shelby remarks that coping with business reverses is "like jumping from one bog to another, all through a swamp; borrow of one to pay another, and then borrow of another to pay one,—and these confounded notes falling due before a man has time to smoke a cigar and turn round,—dunning letters and dunning messages,—all scamper and scurry."

11. Greeley, *Recollections of a Busy Life*, 141.

12. C-F 2103. Other southern New York bankrupts who contracted a significant proportion of debts as the result of shinning among business associates included the former Brooklyn saddler Sheldon P. Church; the Newburgh, Orange County, freighter Oliver Davis; the New York City oil dealer James McAlister; the former Troy merchant George W. Mayhew; the Brooklyn builder Asa Stebbins; and the Kingston tavern keepers and butchers David and William Vreedenbergh (C-Fs 448, 606, 1416, 1507, 2326, 2327).

13. Debt and Asset Schedules, Deposition of George C. Thomas, C-F 2198. Reliance on family members was common both among bankrupts who had easy recourse to other means of assistance and among those who lacked such means. Compare the records of large-scale economic operators, like Edward and Henry Heyer, the New York City hardware merchants; Benjamin Franklin Robinson, a New York City merchant tailor; and John Satterlee, a New York City banker and former merchant, with those of bankrupts who ran more modest enterprises, such as James Jarvis, a New York City shoemaker; Edward Kellogg, the former Binghamton merchant; and Harvey Pettit, a Poughkeepsie saddle and harness maker (C-Fs 1021, 1870, 1933, 1172, 1231, 1745). For similar examples of antebellum entrepreneurs whose business reverses eventually forced them to turn to family members for financial aid, see Clark, *Roots of Rural Capitalism*, 244, and Wohl, "Henry Noble Day," 188–91.

14. Debt and Asset Schedules, Deposition of George Ferguson, C-F 747. For other failed attempts to avoid default through the increase of business, see the bankruptcy records of the merchant tailors George Andrews and Jeremiah Lamphier; the cabinetmaker William T. Palmer; and the merchants Robert Ogden, John Scudder, and Edwin Wilcox, all of New York City (C-Fs 37, 1704, 1675).

15. Debt and Asset Schedules, Depositions of Carlos P. Houghton, Daniel Day, C-F 1082.

16. BV Houghton & Day, Letterbook, Manuscript Department, N-YHS. Quotations from Oct. 18, 1839, letter to Kasson & Hoyt; Sept. 18, 1839, letter to C. Earll; Oct. 18, 1839, letter to Pearson & Laurence; and Nov. 15, 1839, letter to Amos Cornwall.

17. Letterbooks, Mar. 27, 1837–Nov. 11, 1837; Dec. 11, 1839–Feb. 15, 1841, R. Hoe & Co. Papers, Columbia University Rare Book and Manuscript Library. See in particular June 28, 1837, to G. L. Whitney of Detroit; July 10, 1837, to Miner & Horton of Peekskill, New York; Sept. 5, 1837, to D. & J. Ames of Springfield; Sept. 21, 1837, to Snow & Fisk of Detroit; Sept. 22, 1837, to Samuel Ackerson of Boston; Oct. 11, 1837, to Samuel Atkinson of Philadelphia; May 5, 1840, to A. S. Bowen; Nov. 9, 1840, to A. C. Green of Oswego; and Dec. 1, 1840, to D. & J. Ames.

18. New injections of borrowed capital, expansion, and/or debt extensions most commonly enabled antebellum entrepreneurs to save troubled businesses if they primarily suffered from a dearth of working capital and were able to arrange substantial long-term

financing. For a discussion of several antebellum Massachusetts manufacturers who weathered a monetary crisis through the provision of long-term credit by local merchants, see Clark, *Roots of Rural Capitalism*, 244–46. The quotation is from an April 1, 1837, editorial in the *New York Plaindealer*, reprinted in Leggett, *Democratick Editorials*, 113.

19. On the ramifications of bankruptcy for the lifestyles and social position of urban commercial families, see Kellow, "Duties Are Ours," 160–61, 190–95, and Hewitt, *Women's Activism*, 60.

20. On bankruptcy and "feminization" in eighteenth-century mercantile culture, see Ditz, "Shipwrecked." See also Sandage, "Deadbeats, Drunkards, and Dreamers," 320–22, which discusses the tendency of nineteenth-century credit reporters to "define failure as an emasculated status."

21. On parental expectations of success and fears of failure in antebellum America, see Oakes, *Ruling Race*, 70–73, and Rotundo, "Learning about Manhood," 43–46 (quote on 44). For an example of pecuniary embarrassment leading to a wife's reevaluation of her husband's abilities, as well as a decision to put off having children, see Kellow, "Duties Are Ours," 190–95. For an instance in which bankruptcy reinforced the disapproval of in-laws and led to deep-seated familial estrangement, culminating in a bankrupt's murder of his wife, see the discussion of an 1837 failure by a New Hampshire tanner in Davis, *From Homicide to Slavery*, 5–6. See also *People ex. rel. Barry v. Mercein*, 3 Hill 399 (N.Y. Supreme Court 1842), which recounts the marital separation and custody battle that ensued after the 1838 failure of a New York City merchant. On bankrupts' fears of damaging the "cause of religion," see James, "Josiah Hinds," 24, and Asa Smith, *Guileless Israelite*, 18. The phrase "struggle on" was used by the bankrupt George Ferguson; see his deposition, C-F 747.

22. Quoted in Moore, *Laws of Trade*, 356–57. For Butler's career as a public servant, see *Dictionary of American Biography*, 3:356–57. An early director of the Second Bank of the United States made a similar observation after the panic of 1819, commenting in an 1820 letter that failing businessmen "are like patients in the last stage of consumption, hoping for a favorable change, but growing worse every day until they expire." See Gouge, *Short History of Paper Money*, 2:122.

23. John A. Parker, "Familiar Scenes in the Life of a Clerk," *HMM* 5 (1841): 539. See also the descriptions of struggling antebellum debtors in *Shinning It*; Mrs. C. H. Butler, "The Bankrupt's Daughters," *GM* 25 (1844): 34–35; Arthur, *Debtor and Creditor*; and Melville, *Confidence Man*, 159–60.

24. For discussions of antebellum insane asylum reports as to the leading causes of insanity among inmates, see Davis, *Homicide in American Fiction*, 71, and Rothman, *Discovery of the Asylum*, 111. The quotations are from Edward Jarvis, "On the Comparative Liability of Males and Females to Insanity," *American Journal of Insanity* 7 (1850): 150, cited in Byars, "Making of the Self-Made Man," 107; and Worcester Lunatic Hospital, *Tenth Annual Report* (1843), 62, cited in Rothman, *Discovery of the Asylum*, 116.

25. *Poughkeepsie Journal*, Feb. 9, 1842. For other examples, see the reports of suicides by a Philadelphia merchant in *NYH*, Mar. 22, 1842; an Albany man, in *MCNYE*, Nov. 29, 1842; a publican in Warren County, New York, in *MCNYE*, Dec. 14, 1842; and a Warwick, New York, dry goods merchant in *Poughkeepsie Telegraph*, Feb. 15, 1843. See also the account of an 1825 suicide by a failing Pennsylvania textile manufacturer in Wallace, *Rockdale*, 85–86, and the report of an 1840 suicide by a Buffalo grain merchant in Gerber, *Making of an American Pluralism*, 38.

26. For useful summaries of antebellum legal doctrine pertaining to collateral and mortgages, see Kent, *Commentaries on American Law*, 1st ed., 2:449–56, 4:129–88; and 4th ed., 2:577–85, 4:135–206; and Walker, *Introduction to American Law*, 301–7.

27. Contemporary guides to the antebellum law of debt collection in the several states

include Moore, *Laws of Trade*; Holcombe, *Law of Debtor and Creditor*; and "Laws of Each State Relative to the Collection of Debts," *LMLM* 2 (1854): 3–19. On the creditor's bill in New York, see Edwards, *On Receivers in Chancery*, 268–398. American debtor-creditor law derived from the English common law in most states. See also Walker, *Introduction to American Law*, 504–22. For a succinct exposition of the English legal background, see Coleman, *Debtors and Creditors in America*, 3–5.

28. Examples of southern New York bankrupts who provided their creditors with collateral, generally consisting of stocks or commercial paper, include the former Kinderhook cotton manufacturer David Buffum and the New York City dry goods jobber Frederick Conant (C-Fs 326, 502). Among bankrupts who faced foreclosure on real estate were the former Chicago attorney Joseph Balestier and the New York City woman Mary Ann Harrington (C-Fs 91, 973). Bankrupts who had furniture sold on execution included the New York City lawyer Anthony Dey and the Yorktown railroad contractor John Rutter (C-Fs 644, 1913). Scores of southern New York bankrupts faced debt judgments, sheriff's sales, and chancery-appointed receivers. For an illustrative run of judgments, see the records for New York City carpenter Samuel Atkinson; for a typical sheriff's sale, see the records of Ira Platt, a former Massachusetts stove merchant; and for a chancery-ordered receivership, see the records of the New York City jeweler Jesse W. Benedict (C-Fs 53, 1767, 155).

29. "On a National Bankrupt Law," *American Jurist* 1 (1829): 40; Burrill, *Treatise on the Law*, 104–8. Judge Joseph Story provides an extensive overview of the legal grounds for such priority in an 1842 case, *Ex Parte Foster* 5 LR 55 (CC Mass. 1842).

30. *Ex Parte Foster*, 5 LR 74. See also Weisberg, "Commercial Morality," 75.

31. Debt and Asset Schedules, Depositions of Cassander Frisbee, Charles Hutchinson, C-F 806. The race of diligence created fierce competition among credit reporters once these institutions had come into existence in the 1840s, since early knowledge of a business failure gave creditors a crucial advantage in pursuing their claims through the courts. See Atherton, "Problem of Credit Rating," 542.

32. Debt and Asset Schedules, Deposition of Theodore Brunn, C-F 806. George Ferguson, the Tarrytown shoe manufacturer, negotiated a $2,000 loan several months before his failure through the recommendation of his brother-in-law. Depositions of George Ferguson, Ann Dusenberry, William C. Dusenberry, C-F 747. Other bankrupts who faced charges of misleading their creditors close to the time of their failures include the merchant tailors George Andrews and Jeremiah Lamphier and the mercantile firm of Robert Ogden, John Scudder, and Edwin Wilcox (C-Fs 37, 1675).

33. June 10, 1839, letter to Derby & Andrews of Boston, BV Houghton & Day, Letterbook, N-YHS. T. S. Arthur gave a fictional treatment of this practice in *Two Merchants*, 4–8. Houghton & Day also suffered losses at the hands of at least one other customer who professed solvency despite his precarious position; see the July 19, 1839, letter to J. W. Gilbert concerning the depredations of an upstate New York mercantile firm in BV Houghton & Day, Letterbook, N-YHS.

34. Deposition of John Dayton, C-F 610. A cautionary 1841 novella provided extensive commentary on the willingness of firms to sell to undercapitalized newcomers at the very beginning of their ventures. See *Shinning It*. See also the Massachusetts Legislative Report of 1835, quoted extensively in "Massachusetts Insolvent Law," *American Jurist* 19 (1838): 308–9, which discusses the strategies of some merchants to get rid of old and unwanted stock by launching their clerks on foolhardy business ventures. For a fuller treatment of Dayton & Schuyler's failure, see the discussion of inexperienced proprietors in Chapter 2.

35. Greene, *Perils of Pearl Street*, 81–87. For the machinations of a typical pair of kiters, see the bankruptcy records of the shoe dealer Warren Alden and the crockery dealer Squire P. Dewey, both of New York City (C-Fs 17, 642). According to the antebellum humorist

Joseph Baldwin (*Flush Times*, 94), cross-endorsements were so common in the Old Southwest that after the panics of 1837 and 1839, Alabamians and Mississippians "broke by neighborhoods."

36. Deposition of John Haslett, C-F 30.

37. Examples included Amory & Leeds; the hatters Joseph and Lemuel Brewster; the New York City furniture merchant Smith Ely; and the New York City merchant and land speculator John S. McKibbin (C-Fs 30, 255, 256, 725, 1438). Failing debtors could not always count on this tactic. Creditors of the New York City leather dealer Benjamin Cox rejected his offer of several promissory notes as collateral, since they considered the commercial paper worthless (Amended Asset Schedule, C-F 534).

38. For a similar analysis of accommodation among antebellum members of a given business, social, or family circle, see Freyer, *Producers versus Capitalists*, 69–75.

39. The failure of Burr St. John, a New York City tailor, indicates the price that some creditors paid for turning to the law. Four of St. John's creditors filed creditor's bills against him; but only the first received any payments for his troubles. All of St. John's property not exempted by state law from execution went to a receiver for the benefit of the most diligent creditor. The sale of those assets did not completely satisfy this creditor's debt, so others received nothing on their investment in legal fees and court costs (C-F 2095).

40. The experience of Seneca Odell's creditors highlights this possibility. Odell was a small-scale merchant in the Dutchess County town of Pleasant Valley throughout the 1830s. At least in part because of a series of uncollectible debts from his customers, Odell was unable to pay just under $3,000 in debts to New York City grocers and dry goods dealers in 1838 and 1839. One of his creditors filed a chancery bill in 1839, gaining an undisputed lien on his assets. The court action, however, was in vain; an inventory by the local sheriff indicated that Odell possessed nothing in excess of the assets protected by the state's exemption law (C-F 1671).

41. "Imprisonment for Debt," *NAR* 32 (1831): 494; Moore, *Laws of Trade*, 347–50. For an excellent summation of the difficulties confronting creditors who tried to imprison debtors in the antebellum decades, see Freyer, *Producers versus Capitalists*, 89–90.

42. See in particular the debts of the New York City shoe dealer Warren P. Alden; Amory & Leeds; and the New York City merchant Asa Deming Van Schaik (C-Fs 17, 30, 2304). See also the June 18, 1843, letter from the New York City lawyer John Osborne Sargeant to a Boston client, Isaac Pitman. Pitman, who along with other creditors had retained Sargeant's services in a particularly complex case of debt collection, had previously complained about the resulting legal fee of $120. To Pitman, it was "a hard case to lose property and incur expenses into the bargain." Sargeant's response was that "[t]his is a misfortune that must be borne by those on whom it has fallen. It is incident to all who are obliged to litigate their rights" (BV Sargeant, John Osborne, Letterbook, Manuscript Department, N-YHS). For additional discussions of the expenses associated with antebellum debt collection through the law, see Decker, *Fortunes and Failures*, 51–52, and Oakes, *Ruling Race*, 61–62.

43. Moore, *Laws of Trade*; Edwards, *On Receivers in Chancery*, 269. Judicial process in New York's chancery courts was also notoriously slow and expensive (Basch, *In the Eyes of the Law*, 132). The benefits of a debtor's enjoying friendly relations with a sheriff are suggested by the course of Peter Hasbrouck's bankruptcy. Hasbrouck, the Kingston baker who failed in part because of his poor accounting practices, had several judgments entered against him by June 1842. But the officer charged with levying on his property took his time, giving Hasbrouck as much leeway as possible to arrange his affairs (Petition of Benjamin Hasbrouck, C-F 984). The bankruptcy of Daniel Howell, a Goshen, Orange County, tailor, farmer, and deputy sheriff, indicates other liberties taken by some officers of the court. As a deputy sheriff, Howell levied execution on the property of debtors; but according to the

testimony of several individuals, he had a habit of keeping the proceeds of his sheriff's sales to himself (Depositions of David Sease, Joseph Gott, Adam Lindebaugh, C-F 1093).

44. On the evolution of antebellum debtor relief legislation and the consideration of these laws in the courts, see Warren, *Bankruptcy in United States History*, 87–92; Rothbard, *Panic of 1819*; and Coleman, *Debtors and Creditors in America*.

45. For discussions of indulgence by American creditors in a variety of contexts from the 1810s to the 1860s, see Woodman, *King Cotton*, 41–42; Swierenga, *Pioneers and Profits*, 185, 216; Bushman, *Joseph Smith*, 66; Clark, *Roots of Rural Capitalism*, 166–67; and Gallman, *Mastering Wartime*, 294–97. As Woodman notes with respect to the relationship between southern factors and cotton planters, the imperatives of competition could lead creditors to provide renewals of debt; in a crowded market, the unwillingness to roll over obligations could lead to the loss of business over the long term.

46. C-Fs 1052, 1053; Letterbooks, Mar. 27, 1837–Nov. 11, 1837, Dec. 11, 1839–Feb. 15, 1841, R. Hoe & Co. Papers, Columbia University Rare Book and Manuscript Library. For similar arrangements between pressed debtors and their creditors during periods of widespread financial stringency, see bankruptcy records of the New York City match manufacturer John H. Stevens (C-F 2120); *In Re Potts and Garwood*, 1 *PLJ* 159 (DC ED Pa. 1842); and *In Re Muggridge et al.*, 5 *LR* 351 (DC N.H. 1842).

47. "Massachusetts Insolvent Law," 309.

48. See in particular Feb. 6 and Feb. 13, 1840, letters to J. W. Gilbert, and Feb. 7, 1840, letter to Simon Howe, BV Houghton & Day, Letterbook, N-YHS.

49. Deposition of John Dayton, C-F 610. Several antebellum commentators noted that the more remote a creditor thought the chances of eventual recovery were against a particular debtor, the greater the likelihood he would strike a deal. See in particular the discussion of failure negotiations in "Counting-House Man," *Herbert Tracy*. For other instances of settlements with creditors, see the bankruptcy records of Amory & Leeds; the former New Orleans merchant tailor Temple Hall; and the New York City druggist Oliver Hull (C-Fs 30, 942, 1111). See also the deals struck by Maine merchant Samuel Thurston with several creditors after an 1837 failure, recounted in *John S. Ayer, Assignee, v. Brazier Brastow*, 5 *LR* 498 (DC Maine 1842); and the negotiations between a failing Baltimore merchant and the DuPont family, chronicled in Freyer, *Producers versus Capitalists*, 65. Failing debtors who had suspended business often coupled offers of partial payment with a request for extension on the remainder of their obligations. Difficulties in liquidating assets served as justification for these requests; debtors claimed that they needed time to collect from customers and dispose of stock. As with the tender of partial payment, some creditors granted such extensions. For a typical arrangement, see bankruptcy records of Joseph H. Lester, a former Norwich, Connecticut, merchant (C-F 1354).

50. For discussions of the way assignments worked, see Angell, *Practical Summary of the Law of Assignments*; "Insolvent Law of Massachusetts," 303; Arthur, *Two Merchants*, 19–22; Burrill, *Treatise on the Law*; and Benjamin F. Porter, "The Law of Bankruptcy," *HMM* 28 (1853): 439–44.

51. Antebellum judges consistently held that such legal instruments were valid at common law. American courts also regularly upheld statutory limitations on assignments, such as New York's requirement that all voluntary assignments in trust for creditors be recorded at a deed office, as well as statutory prohibitions on assignments, such as Vermont's 1843 law (Angell, *Practical Summary of the Law of Assignments*, 4–27, 78–95; Burrill, *Treatise on the Law*, 18–92; Edwards, *On Receivers in Chancery*, 280–351).

52. Hopkinson, "Lecture on Commercial Integrity," 376–77. See also "On a National Bankrupt Law," 45, and "Commercial Chronicle and Review," *HMM* 31 (1854): 589–91.

53. The comment is from an opinion of Judge Gibson, chief justice of the Pennsylvania

Supreme Court, in *Thomas v. Jenks*, 5 Rawle's Reports 221, quoted in Burrill, *Treatise on the Law*, 20. Hundreds of southern New York bankrupts executed voluntary assignments after failing. Representative examples include the Saugerteis merchant and freighter William Adams; the former Savannah shoe dealer Horatio Aldrich; the former Springfield, Ohio, hardware merchant Josiah Butler; the onetime Rye shoemaker Howel Clark; the former Poughkeepsie carriage maker John Drom; and the former Newbury Court House, South Carolina, merchant John Johnson (C-Fs 11, 19, 370, 455, 681, 1192).

54. Southern New York bankrupts who made payments in cash or kind on the eve of failure included Amory & Leeds and the New York City cabinetmaker William T. Palmer (C-Fs 30, 1704). See also the actions of a Maine merchant described in *Gardner Dennett v. Nathaniel Mitchell*, 6 *LR* 16 (DC Maine 1843). Among the southern New York petitioners who gave collateral just before or after suspending business were the New York City coal dealers John Ambler and Nehemiah Anderson and the Poughkeepsie saddle and harness maker Harvey Pettit (C-Fs 25, 35, 1745). Bankrupts who executed mortgages included the Kingston baker Peter D. Hasbrouck and the Poughkeepsie boatman Henry Ogden (C-Fs 984, 1673). See also the mortgage granted by a firm of West Troy, New York, pine board manufacturers in 1841 (*Baldwin v. Rosseau and Easton*, 1 *NYLO* 391 [ND N.Y. 1842]). For instances in which bankrupts transferred real estate or stock on the eve of failure, see the records of the New York City merchant John Quackenbos; the Dutchess County iron founder Theodore Sterling; and the New York City match manufacturer John H. Stevens (C-Fs 1809, 2118, 2120).

55. For illustrative preferences accorded through confession of judgment, see the bankruptcy records of the Brooklyn stonecutter David Anderson; the Poughkeepsie merchant Stephen Frost; and the Brooklyn huckster Daniel Youngs (C-Fs 33, 810, 2509). See also the 1842 confession of judgment by a Pittsburgh railroad contractor, discussed in *Lonergan v. Fenlon*, 15 Fed. Cases 803 (DC WD Pa. 1866).

56. There are several thorough descriptions of preferential assignments by contemporaries; see "On a National Bankrupt Law," 45; Angell, *Practical Summary of the Law of Assignments*, 27–40; "Insolvent Law of Massachusetts," 303–8; "Ought Certain Creditors to Be Preferred in Making Assignments?" *HMM* 7 (1842): 273–75; and Burrill, *Treatise on the Law*, 98–110. The many southern New York bankrupts who preferred some creditors in a voluntary assignment included the onetime Newburgh freighter Oliver Davis and the Orange County merchant tailor John W. Welling (C-Fs 606, 2383). For typical instances in which bankrupts appointed a preferred creditor as assignee, see the records of the New York City hatter Francis Amidon; the former New York City merchant James H. Sackett; and the New York City bookbinder Charles Starr (C-Fs 28, 1917, 2103). For detailed evidence about the ways in which assignees secured the interest of preferred creditors, see Depositions of George Whitaker, Hugh Macfarlane (C-F 1459). See also the discussion of the 1832 preferential assignment executed by an Alabama merchant in Atherton, "Problem of Credit Rating," 538.

57. The antebellum legal basis of preferential payments to creditors is clearly laid out in *In Re Chadwick and Leavitt*, 5 *LR* 457 (DC WD Pa. 1842). See also Angell, *Practical Summary of the Law of Assignments*, 27–32, and Burrill, *Treatise on the Law*, 98–103. The most significant statutory limitation on assignments before 1840 was an 1836 Massachusetts law that rendered any preferential assignment null and void. Another important restriction on preferential payments obtained in New York, where individuals who made such payments on the brink of failure excluded themselves from the benefit of the state's insolvency process (Angell, *Practical Summary of the Law of Assignments*, 39–40). This disability, however, did not keep hundreds of New Yorkers from making otherwise legally sanctioned preferential assignments.

58. Oct. 11, 1839, letter to Lyon & Morehouse, BV Houghton & Day, Letterbook,

N-YHS; May 12, 1837, letter to Daniel H. Richards of Milwaukee; May 5, 1840, letter to A. S. Bowen; and Aug. 8, 1840, letter to Thomas W. Harvey of Poughkeepsie, Letterbooks, R. Hoe & Co. Papers, Columbia University Rare Book and Manuscript Library.

59. Debt Schedule; June 25, 1840, Chancery Court Petition of Thomas Taylor & Son; Points for Creditors, Mar. 30, 1843, Hearing; General Statement of the Concerns of Henry H. Leeds; and Depositions of Henry H. Leeds, Jonathon Amory, C-F 30. Other bankrupts who went to similar lengths to satisfy the claims of persistent creditors included the New York City brokers Joseph and Solomon Joseph, who used consigned stock to pay debts, and the New York City merchant tailor Benjamin Franklin Robinson, who applied trust funds that he was administering to the satisfaction of claims against him (C-Fs 1210, 1211, 1870).

60. See Deposition of George Ferguson, C-F 747; *Atkinson v. Farmers' Bank*, which discusses the confession of judgment by a Berks County, Pennsylvania, bankrupt to a local bank; and *Ashby v. Steere*, 2 Fed. Cases 15 (DC R.I. 1846), which discusses the 1841 coerced transfer of store goods by a Rhode Island merchant to his creditor.

61. "Preferring Creditors in Assignment—Its Morality," *HMM* 7 (1842): 527–28. See also Angell, *Practical Summary of the Law of Assignments*, 33; "Looker On," "Preferences by Insolvents," *HMM* 7 (1842): 352–54; and "Insolvency amongst Merchants," *DBR* 16 (1854): 311–19. For the unsuccessful attempt to justify a preference on these grounds in a 1774 British case, see Weisberg, "Commercial Morality," 49.

62. "Preferring Creditors in Assignment," 527; "Looker On," "Preferences by Insolvents," 352–54; "Insolvency amongst Merchants," 315.

63. C-F 2103. See also the preferences made by two Providence, Rhode Island, merchants described in *Hutchins v. Taylor & Taylor*, 5 *LR* 289 (CC R.I. 1842); those made by a northern New York mercantile firm, discussed in *Stewart et al. v. Loomis*, 23 Fed. Cases 66 (DC ND N.Y. 1842); and the bankruptcy records of the New York City coal dealers John Ambler and Nehemiah Anderson and the New York City jewelers Jacob and Jordan Mott (C-Fs 25, 35, 1602, 1603). On failures caused by the granting of accommodation loans or endorsements, see Chapter 1.

64. "Bankruptcy and the Bankrupt Bill," *New York Review* 7 (1840): 442–43. See also Angell, *Practical Summary of the Law of Assignments*, 33; "Insolvent Law of Massachusetts," 307–8; Burrill, *Treatise on the Law*, 105–6; and "Commercial Chronicle and Review," 590–91. Tony Freyer incisively explores the lobbying campaign against preferential payments by urban wholesalers, as well as the political durability of "local control" (his phrase) over bankruptcy administration. See *Producers versus Capitalists*, 83–91. Freyer does not note, however, that wholesalers were similarly prone to make preferences after failure.

65. Among the southern New York bankrupts who favored family members, neighbors, or business friends in their payments were the New York City merchant tailor Joseph Ackerman; the New York City boardinghouse keeper Angeline Brown; the Ulster County tanners Henry and Thurston Cutler; and Carlos P. Houghton (C-Fs 5, 284, 586, 1082).

66. On the successful exertion of pressure by creditor-relatives, see the bankruptcy records of the New York City tailors Francis Baldwin and Daniel Merritt and the Poughkeepsie saddle and harness maker Harvey Pettit (C-Fs 89, 1745). For an example of a confidential lender and endorser successfully extracting a preference through pressure, see *Ashby v. Steere*. For instances in which recipients of preferences were both endorsers or confidential lenders and relatives or friends, see *Albany Exchange Bank v. Johnson and Watrous*, 5 *LR* 313 (ND N.Y. 1842); *In Re Pearce*, 6 *LR* 261 (DC Vt. 1843); and the bankruptcy records of the New York City tailor John Dean and the Peekskill iron founder Judson Gilbert (C-Fs 615, 848).

67. James H. Lanman, "Laws Relative to Debtor and Creditor," *HMM* 4 (1841): 76. These provisions reflected an 1840 widening of the property exemption by the state legislature. See Basch, *In the Eyes of the Law*, 124.

68. Allen's actions came to light only because of a court battle over the ownership of the stock that began seventy-three years after he filed his bankruptcy petition (May 15, 1915, petition of Baltimore lawyer Leigh Bonsal; Aug. 15, 1915, Report of the General Assignee; Nov. 17, 1915, Report of Special Master James McCloughlin; C-F 23).

69. See creditors objections and resulting depositions in the bankruptcy cases of the New York City dry goods dealer James Alden; the New York City boardinghouse keeper Angeline Brown; and the former New Orleans merchant Benjamin Meakings (C-Fs 16, 283, 1516).

70. Debt and Asset Schedules, C-F 1341; Deposition of John Haslett, "General Statement of the Concerns of Henry Leeds," C-F 30.

71. Depositions of Frances Keown, Henry Leeds, William Noyes, Benjamin Blagg; Francis Keown's bank book and check book; Dec. 30, 1839, power of attorney from Keown to Leeds; Aug. 29, 1840, list of Leeds's real estate holdings; Jan. 2, 1837, letter from Amory and Henry Watson to Leeds; Points for Creditors, Mar. 30, 1843, Hearing, C-F 30.

72. The common law did reserve a dower right to women, so that on a husband's death his widow was entitled to a life interest in one-third of his property, regardless of provisions in any will. On nineteenth-century married women's property rights, see Basch, *In the Eyes of the Law*, and Lebsock, *Free Women of Petersburg*, 16–86.

73. Debt and Asset Schedules, Deposition of James H. Sackett, C-F 1917. For a similar trust created by a failing debtor, see the bankruptcy records of George C. Thomas, a New York City merchant (C-F 2198). For an excellent discussion of how fear of looming insolvency often prompted the creation of separate estates for married women, see Lebsock, *Free Women of Petersburg*, 56–67. This practice appears to have been commonplace by the late 1810s; see the commentary in *NWR*, Aug. 14, 1819, quoted in Gouge, *Short History of Paper Money*, 2:113.

74. Beecher, *Seven Lectures to Young Men*, 56–59. For similar conclusions, see Gouge, *Short History of Paper Money*, 1:94–95, and Boardman, *Bible in the Countinghouse*, 189–93.

75. See in particular Cary, *Dependence of the Fine Arts*, 16–17, and Bellows, "Morals of Trade: Number Five," *HMM* 6 (1842): 453.

76. "Law to Prevent Bad Debts," *HMM* 30 (1854): 136; see also "Laws for the Collection of Debts," *HMM* 17 (1848): 440, reprinted from the *Dry Goods Reporter*, and "Of Abolishing Laws for the Collection of Debts," *HMM* 28 (1853): 650, reprinted from the *New York Evening Post*.

77. Clark, *Roots of Rural Capitalism*, 28–38, 156–76; Doyle, *Social Order*, 89–90; Hahn, *Roots of Southern Populism*, 72–77; Faragher, *Sugar Creek*, 133–36; Sellers, *Market Revolution*, 13; Gray, *Yankee West*, 77–79. The attitudes that gave life to this culture of trade may help to explain why some country storekeepers had such great difficulty in collecting from their customers.

78. One should note that the vibrant culture of accommodation among antebellum entrepreneurs echoed the rural mutuality identified by historians like Clark.

79. Circular of Amory & Leeds to Creditors, Feb. 1, 1841, C-F 30.

80. Houghton & Day's correspondence shows a similar reliance on the precepts of the moralists when it suited the firm. See BV, Houghton & Day, Letterbook, N-YHS, especially letters of July 20, 1839, to Denton & Gaul; Jan. 28, Feb. 7, 1840, to G. W. Cornell; and Feb. 7, 1840, to S. W. Howe. Perceptions of "upright" behavior in the face of insolvency also could have an impact on access to credit after bankruptcy. See Chapter 6.

81. A bankrupt's invocation of such conventions, of course, by no means guaranteed generosity from creditors, who increasingly scrutinized the accounting statements that came to accompany circular letters in the 1830s and 1840s. In the case of Amory & Leeds's insolvency, numerous creditors remained unconvinced that the firm had acted with propriety. On theatricality and commerce in America, see Lears, *Fables of Abundance*, 65–74,

and Spears, *100 Years on the Road*, 27–49, 79–111. For incisive discussions of narrative commercial discourse, see Ditz, "Shipwrecked," and Sandage, "Deadbeats, Drunkards, and Dreamers."

82. Barron, *Those Who Stayed Behind*, 115; Doyle, *Social Order*, 184; Burrill, *Treatise on the Law*, 98–113. The term "church commercial" is Freeman Hunt's, who described his calling as "preaching to our parish—the church commercial, scattered over the business world" ("Morals of Commerce, A Lesson for Merchants," *HMM* 34 (1856): 642–43).

Chapter Four

1. Warren, *Bankruptcy in United States History*, 3–21; Coleman, *Debtors and Creditors in America*, 19–20; McCoy, *Elusive Republic*, 178–84.

2. Historians of American bankruptcy law have long noted that the 1841 statute dramatically improved the legal position of debtors. See Noel, "A History of the Bankruptcy Clause," 138–44; Warren, *Bankruptcy in United States History*, 60–85; Beesley, "Politics of Bankruptcy," 108–30; and Coleman, *Debtors and Creditors in America*, 22–24. These scholars, however, have slighted the features of the 1841 act that placed constraints on debtors and all but ignored the role of the federal judiciary in favoring the interests of debtors through interpretation and application of the legislation's ambiguities, as well as the efforts of numerous creditors to turn provisions of the legislation to their own advantage. The regulatory strains of the law anticipated similar features of later bankruptcy legislation in 1867 and 1898. On these statutes, and especially the latter one, see Hansen, "Commercial Associations."

3. This approach to popular legal consciousness draws heavily on Hartog, "Pigs and Positivism."

4. "On a National Bankrupt Law," *American Jurist* 1 (1829): 35–58; "Bankruptcy, and the Bankrupt Bill," *New York Review* 7 (1840): 442–43, 466–67; Moore, *Laws of Trade*, 350–60; *Expediency of a Uniform Bankrupt Law*, 3–13; [Stilwell], *Appeal to the Members of Congress*; Benjamin F. Porter, "The Law of Bankruptcy," *HMM* 28 (1853): 439–44; "A General Bankrupt Law," *Law Reporter* 21 (1858): 385–86. See also the discussion of congressional bankruptcy debates in Warren, *Bankruptcy in United States History*, 1–91.

5. "On a National Bankrupt Law," 44–50; Hopkinson, "Lecture on Commercial Integrity," *HMM* 1 (1839): 378; *Expediency of a Uniform Bankrupt Law*, 15–17; "The Late Bankrupt Law," *PLJ* 3 (1844): 5–8; Porter, "Law of Bankruptcy."

6. "On a National Bankrupt Law," 35–41; Moore, *Laws of Trade*, x–xi; Joshua M. Van Cott, "A General Bankrupt Law," *HMM* 4 (1841): 31; Porter, "Law of Bankruptcy," 442; "General Bankrupt Law," 386–87.

7. Congressional inaction resulted from other sources as well, including: opposition from many farmers, who viewed any bankruptcy system as morally suspect, and from western merchants, who feared being vulnerable to involuntary petitions from eastern suppliers; critical memories of the Federalist Bankruptcy Act of 1800; periodic debtor relief provided by state legislatures during the 1820s and 1830s, such as stay and appraisal laws, abolition of imprisonment for debt, and insolvency processes that could discharge obligations to in-state creditors, all of which lessened pressure on Congress to exercise the bankruptcy power; and deep disputes among proponents of a national bankruptcy system on matters of detail. These disagreements ranged from the constitutionality and propriety of voluntary bankruptcy, to the wisdom of extending federal bankruptcy proceedings to insolvent corporations, to the questions of whether discharges should be contingent on creditor consent and whether assignees should be appointed by creditors or the federal courts. See Warren, *Bankruptcy in United States History*, 26–92; Rothbard, *Panic of 1819*; Beesley, "Politics of

Bankruptcy," 313–43; Coleman, *Debtors and Creditors in America*, 16–24, 274–86; Ciment, "In Light of Failure," 191–205, 245–64; Freyer, *Producers versus Capitalists*, 86–90; and Balleisen, "Navigating Failure," 187–91.

8. Such estimates of American bankrupts became a cliché in the speeches and writings of antebellum supporters of national bankruptcy legislation. See *Expediency of a Uniform Bankrupt Law*, 23; Van Cott, "General Bankrupt Law," 34; 1840 speeches by Sens. Norvell, Strange, Webster, Tallmadge, and Clay, *ACG*, 26th Cong., 1st sess., 464, 542, 796, 798, 816; 1841 speeches by Sen. Tallmadge and Reps. Fessenden and Barnard, *ACG*, 27th Cong., 1st sess., 468, 471, 498–99; 1842 speeches by Sens. Berrien and Choate, *ACG*, 27th Cong., 2d sess., 103, 105; and *New Orleans Bee*, Aug. 30, 1842. On bankruptcy politics in 1840, see Warren, *Bankruptcy in United States History*, 59–69, and Beesley, "Politics of Bankruptcy," 88–108.

9. *Niles' Weekly Register* provided a step-by-step account of the congressional maneuvering that culminated in the adoption of the 1841 act on September 4, 1841. See also Warren, *Bankruptcy in United States History*, 70–79, and Beesley, "Politics of Bankruptcy," 110–17. The different political context after the panic of 1819 goes a long way to explaining why this earlier economic downswing did not lead to bankruptcy reform. In the early 1820s, party politics had all but disappeared at the national level, removing the incentive for party power brokers to seize upon bankruptcy as a compelling election issue. Critical memory of the Bankruptcy Act of 1800 was also relatively fresh.

10. *Act to Establish a Uniform System of Bankruptcy*, secs. 1–2, 4, 6–7, 14. Creditors did have the option to file dissents to motions of petitioners for discharges. A majority of creditors in number who together held at least half of an applicants' total debts could block a discharge, even if the bankruptcy judge had overruled all objections to a given petition. Any applicant, however, could overcome a dissent by demanding a jury trial. In such a trial, the issue would be whether or not the petitioner had violated some provision in the bankruptcy statute. Thus a creditor's dissent could stand in the way of only a petitioner judged to have contravened the act.

11. The United States Bankruptcy Act of 1800, which only allowed for involuntary bankruptcy, required that two-thirds of a bankrupt's creditors consent to a discharge. Other previous bankruptcy or insolvency systems that held out the possibility of a release, but demanded the consent of creditors, included the British bankruptcy system, which was limited to traders and only provided for involuntary proceedings, and which mandated the assent of four-fifths of creditors in value during the first four decades of the nineteenth century; the French system, which required the consent of half the creditors and still left a number of civil disabilities until the debts were paid in full; the systems in Portugal, Spain, Holland, Scotland, Prussia, and Russia, which provided varying degrees of release; and the Maryland and New York insolvency systems, under which insolvents needed the consent of two-thirds of their in-state creditors. The British insolvency system and most insolvency laws in the American states only provided for immunity from imprisonment for debt, leaving unpaid obligations in force. Throughout the early decades of the nineteenth century, the state legislatures of Rhode Island, Connecticut, Vermont, and Maryland granted special discharges regardless of creditor consent. Only in Massachusetts, after the adoption of the 1838 Insolvency Act, could bankrupts gain a discharge through the normal course of law without the consent of creditors; yet this statute did not cover out-of-state creditors ("Bankrupt Laws," *NAR* 7 [1818]: 35–36; "Bankrupt and Insolvent Laws," *American Jurist* 3 [1830]: 219–34; "Bankrupt," *Encyclopedia Americana*, 1:550–54; Charles Clark, "The Russian Insolvency Laws," *HMM* 6 [1842]: 419–25; "The Law of Attachment in the Several States of the United States," *Bankers' Magazine* 12 [1857]: 193–95; Richard Brown, "Comparative Legislation in Bankruptcy," 264–67; Coleman, *Debtors and Creditors in America*,

65–129, 171–76). For a representative petition to Congress calling for the requirement of creditor consent to discharges, see "Memorial of New York City Chamber of Commerce."

12. *Act to Establish a Uniform System of Bankruptcy*, secs. 2, 4.

13. Ibid., sec. 1.

14. Clark, "Russian Insolvency Laws," 419–25; Brown, "Comparative Legislation in Bankruptcy," 264–68; Ch'en, *Insolvency of the Chinese Hong Merchants*, 178–218. The 1841 act mandated twenty days notice before a hearing on a motion for a bankruptcy decree, and an additional seventy days notice before a hearing on a motion for a discharge (*Act to Establish a Uniform System of Bankruptcy*, secs. 4, 7).

15. *ACG*, 27th Cong., 2d sess. (1841), 30–31.

16. *Journal of Commerce*, Feb. 5, 1842; see also *MCNYE*, Feb. 4, 1842; *NYH*, Feb. 5, Mar. 21, 1842; *Poughkeepsie Telegraph*, Feb. 9, 1842; *In Re Benjamin Randall et al.*, 5 LR 115 (CC Mass. 1842); and bankruptcy records of Edmund Arnoux, a New York City tailor, and John C. Bloom, a New York City clerk (C-Fs 49, 202). For an attempt to arrange such a compromise, which in this case did not succeed in forestalling a bankruptcy application, see John Osborne Sargeant to Dudley Selden, Sept. 19, 1842, BV Sargeant, John Osborne, Letterbook, Manuscript Department, N-YHS. A contributor to a New York City newspaper maintained in early 1843 that the law had resulted in at least 20,000 compositions; Sen. Berrien, Judiciary Committee chairman and the leader of antirepeal forces in the Senate, thought the number was higher still ("Veto," *Journal of Commerce*, Jan. 25, 1843; *CG*, 27th Cong., 3d sess., 342). See also the responses of Judge Betts and Judge Story, in *Report . . . in Relation to the Operation of the Bankrupt Law*, 10, 27; and the reprinted article from the *Philadelphia Gazette* in "The Bankrupt Law," *NWR*, Nov. 5, 1842.

17. *Act to Establish a Uniform System of Bankruptcy*, sec. 3. For leading cases on the rights of secured creditors under the 1841 act, see *In Re Benjamin B. Grant et al.*, 5 LR 303 (CC Mass. 1842); *In Re Kerlin*, 3 Howard 326 (1843); *In Re Jacob F. Hahnlen*, 1 PLJ 10 (DC ED Pa. 1842); and *Mitchell v. Winslow et al.*, 6 LR 347 (CC Maine 1843). The right of a bankrupt's creditor to foreclose on a mortgage did have limits. Federal judges could void mortgages given by bankrupts if they constituted illegal preferences, as well as order a bankrupt's mortgaged assets to be sold by the bankruptcy assignee, preempting the role of the state courts in foreclosure (*Ex Parte City Bank of New Orleans, In Re William Christy*, 3 Howard 292 [1845]; *Norton's Assignee v. Boyd et al.*, 3 Howard 426 [1845]).

The 1841 act constrained lien holders in one important respect. Creditors who attacked the property of bankrupts in state courts had to choose between continuing those suits or applying to the bankruptcy court for payment from their debtors' estates. If creditors chose the latter option, they lost the legal right to press their liens in state tribunals and had to surrender any assets of bankrupts in their possession to the relevant bankruptcy assignee (*Act to Establish a Uniform System of Bankruptcy*, sec. 5; *Briggs v. Stevens*, 7 LR 281 [DC ND N.Y. 1844]; *In Re Cohaus*, 6 Fed. Cases 12 [CC D.C. 1842]). As the likely dividends from a bankrupt's estate did not often match the probable return from foreclosing a mortgage or levying on a debtor's possessions, creditors with liens overwhelmingly shied away from the bankruptcy court. In at least a few instances, secured creditors proved their debt against a bankrupt but then petitioned to withdraw their proof after discovering that their action prohibited them from pursuing their claims in state courts (*Ex Parte Lapsley*, 1 PLJ 245 [DC ED Pa. 1842]; *In Re Simon W. Lychenheim, MCNYE*, Apr. 6, 1843 [DC SD N.Y.]).

18. Wells delivered his ruling in the case of *In Re Klein* in September 1842; see *NWR*, Nov. 5, 1842, and 1 PLJ 344 (DC Mo. 1842). By the time circuit court judge Catron overruled Wells on appeal in April 1843, Congress had repealed the 1841 act. Thus Wells's action essentially prevented residents of Missouri from obtaining bankruptcy relief (*NWR*, May 13, 1843). For Catron's opinion, see 1 Howard 277 (CC Mo. 1843). At least two other federal

judges—Judge McKinley, in Louisiana's circuit court, and Judge Betts, in southern New York's district court—specifically ruled that the entire Bankruptcy Act was constitutional (Report of unnamed case, *NWR*, May 6, 1843 [CC La.]; *In Re Zerega*, *NYH*, Mar. 4, 1842 [DC SD N.Y.]).

19. The following analysis of judicial application is based on an exhaustive consideration of published bankruptcy opinions by federal judges, which are heavily weighted toward the Northeast and Old Northwest, as well as an intensive examination of judicial decision making in the southern federal district of New York, based on manuscript court records.

20. *In Re John C. Tebbets*, 5 *LR* 268 (CC Mass. 1842); *In Re Cassander Frisbee*, *NYH*, Mar. 8, 1842 (DC SD N.Y.); Creditors' Objections, Betts Ruling, C-F 806. See also *In Re John Moffat*, *NYH*, Mar. 8, 1842 (DC SD N.Y.); Betts Rulings in cases of Aaron Abrahams, Charles Oakley (C-Fs 2 1/2, 1663); *In Re Jacob Mott*, *NYH*, Nov. 4, 1842 (DC SD N.Y.); *In Re Robert Malcolm*, 4 *LR* 488 (DC SD N.Y. 1842); *In Re Horace Plimpton*, 4 *LR* 499 (DC SD N.Y. 1842); and *In Re Leonard Gosling*, *NYH*, Oct. 22, 1842 (DC SD N.Y.). This stance diverged strikingly from the practice of early- and mid-nineteenth-century English insolvency courts—the courts in which English debtors who were not merchants sought legal relief, which through midcentury was limited to release from imprisonment for debt. Across the Atlantic, English insolvency judges strictly enforced formal requirements in the presentation of debtors' petitions, allowing resubmissions only if insolvent debtors could pay the costs incurred by opposing creditors (Lester, *Victorian Insolvency*, 95).

21. Betts Rulings in the cases of Frost Brundage, Levi Dodge, Joseph L. Joseph, Daniel B. Tallmadge, C-Fs 317, 655, 1210, 2167; *Ex Parte John W. Hull and Abraham Smith*, 1 *NYLO* 1 (DC SD N.Y. 1842); report of unnamed case, *MCNYE*, June 18, 1842 (DC N.J.); *In Re Nathaniel B. Frost*, *MCNYE*, Mar. 9, 1842 (DC SD N.Y.); *In Re Newman*, *NYH*, Sept. 9, 1842 (DC SD N.Y.); *In Re George Livermore*, 5 *LR* 370 (DC SD N.Y. 1842); *In Re George Richmond*, *NYH*, June 12, 1842 (DC SD N.Y.); *In Re Benjamin March*, *NYH*, Nov. 4, 1842 (DC SD N.Y.).

22. Betts Ruling in the case of Daniel Delevan, C-F 628.

23. *In Re Alonzo Pearce*, 6 *LR* 261 (DC Vt. 1843); *In Re Mark Banks*, 1 *NYLO* 274 (DC SD N.Y. 1842); Creditors Objections, Depositions, Thompson Ruling in the case of William Hillyer, C-F 1041.

24. *Hutchins v. Taylor et al.*, 5 *LR* 288 (CC R.I. 1842); *Albany Exchange Bank v. Johnson and Watrous*, 5 *LR* 313 (DC ND N.Y. 1842); *Dennett v. Mitchell*, 6 *LR* 16 (DC Maine 1843); *Gasset et al. v. Morse and Chapman*, 3 *NYLO* 350 (DC Vt. 1845); *Ex Parte the Creditors of Breneman*, 1 *PLJ* 36 (DC ED Pa. 1842); *Stewart et al. v. Loomis*, 23 Fed. Cases 66 (DC ND N.Y. 1842); *Ex Parte the Creditors of Flack*, *NWR*, Nov. 5, 1842 (DC Md.). Some federal judges narrowed the legal meaning of the phrase "in contemplation of bankruptcy" even further, insisting that it referred to an intention to submit a bankruptcy application under the 1841 statute, thus exempting any transactions that occurred before congressional passage of the legislation (*In Re Charles H. Delevan*, *NYH*, Aug. 15, 1842 [DC SD N.Y.]; *Ex Parte the Creditors of James Bonnet, Jr.*, 1 *NYLO* 310 [DC SD N.Y. 1843]; *Buckingham et al. v. McLean*, 13 Howard 151 [1851]).

25. *In Re Samuel S. Cotton*, 6 *LR* 546 (CC Conn. 1843); *Spalding v. State of New York*, 4 Howard 21 (1846); *In Re John Hardison*, 5 *LR* 255 (CC ED Va. 1842); *In Re Hezekiah B. Crease*, 5 *LR* 408 (DC WD Va. 1842); *In Re Parker*, 1 *PLJ* 370 (CC ED Pa. 1842); *In Re Jonathon Cheney*, 5 *LR* 19 (CC Mass. 1842); *In Re Edson Comstock*, 5 *LR* 163 (DC Vt. 1842); *Ex Parte Hoskin*, 1 *PLJ* 287 (DC ED Pa. 1842); "The Bankrupt Law," *NWR*, Nov. 5, 1842; report of unnamed case, 5 *LR* 136 (DC N.J. 1842). In at least five states, voluntary applicants who owed fiduciary debts could still petition for a release from the other claims against them. The Supreme Court adopted the more lenient interpretation in 1844. See *In Re Levi H. Young*, 5 *LR* 128 (DC Conn. 1842); *In Re John C. Tebbets*, 259; *In Re Horace Lord*, 5 *LR* 258

(CC Ohio 1842); *In Re Samuel G. Wheeler, MCNYE*, Apr. 23, 1842 (DC S.C.); *In Re George Brown, NYH*, Mar. 22, May 12, 1842 (DC SD N.Y.); *In Re Samuel R. Brooks, NYH*, Mar. 24, May 12, 1842 (DC SD N.Y.); *In Re William Booth, NYH*, Nov. 12, 1842 (DC SD N.Y.); and *Chapman v. Forsyth*, 2 Howard 202 (1844). The habeas corpus decisions made clear that federal judges would grant the writ to allow imprisoned bankrupts to attend necessary business in bankruptcy court. In addition, not all federal judges refused to free bankrupts imprisoned under state debt law. See *United States v. Dobbins*, 5 *LR* 81 (DC WD Pa. 1842), and *In Re Grenville T. Winthrop*, 5 *LR* 24 (DC Mass. 1842).

26. *In Re Alexander Greaves*, 1 *NYLO* 213 (DC SD N.Y. 1842); bankruptcy records of David Dodge, an Orange County railroad contractor; Roswell Tuthill, an Orange County mason; and James Van Duzer, an Orange County farmer (C-Fs 654, 2250, 2288). Other voluntary applicants of very small means never completed their petitions, possibly because of poverty. See the records for Lawrence Bates, a Columbia County farmer; Simon Bearbieur, a Poughkeepsie shoemaker; and John Beelman, a Flatbush farmer (C-Fs 123, 133, 141). Betts's reasoning on this issue pertained especially to the requirement that petitioners pay the assignee's fees. This court official had the task of ascertaining whether petitioners had surrendered all their property. If he did not receive his compensation, he could not certify to the court that applicants had no property. Betts maintained that allowing applicants who alleged poverty to bypass the assignee would create a procedural loophole subject to abuse— petitioners who were not wholly destitute could claim to be, thereby easing the task of concealing property from the court.

27. Debt and Asset Schedules, Deposition of John Bailey, C-F 72.

28. *In Re John Bailey*, 1 *NYLO* 18 (DC SD N.Y. 1842). For a similar case, see *In Re John Q. McCarty, NYH*, Aug. 15, 1842 (DC SD N.Y.). By the same token, the sworn testimony by a bankrupt that he had lost $2,500 in banknotes, no matter how far-fetched, protected him from allegations that he had concealed property, as long as the objecting creditors could not show that the bankrupt's testimony was false. See the creditors' objections, depositions, and judicial rulings in the bankruptcy case of Aaron Abrahams (C-F 2 1/2).

29. Objections of Seth Driggs in the case of Hugh Macfarlane, C-F 1458.

30. Betts Ruling, C-F 1458; *In Re Macfarlane*, 16 Fed. Cases 89 (DC SD N.Y. 1842). Betts also applied Judge Smith Thompson's position on fraud before the passage of the Bankruptcy Act in *In Re Charles H. Delevan* and *In Re John Q. McCarty*.

31. For a discussion of antebellum approaches to statutory construction based on the relationship between legislative "parts" and "wholes," see Sedgwick, *Treatise on the Rules*, 199–201.

32. On the interpretive traditions of reading ambiguous statutory provisions in light of the common-law rules in place before the adoption of the statute, and older statutes on the same subject matter (*in pari materia*), even when the earlier statutes had been repealed, see ibid., 209–12, 267–79.

33. Oaks and Bentley, "Joseph Smith and the Legal Process," 180.

34. For a discussion of Story's role in drafting the 1841 act, see Swisher, *History of the Supreme Court*, 132–35; on Moore's sentiments, see *Report . . . in Relation to the Operation of the Bankrupt Law*, 147; for Betts's interpretation of historical context, see *In Re the Creditors of John W. Hull and Abraham Smith*, 1 *NYLO* 1 (DC SD N.Y. 1842). Harry Baldwin, a Jacksonian Supreme Court justice, indicated a similar understanding of the Bankruptcy Act's goals. See *Report . . . in Relation to the Operation of the Bankrupt Law*, 70. See also "Bankrupt Law," *PLJ* 1 (1842): 286, which noted that "the Courts of the United States, guided by a desire to carry out the intention of Congress in passing the act, have adopted a Practice calculated to relieve the unfortunate but honest debtor, from the weight of obligations."

35. *Milledgeville Federal Union*, Sept. 27, 1842.

36. *In Re John George Smith, NYH,* Mar. 26, 1842 (DC SD N.Y.). Federal judges in western Virginia and North Carolina also made mention of the great amount of bankruptcy work they confronted (*Report . . . in Relation to the Operation of the Bankrupt Law,* 56, 154).

37. *Wakeman v. Hoyt,* 5 *LR* 309 (CC Conn. 1842). For other examples of successful involuntary petitions outside southern New York, see *Hutchins v. Taylor et al.; Arnold et al. v. Maynard,* 5 *LR* 296 (CC Mass. 1842); *Albany Exchange Bank v. Johnson and Watrous; In Re the Creditors of Ezekiel Daws, MCNYE,* Sept. 22, 1842 (DC ED Va.); the report of an unnamed South Carolina case, *MCNYE,* Nov. 8, 1842 (DC S.C.); and *Planters' Bank and John McKeage v. Galbraith, Cromwell & Co,* 5 *LR* (1842): 134–35 (DC MD Tenn.). Successful involuntary petitions in Judge Betts's court included those against the New York City merchant tailors George Andrews and Jeremiah Lamphier; the New York City furniture dealer Smith Ely; the Kingston baker Peter Hasbrouck; and the New York City merchants Robert Ogden, John Scudder, and Edwin Wilcox (C-Fs 37, 984, 1675).

38. *In Re Quackenbos,* 20 Fed. Cases 104 (DC SD N.Y. 1842); see also *In Re Johnson,* 13 Fed. Cases 718 (DC Ky. 1842); *In Re Irwine,* 1 *PLJ* 291 (CC ED Pa. 1842); *In Re Alonzo Pearce; Aspinwall's Case,* 3 *PLJ* 212 (DC ED Pa. 1844); and *In Re Daniel J. Perley,* 4 *NYLO* 255 (DC Maine 1846). Voluntary bankrupts whose motions for a decree or a discharge were denied by Judge Betts included the Tarrytown shoe manufacturer George Ferguson; the New York City commission merchant Henry Leeds; and the Brooklyn huckster Daniel Youngs (C-Fs 747, 1341, 2509).

39. This calculation is derived from the two congressional reports on the functioning of the bankruptcy system created by the 1841 act, which exclude statistics from eight federal districts. In addition, 5,450 of the 41,108 applications in the thirty-three reporting districts were still pending at the time of the last report. These statistical omissions make a precise calculation impossible. Of the 35,444 applications disposed of in the reporting districts, 968, or 2.7 percent, were refused discharges. See *Letter . . . Relative to the . . . Bankrupt Law; Letter . . . Showing Proceedings under the Bankrupt Act.*

40. Creditors' Petition, C-F 660.

41. Creditors' Motion to Withdraw Petition, C-F 660. Payment may have come from James Dolton, whose preferential treatment would have been in jeopardy if the bankruptcy proceedings continued.

42. 83.3 percent of the involuntary petitions offered by creditors did not proceed to a bankruptcy decree. This figure is calculated from a random sample of the 1841 bankruptcy docket books in New York's southern district (Entry 118, Bankruptcy Records, Act of 1841, United States District Court for the Southern Federal District of New York). The sample included 509 bankrupts, just under 20 percent of the individuals in the jurisdiction who either filed for relief or had bankruptcy proceedings initiated against them. Of the sample, eighteen debtors, or 3 percent, were involuntary bankrupts. (This proportion is the same as that for the entire bankruptcy docket of the southern federal district.) Only three of the eighteen were decreed bankrupts. Cases in which petitioning creditors formally withdrew their applications included those against John Balch, a New York City merchant; George, Richard, and William Crook, New York City merchants; Stephen Frost, a Poughkeepsie merchant; Pulaski Jacks and Oscar Dibble, partners in New York City and Savannah mercantile firms; and Benjamin Meakings, a former New Orleans merchant (C-Fs 86, 563, 810, 1156, 1516). For other evidence of settlements compelled by the filing of involuntary petitions, see speech of Rep. Underwood, *CG,* 27th Cong., 3d sess. (1842), 71; *Ex Parte the Creditors of R. & L. Calendar,* 1 *NYLO* 200 (DC Conn. 1842).

43. Creditor's Objections, Creditor's Notice of Withdrawal of Objections, C-F 913; Bankruptcy Papers of Micah Seabury, box 39, CTP. Griggs's payment to Bend emerged during a subsequent court case in the New York Supreme Court (*Chamberlin et al. v. Griggs,* 3 Denio 9 [1846]).

44. Figures are also calculated from the random sample of the bankruptcy docket books for southern New York. Out of the sample, 491 bankrupts filed voluntary petitions, of whom 84 faced opposition from at least one creditor. In 48 of these cases, creditors withdrew their objections.

45. George Manley, for example, initially objected to the bankruptcy petition of George W. Soule, a New York City broker, alleging the creation of an illegal preference through Soule's execution of a mortgage on his furniture, as well as willful concealment of other assets. Manley soon withdrew his objections, explaining that he had "satisfied myself that said Soule had acted fairly and honestly." This statement, of course, might simply have been part of a settlement between the bankrupt broker and his creditor (Creditor's Objections, Withdrawal of Creditor's Objections, C-F 2077). The Philadelphia mercantile firm's instructions are in the bankruptcy records of Samuel Reeve (C-F 1832).

46. For instances in which creditors withdrew objections after Betts rejected motions for the granting of discharges, see the bankruptcy records of James Alden, Jonathon Amory, and Smith Ely (C-Fs 16, 30, 725). For examples of bankrupts whose creditors withdrew objections after presenting strong evidence of fraud, see the records of the New York City lawyer and speculator Anthony Dey; the Goshen tailor and deputy sheriff Daniel Howell; the New York City mercantile partners Robert Ogden, John Scudder, and Edwin Wilcox; and the Warwarsing tanner Henry Southwick (C-Fs 644, 1043, 1675, 2081).

47. "The Bankrupt Law," *Journal of Commerce*, Dec. 22, 1842. There is reason to question whether the practice of skirting the objections of creditors through negotiated settlements was as prevalent in western parts of the country as it appears to have been in the Northeast. In the 1842 Senate report, Judge Irwin, who presided over the western district of Pennsylvania, maintained that creditors had objected to only 56 of the more than 1,600 voluntary petitions in his jurisdiction—a rate of only 3.5 percent (*Report . . . in Relation to the Operation of the Bankrupt Law*, 50). A lower incidence of formal objections suggests fewer opportunities for out-of-court arrangements.

48. *Poughkeepsie Telegraph*, Feb. 9, 1842, reprinted from the *New York Sun*. *NYH*, Dec. 12, 13, 26, 1842. For similar sentiments, see *NWR*, Nov. 5, 1842, quoting from an article in the *Baltimore Republican*; speeches of Rep. Ferris and Sen. Buchanan, *CG*, 27th Cong., 3d sess., 109, 347–48; and the statements of Democratic politicians in North Carolina, Virginia, and Tennessee, discussed in Beesley, "Politics of Bankruptcy," 133–40. The term "jubilee" refers here to the biblical practice of the Israelites, in which every fiftieth year brought about the emancipation of bondsmen and the redemption of mortgaged property.

49. *Act to Establish a Uniform System of Bankruptcy*, secs. 3, 5. Thus if the amount left in a bankrupt's estate after the payment of court costs equaled 20 percent of proved debts, then each of these creditors would receive 20 percent of the amount owed them. The statute provided for two classes of preferred creditors—the U.S. government and a bankrupt's employees, up to the first $25 owed for labor.

50. *ACG*, 27th Cong., 2d sess. (1841), 30.

51. *Letter . . . , Relative to the . . . Bankrupt Law; Letter . . . Showing Proceedings under the Bankrupt Act*. The figure for the southern district of New York was 1 percent; most southern New York bankruptcies did not result in the payment of any dividends.

52. See the petitions from the state legislatures of Mississippi, Connecticut, and New Hampshire (Senate Doc. Nos. 276, 361, 27th Cong., 2d sess. [1842]; Senate Doc. No. 70, 27th Cong., 3d sess. ([1843]).

53. *New Orleans Bee*, Dec. 26, 1842; *Journal of Commerce*, Jan. 25, 1843. See also *Journal of Commerce*, Dec. 17, Dec. 31, 1842, Feb. 28, 1843; and *MCNYE*, Dec. 12, Dec. 27, 1842, Jan. 20, Feb. 4, 1843.

54. *Report . . . in Relation to the Operation of the Bankrupt Law*, 12, 30. See also the comments of a wide range of judges and other federal officials from around the country, at 3,

9, 12, 22, 27, 30, 50, 53, 54, 61, 62, 67, 70, 72, 145, 147, 152, 161, 163, and 166. A few respondents, such as district judges from Virginia, Indiana, and Missouri, Supreme Court justice Daniel, and U.S. attorneys from Vermont and Virginia, described the law as having pernicious consequences, but they were very much in the minority; their analyses are at 17, 18, 24, 56, 74, 156, 175.

55. Of the sample of 503 southern New York bankrupts, good evidence of time of failure—indicated by an assignment for the benefit of creditors, a crescendo of debt judgments, a state insolvency petition, or state chancery proceedings—exists for 457. Of these, 269, or almost 3 in 5, failed in 1840 or earlier.

56. Since most bankruptcy applicants did not indicate on their petitions how much creditors might have realized through prior liquidation of assets, the statistics provided by federal bankruptcy officials substantially undercount the payments that creditors of bankrupts actually received. Although there is no way to provide a precise calculation of the payments gleaned by diligent creditors outside the bankruptcy process, statistics offered by the court clerk of the Massachusetts district give some indication of the amounts garnered by the holders of secured obligations. The 3,389 bankrupts in Massachusetts collectively owed almost $35 million and surrendered property that, after liquidation, netted just under $1 million in cash for distribution to creditors. The district's court clerk, however, estimated that secured creditors of bankrupts realized an additional $5 million, roughly five times what the court paid out as dividends. This latter sum still does not take into account dividends that would have been distributed through Massachusetts's insolvency courts ("Bankrupts in Massachusetts," *LR* 9 [1846]: 286). The Sept. 17, 1842, issue of the *Brooklyn Daily Eagle* similarly noted that the general creditors of bankrupts in southern New York received such small dividends because "mortgages and the satisfaction of preferred claimants in some way, absorbs about all." See also Balleisen, "Navigating Failure," 234–46.

57. *Report . . . in Relation to the Operation of the Bankrupt Law*, 53, 61, 68, 151, 161; Senate Judiciary Committee, *Report on the Bankruptcy Law*, 28–29.

58. Warren, *Bankruptcy in United States History*, 81–85; Sellers, *Market Revolution*, 412–13; Holt, *Political Parties and American Political Development*, 190. The significance of the row between President Tyler and probank congressional Whigs comes through clearly in the final debates on the bill to repeal the 1841 Bankruptcy Act. Congressmen spent more time either criticizing President Tyler or lauding him than they did on the merits of repeal. See *CG*, 27th Cong., 3d sess. (1843), 65–176, 341–48, and *ACG*, 27th Cong., 3d sess. (1843), 48–49, 70–74, 82–86, 94–96. The 1842 Senate report provides several indications of the political implications resulting from the 1841 act's exclusion of corporations. Several respondents from western jurisdictions suggested that Congress amend the Bankruptcy Law to include corporations, arguing that such an inclusion would greatly increase the popularity of the law (*Report . . . in Relation to the Operation of the Bankrupt Law*, 53, 61, 73, 74, 163–64, 166).

59. Senate Judiciary Committee, *Report on the Bankruptcy Law*, 20–28.

60. Warren, *Bankruptcy in United States History*, 84–85; Beesley, "Politics of Bankruptcy," 141–46.

61. The passage of stay, appraisal, and exemption laws in several state legislatures further blunted any movement toward federal bankruptcy legislation in the late 1840s or 1850s (Warren, *Bankruptcy in United States History*, 87–105). After the panic of 1857, President Buchanan did propose a federal bankruptcy law, but one that would reach only insolvent banking corporations. This proposal garnered only limited support in Congress, since Republicans wished for more comprehensive legislation and many Democrats opposed the extension of federal control over state banking institutions. See Huston, *Panic of 1857*, 114–18. Republicans did not pass bankruptcy legislation earlier than 1867 largely because of

intraparty divisions over the impact of a bankruptcy system on southern, and especially rebellious, debtors. See Sandage, "Deadbeats, Drunkards, and Dreamers," 229–42.

62. The vast majority of bankruptcy petitioners were men. One extensive examination of over 26,000 case-files created as a result of the 1841 statute has identified 48 female bankrupts (Gross et al., "Ladies in Red," 10). The estimated ratio of bankrupts to overall adult white male population reflects the census figures and demographic interpolations provided in the U.S. Department of Commerce, Bureau of the Census, *Historical Statistics*, Series A: 6–8, 119–34. On the legal force of a bankruptcy certificate, see *Act to Establish a Uniform System of Bankruptcy*, sec. 4.

63. Acknowledgment of Debt by James L. Butler, no date, box 39, CTP. As we have seen, Butler was wrong about the legal implications of the fiduciary debt that he owed, since the Supreme Court eventually ruled that such obligations did not bar a discharge from other debts. Butler's reading of the Bankruptcy Act, however, led him to forestall objections from the business for whom he served as agent.

64. *Ingersoll v. Rhoades*, Hill and Denio Supplement 373 (Supreme Court N.Y. 1844). See also *Dearing v. Moffitt*, 6 Alabama Reports 776 (Perry County Circuit Court 1844).

65. *Thompson v. Hewitt*, 6 Hill 254 (Supreme Court N.Y. 1843); *Donnell v. Swaim*, 3 *PLJ* 393 (District Court, Philadelphia 1844); report of unnamed case, 1 *WLJ* 479 (Court of Common Pleas N.Y.C. 1844); *Farmers & Mechanics Bank v. Flint*, 9 *LR* 472 (Supreme Court Conn. 1846); *Stilwell v. Coope*, 4 Denio 225 (Supreme Court N.Y. 1847); *Stouffer v. Executors of Haines*, 13 *LR* 193 (Middle District, Supreme Court Pa. 1850); *Linton et al. v. Stanton*, 12 Howard 423 (1851); *Porter's Administrator v. Porter*, 14 *LR* 565 (Supreme Court Maine 1852); *Otis v. Gazlin*, 14 *LR* 566 (Supreme Court Maine 1852).

66. J. H. Allen, "The True Mercantile Character," *HMM* 34 (1856): 61. See also Arthur, *Two Merchants*; Arthur, *Debtor and Creditor*, 179–80; "Payment of Debts by Bankrupts," *HMM* 27 (1852): 523; and Logan McKnight, "Insolvency amongst Merchants," *DBR* 16 (1854): 318. For a rare example of a commercial moralist who took the opposite viewpoint, see J. N. Bellows, "Morals of Trade: Number Four," *HMM* 6 (1842): 252–56.

67. Asa Smith, *Guileless Israelite*, 28; "An Instance of Commercial Integrity," *HMM* 11 (1844): 292; "An Example of Mercantile Integrity," *HMM* 11 (1844): 481; "Mercantile Integrity," *HMM* 12 (1845): 394; "An Example of Mercantile Honesty," *HMM* 13 (1845): 105; "Honor to Honesty," *HMM* 13 (1845): 191; "The Honorable Debtor and Enterprising Merchant," *HMM* 20 (1849): 687–88; "Daniel Ayer, an Honest Debtor," *HMM* 21 (1849): 362; "An Honest Merchant," 24 *HMM* (1851): 514; "An Honorable and Honest Merchant," *HMM* 24 (1851): 518; "Mercantile Honor," 29 *HMM* (1853): 138; "Success of an Honest Merchant," *HMM* 35 (1856): 519.

68. These comments were prompted by the financial difficulties of Samuel Ruggles, Strong's father-in-law. See entry for May 27, 1851, in Strong, *Diary of George Templeton Strong*, 48–49. For a similar discussion of "moral obligation" after failure, see Sandage, "Deadbeats, Drunkards, and Dreamers," 90–97.

69. Stilwell to Willie P. Mangum, July 20, 1842, *Papers of Willie Person Mangum*, 373. For an analogous pledge, see the February 18, 1843, letter from Julius Tower to Charlemagne Tower (CTP), in which Julius recounts a conversation with the son of a man who had served as an endorser for Putnam Page, a business associate of the Towers whose bankruptcy was pending at the time. Julius told the son, William Osborn Jr., that he hoped that when Page "gets through" the bankruptcy process, he would "take care" of the debt to Osborn senior. See also R. G. Dun & Co. credit reports on Jesse W. Benedict, Edmund Wiley, and William Garrard. Benedict, a New York City lawyer, promised to pay back $10,000 owed to a favored creditor after gaining his bankruptcy discharge and had almost discharged the indebtedness by 1848. A tailor, Wiley failed in New York City and then moved to Springfield, Illinois,

where he petitioned for bankruptcy and eventually paid the discharged debts of Illinois creditors. Garrard, a Columbus, Georgia, commission merchant and cotton buyer, similarly made clear an intent to pay his old debts to local creditors. See Dun, New York, 465:120, Illinois, 198:23, and Georgia, 23:86.

70. *ACG*, 27th Cong., 2d sess. (1842), 128; report of unnamed case, 1 *WLJ* 523 (1843); *Wattles v. Lalor*, 1 *WLJ* 315. Cases in which state courts found the 1841 act to be constitutional include *Sackett v. Andross*, 2 *NYLO* 11 (Supreme Court N.Y. 1843), and *Keen v. Mould*, 5 *WLJ* 215 (Supreme Court Ohio 1847).

71. *Morse v. City of Lowell*, 2 *WLJ* 224 (Supreme Court Mass. 1845); *Flagg v. Ely*, 4 *NYLO* 100 (Supreme Court N.Y. 1846); *Act to Establish a Uniform System of Bankruptcy*, sec. 4. In Indiana and Vermont, state courts also recognized the rights of endorsers to sue the persons for whom they had paid debts, whether or not fellow endorsers or principals had obtained relief in federal bankruptcy court. See *Dunn v. Sparks*, 8 *WLJ* 298 (Supreme Court Ind. 1851); *Wells v. Mace et al.*, 9 *LR* 472 (Supreme Court Vt. 1847). The latter ruling was overturned on appeal to the U.S. Supreme Court. See *Mace v. Wells*, 7 Howard 272 (1849).

72. *Act to Establish a Uniform System of Bankruptcy*, sec. 5; *Lyons et al. v. Executors of Marshall*, 14 *LR* 383 (Supreme Court N.Y. 1851); *Humphreys v. Swett*, 14 *LR* 565 (Supreme Court Maine 1852); *Commercial Bank of Manchester v. Buckner*, 20 Howard 108 (1857).

73. *Hubble & Curran v. Croup*, 2 *WLJ* 240 (Court of Chancery N.Y. 1844); *Brereton v. Hull*, 1 Denio 75 (Supreme Court N.Y. 1845); *Burnside v. Brigham*, 9 *LR* 274 (Supreme Court Mass. 1847); *Price v. Bray*, 7 *PLJ* 465 (Supreme Court N.J. 1847); *Morse v. Cloyes et al.*, 15 *LR* 277 (Supreme Court N.Y. 1851); *Lathrop v. Stewart*, 14 Fed. Cases 1185 (CC SD Ohio 1855).

74. State courts in Maine, Massachusetts, Vermont, Connecticut, New York, New Jersey, Pennsylvania, North Carolina, Tennessee, Alabama, Mississippi, and Ohio upheld this jurisdiction. See the cases cited in Mr. Day's argument for the appellant in *Commercial Bank of Manchester v. Buckner*, 108–13, esp. *Mabry et al. v. Herndon*, 9 *LR* 254 (Supreme Court Ala. 1846). Successful impeachment of discharges occurred in *Beckman v. Wilson*, 4 *WLJ* 303 (Supreme Court Mass. 1847); *Caryl v. Russell*, 13 New York Reports 194 (Court of Appeals N.Y. 1855); *State v. Bethune*, 30 North Carolina Reports 106 (Supreme Court N.C. 1848); and *Mabry et al. v. Herndon*.

75. John Jones to Charlemagne Tower, Feb. 26, 1844, Mar. 13, 1844, CTP. The correspondence leaves unclear whether Roberts agreed to a settlement.

76. *Report . . . in Relation to the Operation of the Bankrupt Law*, 28, 31, 50, 54, 68, 71, 74, 166. See also speeches of Reps. Dawson and Milton Brown, *CG*, 27th Cong., 3d sess. (1842), 86–87; *ACG*, 27th Cong., 3d sess. (1843), 95–96; and Senate Judiciary Committee, *Report on the Bankruptcy Law*, 22–23.

77. Often insolvents who executed such assignments advertised that they included no preferences. For typical notices, see *MCNYE*, June 1, 1842 (assignment of Caleb Brown, of Oxford, New Jersey), and Nov. 3, 1842 (assignment of John Tyler Bingham, a New York City merchant); and *Long Islander*, Oct. 14, 1842 (assignment of Joseph Lewis, of Huntington, New York), quoted in Romano, "Law, Politics, and the Economy," 100. See also "The Bankrupt Law," *New Orleans Bee*, Dec. 7, 1842. The nation's judges disagreed on the question of whether a private assignment without preferences was void if executed after the bankruptcy system came into operation. Compare *Ex Parte Tower*, 1 *NYLO* 8 (DC ND N.Y. 1842), and *McLean, Assignee v. Meline et al.*, 1 *WLJ* 51 (CC Ohio 1843), which ruled such assignments to be void, with *In Re Smith Ely*, 1 *NYLO* 243 (DC SD N.Y. 1843), and *Anonymous*, 1 *PLJ* 323 (CC ED Pa. 1842), which sanctioned them.

78. Speeches of Reps. Everett, Gordon, Wise, Ferris, Pickens, and Rayner, *CG*, 27th

Cong., 3d sess. (1842–43), 65, 68, 72, 110, 116, 156. Whigs who had reversed their position on the 1841 act were especially likely to make this argument.

79. On the 1867 act, which lasted for eleven years before repeal, and the 1898 act, which has remained in force, as amended, to this day, see Warren, *Bankruptcy in United States History*, 95–159; Coleman, *Debtors and Creditors in America*, 24–30; and Hansen, "Commercial Associations."

Chapter Five

1. From 1831 to 1845, Key West salvage crews collectively earned between $32,000 and $174,000 a year. In the 1840s, lawyers there enjoyed annual retainers from northeastern insurance companies of $6,000. Local merchants often gained title to goods worth tens of thousands of dollars for a small fraction of their value. See "Wrecks, Wrecking, and Wreckees," *HMM* 6 (1842): 349–54, and "Key West, and Wrecking for Salvage," *HMM* 14 (1846): 377–78.

2. Novels that focused on great commercial operations gone awry include two by Charles F. Briggs, known to his contemporaries as Harry Franco—*Adventures of Harry Franco*, and *Bankrupt Stories*. Briggs had firsthand experience with a far more mundane bankruptcy, having failed as a grocery merchant in New York during 1842. See also John Jones, *City Merchant*. Fictional accounts of more prosaic bankruptcies were more common, regularly appearing as novels and in short stories published by newspapers and periodicals such as *Godey's Lady's Book* and *Graham's Magazine*. The most prolific writer of failure tales was T. S. Arthur, who enjoyed considerably more fame for his diatribes against strong drink. Nonfictional analyses of failure appeared with regularity in commercial periodicals such as *Hunt's Merchants' Magazine*, *De Bow's Review*, and *Bankers' Magazine*, as well as less specialized periodicals, like the *Democratic Review*, the *American Whig Review*, and the *North American Review*. For an insightful account of antebellum commentaries on financial panics, see Fabian, "Speculation on Distress."

3. The large number of bankruptcies that occurred during the two financial panics of the late 1830s and the ensuing deflation would have increased the possibilities for wrecking even in the absence of a federal bankruptcy system. But by consolidating the legal process of handling business failures, directing thousands of failed Americans and their remaining assets to a discrete number of federal courts, the 1841 act created more structured and less diffuse markets related to insolvency.

4. One can think of the entrenchment of wrecking within the antebellum American economy and the shift in publicly expressed attitudes toward wrecking as "institutional changes" (North, *Institutions*).

5. *CG*, 27th Cong., 1st sess. (1841), 483; *Journal of Commerce*, July 1, 1842. See also speeches of Sen. Anderson and Reps. Lumpkin, Pope, and Williams, *ACG*, 26th Cong., 1st sess. (1840), 622; *CG*, 26th Cong., 1st sess. (1840), 484; *CG*, 27th Cong., 1st sess. (1841), 330, 334; *Journal of Commerce*, Feb. 3–4, 1842; "Regular Operations under the Bankrupt Act," *NYH*, Feb. 5, 1842; "Expenses in Bankruptcy," *NYH*, Jan. 9, 1843; and "The Bankrupt Law Repealed—The Results," *NYH*, Mar. 6, 1843.

6. *Letter . . . Relative to the . . . Bankrupt Law*, 31; *Letter . . . Showing Proceedings under the Bankrupt Act*, 8. According to these reports, court costs incurred throughout the nation totaled $961,632.55. This figure underrepresents the fees received by court officials and newspapers. In addition to the lack of statistics for eight federal districts, two other reporting jurisdictions, Maine and Kentucky, provided only partial tallies of court costs.

7. "Expenses in Bankruptcy"; *Rules and Regulations in Bankruptcy . . . for the Southern*

District of New York, 13–24. The *Morning Courier*, as the paper with the largest circulation in New York City, won the right to publish the notices of every bankrupt in southern New York. Since the district's rules in bankruptcy required each petitioner to advertise in at least three papers, other city dailies and Hudson Valley publications also benefited handsomely.

8. "Expenses in Bankruptcy"; *Report . . . in Relation to the Operation of the Bankrupt Law*, 32, 160; *Fees in . . . Admiralty and Bankruptcy Cases*, 27. In most jurisdictions, court costs for straightforward applications ranged between $30 and $50.

9. *Rules and Regulations in Bankruptcy . . . for the Southern District of New York*, 22–23.

10. "Expenses in Bankruptcy"; *Rules and Regulations in Bankruptcy . . . for the Southern District of New York*, 13.

11. For illustrative costs incurred in the process of declaring a bankruptcy dividend, see bankruptcy records of David Buffum, Squire P. Dewey, John Rutter, Arthur Tappan (C-Fs 326, 642, 1913, 2171). Fees were not uniform in every federal district, but differences were minimal. See *Fees in . . . Admiralty and Bankruptcy Cases*, 24. For examples of bankruptcy estates that generated comparatively high sums of cash but that did not yield sufficient funds to merit dividends to creditors because of court costs, see bankruptcy records of James Alden, Pliny Allen, and Edwin Schenk (C-Fs 16, 21, 1940).

12. For the commissioners appointed in New York's southern and northern federal districts and in Massachusetts, see *Rules and Regulations in Bankruptcy . . . for the Southern District of New York*, 38–40; *Albany Argus*, Jan. 26, 1842; and Peleg Chandler, *Bankrupt Law*, 92–93. On the compensation to southern New York bankruptcy officials, see "Expenses in Bankruptcy" and "Bankrupt Law Repealed."

13. Charlemagne Tower to Aurelian Conkling, July 15, 1844, CTP; Jacob Radcliff to Smith Thompson, Oct. 14, 1841, Misc. MSS Thompson, Smith, Manuscript Department, N-YHS.

14. Bankruptcy records of these three men can be found in C-Fs 389, 2125, 2378. For attacks on Stilwell and Webb for earning so much money from a bankruptcy system that released them from obligations to their own creditors, see *NYH*, Feb. 7, 1842, Jan. 9, 1843; *Brooklyn Daily Eagle*, Mar. 10, 1842; and *Journal of Commerce*, Feb. 5, 1842.

15. Out of a sample of 509 southern New York bankrupts, 57, or just over 11 percent, represented themselves in bankruptcy court. The combination of court costs and legal fees in uncomplicated cases usually totaled around $75. Exceeding two months salary for skilled labor in metropolitan centers, this sum constituted a formidable barrier to bankrupts who were truly destitute and who lacked the ability to borrow funds from friends or family members.

16. C-F 30.

17. On typical antebellum law practices, see Friedman, *History of American Law*, 306–11.

18. For advertisements by these attorneys, see *MCNYE*, Feb. 8, 1842, and *Ulster County Republican*, July 13, 1842. Among the bankruptcy cases from which the New York City firm gained work were those of Angeline Brown, Alpheus Fobes, John Hull and Abraham Smith, and Elijah Prentiss (C-Fs 283, 774, 1110, 1743). Romeyn's clientele was almost exclusively limited to Ulster County, and included Goodrich Baldwin, the creditors of Henry and Thurston Cutler, Minnar Hyatt, Zachariah North, and James Tamney (C-Fs 90, 586, 1343, 1650, 2169).

19. Among Stuart's clients were voluntary petitioners Cassander Frisbee, William Hillyer, and Abraham Hillyer. William Hillyer worked for Frisbee as a clerk at the time of his application, and was a relative of Abraham (C-Fs 806, 1040, 1041). For a list of Poughkeepsie's twenty law offices, see *Poughkeepsie Journal*, June 29, 1842. For listings of other New York City and lower Hudson Valley attorneys who frequently appeared in bankruptcy court, see Balleisen, "Navigating Failure," 292–94.

20. The three cases were those of Cassander Frisbee, Carlos P. Houghton, and Augustus

Zerega (C-Fs 806, 1082, 2510). For press coverage of oral arguments and judicial decisions, see *MCNYE* and *NYH*, Mar. 3, 8, 9, 11, 13, 18, 22, 24, 26, 28, Apr. 11, 14, June 12, Aug. 9, 15, 1842. Among the many other cases in which Joachmissen represented objecting creditors were those of Aaron Abrahams, Aaron Butterfield, George Ferguson, and Harvey Pettit (C-Fs 2 1/2, 374, 747, 1745).

21. For a sample of Clark's caseload, see bankruptcy records of David Dodge, Lorraine Freeman, Joseph Lester, and John Richardson (C-Fs 654, 801, 1354, 1849). Other southern New York attorneys who both petitioned for bankruptcy and developed a bankruptcy practice included Jesse W. Benedict, James Lorimar Graham, Royal Waller, and Clarence D. Sackett.

22. Bankruptcy Records of Charlemagne and Julius Tower, boxes 27, 33, CTP.

23. Julius Tower to Charlemagne Tower, June 20, Nov. 1, 9, 17, 27, 1842, Jan. 4, Feb. 18, 1843; Charlemagne Tower to Charles Sumner, June 13, 1842; to A. G. Dauby, Oct. 31, 1842; and to David Wright, Dec. 8, 16, 1842, Jan. 10, 22, 1843, CTP.

24. Charlemagne Tower to Charles Sumner, June 13, 1842, CTP. Among Tower's numerous bankruptcy-related clients were the voluntary petitioners Micah Seabury, Putnam Page, and William Hanley; and the creditors B. F. Jones of Albany, Butler, Farnwell & Co. of Utica, and John Jones of Utica. See box 39; Tower to David Wright, Dec. 22, 30, 1842; Aurelian Conkling to Tower, Sept. 26, 1842; Julius Tower to Charlemagne, Feb. 18, July 26, 1843; and John Jones to Tower, Feb. 26, Mar. 13, 1844, CTP.

25. Among the attorneys who gained regular bankruptcy work in Boston were William Dehon, Francis G. Loring, Edward G. Loring, A. H. Fiske, William Gray, Henry H. Fuller, Benjamin R. Curtis, and Peleg W. Chandler. In Philadelphia, bankruptcy lawyers included John W. Wallace, William Meredith, A. J. Phillips, and Garrick Mallery. See the bankruptcy cases reported in volumes 4–7 of the *Law Reporter* and in volumes 1–5 of the *Pennsylvania Law Journal*. Edward G. Loring was a master in chancery under the Massachusetts insolvency system in the late 1830s, and William Dehon and A. H. Fiske served as insolvency assignees. See "Table of Those Persons . . . Who Have Taken Advantage of the Insolvent Law of 1838," *LR* 2 (1840): 283. Loring was also a bankruptcy commissioner, as were William Gray and Peleg Chandler (Peleg Chandler, *Bankrupt Law*, 92). In Philadelphia, John W. Wallace was the federal court reporter for the eastern district of Pennsylvania and William Meredith held the post of U.S. district attorney for that same district (*Dictionary of American Biography*, 12:549, 19:324). On the business strategies of central Illinois law firms that specialized in bankruptcy, see Oaks and Bentley, "Joseph Smith and the Legal Process," 177–78.

26. See, for example, Kent, *Commentaries on American Law*, 1st ed.; Angell, *Practical Summary of the Law of Assignments*; Edwards, *On Receivers in Chancery*; and Moore, *Laws of Trade*. On the emerging nineteenth-century American literature of the law, see Friedman, *History of American Law*, 322–33.

27. For an example of the printing of the 1841 act by newspapers, see *Ulster County Republican*, Sept. 1, 1841. In southern New York, the Bankruptcy Law was published by Henry Anstice, a specialist in the provision of law blanks and legal stationery. The printer John S. Voorhies put out Judge Betts's *Rules and Regulations in Bankruptcy*. Anstice, along with competitors Jansen & Bell and Folson & Clayton, printed a wide variety of blank forms for use in bankruptcy proceedings. A few southern New York bankrupts listed the *Rules and Regulations in Bankruptcy* among their assets. See the asset schedules of George North, Randolph Reynolds, and Charles Starr (C-Fs 1649, 1837, 2103).

28. "A Member of the Bar"; Staples, *General Bankrupt Law*; Bicknell, *Commentary on the Bankrupt Law*; Owen, *Treatise on the Law*; Peleg Chandler, *Bankrupt Law*. Both Staples and Bicknell secured work as bankruptcy attorneys in southern New York. A New

Orleans attorney produced a similar guide to the legislation. See *New Orleans Bee*, Feb. 17, 1842.

29. The *Cayuga Patriot* made its bankruptcy reports the focal point of an advertisement in the *Albany Argus*, predicting that "commissioners and assignees under the act, and attorneys practicing in bankruptcy" would find the weekly edition of the *Patriot* "indispensable [*sic*]" (*Albany Argus*, Mar. 26, 1842). *Niles' Weekly Register* also closely followed the development of American bankruptcy law, publishing an extensive collection of bankruptcy reports on November 5, 1842.

30. "Bankrupt Law," *LR* 4 (1842): 498. In the case of two other journals, the provision of bankruptcy reports served as a primary motivation for the launching of the publications. See *NYLO* 1 (1842): 1, and *PLJ* 1 (1842): 15.

31. *PLJ* 1 (1842): 143–45. John W. Wallace may have been related to one of the Philadelphia law magazine's editors, H. E. Wallace. One can follow Peleg Chandler's various bankruptcy-related incarnations in *LR*, vols. 4–7. Owen dedicated his treatise to Betts "with his permission" and later continued his efforts as a bankruptcy counselor in New York City. See, for example, the bankruptcy records of Joseph Atwill (C-F 56).

32. Atherton, "Problem of Credit Rating," 535–58; Wyatt-Brown, "God and Dun & Bradstreet," 436–37; Madison, "Evolution of Commercial Credit Reporting Agencies," 165–66; Norris, *R. G. Dun & Co.*, 8–10.

33. Norris, *R. G. Dun & Co.*, 10–12.

34. Ibid., 14–57; Wyatt-Brown, "God and Dun & Bradstreet," 437–49; Madison, "Evolution of Commercial Credit Reporting Agencies," 166–70; Sandage, "Deadbeats, Drunkards, and Dreamers," 327–408. The partner who suffered the real estate losses was William W. Campbell, the bankrupt who became a bankruptcy commissioner (C-F 389).

35. Lewis Tappan to Lewis Tappan Stoddard, Feb. 6, 1843, quoted in Wyatt-Brown, *Lewis Tappan*, 232. See also "The Mercantile Agency," *HMM* 24 (1851): 46–53; "The Mercantile Agency System," *Bankers' Magazine* 12 (1858): 545–49; and Clark, *Roots of Rural Capitalism*, 215–17. Tappan's aims shared much in common with the goals behind national bankruptcy legislation. See Chapter 4.

36. C-F 2171; Tappan, *Life of Arthur Tappan*, 279–98.

37. C-F 448; Norris, *R. G. Dun & Co.*, 8–10; Foulke, *Sinews of American Commerce*, 332–34, 366–68.

38. For Dusenberry's bankruptcy records, see C-F 695. The launch of the Commercial Agency is discussed in Norris, *R. G. Dun & Co.*, 27. As of 1851, Woodward & Dusenberry remained in the business; see "Mercantile Agency," 46. For Bradstreet's initiation to credit reporting, see Foulke, *Sinews of American Commerce*, 297.

39. *NYH*, Feb. 2, 1842.

40. Advertisements placed by booksellers and the *Law Reporter* itself touted the periodical both for its reports of bankruptcy decisions and for its authoritative and wide-ranging bankruptcy registers. See *MCNYE*, Apr. 11, June 10, 1842. The *New York Legal Observer* and the *Journal of Commerce* also published bankruptcy lists.

41. *Alphabetical List of Applicants*; *List of Bankrupts in . . . the Eastern District of Pennsylvania*; *List of Bankrupts in . . . the Western District of Pennsylvania*.

42. Smith was one of 450 southern New York applicants who did not indicate occupations on bankruptcy applications; as a result, lists of southern New York bankrupts gave only his name and residence (*Alphabetical List of Applicants*, 59). For discussion of geographic mobility among antebellum bankrupts, see Chapter 6.

43. During much of the 1850s, *The Independent*, a New York religious paper, similarly published regular lists of metropolitan business failures. See Sandage, "Deadbeats, Drunkards, and Dreamers," 211.

44. *Act to Establish a Uniform System of Bankruptcy*, sec. 3, 8–11.

45. The overwhelmingly majority of assets sold at bankruptcy sales in southern New York, both at public auction and through private sale, brought $1 or less.

46. For instructive treatments of antebellum mortgage law and the common disputes over legal titles to land, see Friedman, *History of American Law*, 234–48.

47. When bankrupts bought back assets soon after they received a discharge, they probably did so with funds borrowed from relatives or friends.

48. S-B, Auction of July 13, 1843. See also the auction of goods belonging to the bankrupt dry goods firm of Bromley & Wilson, which were also bought by the former proprietors (S-B, Auction of Nov. 9, 1842).

49. Former bankrupts who purchased book-account debts owed to their failed businesses, almost always for less than 10 percent of their face value, included Pliny Allen, a former Troy stove merchant, Edward Norton, a New York City lawyer, and Luman Huntoon, a New York City baker (S-B, Auctions of Dec. 27, 1842, Nov. 1, 1843, June 13, 1844). Bankrupts who repurchased investments included Frederick Gavin Cameron, a New York City oil dealer who bought a patent right in a windlass through a private sale; James McDougall, a New York City merchant who retrieved 490 acres of land in Georgia; and William W. Campbell, the bankruptcy commissioner, who reclaimed all his assets, including several mortgaged tracts of land (C-F 384; S-B, Auctions of Mar. 1, 1843, Mar. 13, 1844).

50. For illustrations of assets purchased by the relatives of bankrupts, see the sale of estates formerly belonging to Joseph Bingham, William L. Booth, and James G. Cox (S-B, Auctions of Dec. 20, 1842, June 2, Nov. 1, 1843). Bankruptcy lawyers who took the opportunity to buy bankruptcy assets include H. M. Western, Jesse W. Benedict (also a bankrupt himself), Richard Reed, and Phillip Burrowes (S-B, Auctions of Dec. 27, 1842, July 12, Nov. 28, 1843, Mar. 13, May 7, 1844). For examples of assets bought by bankrupts' creditors through private sales, see the records of David Anderson and John Simpson McKibbin (C-Fs 33, 1438). See also the records pertaining to the estate of James Lorimar Graham; one of his creditors, J. F. Delaplaine, bought the bulk of his assets (C-F 881, S-B, Auction of Nov. 28, 1843). Relatives and lawyers who bought from bankruptcy estates may have been acting either as agents for bankrupts or for their own benefit.

51. *Schermerhorn v. Talman et al.*, 14 N.Y. Reports 93 (Court of Appeals 1856); Deed of Sale, May 10, 1843, box 39, CTP; *Clark v. Clark and Hackett*, 17 Howard 315 (1854); Oaks and Bentley, "Joseph Smith and the Legal Process," 180–81.

52. For a roster of bankruptcy wreckers in New York City, see Balleisen, "Navigating Failure," 322.

53. For the bankruptcy records of these two wreckers, see C-Fs 203, 751. Bloomer's later career is described in Dun, New York, 368:449.

54. Clute's position is mentioned in Dun, New York, 374:65. For evidence of Burnham's place, see Affidavit of William Coventry H. Waddell, Dec. 29, 1856, C-F 986.

55. S-B, Auction of May 7, 1844. Waddell's 1856 affidavit also mentioned the timing of Burnham's resignation. On Burnham's activity in buying the property of bankrupts from other wreckers, see the bill of sale from Lucius Field to Burnham and William D. McCarty, June 3, 1843, C-F 751. This bill of sale suggests that Waddell's primary auctioneer, McCarty, also may have speculated in bankruptcy assets.

56. Burnham did not redeem the mortgage himself because he knew that his legal claim to the land was questionable. The holder of the mortgage had foreclosed against the bankrupt, William L. Haskins, in 1848. Since Haskins no longer had title to the property at that time, Burnham knew there was a good chance that the courts in Illinois would set aside the foreclosure. He had won a similar case in New York in 1853, gaining the right to redeem the mortgage on a Brooklyn property that he had purchased at a bankruptcy auction, even

though the mortgagee had foreclosed against the bankrupt. In 1856, Burnham retained the services of a Chicago attorney to explore the parcel's market value and legal status. Sensing a good speculative opportunity, that lawyer arranged for his father to buy Burnham's interest and then sought to void the earlier foreclosure in federal court. This suit succeeded on the same grounds that Burnham had won in the New York State courts—for a foreclosure of property surrendered by a bankrupt to stand, the mortgagee had to name the assignee, and not the bankrupt, as the owner (C-F 986; *Burnham v. De Bevorse et al.*, 8 Howard Practice Reports 159 [Supreme Court N.Y. 1853]; *Barron v. Newberry*, 1 Bissel 149 [CC ND Ill. 1857]).

57. For illustrations of such speculation, see the bankruptcy records of James E. P. Dean, from whose bankruptcy estate Clute collected a dividend as a creditor after buying up claims, and those of Arthur Tappan, from whose estate Burnham did likewise (C-Fs 613, 2171). Others in the world of bankruptcy also engaged in this kind of speculation. Philip Burrowes, James E. P. Dean's attorney, bought up a number of claims against his bankrupt client, collecting a dividend alongside Clute. See also the bankruptcy records of Jonathon Amory and Henry Leeds, which detail the speculation of attorney Thomas Wilson in debts owed by Leeds (C-F 30). Through the provision of legal advice to Leeds's nephew, Wilson learned that the uncle had fraudulently conveyed real estate to his sister before petitioning for a bankruptcy discharge. The lawyer then bought up several large claims against Leeds and successfully attacked the real estate in New York's chancery court.

58. For credit reports on these bankruptcy officials, see Dun, New York, 364:65, 374:65, 367:371.

59. Thus the strategies of successful antebellum wreckers make clear that inside information, either about the opportunities presented by particular bankruptcies or about insolvency more generally, dramatically lowered transaction costs associated with wrecking. On transaction costs, see North, *Institutions*, 27–69.

60. Lamoreaux, "Banks, Kinship, and Economic Development," 647–67; Rohrbough, *Land Office Business*, 145–59, 224–32.

61. Lamoreaux, "Banks, Kinship, and Economic Development," 650–52; Rohrbough, *Land Office Business*, 151–53, 215–32.

62. Gouge, *Short History of Paper Money and Banking*, 1:40, 24, 30.

63. See Jackson, *Victim of Chancery*, which includes an extended portrayal of Mr. Gouge, a lawyer who specializes in buying up claims against bankrupts, getting himself appointed assignee of the insolvent's assets, and then milking the estate for fees and gaining information about assets worth purchasing at auction; and N. Beverly Tucker's story *Gertrude*, serialized in the *Southern Literary Messenger* during 1844 and 1845, which chronicles the strategies of the real estate operator Mr. McScrew, who makes a career out of waiting for periodic financial panics, during which he forecloses against anyone unable to meet mortgage payments due him and seeks to find bargains at court-mandated auctions.

64. "Commercial Panic Makers," *HMM* 19 (1848): 234. The reproachful cultural interpretation of wrecking bears some resemblance to the treatment of domestic slave traders, who received even greater and far more frequent condemnation from northern novelists and social commentators. See Tadman, *Speculators and Slaves*, esp. 179–85.

65. "Descent of the Lady-Birds," *Harper's Weekly*, Nov. 7, 1857.

66. These ethical strictures permeate both Gouge's *Short History of Paper Money and Banking* and *Hunt's Merchants' Magazine* (up to Freeman Hunt's death in 1858), as well as Hunt's 1856 compilation of short commentaries, *Worth and Wealth*. For the lineage of this distinction between productive economic activity and unproductive speculation or manipulation, see McCoy, *Elusive Republic*, 166–84, and Weisberg, "Commercial Morality," 5–61. On the significance of the distinction in antebellum America, see Wyllie, *Self-Made Man in*

America, 70–79; Goodman, "Ethics and Enterprise," 439–49; Cawelti, *Apostles of the Self-Made Man*, 39–75; Richard Weiss, *American Myth of Success*, 36–41; and Gerber, *Making of an American Pluralism*, 55–62. Gouge and Hunt, of course, had very different ideas about how to curb reliance on credit, the former advocating the abolition of incorporated (though not private) banking, and the latter placing his faith in a range of measures, such as bankruptcy laws, credit-reporting agencies, the elimination of legal machinery for the collection of debts, and the dissemination of advice against speculative business ventures.

67. John Jones, *City Merchant*.

68. Freedley, *Practical Treatise on Business*. See also Ann Fabian's discussion of Freedley's 1859 work, *Opportunities for Industry and the Safe Investment of Capital*, in "Speculation on Distress," 134–36.

69. Thus cultural responses to the panic of 1857 diverged markedly from those to the panic of 1837. The earlier panic elicited numerous theological interpretations of financial distress as a providential visitation from God, warning Americans to eschew sinful pride and unseemly haste to be rich. Although similar analyses occurred in the late 1850s, and the latter crisis prompted waves of urban religious revivals in the northeast, a growing number of economic commentators discussed the onset of "hard times" in 1857 within a naturalistic framework, divorcing analysis of political economy from religious considerations. See Fabian, "Speculation on Distress," 131–35. On the urban revivals of 1858, see "The Revival of 1858," *Freewill Baptist Quarterly* 7 (1859): 53–67, and Timothy Smith, *Revivalism and Social Reform*, 63–72. For instructive accounts of the contested manner in which various nineteenth-century economic transformations came to be implicitly accepted by many Americans as "second nature," see Kirkland, *Dream and Thought*; Zelizer, *Morals and Markets*; Fabian, *Card Sharps*; Cronon, *Nature's Metropolis*; and Sheriff, *Artificial River*.

70. In the decades after the Civil War, as commercial thinkers came to terms with both the rise of an industrial economy and the related emergence of Social Darwinism, attitudes toward wreckers and wrecking evolved further, as evidenced by the advice that Secretary of the Treasury Andrew Mellon gave to President Hoover in the aftermath of the 1929 stock market crash. Strongly opposed to the extension of public relief, Mellon advocated that "the government must keep its hands off and let the slump liquidate itself," a process that would allow "[v]alues [to] be adjusted, and enterprising people [to] pick up the wrecks from less competent people" (Herbert Hoover, *The Memoirs of Herbert Hoover* [New York, 1952], 3:30, quoted in Kindleberger, *Manias, Panics, and Crashes*, 154). Whereas John Beauchamp Jones and Edwin Freedley merely refused to characterize wrecking as filthy, contemptible work, suggesting that it constituted a natural outlet for the human impulse to seek gain, Andrew Mellon viewed the enterprise as fulfilling a crucial economic function. In essence, Mellon *did* see the wrecker as a vulture capitalist—a specialized scavenger who performed a vital role within the ecology of the marketplace, returning the remains of deceased enterprises to economic circulation.

71. Although wrecking occurred throughout the antebellum period, only in the 1830s did some Americans begin to treat financial scavenging, and especially the buying and selling of assets in bankruptcy estates, as a career. Similarly, only in that decade did entrepreneurs begin to adopt organizational strategies to profit from the widespread experience of bankruptcy, such as through the development of credit-reporting agencies.

72. Not every American at midcentury was equally likely to find complimentary treatments of vulture capitalism compelling. For many members of working-class or farm households, the activities of wreckers would have continued to seem like the epitome of unproductive, manipulative labor. Working-class Americans, moreover, would have been far more likely to think of business failures and financial panics in terms of the unemployment they created, rather than the entrepreneurial possibilities they fostered. On the ideological sen-

sibilities of these groups, see Keyssar, *Out of Work*; Laurie, *Artisans into Workers*; Sellers, *Market Revolution*; and Clark, *Roots of Rural Capitalism*.

Chapter Six

1. *Expediency of a Uniform Bankrupt Law*, 9–11. See also "On a National Bankrupt Law," *American Jurist* 1 (1829): 44; Joshua M. Van Cott, "A General Bankrupt Law," *HMM* 4 (1841): 30; letter from J. D. F., *Poughkeepsie Journal*, Feb. 10, 1841; and "Message from the President of the United States."

2. *Expediency of a Uniform Bankrupt Law*, 13. See also "Memorial of Citizens of Syracuse," and B. F. Lee to Willie P. Mangum, Jan. 1842, and Augustus F. Ball to Mangum, Jan. 21, 1842, *Papers of Willie Person Mangum*, 260, 274. For an incisive overview of antebellum reform, including the importance of slavery as a governing metaphor, see Walters, *American Reformers*.

3. *CG*, 27th Cong., 1st sess. (1841), 318. For similar sentiments, see speeches of Sens. Webster and Smith, and Reps. Fessenden, Milton Brown, Howard, Barnard, and Granger, *ACG*, 26th Cong., 1st sess. (1840), 796, 836; *ACG*, 27th Cong., 1st sess. (1841), 371, 482, 493, 498–99; and *CG*, 27th Cong., 2d sess. (1842), 139. See also the May 11, 1840, letter from Ebenezer Jesup Jr. and others to Daniel Webster, reprinted in *Papers of Daniel Webster*, 301–2; and the remarkable poem, "The Debtor," by Samuel Woodworth, published in the *Ladies' Companion* 20 (1844): 99. Jesup, who along with other signers of the letter to Webster, applied for relief in southern New York under the 1841 act, pleaded for Congress to "release us from a bondage more insupportable than the inherited servitude of the Southern slave." Woodworth's poem compared "the slave," who "inhales the morning's healthful breeze, And gambols gaily o'er the verdant plain," with "the debtor," who "tastes no joys like these, But breathes the foeted atmosphere of pain."

4. For the best analysis of the frequency of court-mandated sales resulting from debt judgments, tax delinquencies, or insolvent probate estates, as well as the percentage of all slave sales resulting from legal actions relating to debt, see Russell, "South Carolina's Largest Slave Auctioneering Firm." On the terms of settlements between particularly canny debtors and their creditors, see Chapter 3.

5. For a discussion of enslavement through debt among both the ancient Greeks and Israelites, see Patterson, *Slavery and Social Death*, 126–28. On the continued existence of imprisonment for debt in the late antebellum period, despite a gathering reform movement to abolish the institution, see Bauer, "Movement against Imprisonment for Debt." Antebellum identification of bankruptcy as a form of slavery reinforces David Brion Davis's argument that "from antiquity to modern times, the concept of slavery has been encrusted with complex metaphorical, allegorical, and anagogical meanings," and that one must be careful in treating "metaphorical extensions" of slavery as only "hyperbole or rhetorical artifice" (*Slavery and Human Progress*, 18–19).

6. Jackson, *Victim of Chancery*, 11; speech of Rep. Nesbit, *ACG*, 27th Cong., 1st sess. (1841), 479. See also "On a National Bankrupt Law," 44; *Expediency of the Bankrupt Law*, 15; Moore, *Laws of Trade*, 358; Van Cott, "General Bankrupt Law," 30, 34; letter from J. D. F.; and "The Bankrupt Law," *New Orleans Bee*, Aug. 30, 1841, Feb. 1, 1842. For an astute and more sustained analysis of the cultural linkages among bankruptcy, slavery, and emancipation that focuses particularly on the period leading up to the Bankruptcy Act of 1867, see Sandage, "Deadbeats, Drunkards, and Dreamers," 116–266.

7. The most influential discussion of this theme in nineteenth-century American political economy and law remains Hurst, *Law and the Conditions of Freedom*. See also Friedman, *History of American Law*. As Hurst cautions, policies and legal doctrines initially justified

on the grounds of broadened entrepreneurial opportunity did not always lead to such consequences, especially in the long run.

8. Lyman Spalding Journal, vol. 2, Oct. 12, 1842, Arents Library; Charlemagne Tower to Eddy Tower, June 14, 1843, CTP. Carol Sheriff alerted me to the journal entry from Spalding.

9. On mid-nineteenth-century treatment of bankrupts in Russia, Hong Kong, and the German principalities, see *NWR*, May 1, 1847; Ch'en, *Insolvency of the Chinese Hong Merchants*, 179–82; and Hunt, ed., *Worth and Wealth*, 394.

10. Advertisement of John Bissell, *MCNYE*, Feb. 25, 1842. See also *New Orleans Bee*, June 11, 1842, which discusses a failed New York merchant who arranged a private discharge from his creditors as a means of avoiding reliance on the federal bankruptcy process.

11. *Milledgeville Federal Union*, Aug. 23, 1842.

12. On the "Shirkshire Road," see Clark, *Roots of Rural Capitalism*, 126. Examples of antebellum fiction that sent indebted characters off to Texas include *Shinning It*, 32; Jackson, *Victim of Chancery*, 174–80; and T. S. Arthur, "There, I Knew It," *GLB* 24 (1842): 276. See also Baldwin, *Flush Times*, 92–93; Hogan, *Texas Republic*, 3–5; Stampp, *Peculiar Institution*, 203; and Watson, *Liberty and Power*, 206. In the wake of the panics of 1837 and 1839, the still-independent Republic of Texas served as a legal haven for American debtors. As difficult as it might have been for creditors to track down and collect from a debtor who had left for another state, the debtor who lived in the foreign country of Texas presented even greater logistical problems. In 1841, the Texas legislature enhanced the republic's attractiveness to debtors by passing a law that recognized the legality of any insolvency discharge gained outside the country. Thus if a resident of Louisiana or Massachusetts earned a discharge under that state's insolvency system and then moved to Texas, creditors, whether Texan or American, could not recover against the debtor in Texas courts (*Oakey v. Bennet et al.*, 11 Howard 33 [1850]). For discussions of the westward movement of failed debtors at various points in the first six decades of the nineteenth century, see Turner, *United States, 1830–1850*, 267; Bauer, "Movement against Imprisonment for Debt," 212–13; Silsby, "Frontier Attitudes and Debt Collection," 157; Decker, *Fortunes and Failures*, 15, 98; and Wiebe, *Opening of American Society*, 278–79. Even the bankruptcy records of southern New Yorkers provide copious traces of westward migration by individuals who failed in the east, as several New York bankrupts left for the west shortly after initiating bankruptcy proceedings and many more mentioned the westward migration of failed partners or debtors. See Balleisen, "Navigating Failure," 349–51.

13. For examples, see the records of George Bennett, Israel Bower, David Buffum, Howel Clark, Henry Cropsey, James Jones, James Howard Longbotham, Henry McKinstry, and Abraham Merritt (C-Fs 161, 229, 326, 455, 565, 1204, 1384, 1440, 1524).

14. For representative instances of bankrupts who moved to southern New York from various regions of the country, and for statistical breakdowns of migratory bankrupts in the sample by the region in which they failed, see Balleisen, "Navigating Failure," 343–53, 493–97. See also Map 2.

15. See the bankruptcy lists for Massachusetts and Rhode Island in the *Law Reporter*; the bankruptcy notices in the *Albany Argus*, esp. on Mar. 3, May 3, June 17, July 28, Aug. 25, Aug. 26, Nov. 5, 1842, Jan. 17, 1843; and similar notices in the *Milledgeville Federal Union*, esp. Mar. 23, July 19, Nov. 15, 1842, Jan. 26, 1843.

16. Halttunen, *Confidence Men*, 33–40; Blackmar, *Manhattan for Rent*.

17. On the frequent mention in antebellum bankruptcy records of migration by the insolvent partners, business associates, and debtors of petitioning bankrupts, see Balleisen, "Navigating Failure," 344–45. The exact percentage of bankrupts from the sample who encountered financial embarrassment at a previous place of residence is 31.8 percent. One must treat the figures generated from the sample with some caution, as the selection of

sample members was by no means random. The process of selecting case-files for examination, however, did not involve any obvious bias for or against geographic mobility. For a detailed discussion of research strategy, including the rationale behind the selection of bankruptcy case-files, see the Note on Research Method. Newspaper notices suggest that another twenty-eight bankrupts who were not in the sample also moved before filing for bankruptcy in New York's southern federal district. Geographic movement after the initiation of bankruptcy petitions occasionally appeared in court records because of later court proceedings. Edwin Schenk, for example, filed for bankruptcy in New York City on December 3, 1842, after failing as an oil merchant. The following November, the bankruptcy assignee required some information from Schenk and received a court order for him to give a deposition. The deposition occurred on the 27th of that month, in Columbus, Ohio, where Schenk then resided (C-F 1940).

18. *Letter . . . Relative to the . . . Bankrupt Law*, 20. The clerk offered this remark in explanation of the negligible amount of property surrendered by Illinois bankrupts. On patterns of social and geographic mobility, see Thernstrom, *Progress and Poverty* and *Other Bostonians*; Thernstrom and Knights, "Men in Motion"; Blumin, "Mobility and Change in Ante-bellum Philadelphia" and *Urban Threshold*; Katz, *People of Hamilton*; Katz, Doucet, and Stern, "Migration and the Social Order"; Griffen and Griffen, *Natives and Newcomers*; Decker, *Fortunes and Failures*; and Dublin, "Rural-Urban Migrants."

19. C-F 2288. For a similar example, see bankruptcy records of Roswell Tuthill (C-F 2250).

20. In 1848, a first-class trip from Detroit to Boston, by lake steamer and railroad, cost $25; by traveling in steerage on the lake steamer and via canal packet between Buffalo and Albany, the cost would have been far less. The cost of travel was more expensive in the 1830s and early 1840s, but not by more than 50 percent. In 1843, the nine-day journey from Decatur to Charleston, South Carolina, by stage and railroad, and then from Charleston to New York City by coastal steamer and rail, cost $62, including lodging and meals. An alternative route, via Nashville, Louisville, and Wheeling, cost $72. In 1820, the trip from Louisville to New Orleans by steamboat cost $75; this cost fell rapidly over the next four decades. Passenger rates on canals during the 1840s and 1850s ranged between 1.5 and 4 cents a mile, depending on the class of service; stage rates ranged between 5 and 7 cents a mile; and railroad rates ranged between 2.5 and 4 cents a mile. Thus even on stages, $30 bought an antebellum American a couple of hundred miles worth of travel, including meals and lodging (MacGill, *History of Transportation*, 76–77, 574–80; Taylor, *Transportation Revolution*, 141–44).

21. On geographic mobility among the antebellum poor, see Thernstrom and Knights, "Men in Motion"; Thernstrom, *Other Bostonians*, 220–61; and Prude, *Coming of Industrial Order*, 145–56, 222–35.

22. C-F 255; Asa Smith, *Guileless Israelite*. For additional examples of older nonmigratory bankrupts, see the records of Charles Starr, Robert Swartwout, Arthur Tappan, and George C. Thomas (C-Fs 2103, 2160, 2171, 2198). Relatively young migratory bankrupts included Joseph Balestier, a lawyer who moved to New York City from Chicago after a failure in 1839; Effingham Cock, a storekeeper who failed in Alton, Illinois, after the panic of 1837 and then moved to New York City; and Robert Ogden, whose mercantile firm failed in New York City in 1842, leading to his move to New Orleans (C-Fs 91, 476, 1675).

23. For Berthoud's credit reports, see Dun, Missouri, 36:82; for an indication of the nature of his business in St. Louis, see his advertisement, *MCNYE*, Feb. 27, 1843. References to prior bankruptcies, while not universal, were extremely common in R. G. Dun credit reports. For representative examples, see reports on James Saulsbury, Richard H. Beach, Samuel W. Benedict, and Stiles Curtis (Dun, Georgia, 3:152; Dun, Illinois, 198:72; Dun, New York, 318:302; 268:542). See also Lamoreaux, *Insider Lending*, 74–75. For instances in

which credit reporters remained aware of past failure despite migration, see Dun, Illinois, 198:23, which recounts the failure of Edmund Wiley as a merchant tailor in New York City before his move to Springfield; Dun, New York, 364:30, which chronicles the Illinois failure of Effingham Cock before he went into the dry goods business in New York City; Decker, *Fortunes and Failures*, 16; and Sandage, "Deadbeats, Drunkards, and Dreamers," 287-98.

24. On Ring and the Heyers, see C-Fs 1857, 1021, and Dun, New York, 224:26; 316:42. Other bankrupts also received timely aid through inheritance, including Goodrich Baldwin, an Ulster County farmer, and Mark Cornell, a New York City grocer who moved to Pough-keepsie after his failure, eventually returning to New York City (C-Fs 89, 522; Deed of Sale, May 2, 1850, Ulster County Deeds, 75:691; Dun, New York, 319:470). For an example of a bankrupt who returned to the business world through partnership with a relative, in this instance a brother-in-law, see bankruptcy records of and credit reports on John L. Vande-water (C-F 2277; Dun, New York, 367:381). For an illustration of relatives injecting capital into the business venture of a former bankrupt, see the partnership notice of Clark & Coleman, *MCNYE*, Apr. 24, 1843. The new firm included Spencer M. Clark, a New York City bankrupt, as one of the general partners; the capital, however, came from Clark's relatives in Hartford, Connecticut, who put up $10,000. See also Freyer, *Producers versus Capitalists*, 73, which recounts the extension of credit by a relative to a bankrupt Baltimore merchant. For instances of bankrupts who took over businesses run by relatives, see the business notice proclaiming the dissolution of P. Bowne & Co in favor of Samuel Bowne, *MCNYE*, Jan. 4, 1843, and the business notice of Nathaniel Weed's "retirement," in favor of Charles W. Weed, Augustus E. Masters, and Marcus W. Weed, *MCNYE*, Mar. 7, 1843. Bowne, Charles Weed, and Masters all appeared on the bankruptcy lists for southern New York.

25. Sylvester, *History of Ulster County*, 242. Two other southern New York bankrupts who returned to business through the aid of patrons were Edward C. Southwick and Samuel I. Tobias. A tanner, Southwick was "backed" by a "friend" who bought his tannery after his failure (Dun, New York, 73:67). Tobias served as an agent for the New York City mercantile firm of Neustadt and Barnet while he awaited his bankruptcy discharge in 1842. After receiving his release, Tobias announced that he was once again transacting business on his own responsibility, selling watches, cutlery, and jewelry, the same items sold by Neustadt and Barnet. The merchandise probably came from his former employers on credit. The firm was obligated to Tobias, as he had given an important deposition on its behalf in the bankruptcy case of Aaron Abrahams (Deposition of Samuel Tobias, C-F 2 1/2; *MCNYE*, Jan. 5, 1843). For examples of private settlements that left antebellum bankrupts with sufficient capital for new enterprises, chiefly through the restructuring of debt terms rather than legal releases, see the bankruptcy records of George Ferguson and Joseph Lester (C-Fs 747, 1354).

26. Julius Tower to Charlemagne Tower, June 21, Sept. 1, Sept. 10, Sept. 26, Nov. 1, Nov. 3, Nov. 12, 1842, July 26, 1843, CTP. For more detailed discussions of the Towers' failure and the resulting legal disputes over their bankruptcy, see Chapters 1 and 5.

27. C-F 1231; Baldwin, *Flush Times*, 94-95. For other examples of southern New York bankrupts who moved in with in-laws or parents after their failures, see the records of Jonathon Amory, who moved from New York City to Boston; Alfred Carpenter, who moved from Brooklyn to the Ulster County town of Plattekill; and Thomas Frame, who moved from New York City to Flushing (C-Fs 30, 399, 794).

28. C-F 942. Hall's debt schedule includes an obligation of $156 due to one Andrew Hall for board; his asset schedule includes a debt of $25 owed by the same Andrew Hall for wages. For more detailed discussion of migration by bankrupts to places where they could draw on the assistance of family members, see Balleisen, "Navigating Failure," 355-61.

29. "Sullivan's Discourse before the Boston Mercantile Association," *Christian Examiner* 8 (1832): 25. Antebellum debates over bankruptcy legislation suggest that the impulse to

aid bankrupt business associates was common. Proponents of such legislation argued that after receiving legal releases, bankrupts could expect substantial assistance from "friends," who in the absence of discharges would not extend advances of capital. Without releases, bankruptcy reformers noted, creditors of bankrupts could pounce on any money that came into their possession. See speeches of Reps. Fessenden and Milton Brown, *ACG*, 27th Cong., 1st. sess. (1841), 471, 482; and Benjamin F. Porter, "The Law of Bankruptcy," *HMM* 28 (1853): 440.

30. *NWR*, Jan. 25, 1823. See also Frost, *Young Merchant*, 194–95; Arthur, *Two Merchants*, 25–32, and *Debtor and Creditor*; and Horace G. Wood, "The Investment; or, The Two Merchants," in Hunt, ed., *Worth and Wealth*, 124–28. On the English lineage of these ideals, which go back at least to the commercial ruminations of Daniel Defoe, see Weisberg, "Commercial Morality," 8–29. For an indication of how this ethic influenced mid-nineteenth-century English commercial culture, see Evans, *History of the Commercial Crisis*, xc.

31. For typical credit reports on former bankrupts who failed as a result of endorsements, see the evaluations of Minot Morgan, a New York City flour dealer; John H. Scudder, a New York City flour dealer; and Edward C. Southwick, a Poughkeepsie tanner and leather dealer (Dun, New York, 368:409; 319:421; 73:67). For an illustrative assessment of proprietors who failed "honorably," see the initial reports on Jesse W. Benedict, a New York City jeweler and lawyer (Dun, New York, 465:20). For examples of bankrupts who received damning credit evaluations as a result of their questionable behavior, see the reports on St. Louis merchant Nicholas Berthoud, New York liquor dealer Stiles Curtis, and Poughkeepsie dry goods dealer Joseph Wright (Dun, Missouri v. 36:82; Dun, New York, 268:542; 73:67).

32. C-F 1716.

33. Anthony Dey and Abraham Hillyer both turned to James Watson Webb, editor of the *Morning Courier and New York Enquirer*, in order to counter portrayals of their respective bankruptcies as involving questionable conduct. A New York City lawyer, Dey was the object of a scathing satire by the *New York Herald* on December 12, 1842. The *Herald* published his asset and debt schedules in full, maintained that he had led an extravagant lifestyle to the detriment of scores of artisans and small shopkeepers, and intimated that he had made preferential payments to relatives after his failure. Hillyer, a New York City deputy sheriff, felt aggrieved by a court report of *In Re Hillyer*, which detailed the suspicious commercial actions of William Hillyer but did not provide a first name for the bankrupt concerned. Webb took up the cause of each of these men, branding Bennett's treatment of Dey "scurrilous" and distinguishing Abraham Hillyer—"a worthy man" against whom "there was no imputation of fraud"—from his namesake (*MCNYE*, Dec. 13, Dec. 19, 1842). For examples of pamphlets written by bankrupts to respond to charges of dishonesty and fraud, see Dunscomb, *To the Electors of the Eighth Ward*, and Reed, *Notice to Creditors*. Anthony Dey tried to vindicate himself by suing James Gordon Bennett for libel, but the suit resulted in a hung jury. For coverage of the case, see *NYH*, *MCNYE*, Feb. 8–10, 1843. See also Cooper, *Autobiography of a Pocket Handkerchief*, 89–91, which details the plans of a failed land speculator "to preserve his character" and reputation through public displays of retrenchment.

34. Bankruptcy Notice of Martin K. Bridges, *MCNYE*, Mar. 26, 1842; C-F 1780. Lawyers and physicians were particularly likely to continue work in their profession when they failed as the result of unfortunate investments. For examples, see the bankruptcy records of James Lorimar Graham, Peter B. Manchester, and Granville Sharp Pattison (C-Fs 881, 1481, 1716). See also the discussion of an Alabamian's turn to botanic medicine after a mercantile failure in James, "Josiah Hinds," 24.

35. For an example of an insolvent debtor resuming business in petty trade, see Freyer, *Producers versus Capitalists*, 68. For the involuntary bankruptcy proceedings against Voorhies, see C-F 2324. His later business dealings are chronicled in Dun, New York, 340:64.

36. Antebellum bankrupts who either continued brokerage work after their failures or turned to it soon after bankruptcy included Samuel Bromberg, Edmund Miller, Samuel Reeve, Nicholas Stuyvesant, and George Ward. See C-Fs 269, 1832; advertisements for Ward & Stuyvesant, *MCNYE*, May 19, 1842; and Chapman & Miller copartnership notice, *MCNYE*, Sept. 5, 1842. At least fourteen New York City and Brooklyn bankrupts turned to work as auctioneers immediately after receiving discharges—Anthony J. Bleecker, Thomas H. Buckmaster, Aaron Butterfield, John B. Glover, Royal Gurley, Edgar Jenkins, William H. Jones, Edward H. Ludlow, James M. Miller, Henry Riell, John J. Swift, Richard Van Dyke, and John E. Van Antwerp. See daily advertisements during 1842 and 1843, *MCNYE*.

37. On the low capital requirements of many artisanal businesses in the mid-nineteenth century, see Greeley, *Recollections of a Busy Life*, 92; Griffen and Griffen, *Natives and Newcomers*, 171, 184; Wilentz, *Chants Democratic*, 117; and Wiebe, *Opening of American Society*, 261.

38. Depositions of James Lyon, Edward Devlin, C-F 2120. Some individuals who failed as merchants turned to small-scale artisanal operations as a way to earn their living even before receiving their bankruptcy discharges. See the bankruptcy records of Stephen Allen, a Columbia County shoemaker who had failed in New York City as a dry goods dealer; George Bennett, a New York City shoemaker who had failed in Orange County as a shoe dealer; Benjamin Burgess, a New York City wig maker who failed in Boston as a dry goods dealer; and John Mosher, a Dutchess County shoemaker who had failed as a storekeeper (C-Fs 22, 161, 348, 1601). See also the restarts of a German shear maker in Newark, discussed in Freyer, *Producers versus Capitalists*, 72–73.

39. C-Fs 1052, 1053; Letterbooks, Dec. 15, 1842–Apr. 15, 1846, R. Hoe & Co. Papers, Columbia University Rare Book and Manuscript Library; bankruptcy notice, R. Hoe & Co. advertisement, *MCNYE*, May 5, 1843. Chapter 3 discusses the Hoes' attempts to avoid bankruptcy by placing pressure on their debtors to pay. For a similar instance of unparalleled mechanical skill attracting financial backing after an insolvency in the antebellum Philadelphia locomotive industry, see Porter and Livesay, *Merchants and Manufacturers*, 85.

40. Bankruptcy records of George Ferguson, Cassander Frisbee, Henry Scott, Henry Southwick, and Angeline Brown (C-Fs 747, 806, 1950, 2081, 283); Decker, *Fortunes and Failures*, 16, 91–92, 98; Griffen and Griffen, *Natives and Newcomers*, 113–16; Katz, *People of Hamilton*, 203. See also John Delaplaine's memorial complaining about applicants under the 1841 act engaging in this practice (*NYH*, Feb. 2, 1843); Baldwin, *Flush Times*, 93; Freyer, *Forums of Order*, 58–59; Ford, *Origins of Southern Radicalism*, 241. Conveyance of property on the eve of bankruptcy became easier after the adoption of married women's property acts in several states, which complicated the task of creditors when husbands transferred assets into their wives' names. For discussions of how some bankrupts retained capital stakes through hard bargaining with their creditors, see Cooper, *Autobiography of a Pocket Handkerchief*, 89–93; Dun, New York, 211:286, which recounts the adoption of these tactics by Lemuel Marcy, a New York City dealer in millinery goods; "The Explanations of Bankrupts," *HMM* 26 (1852): 91–92; Barnum, *Struggles and Triumphs*, 253–54, 266–67; and Decker, *Fortunes and Failures*, 90–92.

41. For an example of an attempt at such conveyances that were successfully thwarted by creditors, see bankruptcy records of Jonathon Amory and Henry Leeds (C-Fs 30, 1341); and the discussion of their failure in Chapter 3. For a typical credit evaluation advising extreme caution because of a pattern of fraudulent conveyances so as to frustrate creditors, see the assessments of the New York City clothing dealer Michael Kerrigan (Dun, New York, 197:100-BB). See also Decker, *Fortunes and Failures*, 100, and Freyer, *Producers versus Capitalists*, 42.

42. C-F 1175. For a listing of over thirty southern New York bankrupts who failed more than once, see Balleisen, "Navigating Failure," 504–6.

43. Bremer, *Homes of the New World*, 246–47. In this characterization, Bremer understood "Yankees" to be those Americans with ancestry in New England. For similar characterizations, see Greene, *Perils of Pearl Street*, 7, and *Poughkeepsie Telegraph*, May 17, 1837.

Chapter Seven

1. BV Hone, Philip, Diary, vol. 23, Aug. 12, 1845, Manuscript Department, N-YHS.

2. Hower, *History of Macy's*, 11–33; Barnum, *Struggles and Triumphs*, esp. 238–68; Harris, *Humbug!*; Adam, *E Pluribus Barnum*. See also discussion of Henry Heinz's 1875 failure and subsequent emergence as a processed food magnate; and of Henry M. Flagler's 1867 bankruptcy as a Michigan salt maker and later careers as a leading executive of Standard Oil and the chief real estate developer of southern Florida (Alberts, *Good Provider*; Chernow, *Titan*, esp. 106–10).

3. The exact percentage of "successful" entrepreneurs in the sample is 43.5 percent. For numerous examples of southern New York bankrupts who later accumulated substantial wealth, see Balleisen, "Navigating Failure," 380–81; for typically more modest postfailure success stories, see ibid., 382.

4. 17.5 percent of the sample struggled to sustain solvency; 38.9 percent failed outright. For extended illustrations of both categories of postfailure careers, see ibid., 381–83. In order to test the representativeness of the outcomes achieved by southern New York bankrupts who returned to proprietorship, I searched the R. G. Dun ledgers for postfailure credit reports on individuals who appeared before bankruptcy courts under the 1841 act in Sangamon and Morgan Counties in Illinois and Chatham and Muscogee Counties in Georgia, as well as residents of Lynn and Worcester who applied for relief under the Massachusetts Insolvency Act between 1846 and 1848, and residents of San Francisco who applied for relief under California's insolvency system in 1855. The Illinois bankrupts and Massachusetts insolvents were gleaned from lists published in *The Law Reporter*; the roster of Georgia bankrupts came from bankruptcy notices in the *Milledgeville Federal Union*; and the register of failed San Franciscans came from a list published in *Hunt's Merchants' Magazine*. I was able to identify credit reports for thirty-one of these bankrupts/insolvents who later embarked in entrepreneurial ventures. Fifteen, or roughly 48 percent, achieved enduring prosperity, one after a second failure; five, or about 16 percent, did not fail outright but sustained only marginal businesses; and 11, or just over one-third, either ended their proprietary careers insolvent once again or failed and then ran perpetually struggling concerns. This distribution largely mirrors that found in the case of southern New York bankrupts, with a slightly higher proportion of successes, a somewhat smaller proportion of repeat bankruptcies, and a similar proportion of individuals whose businesses never prospered, though they did remain solvent.

Because Dun reports tended not to cover the most marginal businesses with the highest rates of failure (little market existed for credit assessments of such small-scale, locally oriented firms), these statistics may very well overstate rates of postbankruptcy success. On the other hand, as we saw in Chapter 6, nineteenth-century bankrupts often responded to their financial predicaments through migration. Even though credit reporters often tracked business owners as they moved from place to place, one cannot be sure that a credit assessment ending with a terse report of insolvency marked the termination of a given individual's entrepreneurial career.

5. Tocqueville, *Democracy in America*, 2:213.

6. This argument takes issue with the conclusions drawn by Edward Pessen in *Riches, Class, and Power*. Drawing on exhaustive research into the income and property of elites in Boston, Brooklyn, New York, and Philadelphia, Pessen demonstrates that the great majority

of the richest northeasterners in the 1820s were still wealthy twenty, or even thirty, years later. From these findings, Pessen concludes that the contemporary claims of a fluid social structure wholly lacked validity. For complementary critiques of Pessen's generalizations, see Katz, *People of Hamilton*, 188–89, 364, and Griffen and Griffen, *Natives and Newcomers*, 87–88. In a similar vein, see Decker, *Fortunes and Failures*, 90–96.

7. Dun, New York, 228:439, 234:1100-V. For a discussion of the opportunities that the Civil War offered to Philadelphia businessmen who had previously failed, see Gallman, *Mastering Wartime*, 299–328, esp. 319–20.

8. Dun, New York, 124:100. For analogous biographies of long toil without pecuniary reward, see the credit reports on John Martin, a New York City maker of bedsteads; Selah Hiler, a New York City mechanic and manufacturer of stair rods; and Ward Newman, a New York City shoemaker (Dun, New York, 365:113; 316a:184; 189:227). Sample bankrupts who struggled as grocers or liquor dealers in the years after receiving legal discharges include Alfred Booth and Samuel Dutton of Poughkeepsie and Isaac Devoe and George W. Soule of New York City (Dun, New York, 73:5, 66; 341:190; 366:225).

9. Dun, New York, 316:51, 1-DD.

10. For examples of discharged bankrupts whose ability to carve out economic niches on the basis of technical capacity did not translate into financial success, see the credit reports on Charles Gayler, a New York City safe manufacturer, and Israel Kinsman, an inventor of several improvements in tanning and woolen manufacture. For illustrations of former bankrupts who pursued traditional artisanal occupations in competitive markets and still managed to build solid credit ratings and assets in excess of $3,000, see the reports on Leonard Paulson, a New York City tailor, and Edmund G. Johns, a Springfield painter (Dun, New York, 316:30; 376:304; 210:152; and Dun, Illinois, 198:175).

11. Reverend Thomas Shephard, "To Young Men in Mercantile Life, No. III," *The Happy Home* 1 (1855): 295–96.

12. T. S. Arthur, "Don't Be Discouraged," *GLB* 27 (1843): 124. Other tales that fit this pattern include Sarah Hale, "The Broken Merchant," *Atkinson's Casket* 10 (1835): 89; "The Gains of a Losing Business," *American Monthly Magazine*, n.s., 5 (1838): 247–51; L. E. Penhallow, "The Failure: A Peep into Futurity," *GLB* 16 (1838): 40–42; T. S. Arthur, "Blessings in Disguise," *GLB* 21 (1840): 18–20; John H. Parker, "Familiar Scenes in the Life of a Clerk," *HMM* 5 (1841): 540; "The Failure," *The Knickerbocker* 20 (1842): 229–40; C. H. Butler, "The Bankrupt's Daughters," *GM* 25 (1844): 34–39, 54–59; Arthur, *Debtor and Creditor*, and "Shattered by the First Storm," *GLB* 57 (1858): 152–54. See also Boardman, *Bible in the Countinghouse*, 79–80.

13. James, "Josiah Hinds," 24.

14. C-F 502; Dun, New York, 365:111, 369:561. On Conant's bankruptcy, see Chapter 1. Additional examples of former bankrupts who returned to the world of trade and continued to have some connection with "the credit system," but who prospered in part because they limited their exposure to risk, include John Keeler, a New York City varnish maker; James Saulsbury, a onetime Georgia bankrupt and later successful clothing merchant in Macon and New York City; and A. K. Ingraham, a New York City clothier who had failed and received a bankruptcy discharge in Newark, New Jersey (Dun, New York, 367:347; Dun, Georgia, 3:152; Dun, New York, 198:141; BV New York Trade Agency, Credit Book, 11, Manuscript Department, N-YHS).

15. C-F 1354; Dun, New York, 368:430. The other former bankrupt in the firm was John De Graw (C-F 625). De Graw left the firm in 1856, when the death of his son provided him with the opportunity to take over a mercantile operation. Other applicants under the 1841 act who prospered in businesses requiring little or no credit include George W. Dow and William H. Leroy, both New York City brokers; and Charles McClellan, founder of the Poughkeepsie Female Collegiate Institute (Dun, New York, 365:170; 345:522; James Smith,

History of Dutchess County, 410). This strategy could work even for individuals whose insolvency had occurred in circumstances that foreclosed access to credit in later years. Henry Leeds, the New York City commission merchant who had violated nearly every tenet of commercial moralism during his financial collapse, managed to build a remunerative career as an auctioneer, despite his inability to gain a federal discharge. Specializing in the sale of furniture, selling only for consignees, and demanding immediate payment in cash, Leeds and a partner did a brisk business throughout the 1850s and 1860s (Dun, New York, 193:612).

16. One can see echoes of this response by individual proprietors in the communal economic strategies pursued by Mormons after their flight to Utah. During the Mormons' sojourns in Kirtland, Ohio, and Nauvoo, Illinois, church leaders avidly used borrowed funds to establish retail stores and manufacturing workshops, to speculate in land, and to set up private banks, ultimately with disastrous results. These interludes crucially shaped later Mormon political economy, prompting avoidance of any schemes that would enmesh the community in credit relationships with non-Mormons or require the church to extend credit to its members (Flanders, *Nauvoo*, 114–78).

17. "Letter from Cleveland Correspondent," *NYH*, May 8, 1842. See also "Arthur Tappan," *Brooklyn Daily Eagle*, Dec. 12, 1842; "The Bankrupt Law Repealed—The Results," *NYH*, Mar. 6, 1843; and speeches of Sens. Benton and Buchanan and Rep. Rayner, *ACG*, 26th Cong., 1st sess. (1840), 505; *ACG*, 27th Cong., 1st sess. (1841), 206; *CG*, 27th Cong., 3d sess. (1843), 156.

18. See the correspondence between Samuel Throckmorton and Peter Roach, esp. June 15, Aug. 1, Sept. 10, 1852, May 5, Sept. 19, 1857, Throckmorton Papers, Bancroft Library; also see Dun, California, A:122.

19. C-Fs 881, 203; Dun, New York, 372:219; 368:449. Other applicants for relief under the 1841 Bankruptcy Act who later prospered in risky ventures included Stephen Crocker, a resident of New York City who failed twice as a dealer in dry goods before he made a series of successful stock investments; Lorraine Freeman, a New York City real estate speculator and dealer in iron railings; Jeremiah Jackson, a New York City stock broker; William Garrard, a Columbus, Georgia, cotton broker; and Charlemagne Tower, the Oneida County distiller turned bankruptcy lawyer who eventually became a multimillionaire, first through his services as an agent in the accumulation of Pennsylvania coal lands, and then through railroad investments and a massive undertaking to open Minnesota's Vermillion Range to iron mining (Dun, New York, 367:372; 317:219; 344:446; Dun, Georgia, 23:86, 39, 4; Bridges, *Iron Millionaire*). Jackson, Garrard, and Tower were particularly noted for keeping their affairs close to their vest and taking care to protect their assets in negotiating the terms of business deals.

20. The quote, from southern humorist Joseph Baldwin, referred to mercantile enterprises of the 1830s that lacked capital, but also makes sense in this context. See his *Flush Times*, 83. For instances of postbankruptcy returns to hazardous enterprises that led quickly to new failures, see credit reports for Alanson Chase, William L. Haskins, William Holdridge, and William F. Voorhies (Dun, New York, 374:37; 189:219; 188a:49; 340:64).

21. Samuel Throckmorton to Peter Roach, May 5, 1857, Sept. 19, 1857; Dun, California, A:122.

22. Dun, New York, 365:111. The postbankruptcy careers of Charles F. Blake, a New York City ribbon manufacturer, and Charles H. Ring, a New York City drug and liquor merchant, took an analogous course, although both Blake and Ring ended up insolvent. After several decades of a successful cash business, Blake had attained assets estimated by a credit reporter at $50–75,000 in the 1870s. Speculation in Wall Street stocks eventually led to a second bankruptcy application, this time under the Act of 1867. Ring also prospered in his

business until a string of losses in lottery policies led to an assignment for the benefit of his creditors in 1859 (Dun, New York, 124:61, 224:26).

23. Bankruptcy reformers did occasionally note the role that business "friends" might play in providing failed proprietors with a stake of capital to begin anew. As we saw in Chapter 6, moralists stressed that upright conduct amid adversity would make creditors more likely to extend assistance to failing or failed proprietors, while some political supporters of the bankruptcy discharge similarly argued that continuing obligations kept numerous bankrupts from receiving financial advances from business associates. But these observations generally portrayed assistance as merely providing a sum of capital with which to start, rather than as ongoing and variegated aid that often served as crucial preconditions of postfailure prosperity.

24. See bankruptcy records and credit reports on Jesse W. Benedict, Isaac Noe, and William Redmond (C-Fs 155, 1647, 1295; Dun, New York, 465:120; 213:439, 473; 197:55).

25. For an example of a formerly insolvent wholesaler who struggled with cash flow problems before the contribution of capital from a business associate paved the way to profitability, see the credit report on the New York City druggist Edmund P. Clay (Dun, New York, 224:11). On Amidon, see Dun, New York, 228:439; 234:1100-V.

26. C-F 476; Dun, New York, 364:30. Although the credit reporter does not explicitly say so, Lawrence may have extended assistance to the Cocks partly because they were members of the Society of Friends. For an instance of a remarkably similar reliance on endorsements to refloat a business, in this case after two successive insolvencies, see the credit reports on T. K. Earle & Co., a Worcester, Massachusetts, iron manufacturer (Dun, Massachusetts, 104:513).

27. Dun, New York, 604:118; Sylvester, *History of Ulster County*, 242.

28. Dun, New York, 364:30.

29. For an example of a proprietor who, along with his wife, eventually righted a struggling business after shifting its ownership, see the credit reports on Lemuel Marcy, a New York City millinery goods dealer (Dun, New York, 211:286). The quotation is from an 1862 credit report on Edwin Wiley, a Springfield merchant tailor (Dun, Illinois, 198:33). For other instances in which transferring proprietorship did little more than enable firms to struggle on, see credit evaluations of William Kehlbeck, the Brooklyn shoemaker; James Hammond, a New York City lumber dealer; Michael Kerrigan, a New York City clothing dealer; and Richard Beach, a Springfield tailor (Dun, New York, 124:100; 367:367; 197:100-BB; Dun, Illinois, 198:72).

30. For illustrations of former bankrupts who failed again largely because of endorsements to business associates, see the credit reports on Dwight Bishop, a New York City furniture dealer, and Mark Cornell, a New York City butter dealer (New York v. 190:396; 319:417). Heavy reliance on financial backers, of course, created potential vulnerability for any firm, whether or not its proprietors had previously endured insolvency. In the 1850s, for example, Chicago and Saint Louis concerns with close links to northeastern capital experienced higher rates of failure during general financial crises than local businesses that lacked such support. During economywide slumps, northeastern entrepreneurs often closed western branches and used "all available resources to bolster" their primary enterprises (Adler, "Capital and Entrepreneurship," 202–4).

31. For Tower's successful requests for financial assistance, see letters of Aug. 8, 1856, to DeWitt Tower; Jan. 1, 1857, Mar. 6, June 1, 1866, to Julius Tower, Letterbooks, CTP; and Bridges, *Iron Millionaire*, 225–39. For his artful dodging of requests to reciprocate such aid, see letters of Feb. 4, 1852, to DeWitt Tower; Nov. 11, 1857, June 15, 1860, to Julius Tower; Apr. 15, Aug. 20, 1866, Oct. 24, 1867, to DeWitt Tower, Letterbooks, CTP. After Charlemagne successfully concluded negotiations in 1871 for the sale of over 8,000 acres of coal

lands for a client, collecting over $1 million as his fee for those services, he became considerably more willing to extend financial assistance to his brothers. See Bridges, *Iron Millionaire*, 45–97, and Charlemagne Tower's correspondence with Reuben and Julius Tower, 1871–89, Letterbooks, CTP.

32. Dun, New York, 319:470. Additional examples include Isaac Noe and Richard Schell. Noe, the merchant tailor who did so well through his contacts in the Navy Department, found that his good fortune did not last much longer than the conflict between North and South. Toward the end of the war, Noe risked his accumulated profits on a series of speculations outside his business. These investments fared badly, leaving him insolvent by the fall of 1867. Unwilling to face his creditors, he went into hiding, though he emerged several years later as a small-scale clothing subcontractor, with little means and no credit. Schell, a New York City banker who prospered throughout the 1850s and 1860s, owed much of his success to "connections" with "the strongest and most influential men" on Wall Street. These links generally protected Schell from the fluctuations in stocks and bonds, providing him with inside information about when to hedge. The panic of 1873, however, overwhelmed Schell's ability to maneuver ahead of the market. By September of that year, he had failed to meet his obligations; a few years later he filed his second application in federal court for bankruptcy relief (Dun, New York, 213:439; 416:100-T).

33. W. Frothingham, "Stewart, and the Dry Goods Trade of New York," *Continental Monthly* 2 (1862): 529. For similar contemporaneous expressions, see Sandage, "Deadbeats, Drunkards, and Dreamers," 77. This formulation follows the interpretations of Max Weber and Joseph Schumpeter, each of whom stressed that incessant assaults on traditional approaches to economic activity and ongoing breaches of its accustomed boundaries distinguished the post-eighteenth-century economies of western Europe and North America from their earlier counterparts. See Weber, *Protestant Ethic*, 58–75, and Schumpeter, *Capitalism, Socialism, and Democracy*, 81–86.

34. C-F 1649; Dun, New York, 604:155; Sylvester, *History of Ulster County*, 281–88. On postbellum failures by northerners who expected to prosper as cotton growers relying on wage labor, see Powell, *New Masters*, 145–49.

35. C-F 749; Dun, New York, 224:58. For examples of Feuchtwanger's advertising, see *MCNYE*, May 31, June 18, 1842, and *Harper's Weekly*, Apr. 2, 1859. On the marketing strategies of nineteenth-century patent medicine makers, see Barnum, *Humbugs of the World*, 65–72, and Lears, *Fables of Abundance*, 41–46, 88–89. For a discharged bankrupt's career with a similar trajectory, though focused on Arkansas lead mining and oil refining, see Dun, New York, 368:420, which chronicles the ventures of E. F. Jenkins (not the peripatetic Edgar Jenkins discussed in Chapter 6.)

36. Useful overviews of failed boosterism include Wade, *Urban Frontier*, 30–35; Boorstin, *Americans*, 124–24, 161–68; and Cronon, *Nature's Metropolis*, 31–46. For incisive accounts of particular episodes in this vein, see Wohl, "Henry Noble Day," and Flanders, *Nauvoo*, 114–78. On late-eighteenth- and nineteenth-century debates over the relationship between economic development and "progress," see McCoy, *Elusive Republic*; Howe, *Political Culture of the American Whigs*; Wilson, *Space, Time, and Freedom*; and Sellers, *Market Revolution*.

37. These contrasting modes of commercial activity had enduring roots within American business culture. The two entrepreneurial styles emphasized here largely parallel those identified by Thomas Doerflinger in his study of merchants in late colonial and revolutionary Philadelphia. Doerflinger distinguishes between "ascetic accumulators," who sought to avoid risk, live within their means, and slowly amass assets "by assiduously building a base of local customers and conscientiously collecting debts as they fell due," and "opulent adventurers," who pursued "bold ventures" far more likely to bring either ruin or wealth, and who demonstrated an eagerness to "display and consume their winnings in public view

in order to consolidate their social position" (*Vigorous Spirit*, 162–63). In drawing this distinction, Doerflinger explicitly critiques Max Weber's stress on parsimony and risk limitation through rational calculation as hallmarks of the prototypical modern entrepreneur. He persuasively observes that this formulation ignored many innovative businessmen's proclivities for ostentatious consumption and risk taking. At the same time, Doerflinger's analysis ignores Weber's discussion of capitalist assaults on economic "traditionalism," whether related to work organization, management structures, or marketing techniques. The "ascetic accumulators" discussed in *Vigorous Spirit* stick to well-established channels of trade or handicraft manufacturing, pursuing tried-and-true business methods. They stand more as examples of what Weber's capitalists uprooted through relentless competition rather than as bearers of the modern capitalist ethos. See *Protestant Ethic*, 58–75. As the following text indicates, moreover, an inclination to limit risk among antebellum proprietors who had experienced insolvency often encouraged the fashioning or acceptance of new approaches to business operations.

38. On the significance of ongoing specialization in the nineteenth-century mercantile economy, see Alfred Chandler, *Visible Hand*, 19–48; Decker, *Fortunes and Failures*, 186–88; and Blumin, *Emergence of the Middle Class*, 78–83. A few metropolitan merchants such as Alexander T. Stewart turned aggressively to high-volume cash selling as early as the 1820s, but few entrepreneurs could afford to adopt such a strategy before midcentury (Resseguie, "Alexander Turney Stewart," 306–8). For discussions of the more general turn to cash trade in the late antebellum period, see Clark, *Roots of Rural Capitalism*, 220–27; Doyle, *Social Order*, 89–90; Faragher, *Sugar Creek*, 216–17; and Griffen and Griffen, *Natives and Newcomers*, 131.

39. For representative credit reports, see those on two New York City tailors, Aaron Chicester and Leonard Paulson (Dun, New York, 365:113; 210:152).

40. Roughly one in eight Dun reports on former bankrupts in the sample provide evidence of reliance on either separate estates or the provisions of married women's property statutes. For examples, see assessments on Samuel Benedict, John W. Hull, and John F. Tucker (Dun, New York, 318:302; 340:79; Dun, Georgia, 28:184).

41. *Arthur's Home Magazine* 5 (1855): 342.

Chapter Eight

1. E. M. Gibson, "Going into Business," *Ballou's Magazine* 1 (1855): 37–41.

2. For examples of antebellum authors who suggested the economic and psychological advantages of salaried work over proprietorship, see T. S. Arthur, "Marrying a Merchant," *GLB* 25 (1842): 160–66; *Shinning It*; "The Value of a Clerkship in New York," *HMM* 20 (1849): 570; T. S. Arthur, "Taking Boarders," *GLB* 42 (1851): 13–20, 81–87, 160–67; "Counting-House Man," *Herbert Tracy*, 180; and Hunt, ed., *Worth and Wealth*, 315–17. See also Henry David Thoreau's argument in *Walden* that the "occupation of a day laborer was the most independent of any." According to Thoreau, the "laborer's day ends with the going down of the sun, and he is then free to devote himself to his chosen pursuit, independent of his labor; but his employer, who speculates from month to month, has no respite from one end of the year to the other" (*Portable Thoreau*, 324–25).

3. In the past thirty-five years, historians of revolutionary and nineteenth-century America have investigated almost every imaginable variety of "republicanism." For an incisive overview of the historiography, see Rodgers, "Republicanism," 11–38.

4. On the extension of suffrage to all adult males, see Rodgers, *Contested Truths*, 80–111, and Montgomery, *Citizen Worker*, esp. 1–25.

5. Gibson, "Going into Business." For a similar suggestion that neither "a convict in State

prison" nor "a slave in a rice-swamp" faced the degree of "torment" created by business owners who "pass[ed] through life under the harrow of debt," see Greeley, *Recollections of a Busy Life*, 96.

6. Henry F. French, "Stick to the Farm," *Country Gentleman*, Apr. 27, 1854, quoted in Barron, *Those Who Stayed Behind*, 33. For the persistence of these pleas in western Massachusetts throughout the antebellum period and in the Midwest after the Civil War, see Clark, *Roots of Rural Capitalism*, 162–63, and Cronon, *Nature's Metropolis*, 357–59. Postbellum success manuals, which were typically aimed at a rural readership, similarly argued that high rates of failure in cities should prompt country boys to look for opportunities in their own communities (Hilkey, *Character Is Capital*, 102–4).

7. "Independence" thus merits the status of a "keyword" in nineteenth-century American culture. This concept helped to structure social aspirations, perceptions of social reality, and political rhetoric; at the same time, it provided grist for cultural conflict and evolution, as individuals appropriated and modified prevailing ideas in response to changing circumstances and interests. On the nature of "keywords," see Williams, *Keywords*, and Rodgers, *Contested Truths*.

8. As discussed in Chapter 6, some bankrupts were able to continue entrepreneurial activity by transacting business in the name of a relative or associate. For an example of a bankrupt's reliance on his wife's protected property, see the bankruptcy records of William Blydenburgh, who failed as a New York City merchant in 1827. For the next fifteen years, Blydenburgh's family was "supported out of a farm and property vested in the hands of Trustees for his wife, appointed under a marriage settlement of the property devised to her from her father's estate" (Asset Schedule, C-F 207). For illustrations of postfailure retreats to the households of parents or in-laws, see the bankruptcy records of Alfred Carpenter, Edward Kellogg, and Thomas Frame (C-Fs 399, 1231, 794).

9. C-F 534. Henry Reynolds and Samuel Dutton also found postfailure employment in the nascent world of American corporations, the former as a Kingston bank officer, the latter as secretary of a Poughkeepsie insurance company (C-Fs 1836, 696; *Commemorative Biographical Record of Ulster County*, 437–38; Dun, New York, 73:5). For a trenchant discussion of corporate offices as a safety net for unfortunate members of the antebellum business class in Philadelphia and its immediate hinterland, see Wallace, *Rockdale*, 19, 49–50, 96–97.

10. [Stilwell], *Appeal to the Members of Congress*, 5.

11. For illustrative bankrupts who successfully sought out governmental positions, see Israel Bower, a butcher who had failed in Sullivan County before gaining appointment as a New York City street inspector; Andrew Merwin, a Brooklyn deputy sheriff who had failed in dry goods; Oliver Davis, a Newburgh freighter turned postmaster; Ephraim Hall, who failed as a carpenter in Sing Sing before taking on duties as a prison keeper; and John Hunt, a failed Boston merchant who obtained a job as a customs inspector in New York City (C-Fs 229, 399, 606, 946, 1118). On bankrupts who became bankruptcy officials, see Chapter 5. Southern New York bankrupts who sought elective office after their failures included Alba Kimball, an insolvent New York City Whig who in 1843 ran for the position of ward tax assessor; William W. Campbell, who after stints as a bankruptcy commissioner, commissioner of deeds, and master of chancery in New York City, was elected to the U.S. Congress in 1845; and Theophilus Gillender, a New York City publisher who moved to Hyde Park, in Dutchess County, where he won election as a town clerk in 1843 and later as a town supervisor. See Whig election slate, *MCNYE*, Apr. 8, 1843; "Obituaries of William W. Campbell," Scrapbook, Campbell-Mumford Papers, Manuscript Department, N-YHS; and James Smith, *History of Dutchess County*, 304. The tendency of bankrupts to turn to politics and office seeking also prevailed in Georgia. See the occupations listed for bankrupts in the *Milledgeville Federal Union* during 1842 and early 1843.

12. The diary of Frederick Westbrook, the New York City lawyer whose expensive tastes nearly led to bankruptcy, provides detailed evidence of the strategies required of a suppli-cant, in this case by someone who skirted insolvency through office seeking (Westbrook Diary, New York Public Library, esp. Mar. 8, 10, Apr. 12, 18, Aug. 1, 31, Oct. 20, 27, Nov. 3, 4, 7, 23, Dec. 12, 20, 21, 1842; Jan. 6, Mar. 18, Apr. 10, 11, 18, 20, May 1, 8, 13, 1843). For examples of bankrupts who expended considerable energy in the search for patronage appointments and electoral nominations, see Julius Tower to Charlemagne Tower, Dec. 18, 1843, CTP; and Samuel Blatchford to Robert Swartwout, Nov. 18, 1839; Erastus Root to Swartwout, Dec. 1, 1839; Swartwout to William Seward, Jan. 8, 1840; Swartwout to Seward, Feb. 5, 1840; Swartwout to John Young, Dec. 30, 1847; Memorandum, Feb. 1840; Appoint-ment to customhouse measurer, June 4, 1841; Memorandum, July 31, 1841; Third Ward Election Handbill, Mar. 1848, all in Swartwout Papers, New York Public Library.

13. *MCNYE*, Mar. 4, 1843. The Democratic electoral triumph resulted in other instances in which bankrupts with allegiance to Tammany Hall ousted bankrupts who had tied their futures to the party of William Seward. On March 13, William W. Campbell lost his position as commissioner of deeds; Edmund Elmendorf Jr., also an attorney with a recently obtained bankruptcy discharge, replaced him (*MCNYE*, Mar. 13, 1843).

14. *Alphabetical List of Applicants*. See also the statistics compiled by the district clerk in New York's southern federal district in 1845, in *NWR*, Nov. 22, 1845. Within a week of the bankruptcy system's inauguration, one New York City paper drew attention to the large proportion of bankrupts who listed their occupations as clerk, noting that these individuals "have been *Merchants*, and many of them Merchants of eminence, who are now earning a support for themselves and their families as 'Clerks'" (*MCNYE*, Feb. 2, 1842; emphasis in the original). For an illustration of a southern New York bankrupt who was working as a clerk in 1843, although he listed the occupation in which he had failed on his bankruptcy petition, see the bankruptcy records of Uriah Gregory (C-F 903). On his bankruptcy application, Gregory listed himself as a "late freighter" from Poughkeepsie; but as a lawyer's motion in another bankruptcy case indicates, his employment after receiving a discharge was as a clerk with the Housatonic Railroad Co. See Motion of J. N. Hammersly, June 17, 1843, C-F 1745.

15. For typical examples of southern New York bankrupts who secured salaried positions outside of stores or countinghouses, see the bankruptcy records of Richard Fury, a failed merchant who gained work as a steamboat captain; Isiah McKibbin, a former stagecoach operator in Troy who turned to stagecoach driving; Peter Roach, a New York City merchant who gained a position as foreman at a sawmill; and Cornwell Sands Roe, a freighter and speculator who became a towboat captain (C-Fs 818, 1437, 1881; Dun, New York, 367:326). Scores of bankruptcy applicants in southern New York listed occupations suggesting that they were working for a wage. See *Alphabetical List of Applicants*. Given the imprecision of occupational titles in the antebellum years, however, one cannot be sure that someone listed as a "shoemaker" was working as a journeyman, as opposed to running a small repair shop. For clear-cut examples of bankrupts who were earning wages at the time of their bankruptcy applications, see the records of Enos Cuthbert, a New York City mariner; Stephen Munson, formerly a Newark master carpenter but in 1842 a New York City journeyman carpenter; and Lodawick Weller, a failed New York City grocer who listed himself as a Huntington, Long Island, boot- and shoemaker. Even in southern New York, a handful of bankrupts, like Cyrus Boyd, turned to tenant farming as a postfailure endeavor (C-Fs 585, 1612, 2382, 237). For the best treatment of unemployment in nineteenth-century America, including a comparison of the incidence of unemployment among manual workers and nonmanual employees, see Keyssar, *Out of Work*, esp. 39–110.

16. The term "agent" is used here in a restrictive sense, excluding such commercial

middlemen as auctioneers, commission merchants, factors, and many brokers. These mercantile representatives typically extended credit to customers and consignees and, in the case of commission merchants and factors, frequently traded on their own account. Thus they retained a substantial degree of financial "responsibility," unlike less independent commercial emissaries. For discussions of compensation for agents, see Story, *Commentaries on the Law of Agency*, 190–95; Stalson, *Marketing Life Insurance*, 161–77; and Spears, *100 Years on the Road*, 55.

17. For an overview of the mid-nineteenth-century law of agency, see Story, *Commentaries on the Law of Agency*.

18. *Alphabetical List of Applicants*. Henry Ogden's employment as an agent for the ferry company emerges in Deposition of William Ogden, C-F 1673. For additional examples of bankrupts who did not list their positions as agents on their bankruptcy applications, see records of William Hillyer, C-F 1041, and *In Re George Brown*, 5 *LR* 121 (DC SD N.Y. 1842).

19. Asset and Debt Schedules; Pennsylvania Insolvency Application, Oct. 1, 1841; Affidavit of Israel Kinsman, Jan. 1, 1843; all in C-F 1271; C-Fs 929, 2182.

20. Robert Swartwout to William Seward, Jan. 8, 1840, Swartwout Papers, New York Public Library.

21. For a typical acclamation of a businessman's rise to affluence, see the biographical sketch of Charles Oakford, a Philadelphia hatter, in "A Career of Industry: With Some Account of Hats and Hatting," *GLB* 49 (1854): 149–56. For examples of laudatory discussions of individuals who responded to bankruptcy with renewed entrepreneurial activity, see Chapters 6 and 7. On political rhetoric concerning individual mobility, see Foner, *Free Soil, Free Labor, Free Men*.

22. Hunt, ed., *Worth and Wealth*, 316, 367–68. See also "Self-Support, the Road to Fame and Fortune," *HMM* 36 (1857): 388–89.

23. *Doggett's New York City Directory*, 1845. For illustrations of former bankrupts who moved out of agency and back to their old line of trade, see credit reports on the furniture dealer Dwight Bishop and the lumber dealers William Dunning and Lyman Taylor, all of New York City (Dun, New York, 190:396; 366:289; 367:321). A number of bankrupts discussed in Chapter 7 also followed this pattern. They include William Teller and Andrew Near, who worked as journeymen tanners in Kingston after their respective failures and before gaining a new chance as proprietors in 1846; Isaac Noe, who worked as a cutter and workshop foreman after his misfortunes and before eventually entering into a new venture in the early 1850s; and Joseph Lester, who gained experience for his successful business in the storage and private inspection of ash through work as a public inspector of pot and pearl ash. See also the correspondence from Julius Tower to his brother Charlemagne, discussed in Chapter 6, in which Julius both describes his work as a clerk for an Albany flour merchant and communicates fervent desire to reestablish himself on his own account.

24. C-Fs 1507, 1905; Dun, New York, 374:96; James Smith, *History of Dutchess County*, xxv. The numerous southern New York bankrupts who retained public offices for years after their failures include William Cruger, John E. Hunt, Henry McKinstry, and George C. Thomas, all of whom earned salaries from the New York Customs House; Abraham Hillyer, who after over a decade as a New York County deputy sheriff received a federal appointment as a U.S. marshal; Peter Dreyer, who earned a salary as a city surveyor and architect; Zelotus Willson, who served as a city tax collector; Vanbrugh Livingston, who held various posts in the New York City customhouse and worked as a pension agent; and Isaac Bower, who spent a number of years working as a New York City street inspector and policeman. See listings in *Doggett's*, *Rode's*, and *Trow's* directories for New York City, 1845, 1848, 1852, 1856, 1858, and 1860; and Dun, New York, 385:1204. For indications of the enduring attractions of agency after insolvency, see the bankruptcy records of and later credit reports on Stiles

Curtis, Otis P. Jewett, and Alfred Kershaw (C-Fs 584, 1182, 1238; Dun, New York, 268:542; 369:501; 341:189). For further illustrations of extended postfailure service in clerical posts, see the 1850 and 1860 U.S. census listings for Peter Brusie of Hudson, New York, and Samuel Roosa Spelman of New York City; and Dun, New York, 340:79, which tracks John W. Hull's turn to clerkships in the 1840s and 1850s after multiple failures.

25. In Georgia, for example, former bankrupts James A. Fawns and William E. Long of Savannah maintained employment through the late 1840s and 1850s as a steamboat company agent and a bank discount clerk/bookkeeper, respectively; during the same period, Michael N. Clarke of Columbus served as a land agent. For their bankruptcy notices, see the *Milledgeville Federal Union*, Mar. 2, July 26, Sept. 27, 1842; for their later careers, see *Directory of the City of Savannah*, 1849, 1850, 1858, 1859, and 1860; and Dun, Georgia, 23:49. In Springfield, Illinois, Horace F. Ash responded to his failure by becoming an agent for land transactions and debt collection (Dun, Illinois, 198:72). A number of Bostonians who filed for insolvency between 1846 and 1848 later held salaried positions for long stretches. See insolvency notices in the *Law Reporter* and Boston city directory listings in the 1850s for William L. Frothingham, Charles Howe, Samuel M. King, Samuel S. Miles, John McCallum, George W. Pearson, and Elijah K. Spoor.

26. C-F 1236; Dun, New York, 224:38, 100-A64.

27. Gibson, "Going into Business," 41; Hunt, ed., *Worth and Wealth*, 570. See also Arthur, *Two Merchants*, "Don't Be Discouraged," *GLB* 27 (1843): 121-24, and "Passing through the Fire," *Arthur's Home Magazine* 6 (1855): 196-202.

28. Cawelti, *Apostles of the Self-Made Man*, 39-75; Horlick, *Country Boys and Merchant Princes*, esp. 106-46, 179-209; quotation on 188.

29. Rogers, " 'Man to Loan $1500 and Serve as Clerk,' " 34-63.

30. Ibid., 43-56.

31. "Value of a Clerkship in New York," 570. In his examination of job-loan trades in San Francisco, F. Halsey Rogers explains the unwillingness of salaried workers to use their savings to go into business themselves by suggesting that they had only recently arrived in the city. Without sufficient knowledge of the California marketplace, these newcomers accepted white-collar employment as a way station to independent proprietorship. But Rogers provides no evidence that the employees who provided loans were recent migrants, or that they quickly opened their own stores. See " 'Man to Loan $1500 and Serve as Clerk,' " 56.

32. C-F 610; Dun, New York, 198:141; 203:633, 700-BB; 212:400-P; 215:700-A21, 700-A50, 700-A73.

33. For a typical credit assessment describing this transition, see the 1851 report on George W. White, BV New York Trade Agency, Credit Book, 24, Manuscript Department, N-YHS. See also Griffen and Griffen, *Natives and Newcomers*, 57, 112-13, 128-38; Decker, *Fortunes and Failures*, 94-96, 140-41; and Sandage, "Deadbeats, Drunkards, and Dreamers," 166, 180, 212, 284, 292, 456. On the motivations of male applicants for jobs in the federal government, see Aron, *Ladies and Gentlemen of the Civil Service*, 24-27. On formerly bankrupt drummers, see Cronon, *Nature's Metropolis*, 185. For fictional discussions of such moves, see Greene, *Perils of Pearl Street*; Sawyer, *Merchant's Widow*; Arthur, "Don't Be Discouraged"; C. H. Butler, "The Bankrupt's Daughters," *GM* 25 (1844): 39; Briggs, *Bankrupt Stories*, 175; and T. S. Arthur, "Jacob Jones; or, The Man Who Couldn't Get Along in the World," *GM* 32 (1848): 18, and *Debtor's Daughter*. Antebellum writers of fiction rarely had their characters returning to blue-collar wage work. For an exception, see *Shinning It*.

34. Ryan, *Cradle of the Middle Class*, 61-242; Blumin, *Emergence of the Middle Class*, esp. 66-257.

35. "The Broken Merchants," *Ladies' Companion* 7 (1837): 59–62; L. E. Penhallow, "The Failure: A Peep into Futurity," *GLB* 16 (1838); "Hard Times," *Ladies' Companion* 13 (1840): 43–45; T. S. Arthur, "Blessings in Disguise," *GLB* 21 (1840): 15–20; "The Failure," *The Knickerbocker* 20 (1842): 229–40; Mrs. Thayer, "Hard Times; or, Practical Economy," *Poughkeepsie Journal*, Aug. 10, 1842; Arthur, "Marrying a Merchant"; Butler, "Bankrupt's Daughters," 34–59; Catherine Elizabeth, "Reverse of Fortune the Test of Character," *GM* 39 (1851: 289–95); "The Tradesman's Crisis," *Arthur's Home Magazine* 9 (1857): 108–10. See also Cogan, *All-American Girl*, 108–11.

36. *The Merchant's Widow*, a short novel written by Caroline Sawyer in 1841, most vigorously characterized education for girls as insurance against later financial adversity. The protagonist of the story, a Mrs. Seton, grows up in a wealthy Savannah family. As a result of her family's reliance on slaves for household chores, she develops few skills before marrying a Mobile merchant at the age of fifteen. Some years later, both her husband and her father fail in the wake of the panic of 1837. The Setons then move to New York City in search of mercantile employment, but Mr. Seton soon dies from an illness. Unable to obtain work, Mrs. Seton turns to begging as a means of feeding her daughters until she receives assistance from a friend of her husband's family. Once she has received this aid, she vows to provide extensive education for her daughters, so that they never find themselves in a similar position. See also Jackson, *Victim of Chancery*; Butler, "Bankrupt's Daughters"; and Arthur, *Two Merchants*, esp. 23–32, *Ruined Family*, *Debtor's Daughter*, and *Debtor and Creditor*. Of the female characters in these stories who seek employment as a result of a husband's or father's failure, those who find work as teachers or governesses do much better than those who try to sew, bind shoes, or keep a boardinghouse. See also the fiction and advice literature discussed in Cogan, *All-American Girl*, 91–93, 206.

37. Such examples include the wife of Israel Bower, whose keeping of a boardinghouse provided more income than her husband's postbankruptcy career as a New York City policeman; the wife of Isaac Russell, whose grocery business supported the family after Isaac ceased to serve as Rhinebeck postmaster; and the author and abolitionist Lydia Marie Child, whose writings furnished the bulk of income for herself and at times for her husband, David, after his failed ventures as a lawyer, editor, and producer of beet sugar (Dun, New York, 385:1204; 68:208; Kellow, "Duties Are Ours," 396–453). Business failures by husbands or fathers continued to compel women to seek income-producing occupations later in the century. See Aron, *Ladies and Gentlemen of the Civil Service*, 48–52, and Sandage, "Deadbeats, Drunkards, and Dreamers," 298, 320–22, 469–72.

38. For a discussion of rates of business failure, see the Introduction.

39. For an excellent account of these family strategies, see Ryan, *Cradle of the Middle Class*, 145–85. There were, of course, other reasons that so many antebellum Americans embraced the values and self-definitions that set them apart from both the wealthy and the working class. The rejection of a patriarchal household as unrepublican and the emergence of a Protestant culture of revivalism played their part, as did the development of an ideal of female domesticity and the large-scale European immigration of the 1840s and 1850s. See generally Ryan, *Cradle of the Middle Class*, and Blumin, *Emergence of the Middle Class*.

40. As early as the 1850s, decadal rates of occupational upward mobility for clerks in several northeastern cities measured only 30 percent, and the ranks of salaried nonmanual workers in a city such as Philadelphia had begun to include significant numbers of men in their thirties and forties (Blumin, *Emergence of the Middle Class*, 76–77, 120–21). The most dramatic expansion of white-collar work and an associated class of lifelong salaried, nonmanual workers, however, occurred in the postbellum decades. This trend accelerated in the 1870s, when the proportion of white-collar workers in the labor force began to post enduring gains of 50 percent a decade (Kocka, *White-Collar Workers*, 44, 55; Zunz, *Making America*

Corporate, 126–48; Blumin, *Emergence of the Middle Class*, 258–97; Griffen and Griffen, *Natives and Newcomers*, 118–38; Aron, *Ladies and Gentlemen of the Civil Service*). For a suggestive discussion of the economic constraints facing white-collar employees in late-nineteenth-century America, see John Cawelti's treatment of the Horatio Alger stories in *Apostles of the Self-Made Man*, 101–23.

41. Aron, *Ladies and Gentlemen of the Civil Service*, 25–39.

42. On the income and purchasing power of white-collar salaried positions, patterns of middle-class consumption, and the conditions of salaried work, see Blumin, *Emergence of the Middle Class*, esp. 83–107, 112–13, 138–91, 273–75. As Cindy Aron (*Ladies and Gentlemen of the Civil Service*, 21–25) demonstrates, possession of such comparatively well-paid jobs did not necessarily free mid-nineteenth-century employees from financial worries. Members of the federal civil service frequently borrowed money to sustain their standard of living and regularly confronted pressure from retailers who sought the assistance of the federal government in collecting the debts of its employees. In addition, as Mary Ryan (*Cradle of the Middle Class*, 172–73) and Jeanne Boydston (*Home and Work*, 87–88, 136–37) stress, the maintenance of middle-class lifestyles and particularly the provision of extensive education to sons often depended on income contributed by wives and daughters. Still, with comparatively low rates of unemployment and with yearly incomes equal to or higher than those earned by skilled, fully employed manual workers, white-collar salaried employees enjoyed considerable material advantages over most wage earners.

43. For a fascinating expression of such a sensibility toward the end of the nineteenth century, see the Dec. 1, 1890, letter from J. W. Bomgardner to John D. Rockefeller, quoted in Sandage, "Deadbeats, Drunkards, and Dreamers," 417. After failing during the panic of 1873 as a miller and then struggling for almost two decades as a grain dealer, Bomgardner wrote to Rockefeller in search of a corporate job, hoping not "for a *soft* and *easy* place" but rather "a little rest from this care and anxiety."

Epilogue

1. Henry B. Hyde to Lester M. Clark, Feb. 3, 1871, Letterbook A-2, Hyde Papers, Equitable Life Assurance Society Collection, Baker Library; Buley, *Equitable Life Assurance Society*, 49.

2. C-Fs 1138, 1198.

3. Zelizer, *Morals and Markets*, esp. 9–25, 91–147; Clough, *Century of American Life Insurance*, 29–30.

4. Stalson, *Marketing Life Insurance*, 360–63, 383–84; Williamson and Smalley, *Northwestern Mutual Life*, 6–13; Buley, *Equitable Life Assurance Society*, 45–538. Historical examinations of early life insurance companies, which overwhelmingly consist of works commissioned by the corporations themselves, invariably discuss the links between Johnston and the two Hydes, though none discusses the two older men's business failures. Three other bankrupt New York City merchants, Robert L. Patterson, Pliny Freeman, and Frederick Winston, also played crucial roles in early mutual life companies. Patterson and Freeman each failed after the panic of 1839, after which the former initiated the founding of the Mutual Benefit Life in Newark, New Jersey, and the latter helped to instigate and then run the Nautilus Mutual Life, which eventually became New York Life. Accused of mismanagement in 1863, Freeman was forced out of the company. He then founded the Globe Mutual Life, which eventually failed in the mid-1870s. Shortly before Winston's mercantile firm failed in 1853, he received appointment as the president of the Mutual Life. Despite enduring personal indebtedness resulting from this insolvency, Winston exercised firm control over the

company until his death in 1885 (C-F 803; Dun, New York, 197:24; Ward, *Down the Years*, 26–29; Abbott, *Story of Life Insurance*, 35; Stalson, *Marketing Life Insurance*, 211; Hendrick, *Story of Life Insurance*, 81–91, 126, 171–90).

5. Stalson, *Marketing Life Insurance*, 280–81; Clough, *Century of American Life Insurance*, 93–95; Henry B. Hyde to Mr. Garland, San Francisco agent, Apr. 9, 1874, Letterbook 4-A, Hyde Papers, Equitable Life Assurance Society Collection, Baker Library. Hyde circulated similar suggestions to agents in the first few years of Equitable's existence, just after the panic of 1857, and again after the panics of 1884 and 1893 (Alexander, *My Half-Century in Life Insurance*, 45–48).

6. Ward, *Down the Years*, 35; Stalson, *Marketing Life Insurance*, 139; Henry B. Hyde, "Fifteen Good Reasons for Insuring My Life" (1860), quoted in Stalson, *Marketing Life Insurance*, 338.

7. Stalson, *Marketing Life Insurance*, 187–92; Clough, *Century of American Life Insurance*, 93–95; Abbott, *Story of Life Insurance*, 42–45; Ward, *Through the Years*, 35.

8. Dun, New York, 244:490; Hendrick, *Story of Life Insurance*, 262–63; Stalson, *Marketing Life Insurance*, 241–54, 353–59; Zelizer, *Morals and Markets*, 91–101, 119–40.

9. C-F 1214; Dun, New York, 244:390.

10. Wilson Williams, "The Great Opportunity for Trained Men," in *Proceedings of The Fourth Annual Meeting of the National Association of Life Underwriters* (1893), 96, quoted in Zelizer, *Markets and Morals*, 132; speech of Richard McCurdy, *Weekly Statement* (1888): 18, quoted in Stalson, *Marketing Life Insurance*, 510; Henry B. Hyde to Mr. Jennison, Apr. 9, 1874, Letterbook 4-A, Hyde Papers, Equitable Life Assurance Society Collection, Baker Library; Hendrick, *Story of Life Insurance*, 263–65.

11. On the sources of life insurance expansion and consolidation after 1870, see Hendrick, *Story of Life Insurance*; Buley, *Equitable Life Assurance Society*; and Keller, *Life Insurance Enterprise*.

12. On continued cultural critiques of salaried white-collar labor, especially as a permanent condition, see Aron, *Ladies and Gentlemen of the Civil Service*, 104, 181–86.

13. Washington Frothingham, "Stewart, and the Dry Goods Trade of New York," *Continental Monthly* 2 (1862): 533. On Frothingham's literary career, see Bridges, *Iron Millionaire*, 128. John D. Rockefeller's Standard Oil Company similarly made a practice of hiring former managers of struggling oil refineries as salaried employees, especially after buying out such concerns. Though Rockefeller often made such job offers in order to take advantage of technical or entrepreneurial expertise, he also wished to keep failed refiners from starting up new refineries, which would diminish his company's ability to prevent excess capacity in the industry (Chernow, *Titan*, 144–46, 162). The vast corps of commercial drummers who fanned out across the United States in the postbellum decades, serving as pivotal sales representatives of large-scale metropolitan wholesalers, also may have included a significant number of former bankrupts. These individuals faced recurrent criticism for their apparent rootlessness and dependence on distant, powerful economic masters, yet their numbers increased dramatically after 1870. On contemporary assessments of drumming, see Spears, *100 Years on the Road*; for examples of bankrupts turned traveling salesmen, see Cronon, *Nature's Metropolis*, 185.

14. Not surprisingly, other contemporaries offered less sanguine interpretations of A. T. Stewart's hiring practices. Reflecting at the turn of the century on the transition that so many nineteenth-century bankrupts made from proprietors to salaried employees, former secretary of war Henry Stimson lamented "the change of bearing" associated with this alteration in status. Stimson allowed that these former businessmen may have gained substantial economic security; but they did so at considerable cost, losing the "self-respect" that flowed from meeting the responsibilities and challenges of independent enterprise ("Small Business as a School of Manhood," 338–40).

Note on Research Method

1. *Alphabetical List of Applicants.*

2. For an excellent and concise discussion of the difficulties confronting the would-be record linker, as well as copious citations to other relevant analyses, see Conzen, "Quantification and the New Urban History," *Journal of Interdisciplinary History* 13 (1983) 662–63.

3. C-F 191; Dun, New York, 210:113.

Bibliography

Primary Sources

MANUSCRIPT COLLECTIONS

Arents Library, Syracuse University, Syracuse, New York
   Lyman Spalding Journal
Baker Library, Harvard Business School, Boston, Massachusetts
   R. G. Dun & Co. Collection, Nineteenth-Century Credit Ledgers
   Equitable Life Assurance Society Collection
     Henry B. Hyde Papers
Bancroft Library, University of California at Berkeley, Berkeley, California
   Samuel R. Throckmorton Papers
Columbia University Rare Book and Manuscript Library, New York City
   R. Hoe & Co. Papers
   Charlemagne Tower Papers
The New-York Historical Society, New York City
   Campbell-Mumford Papers
   Misc. MSS Curtis, Edward
   BV Hone, Philip, Diary, 1828–51
   BV Houghton & Day, Letterbook, June 10, 1839–Sept. 1, 1840
   Mott Family Papers
   BV New York Trade Agency
   BV Sargeant, John Osborne, Letterbook, 1842–48
   Misc. MSS Thompson, Smith
   BV Wilbur, Marcus
New York Public Library, New York City
   Manuscripts and Archives Division, Astor, Lenox and Tilden Foundations
     Gansevoort-Lansing Collection
     Robert Swartwout Papers
     Frederick E. Westbrook Diary, Jan. 1, 1840–Dec. 31, 1843
     Marcus Wilbur Miscellaneous Papers

MANUSCRIPT FEDERAL COURT RECORDS

Bankruptcy Records, Act of 1841, United States District Court for the Southern Federal
    District of New York, National Archives and Record Administration, Northeast
    Region, New York City
   Case-files, Entry 117
   Dockets, Entry 118
   Indexes to Dockets, Entry 119

Docket of Suits by Assignees, Entry 120
Certificates of Discharge, Entry 123
Record of Assets and Sales, Entry 126
Record of Sales (Sales Book), Entry 127

OTHER GOVERNMENT DOCUMENTS

Congressional Globe and *Appendix to the Congressional Globe*. 1840–43.
Fees in United States Circuit and District Courts in Admiralty and Bankruptcy Cases.
    House Doc. No. 172, 27th Cong., 3d sess., 1843.
Letter from the Secretary of State, . . . Relative to the Application and Discharge of Persons
    under the Bankrupt Law. House Doc. No. 223, 29th Cong., 1st sess., 1846.
Letter from the Secretary of State, Transmitting Statements Showing Proceedings under the
    Bankrupt Act. House Doc. No. 99, 29th Cong., 2nd sess., 1847.
Memorial of Citizens of Baltimore. Senate Doc. No. 49, 27th Cong., 1st sess., 1841.
Memorial of Citizens of Buckingham County, Virginia. Senate Doc. No. 95, 27th Cong., 1st
    sess., 1841.
Memorial of Citizens of Philadelphia. Senate Doc. No. 169, 26th Cong., 2d sess., 1841.
Memorial of Citizens of Rochester. Senate Doc. No. 82, 27th Cong., 1st sess., 1841.
Memorial of Citizens of Syracuse. Senate Doc. 71, 27th Cong., 1st sess., 1841.
Memorial of Connecticut Legislature. Senate Doc. No. 361, 27th Cong., 2d sess., 1842.
Memorial of Electors of Dutchess County. Senate Doc. No. 565, 26th Cong., 1st sess.,
    1840.
Memorial of Louisville Chamber of Commerce. Senate Doc. No. 117, 26th Cong., 2d sess.,
    1841.
Memorial of Mississippi Legislature. Senate Doc. No. 276, 27th Cong., 2d sess., 1842.
Memorial of New Hampshire Legislature. Senate Doc. No. 70, 27th Cong., 3d sess., 1843.
Memorial of New Orleans Chamber of Commerce. Senate Doc. No. 43, 26th Cong., 2d
    sess., 1841.
Memorial of New York City Board of Trade. Sen. Doc. No. 506, 26th Cong., 1st sess.,
    1840.
Memorial of New York City Chamber of Commerce. Senate Doc. No. 170, 26th Cong., 2d
    sess., 1841.
Memorial of New York City Mechanics. Senate Doc. No. 120, 26th Cong., 2d sess., 1841.
Memorial of New York City Merchants. Senate Doc. No. 42, 26th Cong., 2d sess., 1841.
Memorial of New York City Merchants Exchange. Senate Doc. No. 282, 26th Cong., 1st
    sess., 1840.
Memorial of New York City Philanthropic Law Reform Association. Senate Doc. No. 130,
    26th Cong., 2d sess., 1841.
Memorial of a Number of Citizens of the City of New York. Senate Doc. No. 543, 26th
    Cong., 1st sess., 1840.
Memorial of Saint Louis Residents. Senate Doc. No. 81, 26th Cong., 2d sess., 1841.
Message from the President of the United States, Transmitting a Memorial of 2,961 Citizens
    of the City of New York. House Doc. No. 29, 27th Cong., 1st. sess., 1841.
Report from the Secretary of State, in Compliance with a Resolution of the Senate, in
    Relation to the Operation of the Bankrupt Law. Senate Doc. No. 19, 27th Cong., 2d
    sess., 1842.
Rules and Regulations in Bankruptcy, Adopted by the Circuit and District Courts of the
    United States, for the Southern District of New York, January 4th, 1842. New York, 1842.
Rules and Regulations in Bankruptcy, Adopted by the District of the United States, for the
    District of Georgia, February 8, 1842. Savannah, 1842.

*Rules of the District Court of the United States, for the District of Connecticut, in
    Bankruptcy; Together with a List of Appointments by the Court, and a Tariff of Fees.*
    Hartford, 1842.
Senate Judiciary Committee. *Report on the Bankruptcy Law.* Senate Doc. No. 121, 27th
    Cong., 3d sess., 1843.
Ulster County, New York. Deed Books, 1830–80.
United States Census Office. Manuscript Census, 1850 and 1860, New York State.
United States Department of Commerce, Bureau of the Census. *Historical Statistics of the
    United States: Colonial Times to 1970.* Washington, 1975.

NEWSPAPERS, PERIODICALS, CITY DIRECTORIES, AND ENCYCLOPEDIAS

Albany Argus, 1841–43
American Jurist, 1828–43
American Law Magazine, 1842–46
American Monthly Magazine, 1833–38
American Quarterly Review, 1827–37
American Whig Review, 1845–52
Arthur's Home Magazine, 1853–57
Atkinson's Casket, 1832–36
Ballou's Magazine, 1855–60
Bankers' Magazine (New York), 1846–60
Boston Directory, 1845–47, 1850, 1853, 1856, 1859
Brooklyn Daily Eagle, 1841–43
Christian Examiner, 1824–60
Continental Monthly, 1862
De Bow's Review, 1846–60
Democratic Review (also *United States Magazine and Democratic Review*), 1838–59
Directory of the City of Lynn, 1851, 1853, 1855, 1857, 1859
Directory of the City of Savannah, 1848–50, 1858–60
Doggett's New York City Directory, 1846, 1848
Encyclopedia Americana, 1830
Godey's Lady's Book, 1830–60
Graham's Magazine, 1832–52
The Happy Home, 1855
Harper's Weekly, 1857–60
Hunt's Merchants' Magazine, 1839–65
Journal of Commerce, 1841–43
The Knickerbocker, 1833–60
Ladies' Companion, 1834–44
Law Reporter (also *Monthly Law Reporter*), 1838–60
Livingston's Monthly Law Magazine, 1853–54
Louisiana Law Journal, 1842
Milledgeville Federal Union, 1842–43
Morning Courier and New York Enquirer, 1841–43
New Orleans Bee, 1841–43
New York Evangelist, 1852
New York Herald, 1835–43
New York Legal Observer, 1842–46
New York Review, 1837–42
North American Review, 1815–60

Pennsylvania Law Journal, 1842–47
Poughkeepsie Journal, 1837–43
Poughkeepsie Telegraph, 1837–43
Rode's New York City Directory, 1852
San Francisco City Directory, 1854, 1856, 1858, 1859
Southern Literary Messenger, 1844–45
Southern Quarterly Review, 1842–56
Springfield (Illinois) City Directory, 1855, 1857, 1859
Trow's New York City Directory, 1856, 1858, 1860
Ulster County Republican, 1841–43
Western Law Journal, 1843–53
Worcester Almanac, Directory, and Business Advertiser, 1850, 1854, 1857, 1859.

STATUTES AND LEGAL TREATISES

An Act to Establish a Uniform System of Bankruptcy Throughout the United States. New
    York, 1842.
Angell, Joseph K. *A Practical Summary of the Law of Assignments in Trust for the Benefit
    of Creditors*. Boston, 1835.
Bicknell, George A., Jr. *Commentary on the Bankrupt Law of 1841, Showing Its Operation
    and Effect*. New York, 1841.
Burrill, Alexander. *A Treatise on the Law and Practice of Voluntary Assignments for the
    Benefit of Creditors; with an Appendix of Forms*. New York, 1853.
Chandler, Peleg W. *The Bankrupt Law of the United States, with an Outline of the System;
    Together with the Rules and Forms in Massachusetts*. Boston, 1842.
Edwards, Charles. *On Receivers in Chancery, with Precedents*. New York, 1839.
Holcombe, James P. *The Law of Debtor and Creditor in the United States and Canada,
    Adapted to the Wants of Merchants and Lawyers*. New York, 1848.
Kent, James. *Commentaries on American Law*. 4 vols. 1st ed. New York, 1827–30.
———. *Commentaries on American Law*. 4 vols. 4th ed. New York, 1840.
"A Member of the Bar." *The Bankrupt Law of the United States, Passed August 19, 1841.
    With a Commentary Containing a Full Explanation of the Law of Bankruptcy*.
    Philadelphia, 1841.
Moore, Jacob B. *The Laws of Trade in the United States, Being an Abstract of the Statutes
    of the Several States and Territories, Concerning Debtors and Creditors*. New York, 1840.
Owen, Samuel. *A Treatise on the Law and Practice of Bankruptcy*. New York, 1842.
Sedgwick, Theodore. *A Treatise on the Rules which Govern the Interpretation and
    Construction of Statutory and Constitutional Law*. 2d ed. New York, 1874.
Staples, J. B. *The General Bankrupt Law, with an Introduction, Containing Some
    Observations Upon Its Constitutionality, Expediency, &c*. New York, 1841.
Story, Joseph. *Commentaries on the Law of Agency*. 2d ed. Boston, 1844.
Walker, Timothy. *Introduction to American Law*. Philadelphia, 1837.

BOOKS AND PAMPHLETS

Alexander, William. *My Half-Century in Life Insurance*. New York, 1935.
*Alphabetical List of Applicants for the Benefit of the Bankrupt Act (Passed August 19, 1841)
    within the Southern District of New York, Carefully Compiled from the Petitions on File
    in the United States District Clerk's Office*. New York, 1843.
Arthur, Timothy Shay. *Debtor and Creditor: A Tale of the Times*. Philadelphia, 1850.
———. *The Debtor's Daughter; or, Life and Its Changes*. Philadelphia, 1850.

——. *Making Haste to Be Rich; or, The Temptation and the Fall*. New York, 1848.

——. *The Ruined Family and Other Tales*. Philadelphia, 1843.

——. *Temperance Tales; or, Six Nights with the Washingtonians*. Philadelphia, 1843.

——. *Two Merchants; or, Solvent and Insolvent*. Philadelphia, 1843.

Balestier, Joseph N. *The Annals of Chicago: A Lecture Delivered before the Chicago Lyceum, January 21, 1840*. Chicago, 1840. Reprint, Chicago, 1876.

Baldwin, Joseph C. *The Flush Times of Alabama and Mississippi: A Series of Sketches*. New York, 1853. Reprint, Baton Rouge, 1987.

Barnum, Phineas T. *The Humbugs of the World: An Account of Humbugs, Delusions, Impositions, Quackeries, Deceits, and Deceivers Generally, in All Ages*. New York, 1866.

——. *Struggles and Triumphs; or, Forty Years' Recollections of P. T. Barnum, Written by Himself*. Edited by Carl Bode. Hartford, 1869. Reprint, New York, 1981.

Beecher, Henry Ward. *Seven Lectures to Young Men*. Cincinnati, 1845.

Boardman, Henry A. *The Bible in the Countinghouse: A Course of Lectures to Merchants*. Philadelphia, 1853.

Bremer, Frederika. *The Homes of the New World: Impressions of America*. Translated by Mary Howitt. New York, 1853.

Briggs, Charles Frederick. *The Adventures of Harry Franco, A Tale of the Panic*. New York, 1839.

——. *Bankrupt Stories; or, The Haunted Merchant*. New York, 1843.

Brooke, Reverend John T. *Debt: Or Morality of the Credit System. A Sermon*. Cincinnati, 1841.

Brown, Hannah. *Farmer Housten and the Speculator: A Tale of New England*. Portland, 1839.

Brown, John W. *Constance; or, The Merchant's Daughter: A Tale of the Times*. New York, 1841.

Cary, Thomas Greaves. *The Dependence of the Fine Arts for Encouragement, in a Republic, on the Security of Property; with an Enquiry into the Causes of Frequent Failure among Men of Business: An Address Delivered before the Boston Mercantile Library Association, November 13, 1844*. Boston, 1845.

Chevalier, Michael. *Society, Manners, and Politics in the United States: Being a Series of Letters on North America*. Boston, 1839.

"A Citizen of Boston." *Experimental Knowledge: Letter to a Man in Bankruptcy*. Boston, 1849.

Cooper, James Fenimore. *Autobiography of a Pocket Handkerchief*. New York, 1843. Reprint, New York, 1949.

"A Counting-House Man." *Herbert Tracy; or, The Trials of Mercantile Life and the Morality of Trade*. New York, 1851.

Defoe, Daniel. *The Complete English Tradesman in Familiar Letters*. 2 vols. London, 1727. Reprint, New York, 1969.

Dickinson, Emily. *The Poems of Emily Dickinson*. Vol. 1. Edited by Thomas H. Johnson. Cambridge, 1955.

Dunscomb, Daniel E. *To the Electors of the Eighth Ward, as Constituted in the Years 1825 & 1826, and the Community Generally*. New York, 1838.

Dyott, Thomas W. *An Exposition of the System of Moral and Mental Labor, Established at the Glass Factory of Dyottsville, in the County of Philadelphia*. Philadelphia, 1833.

Evans, D. Morier. *The Commercial Crisis, 1847–1848*. 2d ed. London, 1849. Reprint, New York, 1969.

——. *The History of the Commercial Crisis, 1857–1858, and the Stock Exchange Panic of 1859*. London, 1860. Reprint, New York, 1969.

The Expediency of a Uniform Bankrupt Law. New York, 1840.

Foster, B. F. *A Practical System of Book-keeping by Single Entry*. New York, 1845.

Fragile Empires: The Texas Correspondence of Samuel Swartwout and James Morgan, 1836–1856. Edited by Feris A. Bass Jr. and B. R. Brunson. Austin, 1984.

Freedley, Edwin T. *A Practical Treatise on Business; or How to Get, Save, Spend, Give, Lend, and Bequeath Money, with an Inquiry into the Chances of Success and the Causes of Failure in Business*. Philadelphia, 1852.

Frost, John. *The Young Merchant*. Philadelphia, 1839.

Gouge, William. *A Short History of Paper Money and Banking in the United States*. 2 vols. Philadelphia, 1833.

Greeley, Horace. *Recollections of a Busy Life*. New York, 1868.

Greene, Asa. *The Perils of Pearl Street, Including a Taste of the Dangers of Wall Street*. New York, 1834.

Griffith, Mary. *The Two Defaulters; or, A Picture of the Times*. New York, 1842.

Grund, Francis J. *The Americans in Their Moral, Social, and Political Relations*. Boston, 1837. Reprint, New York, 1968.

The Highly Interesting and Important Trial of Dr. T. W. Dyott, the Banker, for Fraudulent Insolvency. Philadelphia, 1839.

Hone, Philip. *The Diary of Philip Hone, 1828–1851*. 2 vols. Edited by Allan Nevins. New York, 1927.

Hunt, Freeman, ed. *Worth and Wealth: A Collection of Maxims, Morals and Miscellanies for Merchants and Men of Business*. New York, 1856.

Jackson, Frederick. *A Victim of Chancery; or, A Debtor's Experience*. New York, 1841.

——. *A Week in Wall Street, by One Who Knows*. New York, 1841.

Jones, John Beauchamp. *The City Merchant; or, The Mysterious Failure*. Philadelphia, 1851.

Jones, Thomas. *The Principles and Practice of Book-Keeping, Embracing an Entirely New and Improved Method of Imparting the Science*. New York, 1841.

Leggett, William. *Democratick Editorials: Essays in Jacksonian Political Economy*. Edited by Lawrence H. White. Indianapolis, 1984.

Life and Letters of Joseph Story. 2 vols. Edited by William W. Story. Boston, 1851.

List of Bankrupts in the United States Court for the Eastern District of Pennsylvania. Pittsburgh, 1844.

List of Bankrupts in the United States Court for the Western District of Pennsylvania. Pittsburgh, 1844.

Martineau, Harriet. *Society in America*. London, 1837.

Melville, Herman. *The Confidence Man: His Masquerade*. Edited by Hershel Parker. New York, 1857. Reprint, New York, 1971.

The Papers of Willie Person Mangum. Vol. 3, 1839–43. Edited by Henry T. Shanks. Raleigh, 1953.

The Papers of Daniel Webster: Legal Papers. Vol. 2, *The Boston Practice*. Edited by Alfred S. Konefsky and Andrew J. King. Hanover, N.H., 1983.

Reed, Willoughby H. *Notice to Creditors*. Philadelphia, 1855.

Sawyer, Caroline. *The Merchant's Widow*. New York, 1841.

Shinning It, A Tale of the Tape-Cutter; or, The Mechanic Turned Merchant, by One Who Knows. New York, 1841.

Smith, Reverend Asa D. *The Guileless Israelite: A Sermon on Occasion of the Death of Mr. Joseph Brewster*. New York, 1851.

[Stilwell, Silas M.] *An Appeal to the Members of Congress, in Favor of a Bankrupt Law*. New York, 1841.

Stowe, Harriet Beecher. *Uncle Tom's Cabin: Or, Life among the Lowly*. Boston, 1852. Reprint, New York, 1981.

Strong, George Templeton. *The Diary of George Templeton Strong*. Vol. 2, *The Turbulent Fifties*. Edited by Allan Nevins and Milton H. Thomas. New York, 1952.

Tappan, Lewis. *The Life of Arthur Tappan*. New York, 1871.

Thoreau, Henry David. *The Portable Thoreau*. Edited by Carl Bode. New York, 1982.

Tocqueville, Alexis de. *Democracy in America*. 2 vols. New York, 1835, 1840. Reprint, New York, 1945.

Tyng, Stephen H. *The Man of Business, Considered in His Various Relations*. New York, 1857.

Tuthill, Mrs. L. C. *Success in Life: The Merchant*. New York, 1850.

Webster, Noah. *An American Dictionary of the English Language*, 3d ed. Revised and edited by Chauncey Goodrich. Springfield, Mass., 1853.

Secondary Sources

BOOKS

Abbott, Lawrence. *The Story of Life Insurance: A History of the Origin and Development of the New York Life Insurance Company from 1845 to 1929*. New York, 1930.

Alberts, Robert. *The Good Provider: H. J. Heinz and His 57 Varieties*. Boston, 1973.

Albion, Robert Greenhalgh. *The Rise of New York Port*. New York, 1939.

Adam, Bluford. *E Pluribus Barnum: The Great Showman and the Making of U.S. Popular Culture*. Minneapolis, 1997.

Appleby, Joyce. *Capitalism and a New Social Order: The Republican Vision of the 1790s*. New York, 1984.

Aron, Cindy Sondik. *Ladies and Gentlemen of the Civil Service: Middle-Class Workers in Victorian America*. New York, 1987.

Ashworth, John. *"Agrarians" and "Aristocrats": Party Political Ideology in the United States, 1837–1846*. London, 1983. Reprint, New York, 1987.

Atherton, Lewis E. *The Frontier Merchant in Mid-America*. Columbia, Mo., 1971.

Barron, Hal S. *Those Who Stayed Behind: Rural Society in Nineteenth-Century New England*. New York, 1984.

Basch, Norma. *In the Eyes of the Law: Women, Marriage, and Property in Nineteenth-Century New York*. Ithaca, N.Y., 1982.

Blackmar, Elizabeth. *Manhattan for Rent, 1785–1850*. Ithaca, N.Y., 1989.

Blumin, Stuart. *The Emergence of the Middle Class: Social Experience in the American City, 1760–1900*. New York, 1989.

——. *The Urban Threshold: Growth and Change in a Nineteenth-Century American Community*. Chicago, 1978.

Boorstin, Daniel. *The Americans: The National Experience*. New York, 1965.

Boydston, Jeanne. *Home and Work: Housewives, Wages, and the Ideology of Labor in the Early Republic*. New York, 1990.

Bridges, Hal. *Iron Millionaire: Life of Charlemagne Tower*. Philadelphia, 1952.

Buck, Norman S. *The Development of the Organization of Anglo-American Trade*. New Haven, 1925.

Buley, R. Carlyle. *The Equitable Life Assurance Society of the United States, 1859–1964*, Vol. 1. New York, 1967.

Bushman, Richard L. *Joseph Smith and the Beginnings of Mormonism*. Urbana, 1984.

Cawelti, John. *Apostles of the Self-Made Man*. Chicago, 1965.

Chandler, Alfred D., Jr. *The Visible Hand: The Managerial Revolution in American Business*. Cambridge, 1977.

Ch'en, Kuo-Tung Anthony. *The Insolvency of the Chinese Hong Merchants, 1760–1843*. Nankang, Tapei, 1990.

Chernow, Ron. *Titan: The Life of John D. Rockefeller, Sr.* New York, 1998.

Clark, Christopher. *The Roots of Rural Capitalism: Western Massachusetts, 1780–1860*. Ithaca, N.Y., 1990.

Clough, Shephard. *A Century of American Life Insurance: A History of the Mutual Life Insurance Company of New York, 1843–1943*. New York, 1946.

Cochran, Thomas C. *Frontiers of Change: Early Industrialism in America*. New York, 1981.

Cogan, Frances. *All-American Girl: The Ideal of Real Womanhood in Mid-Nineteenth-Century America*. Athens, Ga., 1989.

Coleman, Peter. *Debtors and Creditors in America: Insolvency, Imprisonment for Debt, and Bankruptcy, 1607–1900*. Madison, 1974.

Commemorative Biographical Record of Ulster County, New York, Containing Sketches of Prominent and Representative Citizens. Chicago, 1896.

Cronon, William. *Nature's Metropolis: Chicago and the Great West*. New York, 1991.

Crouthamel, James L. *James Watson Webb: A Biography*. Middletown, Conn., 1969.

Davis, David Brion. *From Homicide to Slavery: Studies in American Culture*. New York, 1986.

——. *Homicide in American Fiction, 1798–1860*. Ithaca, N.Y., 1957.

——. *Slavery and Human Progress*. New York, 1984.

Dawley, Alan. *Class and Community: The Industrial Revolution in Lynn*. Cambridge, 1976.

Decker, Peter. *Fortunes and Failures: White-Collar Mobility in Nineteenth-Century San Francisco*. Cambridge, 1978.

Dictionary of American Biography. 19 vols. New York, 1929.

Doerflinger, Thomas. *A Vigorous Spirit of Enterprise: Merchants and Economic Development in Revolutionary Philadelphia*. Chapel Hill, 1986. Reprint, New York, 1987.

Doyle, Don. *The Social Order of a Frontier Community: Jacksonville, Illinois, 1825–1870*. Urbana, 1978.

Dun & Bradstreet. *The Business Failure Record*. New York, 1997.

Fabian, Ann. *Card Sharps, Dream Books, and Bucket Shops: Gambling in Nineteenth-Century America*. Ithaca, N.Y., 1990.

Faler, Paul. *Mechanics and Manufacturers in the Early Industrial Revolution: Lynn, Massachusetts, 1780–1860*. Albany, 1981.

Faragher, John Mack. *Sugar Creek: Life on the Illinois Prairie*. New Haven, 1986.

Flanders, Robert Bruce. *Nauvoo: Kingdom on the Mississippi*. Urbana, 1965.

Foner, Eric. *Free Soil, Free Labor, Free Men: The Ideology of the Republican Party before the Civil War*. New York, 1970.

Ford, Lacy K., Jr. *Origins of Southern Radicalism: The South Carolina Upcountry, 1800–1860*. New York, 1988.

Foulke, Roy A. *The Sinews of American Commerce*. New York, 1941.

Freyer, Tony. *Forums of Order: The Federal Courts and Business in American History*. Greenwich, Conn., 1979.

——. *Producers versus Capitalists: Constitutional Conflict in Antebellum America*. Charlottesville, 1994.

Friedman, Lawrence. *A History of American Law*. 2d ed. New York, 1985.

Gallman, J. Matthew. *Mastering Wartime: A Social History of Philadelphia during the Civil War*. New York, 1990.

Gates, Paul W. *The Farmer's Age: Agriculture, 1815–1860*. New York, 1960. Reprint, New York, 1968.

Gerber, David. *The Making of an American Pluralism: Buffalo, New York, 1825–1860*. Urbana, 1989.

Gray, Susan. *The Yankee West: Community Life on the Michigan Frontier*. Chapel Hill, 1996.

Griffen, Clyde, and Sally Griffen. *Natives and Newcomers: The Ordering of Opportunity in Mid-Nineteenth-Century Poughkeepsie*. Cambridge, 1978.

Hahn, Steven. *The Roots of Southern Populism: Yeoman Farmers and the Transformation of Georgia Upcountry, 1850–1890*. New York, 1983.

Hahn, Steven, and Jonathon Prude, eds. *The Countryside in the Age of Capitalist Transformation: Essays in the Social History of Rural America*. Chapel Hill, 1985.

Halttunen, Karen. *Confidence Men and Painted Women: A Study of Middle-Class Culture in America, 1830–1870*. New Haven, 1982.

Hammond, Bray. *Banks and Politics in America: From the Revolution to the Civil War*. Princeton, 1957.

Harris, Neil. *Humbug: The Art of P. T. Barnum*. Chicago, 1973.

Hartz, Louis. *Economic Policy and Democratic Thought: Pennsylvania, 1776–1860*. Cambridge, 1948. Reprint, Chicago, 1968.

Hendrick, Burton J. *The Story of Life Insurance*. New York, 1907.

Hewitt, Nancy. *Women's Activism and Social Change: Rochester, New York, 1822–1872*. Ithaca, N.Y., 1984.

Hilkey, Judy. *Character Is Capital: Success Manuals and Manhood in Gilded Age America*. Chapel Hill, 1997.

History of Greene County, New York, with Biographical Sketches of Its Prominent Men. New York, 1884.

Hogan, William Ranson. *The Texas Republic: A Social and Economic History*. Norman, Okla., 1946.

Holt, Michael F. *Political Parties and American Political Development from the Age of Jackson to the Age of Lincoln*. Baton Rouge, 1992.

Hoppit, Julian. *Risk and Failure in English Business, 1700–1800*. New York, 1987.

Horlick, Allan Stanley. *Country Boys and Merchant Princes: The Social Control of Young Men in New York*. Lewisburg, Pa., 1975.

Horowitz, Morton. *The Transformation of American Law*. Cambridge, 1977.

Howe, Daniel Walker. *The Political Culture of the American Whigs*. Chicago, 1979.

Hower, Ralph M. *History of Macy's of New York, 1858–1919*. Cambridge, 1943.

Hurst, James Willard. *Law and the Conditions of Freedom in the Nineteenth-Century United States*. Madison, 1956.

Huston, James L. *The Panic of 1857 and the Coming of the Civil War*. Baton Rouge, 1987.

Johnson, Paul. *A Shopkeeper's Millennium: Society and Revivals in Rochester, New York, 1815–1837*. New York, 1978.

Johnson, Paul, and Sean Wilentz. *The Kingdom of Matthias: A Story of Sex and Salvation in 19th-Century America*. New York, 1994.

Katz, Michael B. *The People of Hamilton, Canada West: Family and Class in a Mid-Nineteenth-Century City*. Cambridge, 1978.

Keller, Morton. *The Life Insurance Enterprise, 1885–1910: A Study in the Limits of Corporate Power*. Cambridge, 1963.

Kerber, Linda. *Women of the Republic: Intellect and Ideology in Revolutionary America*. Chapel Hill, 1980. Reprint, New York, 1986.

Keyssar, Alexander. *Out of Work: The First Century of Unemployment in Massachusetts*. New York, 1986.

Kindleberger, Charles P. *Manias, Panics, and Crashes: A History of Financial Crises*. New York, 1989.

Kirkland, Edward. *Dream and Thought in the Business Community, 1860–1900*. Ithaca, N.Y., 1956. Reprint, Chicago, 1990.

Kocka, Jurgen. *White-Collar Workers in America, 1890–1940*. Translated by Maura Kealey. Beverly Hills, 1980.

Kohl, Lawrence Frederick. *The Politics of Individualism: Parties and the American Character in the Jacksonian Era*. New York, 1989.

Kulikoff, Alan. *The Agrarian Origins of American Capitalism*. Charlottesville, 1992.

Kutler, Stanley. *Privilege and Creative Destruction: The Charles River Bridge Case*. Baltimore, 1971.

Lamoreaux, Naomi R. *Insider Lending: Banks, Personal Connections, and Economic Development in Industrial New England*. New York, 1994.

Laurie, Bruce. *Artisans into Workers: Labor in Nineteenth-Century America*. New York, 1989.

———. *Working People of Philadelphia, 1800–1850*. Philadelphia, 1980.

Lears, Jackson. *Fables of Abundance: A Cultural History of Advertising in America*. New York, 1994.

Lebsock, Suzanne. *The Free Women of Petersburg: Status and Culture in a Southern Town, 1784–1860*. New York, 1984.

Lee, Susan Previant and Peter Passell. *A New Economic View of American History*. New York, 1979.

Lester, V. Markham. *Victorian Insolvency: Bankruptcy, Imprisonment for Debt, and Company Winding-Up in Nineteenth-Century England*. New York, 1995.

Lindstrom, Diane. *Economic Development in the Philadelphia Region, 1810–1850*. New York, 1978.

McCoy, Drew. *The Elusive Republic: Political Economy in Jeffersonian America*. Chapel Hill, 1980.

MacGill, Caroline. *History of Transportation in the United States before 1860*. Washington, D.C., 1917.

McGrane, Reginald Charles. *The Panic of 1837: Some Financial Problems of the Jacksonian Era*. Chicago, 1924.

Matthews, R. C. O. *A Study in Trade-Cycle History: Economic Fluctuations in Great Britain, 1833–1842*. London, 1954.

Montgomery, David. *Citizen Worker: The Experience of Workers in the United States with Democracy and the Free Market during the Nineteenth Century*. New York, 1993.

Myers, Marvin. *The Jacksonian Persuasion: Politics and Belief*. Palo Alto, 1957. Reprint, New York, 1960.

Newmeyer, R. Kent. *Supreme Court Justice Joseph Story: Statesman of the Old Republic*. Chapel Hill, 1985.

———. *The Supreme Court under Marshall and Taney*. Arlington, Ill., 1968.

Norris, James D. *R. G. Dun & Co., 1841–1900: The Development of Credit-Reporting in the Nineteenth Century*. Westport, Conn., 1979.

North, Douglass. *The Economic Growth of the United States, 1790–1860*. New York, 1961.

———. *Institutions, Institutional Change and Economic Performance*. New York, 1990.

Oakes, James. *The Ruling Race: A History of American Slaveholders*. New York, 1982.

Patterson, Orlando. *Slavery and Social Death: A Comparative Study*. Cambridge, 1982.

Pessen, Edward. *Riches, Class, and Power: America before the Civil War*. New Brunswick, 1990.

Porter, Glenn, and Harold C. Livesay. *Merchants and Manufacturers: Studies in the*

Changing Structure of Nineteenth-Century Marketing. Baltimore, 1971. Reprint, Chicago, 1989.

Powell, Lawrence. *New Masters: Northern Planters during the Civil War and Reconstruction.* New Haven, 1980.

Prude, Jonathan. *The Coming of Industrial Order: Town and Factory Life in Rural Massachusetts, 1810–1860.* New York, 1983.

Remini, Robert V. *Andrew Jackson.* New York, 1969.

Rodgers, Daniel. *Contested Truths: Keywords in American Politics Since Independence.* New York, 1987.

Rohrbough, Malcolm J. *The Land Office Business: The Settlement and Administration of American Public Lands, 1789–1837.* New York, 1968. Reprint, Belmont, Calif., 1990.

Rose, Ann C. *Transcendentalism as a Social Movement, 1830–1850.* New Haven, 1981.

Rothbard, Murray. *The Panic of 1819: Reactions and Policies.* New York, 1961.

Rothenberg, Winifred. *From Market-Places to a Market Economy: The Transformations of Rural Massachusetts, 1750–1850.* Chicago, 1992.

Rothman, David J. *The Discovery of the Asylum: Social Order and Disorder in the New Republic.* Boston, 1971.

Ryan, Mary. *The Cradle of the Middle Class: The Family in Oneida County, New York, 1790–1865.* New York, 1981.

Schama, Simon. *Dead Certainties: (Unwarranted Speculations).* New York, 1991.

Schumpeter, Joseph. *Capitalism, Socialism, and Democracy.* London, 1942. Reprint, New York, 1976.

——. *The Theory of Economic Development: An Inquiry into Profits, Capital, Credit, Interest, and the Business Cycle.* Translated by Redvers Opie. Cambridge, 1962.

Sellers, Charles. *The Market Revolution: Jacksonian America, 1815–1846.* New York, 1991.

Sheriff, Carol. *The Artificial River: The Erie Canal and the Paradox of Progress, 1817–1862.* New York, 1996.

Sloan, Herbert E. *Principle & Interest: Thomas Jefferson & the Problem of Debt.* New York, 1995.

Smith, James H. *History of Dutchess County, New York, 1683–1882.* Syracuse, 1882.

Spann, Edward K. *The New Metropolis: New York City, 1840–1857.* New York, 1981.

Spears. Timothy. *100 Years on the Road: The Traveling Salesman in American Culture.* New Haven, 1995.

Stalson, J. Owen. *Marketing Life Insurance: Its History in America.* Cambridge, 1942.

Stampp, Kenneth. *The Peculiar Institution: Slavery in the Ante-Bellum South.* New York, 1956.

Stokes, Melvin, and Stephen Conway, eds. *The Market Revolution in America: Social, Political, and Religious Expressions, 1800–1880.* Charlottesville, 1996.

Sullivan, Theresa, Elizabeth Warren, and Jay Lawrence Westbrook, *As We Forgive Our Debtors: Bankruptcy and Consumer Credit in America.* New York, 1989.

Swierenga, Robert P. *Pioneers and Profits: Land Speculation on the Iowa Frontier.* Ames, Iowa, 1968.

Swisher, Carl. *History of the Supreme Court of the United States: The Taney Period, 1836–1864.* New York, 1974.

Sylvester, Nathaniel Barnett. *History of Ulster County, New York, with Illustrations and Biographical Sketches of Its Prominent Men and Pioneers.* Philadelphia, 1880.

Tadman, Michael. *Speculators and Slaves: Masters, Traders, and Slaves in the Old South.* Madison, 1989.

Taylor, George Rogers. *The Transportation Revolution.* New York, 1951. Reprint, Armonk, N.Y., 1977.

Temin, Peter. *The Jacksonian Economy*. New York, 1969.

Thernstrom, Stephan. *The Other Bostonians: Poverty and Progress in the American Metropolis, 1880–1970*. Cambridge, 1973.

———. *Progress and Poverty: Social Mobility in a Nineteenth-Century City*. Cambridge, 1964.

Turner, Frederick Jackson. *The United States, 1830–1850: The Nation and Its Sections*. New York, 1935. Reprint, New York, 1950.

Van Vleck, George W. *The Panic of 1857: An Analytical Study*. New York, 1943.

Wade, Richard C. *The Urban Frontier: Pioneer Life in Early Pittsburgh, Cincinnati, Lexington, Louisville, and St. Louis*. Chicago, 1959.

Wallace, Anthony F. C. *Rockdale: The Growth of an American Village in the Early Industrial Revolution*. New York, 1972.

Walters, Ronald G. *American Reformers, 1815–1860*. New York, 1978.

Ward, William Rankin. *Down the Years: A History of the Mutual Benefit Life Insurance Company, 1845 to 1932*. Camden, N.J., 1932.

Warren, Charles. *Bankruptcy in United States History*. Cambridge, 1935.

Watson, Harry. *Liberty and Power: The Politics of Jacksonian America*. New York, 1990.

Weber, Max. *The Protestant Ethic and the Spirit of Capitalism*. Translated by Talcott Parsons. New York, 1958.

Welter, Rush. *The Mind of America, 1820–1860*. New York, 1975.

Weiss, Barbara. *The Hell of the English*. Cranbury, N.J., 1986.

Weiss, Richard. *The American Myth of Success: From Horatio Alger to Norman Vincent Peale*. New York, 1969. Reprint, Urbana, 1988.

Wiebe, Robert H. *The Opening of American Society: From the Adoption of the Constitution to the Eve of Disunion*. New York, 1985.

Wilentz, Sean. *Chants Democratic: New York City and the Rise of the American Working Class, 1788–1850*. New York, 1984.

Williams, Raymond. *Keywords: A Vocabulary of Culture and Society*. New York, 1976.

Williamson, Harold, and Orange Smalley. *Northwestern Mutual Life: A Century of Trusteeship*. Evanston, Ill., 1957.

Wilson, Major. *Space, Time, and Freedom; the Quest for Nationality and the Irrepressible Conflict, 1815–1861*. Westport, Conn., 1974.

Wood, Gordon. *The Radicalism of the American Revolution*. New York, 1992.

Woodman, Harold. *King Cotton and His Retainers: Financing and Marketing the Cotton Crop of the South, 1800–1925*. Lexington, Ky., 1968. Reprint, Columbia, S.C., 1990.

Wyatt-Brown, Bertram. *Lewis Tappan and the Evangelical War against Slavery*. Cleveland, 1969.

Wyllie, Irvin. *The Self-Made Man in America*. New Brunswick, N.J., 1954.

Zelizer, Viviana A. Rotman. *Morals and Markets: The Development of Life Insurance in the United States*. New York, 1979.

Zunz, Oliver. *Making America Corporate, 1870–1920*. Chicago, 1990.

ARTICLES

Adler, Jeffrey S. "Capital and Entrepreneurship in the Great West." *Journal of Interdisciplinary History* 25 (1994): 189–209.

Aitken, Hugh G. J. "A New Way to Pay Old Debts: A Canadian Experience." In *Men in Business: Essays in the History of Entrepreneurship*, edited by William Miller, 71–90. Cambridge, 1952.

Atherton, Lewis E. "The Problem of Credit Rating in the Ante-Bellum South." *Journal of Southern History* 12 (1946): 534–56.

Blumin, Stuart. "Black Coats to White Collars: Economic Change, Nonmanual Work, and the Social Structure of Industrializing America." In *Small Business in American Life*, edited by Stuart Bruchey, 100–121. Ithaca, N.Y., 1980.

———. "Mobility and Change in Ante-bellum Philadelphia." In *Nineteenth-Century Cities: Essays in the New Social History*, edited by Stephan Thernstrom and Richard Sennett, 165–208. New Haven, 1969.

Brown, Richard. "Comparative Legislation in Bankruptcy." *Journal of Comparative Legislation and International Law* 2 (1900): 251–70.

Bushman, Richard. "Markets and Composite Farms in Early America." *William & Mary Quarterly* 55 (1998): 351–74.

Conzen, Kathleen Neils. "Quantification and the New Urban History." *Journal of Interdisciplinary History* 13 (1983): 653–77.

David, Paul. "The Growth of Real Product in the United States before 1840: New Evidence, Controlled Conjectures." *Journal of Economic History* 27 (1967): 151–97.

Ditz, Toby. "Shipwrecked; or, Masculinity Imperiled: Mercantile Representations of Failure and the Gendered Self in Eighteenth-Century Philadelphia." *Journal of American History* 81 (1994): 51–80.

Dublin, Thomas. "Rural-Urban Migrants in Industrial New England: The Case of Lynn, Massachusetts, in the Mid-Nineteenth Century." *Journal of American History* 73 (1986): 623–44.

Duffy, Ian P. "English Bankrupts, 1571–1861." *American Journal of Legal History* 24 (1980): 283–305.

Fabian, Ann. "Speculation on Distress: The Popular Discourse of the Panics of 1837 and 1857." *Yale Journal of Criticism* 3 (1989): 127–42.

Goodman, Paul. "Ethics and Enterprise: The Values of a Boston Elite." *American Quarterly* 18 (1966): 437–51.

Griffen, Clyde. "Occupational Mobility in Nineteenth-Century America: Problems and Possibilities." *Journal of Social History* 5 (1972): 310–30.

Gross, Karen, Marie Stefanini Newman, and Denise Campbell. "Ladies in Red: Learning from America's First Female Bankrupts." *Journal of American Legal History* 15 (1996): 1–40.

Hartog, Hendrik. "Pigs and Positivism." *Wisconsin Law Review* (1985): 899–935.

Hansen, Bradley. "Commercial Associations and the Creation of a National Economy: The Demand for Federal Bankruptcy Law." *Business History Review* 72 (1998): 86–113.

Henretta, James. "Families and Farms: *Mentalite* in Pre-Industrial America." *William & Mary Quarterly* 35 (1978): 3–32.

Hollander, Stanley C. "Nineteenth-Century Anti-Drummer Legislation in the United States." *Business History Review* 38 (1964): 479–500.

Hutchinson, Ruth G., Arthur R. Hutchinson, and Mabel Newcomer. "A Study in Business Mortality: Length of Life of Business Enterprises in Poughkeepsie, New York, 1843–1936." *American Economic Review* 28 (1938): 497–514.

James, Newton Haskin. "Josiah Hinds: Versatile Pioneer of the Old Southwest." *Journal of Mississippi History* 2 (1940): 22–33.

Katz, Michael B. "Occupational Classification in History." *Journal of Interdisciplinary History* 3 (1972): 63–87.

Katz, Michael B., Michael Doucet, and Mark Stern. "Migration and the Social Order in Erie, County, New York: 1855." *Journal of Interdisciplinary History* 8 (1978): 669–701.

Lamoreaux, Naomi. "Banks, Kinship, and Economic Development: The New England Case." *Journal of Economic History* 46 (1986): 647–67.

Lindstrom, Diane. "American Economic Growth before 1840: New Evidence and New Directions." *Journal of Economic History* 39 (1979): 289–301.

Macesich, George. "International Trade and United States Economic Development Revisited." *Journal of Economic History* 21 (1961): 384–85.

———. "Sources of Monetary Disturbances in the United States, 1834–1845." *Journal of Economic History* 20 (1960): 407–26.

Madison, James H. "The Credit Reports of R. G. Dun & Co. as Historical Sources." *Historical Methods Newsletter* 8 (1975): 128–31.

———. "The Evolution of Commercial Credit Reporting Agencies in Nineteenth-Century America." *Business History Review* 48 (1974): 164–85.

Marriner, Sheila. "English Bankruptcy Records and Statistics before 1850." *Economic History Review* 4 (1980): 351–66.

Merrill, Michael. "Cash Is Good to Eat: Self-Sufficiency and Exchange in the Rural Economy of the United States." *Radical History Review* 4 (1977): 42–71.

Oaks, Dallin H., and Joseph I. Bentley. "Joseph Smith and the Legal Process: In the Wake of the Steamboat *Nauvoo*." *Brigham Young University Studies* 19 (1979): 167–99.

Owens, James K. "Documenting Regional Business History: The Bankruptcy Acts of 1800 and 1841." *Prologue* 21 (1989): 179–85.

Resseguie, Harry E. "Alexander Turney Stewart and the Development of the Department Store, 1823–1876." *Business History Review* 39 (1965): 301–22.

Rezneck, Samuel R. "The Depression of 1819–1822: A Social History." *American Historical Review* 39 (1933): 28–47.

———. "Influence of Depression upon American Opinion, 1857–1859." *Journal of Economic History* 2 (1942): 1–23.

———. "The Social History of an American Depression." *American Historical Review* 40 (1935): 662–87.

Rockoff, Hugh. "Money, Prices, and Banks in the Jacksonian Era." In *The Reinterpretation of American Economic History*, edited by Robert Fogel and Stanley Engerman, 448–58. New York, 1971.

Rodgers, Daniel. "Republicanism: The Career of a Concept." *Journal of American History* 79 (1992): 11–38.

Rogers, F. Halsey. " 'Man to Loan $1500 and Serve as Clerk': Trading Jobs for Loans in Mid-Nineteenth-Century San Francisco." *Journal of Economic History* 54 (1994): 34–63.

Rotundo, E. Anthony. "Learning about Manhood: Gender Ideals and the Middle-Class Family in Nineteenth-Century America." In *Manliness and Morality: Middle-Class Masculinity in Britain and America, 1800–1940*, edited by J. A. Mangan and James Walvin, 35–51. Manchester, 1987.

Russell, Thomas D. "South Carolina's Largest Slave Auctioneering Firm." *Chicago-Kent Law Review* 68 (1993): 1241–82.

Sampson, Roy J. "American Accounting Education, Textbooks and Public Practice Prior to 1900." *Business History Review* 34 (1960): 459–66.

Silsby, Robert W. "Frontier Attitudes and Debt Collection in Western New York." In *The Frontier in American Development: Essays in Honor of Paul Wallace Gates*, edited by David M. Ellis, 141–61. Ithaca, N.Y., 1969.

Smith, Timothy. *Revivalism and Social Reform: American Protestantism on the Eve of the Civil War*. 2d ed. Baltimore, 1980.

Stimson, Henry. "The Small Business as a School of Manhood." *Atlantic Monthly* 93 (1904): 337–40.

Suarez, Raleigh. "Bargains, Bills, and Bankruptcies: Business Activity in Rural Antebellum Louisiana." *Louisiana History* 7 (1966): 189–206.

Sushka, Mary. "The Antebellum Money Market and the Economic Impact of the Bank War." *Journal of Economic History* 36 (1976): 809–35.

Thernstrom, Stephan, and Peter Knights. "Men in Motion: Some Data and Speculations about Urban Population Mobility in Nineteenth-Century America." *Journal of Interdisciplinary History* 1 (1970): 7–35.

Weisberg, Robert. "Commercial Morality, the Merchant Character, and the History of the Voidable Preference." *Stanford Law Review* 39 (1986): 3–138.

Welbourne, E. "Bankruptcy before the Era of Victorian Reform." *Cambridge Historical Journal* 4 (1932): 51–62.

Wohl, R. Richard. "Henry Noble Day: A Study in Good Works, 1808–1890." In *Men in Business: Essays in the History of Entrepreneurship*, edited by William Miller, 153–92. Cambridge, 1952.

Wyatt-Brown, Bertram. "God and Dun & Bradstreet." *Business History Review* (1966): 432–50.

DISSERTATIONS AND UNPUBLISHED PAPERS

Balleisen, Edward. "Navigating Failure in Antebellum America." Ph.D. diss., Yale University, 1995.

Bauer, George Philip. "The Movement against Imprisonment for Debt in the United States." Ph.D. diss., Harvard University, 1937.

Beesley, David. "The Politics of Bankruptcy in the United States, 1837–1845." Ph.D. diss., University of Utah, 1968.

Byars, Ronald Preston. "The Making of the Self-Made Man: The Development of Masculine Roles and Images in Ante-Bellum America." Ph.D. diss., Michigan State University, 1979.

Ciment, James. "In Light of Failure: Bankruptcy, Insolvency, and Financial Failure in New York City, 1790–1860." Ph.D. diss., City University of New York, 1992.

Duffy, Ian P. "Bankruptcy and Insolvency in London in the Late Eighteenth and Early Nineteenth Centuries." Ph.D. diss., Oxford University, 1973.

Kellow, Margaret. "Duties Are Ours: A Life of Lydia Marie Child, 1802–1880." Ph.D. diss., Yale University, 1992.

Lamoreaux, Naomi. "Accounting for Capitalism in Early American History: Farmers, Merchants, Manufacturers, and their Economic Worlds." Paper presented to the 1999 Annual Meeting of the Society for Historians of the Early Republic, Lexington, Kentucky.

Matthews, Barbara. " 'Forgive Us Our Debts': Bankruptcy and Insolvency in America, 1763–1841." Ph.D. diss., Brown University.

Noel, F. Regis. "A History of the Bankruptcy Clause of the Constitution of the United States of America." Ph.D. diss., Catholic University, 1919.

Romano, Mary. "Law, Politics, and the Economy: Changing Patterns of Growth in Debtor-Creditor Laws, New York State, 1785–1860." Ph.D. diss., New York University, 1989.

Sandage, Scott. "Deadbeats, Drunkards, and Dreamers: A Cultural History of Failure in America, 1819–1893." Ph.D. diss., Rutgers University, 1995.

Wermuth, Thomas Sylvester. " 'To Market, to Market': Yeoman Farmers, Merchant Capitalists, and the Transition to Capitalism in the Hudson River Valley, Ulster County, 1760–1840." Ph.D. diss., State University of New York at Binghamton, 1991.

tections for creditors in, 102–19 passim, 128–29, 130–31, 258 (n. 10); premises of, 103–5; constraints on paupers under, 112, 261 (n. 26); and Tyler administration, 114, 123; legacy of, 123–24, 132–33; constitutionality of, 128, 259–60 (n. 18); demand for legal information stimulated by, 143–46; publication of text of, 144, 269 (n. 21); and credit reporting, 148–49

Bankruptcy Act of 1867, 123, 133, 257 (n. 2), 267 (n. 79), 282 (n. 22)

Bankruptcy Act of 1898, 133, 257 (n. 2), 267 (n. 79)

Bankruptcy discharges: 12–13, 124, 258–59 (n. 11); compared to emancipation, 15, 167–68; and release of economic energy, 19, 103, 198–200, 274–75 (n. 7)

Bankruptcy law: specialization in, 18, 141–42, 143, 269 (n. 25); and decentralized political authority, 69; Congress's reluctance to pass, 104, 123–24, 257 (n. 17), 258 (n. 9), 264 (n. 61). *See also* States; *specific bankruptcy acts*

Bankruptcy process: voluntary, 12, 102–15, 119, 123, 132–33, 258–59 (n. 11); involuntary, 12, 101–2, 104–9, 115–17, 123, 258–59 (n. 11)

Banks: bankruptcy among, 2, 3; as source of capital/credit, 17, 27, 31, 46, 73, 84, 127, 214, 239 (nn. 14, 15); and panics of 1830s, 34, 35–38, 39, 40; speculation in stocks of, 53, 54; and 1841 Bankruptcy Act, 106, 107, 122; insiders favored in transactions of, 158–59, 239 (n. 15); and shift to cash basis for business, 200; former bankrupts as officers of, 206

Barnum, P. T., 183–84

Beecher, Henry Ward, 69, 72, 96–97

Bellows, J. N., 72

Benedict, Jesse W., 265 (n. 69)

"Benevolent empire." *See* Christianity: bankrupts and reform causes of

Bennett, James Gordon, 119, 149, 278 (n. 33)

Benton, Thomas Hart "Old Bullion," 20, 107, 120, 128

Berrien (U.S. senator from Georgia), 123, 259 (n. 16)

Berthoud, Nicolas, 173

Betts, Charles, 139

Betts, Samuel Rossiter, 2, 61, 145, 270

(n. 31); treatment of bankruptcy petitions by, 110, 111, 113, 116, 118, 141, 261 (n. 26); on objective of 1841 Bankruptcy Act, 114; on caseload created by 1841 Bankruptcy Act, 115; son of as clerk to, 139; employment of bankrupts by, 140; on constitutionality of 1841 Bankruptcy Act, 260 (n. 18); *Rules and Regulations in Bankruptcy*, 269 (n. 27)

Big business: individual bankruptcy and growth of, 221–27

Birdseye, Victory, 137

Blake, Charles F., 282 (n. 22)

Bloomer, Elisha, 155, 159, 192

Blydenburgh, William, 286 (n. 8)

Bolles, Jesse N., 190

Bonesteel, Virgil, 141

Boston, Mass.: widespread bankruptcy in, 3; bankruptcy commissioners in, 139; bankruptcy lawyers in, 143, 269 (n. 25); publication of bankruptcy decisions in, 145; publication of bankrupts' names in, 149; migration of bankrupts to, 171; elites in, 280–81 (n. 6)

Boyd, David, 29

Boyd & Pond, 29

Bradstreet, John, 148

Bremer, Frederika, 182, 183, 201

Brewster, Joseph, 54–56, 126, 172–73

Brewster, Lemuel, 54–56

Bridges, Martin K., 177

Briggs, Charles F. (pseud. Harry Franco), 267 (n. 2)

Brokers: bankruptcy among, 7, 229; as source of capital/credit, 17, 30, 31, 46, 73, 84, 127; and panics of 1830s, 34, 35, 37; as speculators, 53; and 1841 Bankruptcy Act, 106; former bankrupts as, 177–78, 184, 189

Brooke, John T., 25, 26, 27, 46, 48

Brooklyn, N.Y., 8, 139, 154, 170–71, 192, 280–81 (n. 6)

Brown, Angeline, 29

Bruyn, A. H., 174, 175, 195

Buchanan, James, 124, 264 (n. 61)

Burnham, Gordon, 155–57, 158, 271–72 (nn. 56, 57)

Burrowes, Philip, 272 (n. 57)

Business cycle, 5, 8, 31–33, 185, 194–95, 198, 223, 240 (n. 20); and booms, 5, 33–34, 53–57, 63, 185, 194–95; bankruptcy

and 1800 Bankruptcy Act, 101; general reluctance to pass bankruptcy legislation, 103, 257 (n. 7), 264–65 (n. 61); criticism of 1841 Bankruptcy Act in, 107, 109, 137; repeal of 1841 Bankruptcy Act by, 120–23, 264 (n. 58); and post–Civil War bankruptcy legislation, 133, 264–65 (n. 61)

Conkling, Alfred, 139, 143, 241 (n. 40)

Connecticut, 138, 258 (n. 11)

Constitution, U.S., 109

Consumption, excessive: commercial moralists' warnings against, 60–61, 188, 247 (n. 37); as cause of bankruptcy, 60–64, 246–47 (n. 32)

Cooper, Charles, 208

Cornwall, Amos, 76

Court officials: profit from operations of bankruptcy system, 18, 120, 137–39, 143; fees and duties of, 112, 119–20; and defense of 1841 Bankruptcy Act, 122; patronage and, 139; former bankrupts as, 139–40, 145, 230

Court processes: and private settlements, 19, 86–90, 107–8, 115–19; costs of, 85, 89, 92, 120, 130, 138–39, 267 (n. 6); drawbacks of for creditors, 85–86, 89; and caseloads, 115, 139; newspaper and law journal reporting on, 144–46

Cox, Benjamin, 207, 252 (n. 37)

Credit: pervasiveness of in antebellum economy, 2, 27, 81, 98; access of former bankrupts to, 14, 15, 173, 174, 177, 178–79, 181, 184, 196–97, 198, 200; former bankrupts' curtailed reliance on, 16, 181, 189–91, 194, 195, 200–201, 209–10, 215, 216, 282 (n. 15); personal networks as source of, 17, 72–75, 84; as substitute for specie/capital, 27, 32; and cash flow problems, 45–46, 57–58; and excessive consumption, 60, 61; commercial moralists' view of, 70–73, 97; 1841 Bankruptcy Act and supply of, 102, 131–32; and job-loan trades, 214. *See also* Creditors; Credit reporting; Credit system

Creditors: as debtors simultaneously, 2, 81, 86; and involuntary bankruptcy, 2, 104–5, 106, 108, 109–10, 115–17; bankrupts favored over by 1841 Bankruptcy Act, 12, 102–20 passim, 129, 131, 133, 259 (n. 17); favored over bankrupts in European

insolvency laws, 12, 105, 258 (n. 11); distribution of debtors' assets to, 13, 18, 70, 80–82, 89, 103, 116, 120, 122, 139, 264 (n. 56); preferment among, 13, 72, 73, 90–94, 103, 105, 106, 108, 111, 116, 118, 119, 127–28, 129, 130–31, 132, 254 (n. 57); vs. debtors in state insolvency processes, 13, 105; family and friends as preferred class of, 17, 90, 91, 93, 94, 103, 111, 131; advocates of equal treatment of, 17–18, 70, 103; and security for loans, 30–31, 45, 84, 132; commercial moralists on obligations to, 70–72, 89, 103, 106, 126, 128; commercial moralists on obligations of, 70–72, 175–76; competition among for debtors' assets, 72, 80, 81–83, 85, 87, 91–92, 97, 252 (n. 39); strategies for securing claims of, 80–90, 115–19, 124–30; drawbacks to legal action for, 85–86, 89; and voluntary assignments, 89–91, 106; concealment of assets from, 95–96, 103, 106, 110, 111, 118, 129, 130, 179, 261 (n. 28); and 1800 Bankruptcy Act, 101; protections for under 1841 Bankruptcy Act, 102, 104–6, 108, 112, 115–19, 128–29, 130–31, 258 (n. 10); and judicial interpretation of 1841 Bankruptcy Act, 109–16, 128–29; and resurrection of canceled debts, 124–30; and wreckers, 137, 138, 139, 141, 157

Creditors' bills, 81, 85

Credit reporting, 173, 196, 201, 229; rise of, 146–51, 168, 273 (n. 71); differentiation among bankrupts in, 176; and role of connections in business world, 196; and life insurance agents, 225; use of for this study, 231–32, 280 (n. 4); competition in, 251 (n. 31)

Credit system: and market economy, 5, 27, 65–66, 216; criticism of, 20–21, 25, 159, 160, 165, 203–4, 216–17, 273 (n. 66); definition and workings of, 27–32; as factor in widespread bankruptcy, 32–48, 49; commercial hazards attendant to, 41–48; and independent proprietorship, 65–66, 205; and emotion-laden narratives, 98–99, 197; and 1841 Bankruptcy Act, 130–32; and credit reporting, 147; former bankrupts' avoidance of, 189–91, 200–201; salaried employment as protection from dangers of, 204. *See also* Credit

Daniel, Peter V., 264 (n. 54)
Day, Daniel, 76
Dayton, John, 45, 51, 59, 83, 215
Dayton & Schuyler, 45, 83, 87–89
De Bow's Review, 267 (n. 2)
Defoe, Daniel: *The Complete English Tradesman*, 70–71
Dehon, William, 269 (n. 25)
Democratic Review, 267 (n. 2)
Democrats, 166, 194; as bankrupts, 7; attitudes toward integrated market economy, 20, 21, 236 (n. 24); and repeal of 1841 Bankruptcy Act, 102, 123; Jeffersonian, and repeal of 1800 Bankruptcy Act, 103; opposition to bankruptcy legislation, 104, 123, 264 (n. 61); criticism of 1841 Bankruptcy Act, 107, 109, 115, 119, 120–21, 122, 123, 137; and judicial enforcement of 1841 Bankruptcy Act, 114–15; criticism of wrecking, 159; and patronage jobs, 208
Dey, Anthony, 278 (n. 33)
Dickerson, Philemon, 110
Discounting, 30, 31, 46, 58, 73, 75, 84, 239 (n. 14)
Dolton, William, 117
Driggs, Seth, 113
Dun & Bradstreet, 234 (n. 7)
Dusenberry, William Coxe, 148
Dutcher, Salem, 141
Dutchess County, N.Y., 8, 141, 230
Dyott, Thomas W., 245 (n. 20)

E. & W. Cock, 195, 196, 283 (n. 26)
Elmendorf, Edmund, Jr., 287 (n. 13)
Endorsements, 46, 197, 266 (n. 71); and access to capital/credit, 17, 73, 195–96; defined, 30–31; and preferment among creditors, 92–93, 94; as cause of bankruptcy, 176, 212, 236 (n. 19), 252 (n. 35)
Entrepreneurship: risks of, 2, 47, 206; and credit system, 5, 27–32, 74; celebration of in American society, 14, 206, 211; role of family and social networks in, 17; among former bankrupts, 19, 198–201, 227; and competition, 43; and commercial moralists, 69–72; wrecking as form of, 136–37, 159; contrasting styles of, 200, 284–85 (n. 37); and corporate enterprise, 222; Democrats and, 236

(n. 24). *See also* Independent proprietorship
Equitable Life Assurance Company, 223
Europe: treatment of bankrupts in, 12, 13, 107, 130, 168, 258 (n. 11); view of American bankruptcy in, 13, 182, 184; American financial and commercial relations with, 28, 31, 33, 38, 58, 60. *See also* Great Britain

Family/relatives: and business success, 14; and business partnerships, 17; and endorsements, 17, 31, 195–96, 236 (n. 19); as source of aid to entrepreneurs, 17, 50, 73, 74–75, 84, 249 (n. 13); provide help to former bankrupts, 17, 94, 173–75, 176, 181, 185, 190, 194, 196, 197, 206, 271 (n. 47); preferred over other creditors, 17–18, 90, 91, 94, 103, 111, 127–28, 131; bankrupts' conveyance of assets to, 95–96, 179; and patronage, 139, 158; and wrecking, 154; and migration of bankrupts, 172, 173, 174. *See also* Wives
Farmers: bankruptcy among, 2, 3, 7, 159, 229; and economic independence, 13, 15, 20, 204–6; and credit system, 20–21, 26–27, 66, 205; as Democrats, 21; competition among, 44; and market economy, 48, 50, 237–38 (n. 4); undercapitalization among, 58–59; oppose bankruptcy legislation, 257 (n. 7)
Federalists, 101, 257 (n. 7)
Ferguson, George, 75–76, 251 (n. 32)
Feuchtwanger, Lewis, 47, 199–200
Fiction: criticism of excessive consumption in, 60–61; portrayals of bankruptcy in, 78–79, 188–89, 215, 216, 267 (n. 2); portrayal of wreckers in, 159–60, 272 (nn. 63, 64); portrayal of salaried middle class in, 203–4, 215; criticism of excesses of credit system in, 216
Fiction writers: as commercial moralists, 69, 188–89; profit from bankruptcy system, 136; advocate salaried employment, 204; urge women to prepare for possibility of bankruptcy, 216–17, 290 (n. 36)
Fiduciary debts, 106, 112, 124, 128, 260 (n. 25)
Field, Lucius, 155
Fiske, A. H., 269 (n. 24)
Florida, 38

states' curtailment of, 12, 257 (n. 7), 258 (n. 11); calls for abolition of, 15, 127; states' continuation of, 81, 85, 167; and British insolvency system, 258 (n. 11), 260 (n. 20)

Independence, economic: as badge of honor, 13, 14–15; personal consequences of loss of, 13–14, 15, 77–80; cultural implications of, 14–16, 167, 204–6, 286 (n. 7); shifting meaning of, 14–16, 206, 219, 286 (n. 7); and independent proprietorship, 15–16, 49–50, 204–6; and salaried employment, 16, 204, 206, 219; culture of dominates antebellum society, 77, 204–6, 211, 226, 227, 286 (n. 7)

Independent, The, 270 (n. 43)

Independent proprietorship: former bankrupts' avoidance of, 3, 16, 201, 212–16, 217–19, 222, 227; citizenship and, 12, 13, 65, 204–6; and corporate enterprise, 12, 227; vs. wage labor, 14–15, 49, 211; and development of market economy, 15–16; former bankrupts' return to, 15–16, 170–201 passim, 206, 210–12, 216, 227; and economic independence, 15–16, 204–5; limited barriers to attaining, 15, 27–28, 43, 50, 65–66, 177–78; vs. salaried employment, 16, 203–19 passim; high status of in antebellum society, 49–50, 72, 204–5, 211–12; and credit system, 65–66; and commercial agency, 210, 212, 213, 218, 219. *See also* Entrepreneurship

Indiana, 266 (n. 71)

Insanity, 79–80

Insolvency law. *See* States

Internal improvements, 31, 37, 38, 65, 241–42 (n. 41). *See also* Canals; Railroads; Transportation

Irwin (western Pennsylvania district judge), 263 (n. 47)

Jackson, Andrew, 20, 21, 104, 240 (n. 24)

Jackson, Frederick: *A Victim of Chancery*, 272 (n. 36)

J. & L. Joseph & Co., 35, 37

Jansen, A. D., 112

Jarvis, Edward, 79–80

Jefferson, Thomas, 246–47 (nn. 32, 34)

Jenkins, Edgar, 181–82

Jesup, Ebenezer, Jr., 274 (n. 3)

Joachmissen, Philip J., 141

John Haggerty & Sons, 91–92

Johnston, John C., 221–22, 223

Jones, Benjamin P., 174, 175

Jones, John, 130

Jones, John Beauchamp, 160, 162, 273 (n. 70); *The City Merchant; or, The Mysterious Failure*, 160–61

Joseph, Joseph, 35

Joseph, Solomon, 35

Judd, James W. 225

Judson, Andrew, 122

Kehlbeck, William, 186–87

Kellogg, Edward, 54, 174

Kendall, Amos, 236 (n. 23)

Kent, Edward, 212

Kentucky, 122

Keown, Frances, 95

Key West, Fla., 135, 267 (n. 1)

Kingston, N.Y., 8, 230

Kinsman, Israel, 210

Lamphier, Jeremiah, 44–45

Land. *See* Real estate

Lane, Alexander P., 47

Lawrence, Joseph, 195, 283 (n. 26)

Law Reporter, 145, 149, 151, 158, 270 (n. 40)

Lawyers: profit from operations of bankruptcy system, 18, 135–37, 140, 141–43, 154; as speculators, 53; and costs of legal action, 85, 140–41; specialization in bankruptcy practice by, 141–42, 143, 269 (n. 25); former bankrupts as, 141–43, 145, 230, 269 (n. 21); and need for legal information, 144; and credit reporting, 146–47

Leeds, Amos, 95

Leeds, Henry, 58, 95–96, 98, 140, 282 (n. 15)

Legal periodicals, 145, 149, 270 (n. 30). *See also specific periodicals*

Leggett, William, 41

Lester, Joseph H., 190–91, 288 (n. 23)

Life insurance industry, 221, 222–26

Lippit, Joseph Benjamin, 208

London, 147, 149

Long Island, 4, 8

Loring, Edward G., 269 (n. 25)

Louisiana, 109, 138

McKinley (Louisiana circuit court judge), 260 (n. 18)

Macy, Roland H., 183

Maine, 123, 126

Manhood/manliness, 72, 77–78, 167, 226, 248 (n. 6), 250 (n. 20)

Manley, George, 263 (n. 45)

Manufacturers: bankruptcy among, 2, 3, 7, 175, 209, 229, 239 (n. 8); and economic independence, 13; and credit system, 27, 28–29, 31; and panics of 1830s, 39; competition among, 43–44; undercapitalization among, 58–59; and credit reporting, 146; resumption of proprietorship by bankrupts among, 178–79, 186, 187; and commercial agents, 208–9

Market economy/society: bankruptcy and dangers of, 2, 3, 5, 8, 14, 188; credit system as component of, 5, 27, 65–66; and "market revolution," 5, 237–38 (nn. 3, 4); resistance to, 9, 20, 50; and economic independence, 15–16, 65–66, 205, 227; and family and social networks, 17; Americans' adjustment to, 19, 136, 162, 226–27; Democrats and, 20, 236 (n. 24); and 1841 Bankruptcy Act, 130–32; bankrupts take second chance in, 133, 170. *See also* Capitalism, American

Martineau, Harriet, 57

Maryland, 258 (n. 7)

Massachusetts: 3, 170, 254 (n. 57); resistance to integrated market economy in western part of, 97, 200, 286 (n. 6); legal treatment of bankrupts in, 129, 138, 151, 258 (n. 7); payments to creditors in, 138, 264 (n. 56)

Massachusetts Insolvency Act, 151, 212, 258 (n. 11)

Mellon, Andrew, 273 (n. 70)

Men: as vast majority of bankrupts, 6, 265 (n. 62); and dependent vs. independent employment, 49, 205, 217; and advice manuals, 61; and consumption, 61, 247 (n. 39); and doctrine of couverture, 96. *See also* Manhood/manliness

Mercantile Agency, 147–48, 149, 196, 234 (n. 5). *See also* R. G. Dun & Co.

Merchants: bankruptcy among, 2, 3, 4, 7, 159, 175, 181, 209, 229; and economic independence, 13, 78; as both suppliers and consumers of credit, 27, 28, 31–32, 34, 44–45, 51, 52, 76–77; and credit system, 27–29, 31–35, 66, 200, 205; and

panics of 1830s, 33–35, 37, 38, 39, 46; competition among, 43; inexperience as cause of bankruptcy among, 50–51; as speculators, 53, 54, 56–57, 58; marketing activities of as spur to consumption, 60; and voluntary assignments, 90; and 1841 Bankruptcy Act, 105–6, 107, 122; and credit reporting, 146–47; resumption of proprietorship by bankrupts among, 186, 187; and commercial agents, 208–9; and training of clerks, 213; and job-loan trades, 214; western, oppose bankruptcy legislation, 257 (n. 7)

Merwin, Andrew, 28

Michigan, 38

Middle class, urban: bankruptcy and formation of, 4, 16, 201, 206, 215–19, 227; fictional portrayal of, 203–4; former bankrupts in, 206, 227; characteristics of, 215–16, 217, 218–19, 291 (n. 42); and life insurance, 224

Migration: as response to bankruptcy, 8, 20, 170–73, 174–75, 180–81, 275–76 (nn. 12, 17); to escape market society, 20

Mississippi, 38, 126

Missouri, 109, 259 (n. 18)

Money supply, 27, 40, 200

Montreal, Que., 147

Moore, Thomas, 115

Mormons, 282 (n. 16)

Morning Courier and New York Enquirer, 63, 278 (n. 33); publishes bankruptcy notices, 138, 139, 268 (n. 7); reports on bankruptcy proceedings, 144–45, 146; publishes bankrupts' names, 149, 168–69

Mott brothers, 197–98

Mutual Benefit Life, 291 (n. 4)

Mutual Life Insurance Company of New York, 222–23

Mutual Life Insurance Company of Wisconsin (now Northwestern Mutual Life), 223

National Republicans, 103, 114

Nautilus Mutual Life (now New York Life), 291 (n. 4)

Near, Andrew, 174, 195–96, 198, 288 (n. 23)

Negotiation: between debtors and creditors. *See* Court processes: and private settlements

Neustadt & Barnet, 277 (n. 25)

Nevada: mining discoveries in, 200

New Hampshire, 122, 138

New Jersey, 3

New Light Presbyterians, 7, 69

New Orleans, La., 34, 35

New Paltz Ferry Company, 210

Newspapers: bankruptcy notices in, 107, 112, 116, 137, 145, 149, 268 (n. 7); profit from operations of bankruptcy system, 135, 136, 137–38, 139, 140, 143; lawyers' advertisements in, 141, 143; coverage of bankruptcy proceedings in, 141, 144–45, 149, 278 (n. 33); publish text of 1841 Bankruptcy Act, 144, 269 (n. 27); publish bankrupts' names, 149, 270 (n. 43). *See also specific newspapers*

New York (state), 44, 149: filing of creditors' bills in, 81, 85; debtor-creditor law in, 94–95, 127, 129, 254 (n. 57); frequency of bankruptcy in, 119; popular opposition to 1841 Bankruptcy Act in, 122, 123; migration of bankrupts to, 170; former bankrupts as government officials in, 207

New York, N.Y.: widespread bankruptcy in, 1–2, 3, 8, 46, 234 (n. 5); and panics of 1830s, 35–37, 39, 63; clothing trade in, 44; 1835 fire in, 46; bankruptcy commissioners in, 139; merchants and credit reporting in, 146–47, 148, 149; wrecking in, 154, 155–57; migration of bankrupts to, 170–71; 1845 fire in, 183; former bankrupts as government officials in, 207; elite in, 280–81 (n. 6)

New York, U.S. District Court for the Southern District of: makeup of, 4; bankruptcy proceedings in as focus of this study, 4, 6; court records related to 1841 Bankruptcy Act in, 6, 229–32, 235 (n. 9), 237 (n. 3); causes of bankruptcy in, 26; judicial interpretation and enforcement of 1841 Bankruptcy Act in, 110–15; costs of operations of bankruptcy system in, 138, 140; lawyers specializing in bankruptcy practice in, 141–43; wrecking in bankruptcy court in, 154–57. *See also* Betts, Samuel Rossiter; Court officials; Court processes

New York & Harlem Railroad, 207

New York Herald, 6, 119, 146, 148–49, 278 (n. 33)

New York Journal of Commerce, 37, 118–19, 122, 270 (n. 40)

New York Legal Observer, 145, 270 (n. 40)

Nicholl (Georgia district judge), 115

Niles' Weekly Register, 269 (n. 24)

Noe, Isaac, 284 (n. 32), 288 (n. 23)

North, George, 199, 200

North American Review, 267 (n. 2)

North Carolina, 129, 262 (n. 36)

Odell, Seneca, 252 (n. 40)

Ogden, Henry, 210

Ohio, 122, 123

Overtrading, 53, 57–60, 119, 147, 176, 188, 246 (n. 24)

Owen, Samuel, 145, 270 (n. 31)

Panic of 1819, 12, 20, 33, 104

Panic of 1837, 26, 53, 192, 275 (n. 12); bankruptcies resulting from, 5, 7, 102, 148, 174, 181, 185, 195, 210, 245 (n. 20); bankruptcy legislation in wake of, 5, 12, 102, 104; prelude to, 33–34; onset and consequences of, 34–38, 267 (n. 3); cultural response to, 273 (n. 69)

Panic of 1839, 26, 53, 192, 275 (n. 12); bankruptcies resulting from, 5, 7, 102, 185; bankruptcy legislation in wake of, 5, 12, 102, 104; prelude to, 33–34; onset and consequences of, 38–41, 267 (n. 3)

Panic of 1854, 124, 185, 225

Panic of 1857, 33, 160, 185, 194, 214; bankruptcy legislation in wake of, 12, 124, 264 (n. 61); bankruptcies resulting from, 185, 193, 199; cultural response to, 273 (n. 69)

Panic of 1873, 185, 284 (n. 32)

Panics, financial, 5, 7, 18, 32–33, 185, 223; of late 1830s, 16, 46, 86, 99, 152, 221; of 1850s, 162, 195. *See also specific panics*

Parkman, George, 247 (n. 37)

Patterson, Robert L., 291 (n. 4)

Pattison, Granville Sharp, 176

Pells, Zephaniah, 80

Pennsylvania, 3, 123, 126

Pennsylvania Law Journal, 145

Perry's London Bankrupt Gazette, 149

Philadelphia, Pa., 4, 280–81 (n. 7), 284–85 (n. 37), 290 (n. 40); bankruptcy lawyers in, 143, 269 (n. 25); publication of bankruptcy proceedings in, 145; register of

Wallace, H. E., 270 (n. 31)

Wallace, John W., 145, 269 (n. 25), 270 (n. 31)

Watson, William, 29

Webb, James Watson, 63–64, 140, 149, 230, 278 (n. 33)

Webster, Daniel, 103

Webster, John, 247 (n. 32)

Wells, Robert, 109, 259 (n. 18)

West, Jessie, 208

Westbrook, Catherine, 62

Westbrook, Frederick E., 61–63, 287 (n. 12)

Western Law Journal, 145, 248 (n. 1)

Wheeler, Andrew, 54–56

Wheeler, Epenetus, 243 (n. 51)

Whigs, 63, 123, 264 (n. 58); as bankrupts, 7; and commercial moralists, 69, 103, 104, 167; and passage of 1841 Bankruptcy Act, 102, 104–5; and federal bankruptcy system, 103, 108, 109, 114, 115, 120–21, 122, 123, 124, 167; *Hunt's Merchants' Magazine* and, 159; and patronage jobs, 208

White-collar workers. *See* Salaried employment

Wilbur, Marcus, 57, 74

Wiley, Edmund, 265–66 (n. 69)

Wilkinson, William, 141

Wilson, Thomas, 272 (n. 57)

Winston, Frederick, 291–92 (n. 4)

Wise, Henry, 132

Wives: and husbands' financial troubles, 78, 188–89, 216–17; conveyance of husbands' assets to, 96, 179, 201, 279 (n. 40), 286 (n. 8); and dependence of bankrupt husbands on, 217, 290 (n. 37). *See also* Women

Women: and consumption, 60, 247 (n. 39); property rights of, 96, 223, 256 (n. 72), 279 (n. 40), 285 (n. 40); and gendered imagery of wreckers, 160; and safeguards against bankruptcy, 216–17, 290 (nn. 36, 37); and life insurance, 223–24; as bankrupts, 229, 265 (n. 2); and family income, 290 (n. 37), 291 (n. 42). *See also* Wives

Woodward, Samuel, 79–80

Woodworth, Samuel: "The Debtor," 274 (n. 3)

Wrecking: as profit making from bankruptcy system, 18–19, 133, 135–37, 267 (n. 3); types of persons engaged in, 135, 136–43; and evolution of American capitalism, 136, 137, 159, 162, 199; inside information as key to success in, 136–37, 141, 153–54, 155–56, 157–59, 272 (n. 59); criticism of, 137, 159–60, 272 (nn. 63, 64), 273 (n. 72); eventual acceptance of, 137, 160–62, 273 (nn. 70, 71); bankrupts participate in, 139–40, 141–43, 145, 153–55, 159, 162, 192, 199; and demand for legal knowledge, 143–46; and credit reporting, 146–51; in bankruptcy court, 151–57